THE TONGUE-TIED IMAGINATION

The Tongue-Tied Imagination

Decolonizing Literary Modernity in Senegal

Tobias Warner

FORDHAM UNIVERSITY PRESS

New York 2019

Fordham University Press gratefully acknowledges financial assistance and support provided for the publication of this book by the University of California, Davis.

This book was a recipient of the American Comparative Literature Association's Helen Tartar First Book Subvention Award. Fordham University Press is grateful for the funding from this prize that helped facilitate publication.

Fordham University Press has no responsibility for the persistence or accuracy of URLs for external or third-party Internet websites referred to in this publication and does not guarantee that any content on such websites is, or will remain, accurate or appropriate.

Fordham University Press also publishes its books in a variety of electronic formats. Some content that appears in print may not be available in electronic books.

Visit us online at www.fordhampress.com.

Library of Congress Cataloging-in-Publication Data

Names: Warner, Tobias, author.
Title: The tongue-tied imagination : decolonizing literary
    modernity in Senegal / Tobias Warner.
Description: First edition. | New York : Fordham University Press,
    2019. | Includes bibliographical references and index.
Identifiers: LCCN 2018059018| ISBN 9780823284634 (cloth :
    alk. paper) | ISBN 9780823284290 (pbk. : alk. paper)
Subjects: LCSH: Senegalese literature (French)—20th century—
    History and criticism. | Senegalese literature (French)—
    21st century—History and criticism. | Senegalese literature—
    20th century—History and criticism. | Senegalese literature—21st
    century—History and criticism. | Senegal—Languages—Political
    aspects. | Postcolonialism in literature.
Classification: LCC PQ3988.5.S38 W37 2019 | DDC 809.99663—dc23
LC record available at https://lccn.loc.gov/2018059018

Printed in the United States of America
21 20 19   5 4 3 2 1
First edition

for Lauren

CONTENTS

I have opted for the modern transcription system for Wolof established by Arame Fal. For the sake of clarity, I follow the conventional spellings of authors' names that already exist in English and French rather than those used in Wolof (e.g., Diop instead of Jóob, Ndao instead of Ndaw). For passages in Wolof given in older transcription systems, I have chosen to include both the original and a transliteration into Fal's system.

Unless noted below, the letters used in Wolof passages correspond phonetically with their equivalents in English.

Vowels
    à—as in "cat"
    a—as in "cut"
    e—as in "met"
    é—as in "fiancé"
    ë—as in "third"
    i—as in "sit"
    o—as in "mop"
    ó—as in "load"
    u—as in "moo"

A double vowel (uu) means the vowel is long.

Consonants
    c—ch as in "chess"
    ñ—as in "onion," similar to Spanish ñ
    q—strong "k" sound similar to Arabic qāf (ق)
    x—strong "kh" sound similar to Arabic khā" (خ)
    ng or ŋ—nasal "ng" sound, as in "parking"

A double consonant (dd) means the consonant is long.

Adapted from Arame Fal, "Phonetic Correspondences Between Wolof and English."

Unwinding the Language Question

There was an uproar at the first conference devoted to African literature "of French expression." Among the crowd of writers, academics, publishers, and students who were gathered in the Senegalese capital of Dakar in March 1963 to celebrate African literature written in French, the Senegalese novelist and filmmaker Ousmane Sembène attacked the very premise of the event. Sembène demanded to know why the conference was devoted only to writers working in French. Why was literature written in a former colonial language being institutionalized in a nation that was supposed to be undergoing decolonization? Sembène spoke at length and warned that unless African languages became languages of literary expression, "our literature will still be subject to the control of other powers, or other people's good intentions." But he was swiftly challenged by one of his compatriots, Birago Diop, who invited Sembène to repeat his critique in Wolof, the most widely spoken language in Senegal. "I would like to ask M. Sembène Ousmane to repeat the whole of his speech in Wolof," Diop requested wryly. "That is all. Because he talks about cultural imperialism. Let him make the same speech, as eloquently, in Wolof." Sembène, a Wolof speaker as well, admitted that he could repeat some of what he had said, but not all,

for want of terminology, but he insisted that this did not make the Wolof
language poorer. Amid a mounting chorus of interruptions and objections
from other conference-goers, Sembène attempted to turn Diop's question
around by shifting the focus from expression to audience. Sembène proclaimed that he could have written his first novel in Wolof rather than in
French, but then, he wondered, who would have read it and how many
people would the book have reached? As he pondered this state of affairs,
Sembène observed somewhat ruefully, "This is one of the contradictions
of our life."[1]

But could you say it in Wolof? And what audience would you reach if
you did? This exchange captures a thorny problem that would come to be
known as the language question: should one write in a former colonial language or in a vernacular? As the wave of decolonizations crested at mid-
century, similar questions and contradictions bedeviled writers and scholars
across the globe as they sought to build, categorize, and compare literary
traditions in the wake of European colonialism. From India, Kenya, and
Angola to Martinique, South Africa, and Morocco, writers in the second
half of the twentieth century reflected on the language of creative expression in a decolonizing world.[2]

There has always been something untimely about the language question. Like Sembène's intervention in Dakar, debates over the language of
postcolonial literatures have often taken the form of an interruption. This
was especially the case in the field of African literature, where language
debates erupted in the 1960s almost simultaneously around the legitimacy
of francophone and anglophone African writing. A year before Sembène's
outburst at the Dakar conference, the language question materialized in
the aftermath of a similar gathering of African Writers of English Expression at Makerere University in Kampala, Uganda. The June 1962 Makerere conference drew together future literary icons, including Chinua
Achebe, Wole Soyinka, Gabriel Okara, and a young Ngũgĩ wa Thiong'o,
who met to discuss the current state and future trajectory of anglophone
African literature. The conference is perhaps best remembered for unleash-
ing one of postcolonial literature's most recognizable polemics.

"What is African literature?" the Nigerian poet Christopher Okigbo
asked at the very first session at Makerere.[3] The question went off like a
bomb whose echoes continue to reverberate. A little more than a year after
Makerere, Obiajunwa Wali's essay "The Dead End of African Literature?"
appeared in *Transition* in 1963. Wali criticized the conference's focus on
African literature written in English, which he argued would inevitably
"lead nowhere."[4] Wali's provocation ignited a fierce debate that ebbed

and flowed for decades, with notable interventions by Achebe and Ngũgĩ. The debates unfolded differently but no less contentiously on the francophone side.[5]

More than fifty years after the Dakar and Makerere conferences, the language debates have come to feel untimely in a different way. There is now a palpable sense for many writers and critics that the issue of language is a holdover from the past. The contemporary Nigerian writer Helon Habila captured this sentiment in a post for the Caine Prize for African Writing in 2014, in which he marvels that "it feels strange to remember that there was a time, and not too long ago, when some theorists tried to limit what can or cannot be called African literature; some said a work can never be African literature unless it is in an African language."[6] Habila situates the language debates in an in-between temporality—distant from our own literary present and yet not so very long ago.

The language question was once one of the great intractable problems haunting literary decolonization in the twentieth century, but it has since acquired a reputation for being a blind alley of identity politics and narrow nationalism. Although Wali meant to dismiss writing in former colonial languages as a dead end, in the ensuing half century since his polemic appeared, it has been the language debate itself that has often been accused of going nowhere. Many writers simply short-circuit the identitarian framing they detect in the language question with a variety of creative responses.[7] Even some of the original participants in these debates felt that the argument had an oddly static quality to it. Looking back more than a decade later on some of his early 1960s salvos, Achebe admitted that he felt uneasy with his defense of writing in English but that he simply was "unable to see a significantly different or a more emotionally comfortable resolution of that problem."[8] The language debate has come to feel like a script to many, a polemic condemned to rehearse a set of positions that were laid out decades ago.[9]

Academia seems to have grown equally weary of the debate's apparent failure to break new ground. Many students and scholars of postcolonial and African studies will readily acknowledge the language question's historical importance, but I suspect that few believe the debate itself has much new to offer.[10] Classic anthologies of criticism evoke a sense of stasis, and it is not hard to see why. The language debate is sometimes framed as consisting of two choices: an essentialist, nativist return to the vernacular or a more cosmopolitan strategy of appropriating and subverting the former colonial language.[11] When the debate is understood in this way, the contest between the two options seems increasingly predictable. In a helpful and more recent survey of scholarship, Harry Garuba writes that the language issue has been "the most enduring debate in African literature" but that "so much has been written" about its essentialism "that it will be superfluous to labor the point."[12] Garuba is surely right on the first two counts. But his sense that nothing more needs to be said on the language question is a symptom that a critical consensus has become solidified.[13]

World literature is the other field that has recently developed an interest in the language question. But here again, the language issue is thought to have a curiously untimely quality. Led by Pascale Casanova, scholars who track the global circulation of texts, forms, and literary capital have tended to focus on what appears to be the language question's compulsion to repeat the past. Postcolonial language debates are seen to be merely an echo of the vernacular revolutions that shook nineteenth-century Europe. From the perspective of world literature studies, the question becomes why decolonization was still being visited by such derivative ghosts of nationalisms past.[14]

All this speaks to a strong—though by no means universal—sense that the language question has become a kind of zombie debate. Although this feels like a recent development to some, this same undead quality was being attached to the language issue almost from its very inception. J. F. Povey was already declaring in 1965—a mere two years after Wali's essay first appeared—that he did not want "to revive (or at this stage disinter!) the hoary old argument of 'What is African Literature?'"[15] This trajectory is remarkable. Not only did the language question rapidly take on a life of its own, but it was also declared dead and buried nearly as quickly. And it has continued to be both brought back to life and put to rest again countless times since.

I am not interested in reviving the language debates nor in killing them off. Instead, I want to begin by taking their untimeliness more seriously. The language question is untimely because it involves a refusal to inhabit the given conditions of a literary present. It often takes the form of a demand that present conditions be remade otherwise, an insistence that other configurations of literary culture must still be possible, and most paradoxically of all, a claim that the past that has resulted in the present ought not even be the past. The language question defamiliarizes literature itself by forcing us to reflect on how we arrived at present institutional arrangements and what we risk in perpetuating them.

The Tongue-Tied Imagination reopens the language issue by posing a different kind of question. Instead of asking whether language matters, I explore how the language question itself came to matter. Focusing on the case of Senegal, I examine the tensions and exchanges between writers and filmmakers working across French and Wolof. Drawing on extensive archival research and an under-studied corpus of novels, poetry, and films in both languages, I follow the emergence of a politics of language from colonization into the early-independence decades and through to the era of neoliberal development. When we view the language issue in this more expansive temporal lens, we begin to see it differently. Pushing back against a prevailing view of postcolonial language debates as a terrain of nativism, this book argues for the language question as a struggle over the nature and limits of literature itself.

Frantz Fanon once described colonial regimes of language as being like knots that persist.[16] And indeed, language debates have often focused their energies on unraveling the entanglement of a former colonial language in present literary practice. In this book, I frame the language issue in Senegal as a kind of knot and the politics of language as an ongoing series of attempts to dislodge its many threads. This framework entails a two-part strategy: I explore where the language question came from and how writers have responded to it.

In early chapters, I work historically by tracing back to the colonial period the many threads that created the entanglement that exists between Wolof and French. These include the consolidation of Wolof as a written language and the teaching of French literature in colonial classrooms. I also uncover less obvious but equally decisive episodes: the collection of Wolof performance traditions as literary texts, debates about what writing system to use for African languages, and changes in practices of authorship and reading. I demonstrate that the language issue is composed not only of such past transformations but also of practical questions about possible literary futures, from the viability of publishing in Wolof to the question of what audiences can be reached. These are some of the threads— past and future—that bind together a sense of a shared literary present.

In later chapters, I examine how Senegalese writers have engaged creatively with the language question. I pair new readings of well-known francophone authors such as Léopold Senghor, Mariama Bâ, and Boubacar Boris Diop with the more overlooked Wolof-language writers with whom they are in dialogue, such as Cheikh Aliou Ndao and Maam Yunus Dieng. By working in Wolof as well as French, I show how the emergence of Senegal's highly visible francophone literary tradition has been haunted from the very start by the issue of language. But rather than treating French and Wolof as rival or parallel traditions, my focus is on the interchanges between them. Working through this approach, I show that the language question has allowed Senegalese writers to explore the contingency of the literary present and question the terms of their own unfolding tradition.

Attempts at disentangling language and literature uncover something radical—once the dominant language of literary expression is put into question, those concerned start to ask questions that go well beyond language alone: What are the given terms of literary culture? Where did those terms come from, and what can still be done about them? What does it mean for a tradition, a text, or a language to be or to become literary? By provoking such inquiries, the language question reveals a hidden normativity in literary institutions and practices. Language debates work by creating space in which to imagine literature otherwise, but this often leads to the discovery that some knots are not so easily undone. While a knot may constrain or restrict, attempts to untie one sometimes produce not a complete unraveling but rather unexpected attachments that bind together elements in new configurations. Throughout this book, I explore how the politics of language in Senegal have produced not a separation of Wolof and French but rather a spectrum of cross-linguistic creative practices.

Through these readings of the many threads that make up the language question in Senegal, this book unfolds two larger interventions: the first is a call for a more expansive approach to translation; the second is an invitation to rethink our methods of literary comparison. Together, these constitute the book's broader argument and its contribution to conversations across literary studies. By recasting the politics of language as a struggle over literature, I suggest ways of revisiting some of our shared methodological assumptions and critical attachments.

At the core of this book is an argument for an expanded conception of translation. We often think of translation as a transfer of meaning that occurs across a linguistic boundary. But such a view starts to seem terribly insufficient when we consider the language question. To clarify what I mean, let us look again at that 1963 exchange between Diop and Sembène. Diop's challenge—could you say it in Wolof?—is a demand for translation. But Diop's point—which Sembène seems to immediately grasp and concede—is that translation in their case cannot be a simple movement of meaning from one language to another. Sembène demands the decolonization of literature, but Diop implies that this involves more than making a speech or even writing a novel in Wolof. Diop's challenge suggests that decolonizing literature, if it is to mean anything at all, must mean more than objecting to the presently hegemonic language of literary expression. The language question demands a reckoning with the tangle of past transformations and future possibilities that make up the literary present.

To account for the language question and the creative practices it helps spark, our understanding of translation needs to be stretched. We must look beyond the normative, transmission-centered view in at least two ways. The first dimension that must be drawn out is what we can call translation's dynamic embeddedness in circumstance. The possibility of translating is always caught up in a web of shifting presuppositions about language, context, enunciation, medium, audience, and time. To grasp the stakes of Diop's challenge to Sembène, we need an approach to studying translation that is more finely attuned to this penumbra. The second dimension that we need to bring into focus is what we can call translation's internal diversity. The term *translation* conceals a collection of related semiotic practices that convert, recontextualize, or otherwise transform their objects while nevertheless claiming to preserve something about them. To appreciate the kinds of cross-linguistic creative works studied in this book, we must also unravel the internal multiplicity of translation itself.[17]

I call this more expansive perspective on translation *unwinding*. This contains a deliberate echo of the Wolof word for translation, *tekki*, which carries with it the meaning of "unknotting." Drawing on *tekki*, I conceive of translation here as an attempt to unravel a multichannel semiotic knot. Thinking of translation as a kind of untying is a useful analytic counterweight, because it pulls against our tendency to think of translations as always being acts that join things together, transcend boundaries, or leave behind remainders. Discussions of translation are often populated by figures of movement. Translatability and untranslatability, fidelity and license—such oppositions are unthinkable without an implicit view of translation as a transfer of something from one place to another (even a failed one). From *tekki*, I adapt a rather different conceptual vocabulary—instead of an act of transmission, I suggest thinking of translation as a process of unwinding a dense knot, a way of working at a semiotic snarl with no guarantee of undoing it completely, because pulling on one thread may unsettle others in ways we cannot know in advance.

In this book, *translation* names a site of negotiation around the terms of literary culture. I use *translation* to refer not only to the movement of discourse from one language to another, but also to the reconfiguration of literary institutions, practices, and dispositions. In the case of Senegal, I explore how "translations" of textuality, authorship, and reading in the colonial era helped produce the language question as we recognize it today.

I also study how writers and artists who have responded to this question have done so by working through translation in the expanded sense outlined above: by experimenting with creative practices that put into question the givenness of modern literary conventions. These readings allow me to attend to translation as a process of knotting and unknotting by which literary institutions are held together and by which they can be pulled apart.

Dilating the meaning of a familiar term like *translation* is not without risks. Even my most patient reader may well wonder: if all this is to be accommodated under the same banner, then what is *not* translation? To this reasonable concern I reply that my aim in this book is not to redefine translation completely so much as draw our attention to aspects of it that are always present and yet difficult to notice. All translations are premised on institutional, ideological, and practical preconditions that are not reducible to linguistic difference. To disturb these preconditions, as the language question inherently seems to do, is to expose their contingency and raise the possibility of transforming them. The language question yields a disruption of our normative sense of translation as a transfer of semantic meaning. In its wake, we suddenly feel that translation is embedded in past precedent and anticipated futurity. Of course, translations are always bound up with circumstance in this way. But one of the distinctive properties of the language question is to make us perceive the tangle that surrounds them.

This book's more expansive understanding of translation grounds a second, larger argument about one of the fundamental challenges in literary studies—the variability of literature itself. As literary scholars, we tend to proceed as if we can compare texts, genres, and aesthetic categories across time and space by simple reference to the label of "literature." Working through the politics of language unsettles this assumption. By exploring the contingency of literature that the language question exposes, I outline a renewed approach to literary comparison. What would a comparative method look like that did not take for granted the universality or equivalence of the literary? This is the challenge that animates this book. Instead of presuming the commonality of literature in advance, I suggest that the making and unmaking of a literary tradition can be an object of study in its own right.

Language debates are one time-honored way that literary traditions are stitched together and pulled apart. We can think of them as a kind of seam in the fabric of our shared global literary system. But, as I show over the course of this book, this seam pulls in two different directions. First, language debates tend to produce literary commensurability by suturing vernacular traditions into the normative patterns of global literary culture. This often takes place through the reconfiguration of older traditions in text and performance into modern literary ones or the adaptation of existing literary forms for vernacular writing—both phenomena that have been widely described by other scholars. But there is a second tendency to the language question that has so far largely escaped our attention. This takes the form of a propensity to pull away from the production of literary equivalence, to dislocate and open literature up to being rethought and reimagined. This second tendency manifests itself as experiments in poetics and translation that extend across vernacular and dominant languages to suggest ways that literary institutions and practices might be made to work otherwise.

These two tendencies—a normative extension of global literary culture and an antinormative re-imagination of the literary—correspond roughly to the approaches one might expect from the fields of world literature and comparative literature, respectively. World literature, with its emphasis on translatability, will tend to see the language question as a repeatable dynamic that produces new, commensurable literary traditions. Comparative literature, with its attachment to reading in the original and its defense of the untranslatable, will tend to see the language question as an assertion of difference or incommensurability. My intervention connects these two perspectives. Rather than seeing the production of literary commensurability on a global scale as being in opposition to the generation of unassimilable remainders, I argue for understanding these dynamics as two facets of a broader process that helps make a global literary present thinkable.

Language debates are by no means the only site for us to study the transformations of literary conventions and practices, but they are an especially generative one. By exploring the politics of language, we can trace how authorship, reading, addressivity, genre, textuality, and audience are all translated into new spaces and become the terms through which new literary traditions emerge. But the language question also affords us space to notice that such translations of literary institutions and practices necessarily open them up, creating the conditions for their reinvention. *The Tongue-Tied Imagination* argues that the politics of language translates a shared sense of literature into being, by producing both equivalencies in literary culture and the potential for new configurations. By working through an expanded understanding of translation, this book recasts the intersection of world literature and comparative literature as the study of the metamorphosis of literature across time and space.

"What Is African Literature?"

To give substance to my approach, I will offer a brief reading of the two landmark conferences on African literature that took place at Makerere and Dakar in the early 1960s. These gatherings provide a powerful example of the connection between language debates and the variability of literature. Makerere and Dakar represent some of the earliest attempts at institutionalizing modern African literature, and the friction that erupted around those efforts led directly to the polemical language question that we recognize today. And yet these conferences—Makerere especially—are usually remembered quite differently, as the beginning of a language argument that pits African writers against each other on questions of identity and cultural authenticity. In this section, I try to create space for a different interpretation of these foundational gatherings by dispelling some of the mythology that still surrounds them. Working with unpublished transcripts and reports from both meetings, I offer a concise, revisionist history that will help ground the larger argument of this book.

Our sense that the first language debates around African literature took place between writers is a belated reconstruction. The 1962 Makerere conference is a case in point: we tend to remember Makerere as having been a gathering of writers, but in fact the conference brought writers together with academics and publishers to formalize collectively something called African literature. Makerere's sister conference in Dakar followed a similar format. The language debates erupted nearly simultaneously in the francophone and anglophone fields as a result of these mixed gatherings, which were convened with the purpose of formalizing African literature as a creative endeavor, scholarly field, and marketing category.[18]

At Makerere and Dakar, writers, academics, and publishers met to try to hash out what African literature had been, what it was becoming, and (most importantly for them at the time) what it ought to be. These were the first conferences that aimed specifically at consecrating African literature as a field.[19] There were, of course, other foundational pan-African and diasporic writers' conferences during the late 1950s and early 1960s, but none of them shared this format or focus. The issue of language had also been raised before, but it was only in the aftermath of Makerere and Dakar that the question would become a polemic.[20]

We can still detect echoes of the conferences' focus on institutionalization in Okigbo's framing question at the first session of Makerere: "What is African literature?" Ever since Makerere, we have tended to hear this question as an invitation to debate what literature counts as "African."

When we hear it this way, our answers often cluster around identity: what it means for a text, a piece of literature, an author, or a language to *be African*. This trajectory is part of what makes the language question seem so identitarian to many writers and scholars today. But Okigbo's question contained two terms—*African* and *literature*. Only if we imagine that *literature* is the settled aspect of the pairing does it become possible to debate Africanity in isolation. Okigbo's question invited the audience at Makerere to consider what it meant to join these two terms together.[21] At both Makerere and Dakar, the other half of this question, the literature question, was being actively investigated.

African literature as an institutional practice was still taking shape in the early 1960s.[22] There was not a settled sense of what the category might mean or do, and the Makerere and Dakar conferences were convened with the purpose of developing some tentative answers. In other words, Okigbo was asking about a category that was still in formation, and the question was interpreted differently by different participants. For some, "African literature" was the name of a creative endeavor in which they saw themselves as being engaged (or not); for others, it was potentially the name of a field of study; for still others, it was a way of designating an emerging market. These conferences were full of a sense of excitement and potential but also a feeling of foreboding and even resentment among some of the participants, who seem to have had the sense that unwanted structures were already starting to coalesce. It was in this heady atmosphere of radical possibility and imminent institutionalization that the language question would materialize into the form in which we recognize it today.[23]

A particular type of discussion format played a key role in igniting the debate's earliest iterations. Both Dakar and Makerere had mixed sessions that included writers, academics, and sometimes publishers. In these sessions, academics read papers on "contemporary African literature" in which the participants "confronted the writers with their candid views about their works."[24] This arrangement was, to put it mildly, rather awkward. The Congolese poet Tchicaya U Tam'si noted in Dakar that having to listen to papers being given about his work made him feel like he was under a scalpel, that he was "an invalid" while "they [the critics] are the doctors."[25] In these mixed sessions, the independence generation of African writers directly encountered for the first time its developing academic and publishing publics. The collisions that took place gave shape to the language question: both Sembène's intervention and Okigbo's question occurred in these mixed sessions.

Figure 1. The Makerere Conference of English-Speaking African Writers, June 8–17, 1962. Left to right: novelist Chinua Achebe, radio journalist and writer Frances Ademola, editor Theodore Bull, publisher André Deutsch, critic Arthur Drayton, writer Bernard Fonlon, and writer Bob Leshoai. Courtesy of the Special Collections Research Center, University of Chicago Library.

Figure 2. The Makerere Conference of English-Speaking African Writers, June 8–17, 1962. Left to right: scholar and critic Donatus Nwoga, poet Gabriel Okara, poet Christopher Okigbo, writer and journalist Segun Olusola, professor Saunders Redding, playwright Barry Reckord, and editor Neville Rubin. Courtesy of the Special Collections Research Center, University of Chicago Library.

As excruciating as this format was, the strange alchemy of these conversations produced some of the first sustained attempts to establish an authoritative account of African literature. That these attempts failed to produce a lasting consensus is less interesting than the sparks they generated in trying to do so. The conversations were different at Dakar and Makerere, but in both locations the effort of trying to define African literature "of French or English expression" had a paradoxical effect. Each conference produced official resolutions but little in the way of durable agreement. Instead, they generated speculation about the terms, limits, and nature of both literary practices and literary culture. Okigbo captured this best when he noted that the attempt to define African literature in Makerere was always going to "begin to approach absurdity" since it seemed to lead the participants "to modify [their] sense of values in considering literature as literature."[26] Although he meant this dismissively, Okigbo's insight stands. In trying to figure out what "African literature" could possibly mean, the participants in these conferences had a tendency to lose sight and certainty over what *literature* meant for them, as they stumbled again and again into the contingency and variability of literature itself.

These gatherings became fertile ground for explorations of the meaning and nature of literature from a variety of angles—both what *literature* meant in an African context but also more broadly. At times the participants took the debate in this direction unwittingly, while at other moments the sense of uncertainty seems to have been strategic. The questions they asked were many and varied: What textual and performance practices counted as literary? How could one properly delineate genres such as theatre and poetry? Were both modernist works and "folk poetry" to be counted as literary, and which would be more likely to reach a wide public? Was the collection and translation of oral works enough to produce literature, or was some further artistic reconfiguration necessary? How could one tell a literary short story from a folk tale or an anecdote? Participants also discussed the institutional arrangements that subtended literary production; at Makerere, the writers grilled the publishers on the criteria by which African texts would be reviewed and packaged, and worried whether this would in turn have an effect on the kinds of texts writers would produce. In Dakar, the participants debated whether it mattered that existing literary institutions, training, and languages were deeply intertwined with colonial education. Last but very much not least, the participants explored literature's relationship to its audience.[27] So how did the contingency of literature fade from our sense of what was at stake in these conferences and in the language question more broadly? To

Figure 3. The Dakar Conference on African Literature of French Expression, March 26–29, 1963. Left to right: novelist Ousmane Sembène, [unknown], novelist Ousmane Socé, poet and storyteller Birago Diop, novelist Cheikh Hamidou Kane, [unknown]. Courtesy of the Special Collections Research Center, University of Chicago Library.

Figure 4. The Dakar Conference on African Literature of French Expression, March 26–29, 1963. President Léopold Sédar Senghor of Senegal addressing the conference. Courtesy of the Special Collections Research Center, University of Chicago Library.

sketch an answer, we can compare the reception history of Makerere and Dakar.

We sometimes frame Makerere as the beginning of an intense debate over the language issue, but the unpublished report from the conference paints a very different picture. Few discussions seem to have resembled the language debates as we think of them today. The participants spent most of their time and energy surveying the literary landscape as they saw it and trying to figure out what was to be done to formalize African literature.[28] Even when the issue of language was raised, the discussion appears to have been rather mild.

Scholarly and writerly recollections of Makerere are largely based on later print controversies. Makerere first came to be known through a press report and a smattering of articles, but two later polemics would come to redefine what had been at stake.[29] The first of these was sparked by Wali's essay in *Transition*, but the definitive account of Makerere appeared more than two decades later in Ngũgĩ's *Decolonising the Mind*. In this 1986 essay collection, the Kenyan writer famously broke with the English language in favor of Gikuyu. In the pivotal first chapter, Ngũgĩ retroactively stages his awakening to the necessity of a rupture with English by recalling his discomfort as a participant at Makerere. For Ngũgĩ, what was memorable about the conference was the way it slipped problematically from "African Writers of English Expression" into "African Literature" in general. Ngũgĩ was also appalled that some of the participants seemed to assume English was the only natural language of literary expression for African writers.[30] Ngũgĩ was right about Makerere's exclusions, and yet his account of the conference was also somewhat partial. It led the reader to believe that there was little more at stake in the gathering than the focus on anglophone writing. Ngũgĩ did not misrepresent Makerere so much as focus the attention of subsequent scholarship on only one aspect of the gathering—for him, the most important one. Although Ngũgĩ's thinking on the language question has continued to evolve over the intervening decades, his original polemic in *Decolonising the Mind* is sometimes treated as if it encapsulates all that can possibly be at issue in the politics of language—both in African literatures and in postcolonial literatures more broadly—in ways one suspects Ngũgĩ never intended. To chart a different approach to the language question, we have to set aside *Decolonising the Mind* as our touchstone. Our task is not to deny the influence or interest of this text but rather to insist that there have been and continue to be other trajectories.

The reception of the Dakar conference offers a more complex and extreme case of historical revisionism. Although the language question erupted in a far more spectacular fashion at Dakar, this conference is not remembered much at all. This is due to the erasure of the nature of the debate from the two published accounts of this gathering. A partial record of the conference exists in English translation in *African Literature and the Universities*, a 1965 volume by Gerald Moore, one of the outside academics who helped put together the conference. Moore includes some of Sembène's confrontation with Diop, but he or his editorial team also made some rather shocking edits. When we compare Moore's volume with the unpublished transcripts of Dakar, it becomes clear that Moore systematically minimized the mixed nature of the conversation, removing certain academic speakers altogether and reshaping the comments of others.[31] On the whole, his edits made it appear as if Sembène had raised the language issue of his own accord, rather than in reaction to the broader project of the conference.[32]

This is nothing compared to what happened to the French record of the Dakar conference, which was published in the same year by the University of Dakar. *Actes du Colloque sur la littérature africaine d'expression française* is the only published record of the conference that exists in French. But the conversation between Sembène and Diop simply does not appear.[33] The volume consists entirely of the academic papers and formal speeches that were given. Although full transcripts were available, Jacques Golliet of the University of Dakar opted to conserve the contributions that he believed were of a "purely literary interest."[34] This effectively erased a signal moment of language politics from all histories of francophone literature. Of course, a vigorous debate over the politics of language did develop in and around francophone African writing, but we can only speculate at how these elisions altered its course.

Our memories of these two conferences are not so much incorrect as they are symptomatic. The way in which we tell the story of the origins of the language question in African literature becomes an integral part of the dim view that many take of these debates today. We tend to remember the language issue as always having been an exchange between writers over identity, authenticity, and commitment. But in its earliest beginnings as a polemic, the language question was also a complicated intervention into the unfolding institutionalization of the category of African literature. Reconstructing this forgotten history allows us to lay the groundwork for a different approach to both the politics of language and the vernacular writing movements they helped to catalyze. This begins with the very facet of the language question that has faded from our memory—namely, the contingency and institutionality of literature itself.

At the Limits of the Literary

The variability of what we mean by *literature* is not a new problem, nor is it unique to African literatures or postcoloniality. Literary scholars have long worked comparatively, despite the sense that what we all do, mean, and study under the term *literature* is quite different. No one has yet made a definition of literature stick, and I suspect that no one really wants to be asked to do so. For comparative literary disciplines especially, this is a foundational problem; our fields of study take their shape by leaving this question to the side. In recent years, however, there has been a resurgence of scholarly interest in a framework that really ought to have refocused our attention on the variability of what we mean by literature and what it means to compare across literary worlds. I am referring to the concept of world literature, first coined by Johann Wolfgang von Goethe in 1827 to describe his sense that the frontiers between national literatures were eroding and that the "epoch of world literature" was at hand.[35] Goethe's original pronouncement was rather opaque, and only over the last two decades has a great deal of scholarly attention, enthusiasm, and controversy crystallized around the term. For its most ardent supporters, world literature seems to represent the possibility of finally studying literature on a planetary scale. For its critics, it represents the worst of the homogenizing tendencies of neoliberal capitalism and a dangerous step toward only reading and teaching literary works in translation. Amid this quarrel, world literature has started to become a formalized field of study, supported by anthologies, survey courses, journals, and institutes.

The first wave of world literature scholarship that appeared in the late 1990s and early 2000s sought to take up the mantle of wide-ranging comparison from the discipline of comparative literature by valorizing analysis at the extremes of scale. This produced many pivotal interventions and provocations, from David Damrosch's *What Is World Literature?* to Franco Moretti's "Conjectures on World Literature" to Pascale Casanova's *La République mondiale des Lettres* (*The World Republic of Letters*).[36] As divergent as these three scholars' contributions are, each of them helped give world literature its renewed critical currency. For different reasons and ends, Damrosch's, Moretti's, and Casanova's initial contributions to the study of world literature ranged across broad spatial and temporal coordinates. They each relied on units of comparison that were assumed to have a great deal of continuity if not the same basic nature across time and space— reading practices, forms and genres, and literary capital, respectively. This type of framework has been a hallmark of the new world literature

studies. Such an orientation makes a lot of sense; to scale up literary studies, it seems almost obligatory to proceed as if the "data" were really not so
noisy after all. But the framework of world literature would also seem to
demand that we closely examine the contingency of the literary—how literatures can vary across time and space and yet, under certain conditions,
tend to become more and more alike. In its appearance on the critical scene,
though, the first wave of world literature studies was rarely interested in
such questions. To trace the contours of their breathtakingly vast fields of
inquiry, these three scholars felt obliged to set the variability of literature
to the side.[37]

Damrosch gives us a paradigmatic example of such a gesture in *What Is
World Literature?*: "I will have relatively little interest in attempting any
firm definition of literature as such, since this is a question that really only
has meaning within a given literary system. Any global perspective on
literature must acknowledge the tremendous variability in what has counted
as literature from one place to another and from one era to another; in this
sense, literature can best be defined pragmatically as whatever texts a given
community of readers *takes* as literature."[38] Setting aside literature's "tremendous variability" allows Damrosch to produce a far-reaching and
nuanced study of world literature as a mode of circulation and reading. But
it is nonetheless unclear why the global perspective he valorizes must either
descend into an endless search for a definition of the literary or proceed
with whatever understanding is already in use in a given community of
readers. Damrosch has built up a binary choice where there is no need for
one. Surely an acknowledgment that literature does vary across space and
time points instead toward the need to study the conditions of such
variability—how literature, literariness, and literary institutions emerge,
converge, and diverge.

A global perspective on literature can begin with the question of variability. But instead of opposing the universal, global approach to the particular, pragmatic one, we can explore how the universal and the local are
configured together. Here we move toward the problem obliquely. First,
we examine how what appears to us as a very "local" literary tradition has
been produced as equivalent with other such traditions by conforming to
the given terms of a more "global" literary culture. But second, we attend
to the limits of this homogenizing dynamic, to the ways in which efforts
to produce literary commensurability can end up creating space for these
given terms to be put into question. Studying the variability of literature
can mean examining the ways in which new spaces and traditions are
absorbed into our modern literary system such that *literature* comes to seem

an appropriate term for them, but it can also involve attending to contestations of this same dynamic. To cast this in Damrosch's terms, we must insist that literature has meaning not only inside the confines of a given literary system, but also in the friction between different systems and even in the internal friction in what appears to us to be a single system.

To move toward a different perspective on world literature, we need to think not just in terms of space, but of time. How have we come to the sense that there is a common global literary culture that we can compare across? How have traditions with equivalent literary pasts and convergent futures been produced? Are there limits to these homogenizing dynamics? Although a shift from space to time might seem novel, the temporal perspective has been there all along in the background. "The time has come," Erich Auerbach wrote in 1952, "to ask what meaning the phrase 'world literature' can still have if we take it, as Goethe did, to refer both to the present and what we can expect in the future."[39] Auerbach's essay "The Philology of World Literature" predates the current revival by many decades and stages a useful corrective to several trajectories.[40]

Auerbach argues that Goethe's proclamation of the "epoch" of world literature gives us a way of grappling with the temporality of literature on a global scale, not just with its spatial expansion. For Auerbach, the background of Goethe's coinage was the sense that the literary cultures of the world were becoming progressively standardized. Goethe celebrated this, since it meant that the differences between bounded national traditions were being overcome, and scholarship has since often followed his lead. Auerbach, however, was worried about what was at stake if the literatures of the world were to become ever more alike.[41] The emergence of a single literary culture and language spanning the globe would mean that the idea of a world literature would be "simultaneously realized and destroyed."[42] For Auerbach, the idea of world literature demanded that we study the conditions under which literatures develop in convergent ways. To recast his proposal in a slightly different direction than he intended, we might say that the task of criticism in an age of world literature is neither to take the standardization of the literary for granted nor to reject it entirely—it is rather to inquire into this dynamic's conditions of possibility.

Auerbach's essay is consumed with the monumental methodological challenge world literature poses to literary critics. The sheer number of languages and traditions in the world makes it unhelpful to focus on just one language or national tradition, but it will also never be enough to simply aggregate data (which he calls "encyclopedic collecting"). To study the conditions of literature's emergence, Auerbach recommends an approach based on what he describes as "points of departure." These are phenomena that are concrete and comprehensible and yet have the potential for "centrifugal radiation."[43] To study literary culture's increasing standardization alongside its stubborn variability, we need a point of departure that is at once situated within the conditions of emergence of a particular literary world and yet central to a broader problematic.

The language question is this book's point of departure. My inquiry takes shape around the debates over language that emerged in the aftermath of decolonization in Senegal. But after grounding itself in this way, the project then radiates outward to consider where the tendencies that became the politics of language arose from and what has become of them since the 1960s. In this broader framework, the language question becomes an optic through which to study the conditions of emergence of a literary tradition and to inquire into the temporality of world literature.

One aspect of the language question in particular will be crucial for this approach: its capacity to spur the development of vernacular literature movements. Such movements often aim to build a literary tradition in a vernacular language, and as such, they are clearly one mode of the standardization of literary cultures that Auerbach identified as the backdrop of our ability to speak of a world literature. But when we closely study such a movement across a broader timeframe, we start to see a new side to this process. Vernacular literary movements do not only help integrate newly "literary" traditions into a globalized literary modernity, they also tend to open up the possibility of questioning, critiquing, and unraveling the givenness of literature itself.

A politics of language often incorporates two different dynamics: first, it extends the reach of the literary, and second, it makes it possible to throw literature itself radically into question. A Senegalese example will help us see what is at stake for the first tendency. Following the challenge that was issued to Sembène in 1963 to "say it in Wolof," writers, filmmakers, and anthologists began trying to produce a modern literary tradition in Wolof that could intervene in the consolidation of its francophone counterpart. In this spirit, the linguist Pathé Diagne assembled in the 1970s an anthology of world literature in Wolof, the *Teerebtanu ladab ci wàlàf* (*Anthology of Literature in Wolof*). Diagne's anthology includes Wolof translations of established world literature classics, including those by Goethe, Dante, Wilde, Abu Nuwas, Homer, and Sappho. Diagne sets these translations alongside a section on Wolof literature, which includes transcriptions of songs of spiritual devotion meant to be collectively chanted.[44] The aim of Diagne's gesture is to establish that these Wolof texts are equivalently literary with the other works he translated. But this reconfigures shards of older performance genres into literary texts intended for silent, private readers. Performance practices with their own semiotic ideology, traditions of address, and sense of an audience are transformed into literary objects. This is the kind of extra-linguistic translation that vernacular literary movements regularly perform. When writers and activists feel obliged to produce the vernacular as literary, they tend to rework older traditions into a common vocabulary in which authorship, reading, and audience are treated as constants.

Detecting this work of reconfiguration allows us to notice that "literature" does not mean the same thing for the other texts in Diagne's anthology either.[45] From the Upanishads to Claude McKay, Lao Tzu to Leopardi, Novalis to an ancient Egyptian hymn, the texts Diagne translates into Wolof in the *Teerebtanu* are not inherently, interchangeably literary but for the anthology form making them so. Diagne's collection produces the commensurability it claims to describe. This is one source of the untimeliness we all sense in a politics of language: when a vernacular movement gathers up and presents a literary past that is equal to all other literary pasts, the artificiality of this gesture reminds us that all literary traditions have been at some point fashioned in similar ways.

This is the first tendency: vernacular language movements produce literary commensurability. Scholars have long understood this, but we have not fully grasped what is at stake. Benedict Anderson first comprehensively documented this phenomenon, which is often called vernacularization.[46] Anderson's invaluable contribution was to deduce that vernacular movements are modal—translating older textual and performance traditions into literary space is a moveable and repeatable strategy for producing a literary tradition. Anderson associated this dynamic with the rise of nationalism, and this insight has continued to shape our understanding of vernacular literatures and the role they play in a global literary order. We often tend to assume, following Anderson, that vernacular movements are inherently geared toward the production of national, sovereign literary spaces. This is the assumption that underwrites much of Pascale Casanova's *The World Republic of Letters*.[47] Anderson's conclusion is not so much wrong as seriously incomplete. He was correct to observe that vernacular movements can refashion older textual traditions into national ones, just as Casanova was right to note that such a phase is key to new traditions joining a globalized literary space. But both of these scholars miss the paradox inherent in this process. When vernacular movements rework older traditions into literary ones, the translations they perform are not only between languages but between different textual and performance cultures with sometimes incommensurate understandings of the nature of textuality, print, address, and reading. In other words, translating earlier traditions and practices also means reconfiguring them.

By the time the language question appears as such, this process of reconfiguration has usually been well under way. When an argument breaks out about what *language* literature ought to be written in, a great feat of commensurability has already been performed. At the point at which language becomes the issue, the nature and equivalence of *literature* is increasingly being taken as a given. We can see this happen after the Dakar and Makerere conferences: the category of "African literature" emerges most clearly not in the attempts to consciously define it but rather in the arguments over what languages it ought to be written in. This is what we might call the cunning of the language question, to recast Hegel. When the fight becomes over what language "literature" can or ought to be written in, an enormous amount of conceptual terrain has already been conceded by both sides, such that the variability of literature itself is less and less of an issue. Paradoxically, then, both sides in a language debate usually agree on a shared (if implicit) understanding of literature and literary culture, precisely because they are fighting over it. Shifting the debate to language accelerates a rush (on both sides) to translate earlier traditions into literary space. Thus a politics of language serves to naturalize and conceal a more radical process of reconfiguration, as we see in Diagne's anthology.

But there is a second tendency to literary vernacularization that has largely been overlooked by scholarship. The drive to produce the vernacular as literary creates the conditions for putting into question existing literary conventions and institutions. While vernacular movements do strive to demonstrate the equivalence, or at least the commensurability, of literature written in the vernacular, such movements also uncover the contingency of the terms in which they can make these claims. This in turn creates spaces for experimentation and critique where the practices, institutions, and dispositions that constitute our global literary present can be made to seem normative rather than natural. The language question not only tends toward the production of sameness, it also tests the limits of literature's institutionality, forcing writers to ask anew what it means to be an author, who counts as a reader, and how one can write for a public whose shape and sensibilities have yet to be determined.

Another Senegalese example will help us clarify this second tendency. The politics of language in Senegal did not only give rise to attempts to produce literary monuments in vernaculars. It has also taken a second trajectory that draws out the limits of the literary. The Wolof translation of Mariama Bâ's iconic 1979 francophone novel *Une si longue lettre* (*So Long a Letter*) offers us an example. Bâ's text is an undisputed classic of postcolonial, francophone, and world literatures and has been translated into more than sixteen languages since it first appeared. Part of what made the text so well received by a world literary public was its apparent celebration of the self-fashioning powers of writing, literature, and print culture. But when the writer Maam Yunus Dieng translated this text into Wolof, she uncovered a very different interpretation. Dieng's Wolof translation reveals *Letter* to be a text consumed by a deep ambivalence over the given nature of literary conventions such as audience, textuality, and address. By reading *Letter* back through its Wolof translation, as I do in Chapter 6, we start to see that Bâ's novel was also an experiment in testing the contingency of literary culture. Dieng's work is one of many interventions that I study throughout this book that do not fit our preconceived ideas about the politics of language. Vernacular writing and translating are not bound to produce literary equivalence or nativist quests for unmediated cultural rootedness. They also open spaces for interrogating literature itself.

This second tendency is entirely missing from Anderson's account of vernacular movements, which presumes that such movements tend to proceed toward the production of ever greater homogeneity and sameness. Our task is not to discount the value of Anderson's insight but rather to rigorously critique its capacity to limit our ability to recognize other dynamics. When we elevate Anderson's insight to the level of a general law, as Casanova does, we eliminate the possibility of seeing anything else at work in vernacular language movements. This in turn walls us off from a more multifaceted engagement with one of the most widespread dynamics in literary culture.

Before, During, After

This book is divided into three parts, each of which examines a phase of the language debates in Senegal. In Part I, "Colonial Literary Modernity," I look at what happened *before* the language question appeared as such and explore its genesis in the colonial era of French West Africa. Rather than locating the origins of the issue in colonial language policies, I argue that the politics of language emerged out of a broader volatility of literary culture in this era. I focus on fluctuations in three modern literary conventions: textuality, authorship, and reading. In Chapter 1, I examine how the textuality of a missionary's artifact collection spills over into an early anthology of African literature assembled by Léopold Senghor. In Chapter 2, I study how a conflicted mode of authorship that flourished in colonial schools had a profound impact on early francophone literature. In Chapter 3, I show that African newspapers in the colonial era were hotbeds of creative writing, especially explorations of the nature of a future reading public. Moving from textuality to authorship to reading, Part I reconstructs the instability of these three key aspects of literary culture in the late colonial era. My argument here is that the language question neither invented nor discovered on its own the contingency of literature—instead, it refracts a much older, constitutive fracture.

In Part II, "Decolonization and the Language Question," I pivot to re-examining what occurred *during* the language debates that roiled the first few decades of an independent Senegal. Here I focus on what appears to be a familiar version of language politics—a confrontation over the language of artistic expression that pits French against Wolof. But rather than take this antagonistic character at face value, I show that the conflicts and interventions of the 1960s and 1970s undermine our dominant narratives for understanding language politics. In Chapter 4, I reconstruct the battle over how to write the Wolof language, which pitted the francophile administration of the poet-president Senghor against writers and artists who advocated a turn to Wolof—a feud that culminated in the censorship of a Wolof film for spelling its title in a way that Senghor had deemed illegal. In Chapter 5, I examine the reflexive poetic strategies of the first Wolof novel and film, both of which had to be remade in French to reach an audience. Part II rejects a binary understanding of the politics of language as either nativist resistance or cosmopolitan subversion. Instead, it sketches a more complex series of engagements with the nature of literature and the limits of translation.

In Part III, "World Literature, Neoliberalism," I look at events *after* the heyday of the language debates to explore how vernacular writing persists and evolves past the confrontational 1960s and 1970s. The battle lines of the independence era no longer capture what is at stake for contemporary vernacular writers and translators. In Chapter 6, I look at how the Wolof novelist Maam Yunus Dieng translates and rewrites Mariama Bâ's iconic 1979 novel *Une si longue lettre* (*So Long a Letter*), throwing into question the terms by which Bâ's novel became a classic of world literature. In Chapter 7, I explore how the politics of language in Senegal shifted dramatically after the domestic cultural field was devastated by structural adjustment loans imposed by the International Monetary Fund and the World Bank. The language question looks different in an era of neo-liberalism than it did in the heyday of cultural nationalism, and contemporary writers such as Boubacar Boris Diop are exploring ways of reinventing language politics beyond the framework of the nation-state. In the book's epilogue, I read Diop's recent Wolof translation of Aimé Césaire's play *A Season in the Congo* to reflect on the challenge decolonization continues to pose both to the temporality of world literature and to our scholarly practices of comparison.

The broad temporal sweep I have just sketched perhaps suggests a book with a neat, linear chronology. My aim is rather different. The book's structure is an effort to take seriously the ways in which language debates and vernacular writing have shifted and responded to local and world historical developments. But a fundamental feature of the phenomena I trace under the rubric of the language question is that their claims go beyond what we might understand to be their immediate context. So although this book works across what appears to be a progressive temporality—from colonial to postcolonial to neoliberal—the goal is to show how the question of language makes this framework untimely. Beneath this linear architecture, the reader will encounter a rather different structuring device, which takes the form of a series of questions: How can literature accommodate different modes of textuality? What does it mean to speak or write in one's own words? How can one write for a public that is yet to come? These three questions reverberate across all three sections of the project, making historical moments that seem to have little in common speak back to each other and undermining any sense that the past, present, and future of the language question can be kept so neatly separated.

On Method

The methodology of this book can be thought of in terms of different lenses, which shift in and out of use to bring different aspects of a problem into focus. The distinction between these lenses is artificial, and I will often use more than one lens at once. Nevertheless, the question of method is worth elaborating on, given the unique challenges of this subject matter.

The most obvious lens the reader will encounter in this book is linguistic; I work closely with texts in Wolof as well as French. In this approach, my work joins a growing body of scholarship on African-language literatures.[48] And yet most existing studies of Senegalese writing tend to be focused on French texts and archives.[49] Working comparatively across French and

Wolof allows for a different kind of intervention. Scholarship on the language issue can become overly fixated either on polemics written in dominant languages or on the ways in which writers have "indigenized" those former colonial languages.[50] By tracing how texts shift on a granular level as they move between Wolof and French, my work seeks to illuminate a different set of concerns. I am not claiming that the truth of language politics exists only in vernacular texts, nor even that close reading is the only possible approach. My aim is rather to outline a way of reading the transformations of texts, practices, and institutions as they move across languages and circumstances.

The next lens I use is a historical one. Proceeding from the assumption that modern literary culture is not a given or universal category, I treat the emergence of a literary world in Senegal as a contingent achievement that can still be put into question. To this end, I offer micro-histories of particularly decisive episodes—how literature was taught in colonial classrooms, how West African newspapers addressed their audiences, and how prize-winning novels were praised in confidential readers' reports. Archival work is not an end in itself for this project but a way to dislodge certain threads in a broader, shifting assemblage of institutions, practices, and sensibilities.

Another lens will be a materialist one. I pay quite a bit of attention to the unstable materiality of texts and artifacts—for example, how the structure of address of an oral performance is reconfigured as it is collected, transcribed, and anthologized or how a novel's sense of its public seems to bend as the work is serialized, coupled with a new preface, or translated. My aim is to consider literary texts not as works that exist in and reflect a single original context but rather as one point of a continuum of negotiations that stretches from production to reception and beyond.

The final lens is a formalist one. The project assumes that the formal features of written and oral texts activate different subjective formations, arrangements of power, and narrative and temporal structures. In other words, although I argue that modern literary culture is historically contingent, I take seriously the formal dimensions of literary texts and see no incompatibility between a formalist approach and a commitment to historical and archival work. My understanding of formalism, however, does not entail positing the existence of a separate, literary realm in which we can appreciate the work of purified forms in isolation. When our point of departure puts the literary into question, we have to track the ways in which forms themselves warp in translation only to be put back together in ways we might not expect.

One or Many Language Questions?

This book investigates the intersection of Wolof and French. This is far from the only language question in the world, or even the only one in Senegal.[51] A comparative or world literature scholar might object that this focus is too national, while an area studies scholar might complain that it privileges only one of many vernacular languages within one national space.[52] This is the challenge that confronts any attempt to study the language question. However we draw the boundaries of our object of study, we seem to be caught between competing imperatives to stretch our focus outward or narrow it ever more tightly. The sheer fact of linguistic diversity is one reason we already have a preference for transferable models for studying vernacular literature movements. No one can learn every language, so we end up looking for patterns in texts and manifestos that are written in or translated into languages that we already know.

The aim of this book is not to generate another movable model of language politics that will reveal the same truth everywhere. That being said, my argument does have a schematic quality to it. I identify what I take to be two trajectories of the language question, the production of literary commensurability on the one hand and its unraveling on the other. My hope is that this schema resonates elsewhere without being merely repeated. Rather than establishing a pattern that repeats itself identically across time and space, this book argues that the language question can be thought of as a restaging of the literary. When we think of the language question in this way, it then becomes impossible to claim that such a dynamic could ever manifest itself in quite the same way twice. And yet the very sense of a restaging does presume that some kind of commonality exists between iterations—which confirms that strange sense of kinship that many of us detect between vernacular literature movements.

To offer further reassurance to the comparative scholar desirous of a more transnational approach, I would argue that the framework of this book both is and is not national. The politics of language I study here did emerge against a background of nationalism and calls for cultural sovereignty. I take these factors seriously, but my aim is to show that nationalism is an insufficient optic for studying the language question. The book's focus moves outward from the era of cultural nationalism precisely to show that the instability of the literary that became the language question began before the era of nationalist movements and has continued to evolve since.

For the area studies scholar who may still be worried that I am focusing on only one of many African languages in Senegal, let me say this: this is not a history of Senegalese literature nor even of Wolof literature. Any serious attempt at the former would certainly need to work in a more linguistically diverse fashion, while any attempt at the latter would need to construct a much more comprehensive archive of Wolof creative expression. This book is an exploration of the contours of a literary problem space that has come to exist at the intersection of Wolof and French.

I am careful to note throughout the book that a plurality of languages and speech communities exists and has long existed in Senegal. Many of these have had their own language questions. There is, however, a long discursive tradition in Senegal of treating Wolof synecdochically, as if it can represent African languages more broadly. This argument is often made in seemingly benevolent terms by those who would seek to promote Wolof literary activism as a kind of model for other African languages.[53] The impetus behind such rhetoric is more often pan-Africanist than nationalist. Nevertheless, there can be no mistaking that this type of substitution is also a gesture of exclusion. Such privileging of Wolof has long been vigorously contested in Senegal by writers and activists focusing on promoting writing and literacy in other languages.[54]

To be very clear, then, it is not my argument that the Wolof-French intersection can stand in for all the variability and complexity of the language issue. But such a tendency to treat Wolof synecdochically is a trope in the history that I trace here—though by no means the dominant mode. What underlies this tendency to speak of Wolof as if it could stand in for other languages is the linguistic situation of Senegal. Senegal has a large number of regional languages, eighteen of which now share with Wolof the legal status of national languages. Wolof occupies a unique position in this diverse linguistic ecosystem. It has been and still is marginalized (with respect to French, the official language of government and education), but it is also hegemonic (with respect to Senegal's other national languages) and absorptive (especially in urban spaces, where spoken Wolof is porous to vocabulary and syntax from other subregional and globalized idioms). Wolof has for a long time been Senegal's major vehicular language—by some estimates nearly 85 percent of Senegalese speak Wolof.[55] The temptation to treat Wolof as if it could stand in for all other languages besides French has become stronger in recent decades as Senegal has become evermore Wolof speaking—a dynamic scholars have called "Wolofization."[56] I am careful to treat this situation not as natural but as the outcome of a historical process that continues to unfold in relations of power and domination.

My own training and competence in Wolof are unquestionably tied to this dynamic. When I first arrived in Dakar as a student many years ago, I began learning Wolof in part because it was the language of urban space. That I was able to continue studying the language and eventually find a community of scholars who were also working on cultural production in Wolof speaks to its relatively established position in the American academy compared to many other African languages that are rarely taught or studied. As the Makerere and Dakar conferences show, it is never accidental that certain languages or traditions develop into formalized fields of study. So although the production of a Wolof literary tradition has long been a goal for some of the writers studied in this book, my approach is neither to endorse nor to condemn such a project. My focus is rather on studying the internal variability of the politics of language as I find it.

While a drive to produce a literary tradition often animates vernacular writing, a closer examination finds that the paths that are actually taken often lead away from nationalist ends and toward more unexpected and experimental engagements. So while I am careful to document and critique the occasionally hyperbolic claims that have been made for Wolof over the last half century, I also argue that we need to resist the idea that vernacular literary movements are necessarily nativist or exclusionary. Our deeply held suspicion that every vernacular literary project only ever leads to ethnic nationalism is mistaken, and it has badly hindered scholarship on the language question more globally. Here we might take as a counterexample one of the other literary currents of the last century that had a global reach and put the nature of literature into question: modernism. Modernism was multifaceted and not infrequently politically compromised. There were Left and Right modernisms, statist and collectivist modernisms. The radical diversity of what we group under the heading of modernism has never prevented scholars from engaging with modernist writing from a variety of angles. Why must it be otherwise with the language question? Once we can accept that the language question can pull in more than one direction at once, we can finally begin to grapple with what it is: one of the few truly global literary phenomena.

PART I

Colonial Literary Modernity

The Fetish of Textuality: David Boilat's Notebooks and the Making of a Literary Past

In 1843, a curious notebook arrived in Paris at the Geography Society, a French institution that promoted the collection of knowledge about the non-European world. Between the notebook's marbled covers the recipients found a diverse assemblage of texts in a variety of hands, scripts, and hues of ink. Some were mere scraps of paper no larger than a postage stamp, while others had to be carefully unfolded like maps. Some were written in neat Arabic or Latin characters, while in other documents the writing was encased in geometric designs or wound counterclockwise across the page in spirals. All these texts were affixed with red wax to the notebook's pages, giving it the appearance of a collection of pressed flowers.[1] This notebook was sent to the society from Senegal by David Boilat, a métis Catholic priest in Saint-Louis, the tiny island outpost in the mouth of the Senegal River that was the center of French power in preconquest Senegal. Boilat had been born in Saint-Louis in 1814, the child of a European father and a *signare* mother.[2] He had been sent to France by the Catholic Church in 1832 as a member of a group of African students, who were among the earliest targets of the French colonial project of assimilation. Upon his return to

Saint-Louis in 1842, Boilat became the community's abbé, or vicar, and director of some of the colony's schools.[3]

Boilat's notebooks contain a great variety of texts in several languages. There are collections of Wolof performance genres, including *léeb* (tales) and *woy* (songs).[4] There is a copy of an 1843 petition written in French on one side and Arabic and Wolofal on the other (Wolofal is Wolof written in an Arabic-derived script). Boilat's collection also includes letters, poetry, and illuminated manuscripts in a variety of languages, including Arabic, Wolof, and Pulaar. But the members of the society in Paris seem to have been most excited by the collection of *gris gris* that Boilat included.[5] These are talismans often consisting of verses from the Quran or more occult inscriptions, usually written by a *marabout* on pieces of paper.[6] Many of the talismans would likely have been housed in containers made of leather or other materials, so Boilat would have had to extract the papers in order to paste them into his notebook.

The notebooks Boilat sent to the society were quickly forgotten, but Boilat himself would go on to become a well-known figure in scholarship on Senegal.[7] This is due to two books he published after he returned to France. The first is his 1853 *Esquisses sénégalaises* (*Senegalese Sketches*), a proto-anthropological study of the region's peoples and customs. Boilat is also remembered for his 1858 *Grammaire* of the Wolof language, which is the first written by a native speaker.[8] Boilat saw his research on language and culture as laying the groundwork for more extensive French mission-ary work and preparing the way for the colonization that would take place in the latter half of the nineteenth century.[9] In this respect, Boilat was a key contributor to what Valentin Mudimbe called the colonial library. Mu-dimbe located the epistemological underpinnings of European imperial-ism in works by scholars like Boilat who helped make African lifeworlds knowable.[10]

If we reread Boilat's scholarship—his *Grammaire* and his *Esquisses*—alongside his forgotten notebooks, a rather different understanding of the colonial library starts to take shape. Before Boilat became a published scholar, he was training himself to be a text collector—to hear, study, and record the Senegambian social world around him in new ways. When we reconsider Boilat in this way, the colonial library itself starts to look less like a bounded body of knowledge that aimed to "faithfully translate and decipher" its object, as Mudimbe puts it, and more like the residue of a practice of text collecting.[11]

The colonial library also played an important role in the consolidation of many postcolonial literary traditions; in the twentieth century, colonized intellectuals sometimes turned to its studies of indigenous societies in search of evidence of a literary past.[12] This is what happened with Boilat's collections. Nearly a hundred years after he assembled his notebooks, some of Boilat's texts found their way into an early anthology of African literature in French. In this chapter, I reconstruct this remarkable string of transformations—from the inscription of artifacts and performances as texts, to the reframing of texts as literature. The story of Boilat's text collections and their literary afterlife raises questions that will cut to the core of comparative literary studies: Where does a literary past come from? And what are the terms through which such a past can be claimed?

Text Collection as Form

A song, a tale, a talisman, a letter, a petition: these are the remnants of multiple practices of textuality and various genres of speech and performance. But in Boilat's notebooks, each of them is presented as if it were a specimen, giving the entire volume the appearance of a collection of pinned insects. Boilat not only assembled this diverse collection, he proposed a new legibility for its contents. As Boilat pasted his collections into his notebooks, the differences that may have existed between how all these artifacts were created and used were partially effaced by the form of the text collection itself.[13] Wolof *léeb*, or tales, are separated from the call-and-response structure that typically frames them; an isolated song offers us few clues as to its performer or audience; a bilingual petition is stripped of its immediate political context. For their part, the *gris gris* were already recontextualized verses of the Quran, but they were texts that were likely not meant to be read so much as worn on the body and incorporated into everyday life as tokens of protection and adornment.[14] All these artifacts have now been moved from one context into another. Even though some of them were likely nonrepresentational to begin with, they have all been reframed as texts that exist for a reader, even a very distant, future one.

The notebooks show us the crux of Boilat's scholarly activities: he was first and foremost a text collector. Once we see the raw practice of text collecting in his notebooks, we start to detect traces of it in his two published and polished scholarly works. Boilat's Wolof *Grammaire* presents itself to the reader as a scientific study, and yet it is completely dependent on a practice of text collection. Like any linguist of his era, Boilat had to isolate and transcribe utterances that could serve as linguistic evidence. In his *Grammaire*, he includes this data in an appendix that he fills with Wolof tales, songs, and proverbs—a collection of texts not unlike his notebooks. To amass this archive, Boilat had to train himself as an amateur linguist. One source of this training may actually have been the Geography Society, the institution to which he sent his notebooks in the 1840s. In addition to promoting exploration, the society produced guides for scientific amateurs like Boilat. One of these advises an aspiring linguist to "treat a language like a naturalist treats an animal or a plant"—an apt figure for Boilat's text collecting.[15] This type of approach was part of a broader reconfiguration of linguistic study around comparative grammar that occurred in the nineteenth century. In this period, the search for a language's grammar was understood to be the search for the best and most representative usage—grammar was understood to be "a guide to linguistic practice rather than merely a description of it."[16] In Europe, linguists in search of authorities on proper use turned to literature and assembled collections of quotations from famous authors. But in various sites across Africa, early missionary linguists were confronted with communities whose speech genres did not seem to them to conform to the categories of literature. Authors of missionary and colonial grammars often settled on proverbs and folktales as the best alternative, since the varied speech genres they grouped under these categories appeared to them to be more easily extractable from everyday speech.[17] Folklore and proverbs were also thought to be authorless and yet highly illustrative of the mentalities of the speech communities that employed them. But in order for someone like Boilat to collect such evidence, a certain process of purification had to occur. The society's guide contains advice on how to do this. It calls grammar "the skeleton of language" and advises the amateur linguist to imagine himself as a paleontologist reconstructing an animal from a fragment of its skeleton. But where, in spoken language, did the bones begin and the flesh end? In practice, many missionary linguists found that the flesh and skin of linguistic life—what we might call the indexical aspects of speech—were difficult to separate from the grammatical skeleton.[18]

We can see this paradox at work in Boilat's Wolof *Grammaire*. Some of the songs he includes in the appendix to illustrate grammatical concepts are in fact praise songs that appear to have been composed in honor of French colonial administrators on the occasion of military victories. One such song is dedicated to Governor Bouët and his triumph at the battle of Kaska. The last two lines read: Todhie daekae-bae, rey gôre-gnae / Terénae Kaskae néalw. (Toj dëkk ba, rey góor ñi / Tere na Kaska nelaw.) ("He destroyed the city, killed the men / Prohibited sleep in Kaska.")[19] Boilat's commentary focuses only on the song's use of *tere* (to forbid or prevent), and he is chillingly silent on the implied bloodshed. When we approach the *Grammaire*'s appendix not as linguistic data but as an assemblage of texts that were once collected, then the specimens start to reveal once more the circumstances of their transcription, which are embedded in larger histories of violence, colonization, and social upheaval. Like the notebooks, Boilat's Wolof *Grammaire* is an archive of the social world collected as text. But there is a crucial difference between the two: in the notebooks, the practice of collection that Boilat employed is left unvarnished, whereas the *Grammaire* deploys a scholarly apparatus that conceals the very practice that made the scholarship possible. A scientific framework has been retrofitted onto a practice of text collecting, which was itself the product of Boilat's efforts to train himself to reframe the various voices of the social world to be readable in new ways.

A similar dynamic is at play in Boilat's ethnographic memoir, *Esquisses sénégalaises*. The book conceives of itself as a series of portraits of the various peoples who inhabit Senegambia, whom Boilat calls "races." Each chapter takes the reader through a group's physical appearance, customs, dress, religious beliefs, foodways, and so on—all the categories one would expect to find in a nineteenth-century work of proto–social science. But to sift the social world into such categories, Boilat had to busy himself with collecting data. And once again, the practices of collection and reframing that made *Esquisses* possible come into relief most clearly in its appendix. This consists of a series of paintings, done by Boilat himself, that depict various Senegalese "types."[20] (See Figures 5–8)

Of his decision to include these portraits, Boilat writes that he thought they might be necessary "to give my readers more precise ideas" of the peoples he was describing. The point of view of the spectator in the portraits is always positioned to take in the garments, objects, and physical features that Boilat wishes us to notice as belonging to these types—the pointed head wrap that stands for the *signare*, the bottle of wine that is presented as the emblem of the *thiedo* (*ceddo*).[21] Boilat observed that a "certain something that characterizes the physiognomy of a race is reserved for the art of painting . . . It belongs to painting to seize nature on the spot and to report it . . . *in characters that everyone who has eyes can read and understand*" (emphasis mine).[22] This captures the desire that underpins Boilat's many scholarly endeavors. He was constantly in search of a method of framing the representative sample such that its truth would be self-evident to the viewer—a way of framing the specimen such that it would be readable for "everyone who has eyes."

One painting in particular captures the full force of Boilat's practice of recontextualization. In *Toucouleur Man and Woman* (*Homme et Femme*

L.Janta lith.   P.Bertrand, éditeur, rue St André des Arcs 55.   Imp. Lemercier, Paris.

SIGNARE

Figure 5. Signare by David Boilat. Courtesy of the Schomburg Center for Research in Black Culture.

Lkanti lith.   P.Bertrand, éditeur, rue S.t André des Arcs. 53.   Imp. Lemercier, Paris.

THIÉDO.

Figure 6. Thiedo by David Boilat. Courtesy of the Schomburg Center for Research in Black Culture.

Llanta lith.   P.Bertrand, éditeur, rue St André des Arcs, 33.   Imp Lemercier, Paris.

HOMME PEULE.

Figure 7. Homme Peul by David Boilat. Courtesy of the Schomburg Center for Research in Black Culture.

Figure 8. Homme et Femme Toucoulaures by David Boilat. Courtesy of the Schomburg Center for Research in Black Culture.

Toucoulaures) (Figure 8), Boilat depicts a *marabout* creating a *gris gris* for a woman. But the viewer's perspective in this painting also includes a faint glimpse of what is being written in the *gris gris*. What I want to emphasize is not what this composition depicts, but rather the frame it brings to bear on what it represents, the privileged position onto this scene of inscription that it offers the viewer. This is a frame in which one can see and study other practices of textuality. Boilat's portrait seems to promise the readability of other textualities, even though the textual practice it depicts might not be representational at all. In the lengthy gloss Boilat provided for this image, he describes it as a scene of "fetish" making. What is being fetishized here, though, is not the talisman that the *marabout* is creating, but rather *our own viewing position*. The fetish here is the power to stand to one side of this practice and denounce it as "superstitious," as Boilat often did in his writings. The fetish is a perspective on textuality from which improper understandings of the materiality and agency of texts can be criticized.[23] The privilege of this point of view effaces itself in its own claim to naturalness—of course the *gris gris* is a text, Boilat's painting suggests, what else would it be? This may be why Boilat not only collected and confiscated *gris gris* but also opened them before he sent them to Paris, a gesture that seeks to "restore" them to their proper form as objects of mere ink and paper.

This painting captures an impulse that is intimately bound up with Boilat's practice of text collecting—the introduction of a frame in which a variety of practices, bodies, and speech genres all become *texts* that can be quoted, transported, and read in new ways. We see this frame most clearly in the notebooks, but it appears to subtend all of Boilat's scholarship. Of course, Boilat did not singlehandedly invent this reframing gesture, nor was he necessarily successful in his attempt to reconfigure the various textual, scholarly, and performance traditions he gathered. But the form of the text collection does cause the artifacts to *matter* in new ways, and it this new materiality that I want to insist on. The red wax that binds and superimposes the collection offers us a helpful way to grasp this point. Transcriptions, letters, proclamations, songs, poems, and talismans that might not otherwise have been related to each other become collated between two covers, and a potential and commensurable readability hardens around them. The notebooks are the raw flux of data that Boilat would later sift into his research. But they also help reveal that his practice of text collecting was haphazard, partially improvised, and not tightly tethered to any one discipline. Rather than an imposing scholarly edifice, Boilat's

contributions to the colonial library are a tenuous, composite formation—
what Ann Laura Stoler calls a "taxonomy in the making."[24]

The notebooks reveal a practice of amassing artifacts one does not yet
know what to do with but which one has learned to collect as *texts*. When
we reread Boilat's scholarship through the notebooks, all of his works
appear as a series of interlocking collections that are underwritten by a
special kind of translation, one not limited to the transfer of meaning between languages. Boilat's form of translation reconfigures different orders
of practice, embodiment, epistemology, and even ontology. His collation
of artifacts, performances, and adornment practices in the notebooks is a
feat of controlled equivocation, producing commensurability through a
common framework organized around the principle of text itself. By
shifting this assemblage into the notebook form, Boilat establishes himself as his collections' spokesperson. In the process, the very nature of the
contents is transformed. The interactional space of a folktale shifts; the
protective amulet that had been an actor in the social world is converted
into a potential object of study. By rereading Boilat through his notebooks, we uncover a practice of radical translation that aims at generating
a shared sense of textuality.[25]

The Literary Afterlife of a Text Collection

Nearly a century after the notebooks arrived in Paris, a young Senegalese
poet paged through Boilat's Wolof *Grammaire* in search of materials for
an anthology of African literature. The year was 1947, and the poet was
none other than the future president of Senegal, Léopold Sédar Senghor.
Among grammatical proofs that he knew well from his own research on
the Wolof language, Senghor happened upon the appendix of songs and
fables. He tried his hand at new French translations of some of the *léeb* and
woy that Boilat had collected. Senghor then included two of his own translations in his anthology, thereby consecrating as literary what Boilat had
collected merely as text.

The anthology that Senghor was working on is a now-obscure, co-
authored volume, *Les Plus beaux écrits de l'Union française et du maghreb*
(*The Most Beautiful Writings of the French Union and the Maghreb*). The
anthology was meant to illustrate the best writing from the territories of
the French Union, the short-lived federation that replaced the French
Empire between the Second World War and the wave of independences
around 1960. At the time, Senghor was a *député* in the National Assembly

and had been involved in writing the union's constitution.[26] Senghor's contribution to the anthology is a one-hundred-page section on the literature of all "Black Africa."[27] The prefatory essay that Senghor wrote for this section, a piece entitled "Negro-African Civilization," went on to be reprinted as a standalone piece in Senghor's collected writings. The anthology that this essay introduced has never been reprinted. But it is in the pages of the anthology itself that we can see Senghor working on some of his most well-known ideas.

Senghor's section on African literature is a collection of excerpts from heterogeneous time periods and far-flung origins, including translations of Arabic chronicles, Fân and Fulani folklore, Mossi and Kongo myths, and Wolof and Sérère proverbs, as well as contemporary prose, poetry, and theater by Africans writing in French. The majority of the excerpts are taken from the colonial library, from texts like Boilat's *Grammaire*—nonliterary studies of African societies and traditions that happen to include texts that Senghor could reframe as literary. Through this practice of retrieval, Senghor arrived at a comprehensive vision of an African literary past that he would continue to draw on for decades. Senghor's reliance on the colonial library is well documented, but I have no interest in arguing, as others have done, that it is necessarily a kind of weakness or contamination of his project. The point I want to make concerns the way Senghor makes use of Boilat's materials and what this exchange can teach us about the production of a useful literary past.

Boilat's collection shifts as it moves into Senghor's anthology, so it is appropriate that the *léeb* Senghor selects is a tale of metamorphosis. In "La Chenille et le Papillon" ("The Caterpillar and the Butterfly"), a proud butterfly looks down on a caterpillar that crosses its path, contemptuously dismissing the crawling insect for its lowly status, only to have the caterpillar point out that the two are, in fact, kin.[28] One reading of the *léeb* would be that kinship works in unexpected ways—do not be overly fixated on the current form of the entity you see before you, the *léeb* warns, since outward appearances can conceal unexpected bonds. In its movement through Boilat and Senghor's collections, the *léeb* undergoes a metamorphosis of its own. This emerges most clearly in a change to its structure of address. A *léeb* typically begins with an exchange between performer and audience. "Leebòòn," a storyteller calls. "Lëpoon," an audience replies. The exchange that follows frames the coming story as a tale. A *léeb* usually concludes with this phrase: "Foofu la léeb doxe tabbi géej, bakkan bu ko njëkk a fóon tabbi àjjana." (There the tale plunges into the ocean, the first who catches a whiff of it goes to paradise.)[29] These markers define the time and space of the tale and set it apart from any discourse around it. A *léeb* thus already comes equipped with its own conventions of worldedness—established norms for constituting participants into roles and ways of delineating the terms and conditions of a performance.

In Boilat's and Senghor's versions, the call-and-response structure of the *léeb* is preserved and yet completely transformed—they both refer to the formula, but neither one attempts to translate its effect. Boilat mentions the formula but does not call on the reader to participate, because for him this is no longer a *léeb* but a grammatical example. In a similar and yet altogether different way, the call-and-response is silent in Senghor's anthology. We read about the formula and learn about what it does, but this is a gloss. In neither case are we, as readers or listeners, asked to return the call, to participate in the delineation and constitution of an unfolding textual world. Boilat and Senghor translate the *léeb* in terms of its semantic content, but neither one of them translates the exchange between storyteller and audience that constitutes the *léeb* as a worlded narrative. In both cases, the codex format of the book that encloses the tale takes over the framing role. This is not a distortion or a loss so much as a reconfiguration. I am not interested here in romanticizing the *léeb*'s call-and-response formula as an index of a more organic connection between storyteller and audience. What interests me is how the *léeb*'s structure of address and its worldedness shift as it is collected, translated, and anthologized. The texts Boilat gathered were never traces of a purely oral lifeworld free of the meddling mediation of writing; instead, what Boilat collected were earlier practices and performances with their own semiotic ideologies, some written and some spoken or sung. Before they became texts in his collections, these diverse entities were enmeshed and entangled in relations of power and sometimes violence.

There is no better illustration of this than the second text that Senghor takes from Boilat. It is a *woy* with a rather long-winded title: "Song Against the Generals of Walo, After the Bombardment of Ndère, Capital of this Kingdom, by the French army." As the title indicates, this is another Wolof song composed on the occasion of a French military victory. This one commemorates the taking of Ndère during the conquest of Walo, and Boilat tells us it was performed by the inhabitants of Walo to express their disappointment with their leaders, who had failed to defend the region.[30] Neither Boilat nor Senghor have much to say about the song's violent circumstances. But whereas Boilat focuses on the grammatical nuances, Senghor explores the song's poetic qualities. Senghor is especially interested in the exemplary "imitative harmony" of this song, which he says is common "in negro-African poetry."[31] The poetic feature in question is an onomatopoeia—*bim-beuk!*—that the singer uses to evoke the sound of the cannons that were decisive for the French victory. In a remarkable trans-mutation, the gunfire of colonial conquest becomes an exemplar of a po-etic technique that then stands in for qualities of African poetry more generally.

Senghor's anthology not only translates some of Boilat's texts, it also serves to translate Boilat himself. Senghor writes that these texts were col-lected "by the Abbé Boilat, a Senegalese" in his *Grammar of the Wolof Language*.[32] Identifying Boilat as "a Senegalese" conflicts with the more am-biguous ways that Boilat actually presents himself in his writings. In *Es-quisses*, Boilat tells us he is a "child of Senegal" while in his *Grammaire* he merely notes that Wolof is his "maternal tongue" and describes the time he spent in Saint-Louis.[33] Boilat adjusts his self-positioning strategically throughout his work; sometimes he appears closer to his presumably French audience, while at other moments he assumes the role of the native infor-mant to support a particular knowledge claim. Senghor translates Boilat into a figure in a specifically Senegalese literary history. This positioning of Boilat as a kind of pioneer of Senegalese literature has been debated by later literary historians. Bernard Mouralis echoes Senghor in assigning Boilat an "essential place in the literary production of West Africa." Moura-lis claims that Boilat demonstrated "the evident wish to confer on Senegal and Africa the status of a *literary* object."[34] While it seems clear that Boilat wished to make Senegal and West Africa into objects of study to prepare for a more extensive colonization, it is far from clear that he intended to make them into literary objects.[35] In a helpful riposte, David Murphy turns Mouralis's assertion of literariness into a question: "At what point," Murphy asks in reference to Boilat, "does 'Senegalese literature' begin?"[36] Murphy ultimately decides that this is a problematic question, and I would tend to agree. And yet there *is* something about Boilat's work that does touch directly on the issue of literary origins. But here we need to ask a different question. Rather than asking when a literary tradition begins, we need to inquire into the conditions of such an emergence. The exchange between Boilat and Senghor prompts us to examine more closely the transforma-tions of textuality that allow a literary tradition to wrest precursors for itself from an older discursive order and claim them as literary.

The movement of the *léeb* and *woy* from Boilat's text collections into Senghor's anthology captures a translation of text into literature. In this translation, we can detect at least two distinct moments. First, there is Boilat's initial work of collection, a practice that aims at the production of texts, not literature, and that renders the discursive world into text-artifacts for future study. Second, there is Senghor's practice—a second-order form of collection, which aims to retrieve texts as literature. Senghor gathers his resources primarily from the colonial library itself, searching already-bound volumes for excerpts that can serve as examples of African literature. If Boilat's practice is one of text collecting, then Senghor's is one of gleaning—scouring already-bound volumes for texts and transcriptions that can be extracted to serve as literary monuments. Senghor treats all the books from which he excerpts in much the same the way as he treats Boilat's *Grammaire*—as text collections that can be broken apart, worked into a new assemblage, and re-presented as a literary past. In other words, Senghor's claim depends on the form of the text collection into which Boilat has already fastened his findings. This form then allows Senghor to quote, retranslate, and re-present these artifacts as works of literature that can exist alongside others like them.

Let us call Boilat's practice *entextualization* and Senghor's practice *literarization*. By entextualization, I mean here a practice of gathering, assembling, translating, or transcribing that yields a collection whose standard unit of measurement is the text-artifact.[37] By literarization, I mean the conversion of textual resources into literary texts. Entextualization turns a discursive and material world into text-artifacts, while literarization makes such texts into literature.[38] The point of distinguishing between these two dynamics is that scholarship on these types of moments almost always conflates them. We often see entextualization and literarization as one and the same moment, with literature as the necessary telos. What the hand-off between Boilat and Senghor suggests is that a transformation of text into literature consists of two distinct moments of translation. While a literarization depends on an entextualization for its raw material, an entextualization does not need to be oriented toward the production of literary texts at all.[39] Once we start to see the transformation of an older textual order into a literary one as consisting of two moments of translation rather than one, we arrive at a different perspective on the production of a literary past.

Pascale Casanova's *The World Republic of Letters* models an influential approach to this dynamic of literarization. Although we both have in mind the ways in which texts come to be treated as literary, Casanova's sense of literarization is rather different from mine. For her, the focus must be on the processes by which a text is acknowledged as literary by established authorities, a point of view that allows her to keenly track the currents of recognition in her world republic of letters. But to achieve this perspective, she must proceed as if there were already a basic currency of textuality undergirding all literary institutions and practices, everywhere and at all times. Thus Casanova understands literarization as "toute opération— traduction, autotraduction, transcription, écriture directe dans la langue dominante—par laquelle un texte venu d'une contré démunie littéraire-ment parvient à s'imposer comme littéraire auprès des instances légitimes. Quelle que soit la langue dans laquelle ils sont écrits, ces textes doivent 'être traduits,' c'est-à-dire obtenir un certificat de littérarité" (any operation— translation, self-translation, transcription, direct composition in the dom-inant language—by means of which a text from a literarily deprived country comes to be regarded as literary by the legitimate authorities. No matter the language in which they are written, these texts must in one fash-ion or another "be translated" if they are to obtain a certificate of literari-ness).[40] The crucial move here is the use of "text" to describe any input into an operation of literarization. Although Casanova does make it clear elsewhere that literarization "changes the nature" of the texts involved, her focus is on consecration and its transmutation of texts into literature.[41] There would be no difference, for Casanova, between what occurred when Johan Heinrich Voss translated Homer into German, Mazisi Kunene translated Zulu epics into English, Douglas Hyde translated Gaelic oral forms into English, or Boilat and Senghor translated a Wolof *léeb* into French.[42] Once a work enters into a global literary marketplace and is rec-ognized as literary, it is a text like any other in a perfectly equivalent way. In Casanova's optic, only one kind of translation can be said to have taken place in the exchange between Boilat and Senghor—the transformation of a folktale into literature. But when we look more closely, we see a fur-ther set of translations. The *léeb*'s structure of address and the worlded-ness of the performance are altered along a journey from being a text-artifact to a grammatical example to literature.

If all we see in the relay between Boilat and Senghor is the production of literature out of the raw materials of vernacular texts, then we have missed arguably the most important aspect of this process. The transla-tions that occur here are not only between languages but between differ-ent semiotic ideologies that surround the text itself. If entextualization and literarization are collapsed, gestures such as Senghor's will always appear to us as a kind of literary primary accumulation, a scramble to gather all available resources. This allows us to study the intricacies of literary capi-tal in world literary space, as Casanova's work ably demonstrates. But this can have the unfortunate effect of walling us off from any further explo-ration of what the textuality of a given text-artifact was like before it became literature and what it might still become. When we forget that the transformation of text into literature is premised on earlier reconfigurations, we begin to naturalize a certain understanding of textuality as inherent to literature, and we stop being able to envision ways of imagining this situation otherwise.

Casanova's conflation of entextualization and literarization is somewhat understandable, since these two dynamics do have a tendency to go hand in hand. Even my examples show some hints of an overlap. Boilat was not just a text collector; he was also a bit of a gleaner. Although most of the texts he reproduces in his grammar seem to be transcribed from performances, others may be translations back into Wolof of French versions of *léeb* that were produced in the 1820s by Boilat's patron, Baron Jacques-François Roger.[43] Senghor, for his part, was also a text collector—in addition to the excerpts he gathered for his anthology, he includes a small selection of proverbs he collected during field research for his thesis on the Sérère and Wolof languages. So we cannot draw too sharp a distinction here, since text collectors often seem to turn to a library in search of precedents to shape their practice, and gleaners often begin to write down examples from speech. Distinguishing between entextualization and literarization as different processes of translation is less about tracing a clear division that we can always defend and more about developing a heuristic principle. This allows us to observe that the textuality that we impart to texts that *become* literary is a contingent quality—the effect of a transformation that is neither necessary nor final. Thus, for a text to become or be claimed as literary is not a natural realization but a historical achievement of a special kind.

The Boilat-Senghor relay helps illustrate that there is not a singular ontology of textuality that preexists our modern literary world-system. Multiple layers of performance, inscription, transcription, writing, collecting, and reframing must all be laminated together to yield what appears to us as a certain naturalized mode of modern textuality. We are so used to taking this model of textuality for granted that we have trouble detecting that it is the result of a concatenation of different processes. Expanding our understanding of textuality offers a corrective to some of our normative frameworks of literary history. Such a reorientation also encourages thinking about how literary culture can be configured otherwise.

The historicity and contingency of the textuality literature brings with it is central to several of the writers studied later in this book. For the contemporary novelist Boubacar Boris Diop, whom I examine in Chapter 7, it is not a matter of gathering a *léeb* to prove that it is literature but rather of

trying to find a way of translating the call-and-response form, of struggling with the way that a literary frame seems to inevitably refract that
formula. Diop's novel *Doomi Golo* explores, in part, whether such refrac-
tion is necessarily a kind of loss or whether it is possible to translate not
the text of a *léeb* but the addressivity it carried with it—its sense of conjur-
ing *and* implicating its audience. Once we see the textuality of a literary
text as contingent and not determined in advance, we can begin to follow
the ways in which textuality *remains* unstable in texts that now present
themselves as literary. Once we untether literature from a certain narrow
understanding of textuality, a different critical vista opens up. The question ceases to be about when a literary tradition begins and becomes about
whether and how literature might accommodate other textualities.

CHAPTER 2

Para-literary Authorship: Colonial Education and the Uses of Literature

In 1947, Léopold Senghor proclaimed the emergence of a "new negro-African literature of French expression." Today, this phrase will likely seem plucked from Senghor's *Anthologie de la nouvelle poésie nègre et malgache de langue française*, a foundational collection of francophone poetry that helped establish the negritude movement. With its preface by Jean-Paul Sartre, Senghor's *Anthologie* often stands as the epoch-defining statement of the negritude generation's aesthetic intentions. And it is often through this foundational anthology that the story of literary modernity in francophone Africa is told.[1] But Senghor's pronouncement does not come from the *Anthologie*, and the "new literature" he had in mind was not negritude poetry. In fact, the declaration comes from that rather more-forgotten collection, *Les Plus beaux écrits de l'Union française*, which was published a year earlier than the more famous *Anthologie*. As I showed in Chapter 1, Senghor built a vision of an African literary past in his section of *Les Plus beaux écrits* by gleaning excerpts from the colonial library. But Senghor also wanted to isolate and celebrate the tendencies that he thought were most likely to produce a *modern* African literature. Surprisingly, these were not yet to be found in poetry. Although Senghor included a few poems by himself, Léon Damas, and Aimé Césaire, he rather modestly called them the work of "the young generation." This dates his proclamation of a new literature to a moment just before negritude would become negritude, when both the history and future of African literature in French appeared in a very different light than they do today. In 1947, Senghor was still framing his poetry and that of his peers as one small and still embryonic movement that existed in the shadow of a far more robust and recognized tradition of Africans writing in French.[2]

This more-established tradition that Senghor calls a "new literature" consists of writings by Africans who were associated in one way or another with the colonial school system—now-obscure figures such as Dim Delobson, Maximilien Quenum, Mapaté Diagne, and Mamby Sidibé, as well as future novelists such as Paul Hazoumé and Abdoulaye Sadji.[3] These writers were participating in a widespread project of generating new "scientific" knowledge about African societies. Training colonized students and future teachers to write studies of African cultures had been part of the colonial system from its earliest beginnings, but the project was greatly intensified and formalized in the 1930s through 1950s. Many African students and graduates of colonial schools participated. They produced ethnographies; linguistic research; collections of oral traditions; and studies of music, folklore, and sculpture. These works appeared in specialized journals and popular newspapers, and there were prizes and patronage opportunities for the most distinguished contributors.

This outpouring of writing was so closely identified with the colonial school system that Senghor would observe that "our new literature is a literature of school teachers."[4] Today this strange corpus is not widely read. Some scholars are tempted to avoid these ideologically suspect writings altogether in order to begin the story of literary modernity in francophone West Africa with negritude poetry in the 1940s or the rise of the novel in the 1950s.[5] But from the 1930s through the 1950s, this research-driven mode of writing by colonized students and teachers was by far the most established publishing channel for Africans writing in French.

Gathering these writings under the banner of a "new literature" is a surprising gesture, however, since most of these works seem at first distinctly *unliterary*. They are mainly works of social science or translations of oral traditions. And yet Senghor is not wrong: the studies of African cultures that were produced in and around colonial schools *do* often resemble literary works at the level of style, narrative, or rhetoric. But no matter how close the resemblance is, the authors of these works and the venues that published them were usually at pains to disavow any trace of literature. For example, a young schoolteacher writing about a Marka community in 1934 begins by noting that his study "does not have the pretension of being a literary work, but rather an essay of historical documentation." Nevertheless, the teacher's research is told as if it were a piece of realist fiction, narrated in the third person and complete with thick, novelistic descriptions.[6] This was a common strategy of expression for Africans publishing in French in the late colonial period—produce a text that draws extensively on literary techniques while nevertheless denying that your work has any pretensions of literariness. This is one of the most recognizable features of the quasi-scientific body of writing that Senghor hailed as the literary vanguard of French West Africa.[7]

To understand the strange ambivalence toward literature that exists in this corpus, I coin the term *para-literary authorship*. By this I mean narrative modes that are defined by being beside and beyond the literary but that are nevertheless immanently entangled with it. My use of "para" here is deliberate: it connotes a separation but also adjacency and even subordination. Para-literary modes are defined by their nonidentification with existing literary genres but also by their unavowable proximity to them. In advancing this optic, my intent is not to enter into arguments about what counts as literary, nor to essentialize "literature," nor even to suggest that works of ethnography or linguistics cannot be literary. Rather, my point is simply that what was and what was not literary was absolutely at issue in the negotiations between students, teachers, institutions, and publishing venues that shaped this body of writing. So to read this corpus as literature would flatten an important complication that constituted it. By approaching Senghor's "literature of school teachers" as a para-literary corpus, we can study the ways in which these writings interpenetrate with literary genres while retaining a certain distance from them.[8]

Para-literary authorship came into being to negotiate an implicit requirement that existed for many colonized writers: they were expected to write about their own societies from the position of detached observers, but they also had to offer an account of how they themselves had become the modern, colonized subjects who could write in this way. Literary techniques—from the formal or stylistic features of novels to practices of literary translation or citation—offered ways of navigating this racialized double bind. Para-literary modes allowed many colonized writers to make a contingent claim of authorship in French in a period in which this privilege was still fairly rare. In French West Africa, para-literary authorship was characterized by a profound reliance on literary methods and a disavowal of the literariness of one's writing.

In this chapter, I shed light on the possibilities and paradoxes of this mode through an exploration of a large and understudied archive of writings produced by colonized students in the late colonial period. From the 1930s to late 1950s, students at the William Ponty School in Senegal completed their schooling with a special kind of research project. Over the summer break of their third year, these students wrote ethnographies, often of their own communities. Collectively known as the Cahiers Ponty, or Ponty notebooks, these writings were the capstone assignment at the most exclusive institution in the colonial school system in West Africa. Generations of African elites wrote these notebooks, from future teachers and bureaucrats to novelists and presidents. Although nearly eight hundred notebooks were produced, there has been relatively little scholarship on this archive. My own recent article, from which this chapter is adapted, was the first study of the Ponty archive by a literary scholar.[9]

A Ponty notebook was supposed to demonstrate that a student had been sufficiently modernized and yet remained rooted in his African culture. Students were asked to write from a position of rigorous scientific examination and to avoid exercising their literary imaginations. And yet they were also frequently expected to tell the story of their own modernization. Through a survey of this archive and close readings of illustrative examples, I show that the Ponty notebooks are often saturated with a variety of literary techniques, which allow their student-authors to negotiate the complex assignment they were given.

By working through the Ponty notebooks, I outline a new theory of the uses of literature in colonial education. I argue that literary study in French West Africa helped cultivate an unspoken but nonetheless far-ranging grammar for enacting and measuring colonial modernity. As Ann Stoler points out, colonialism often required "proofs of estrangements" and "assessments of sentiments" from colonized subjects.[10] This was certainly true in French West Africa—at school entrance or exit exams and at other key moments of social mobility, colonized students were often asked to demonstrate the nature of their attachments to "French" and "African" cultures. Literary study provided a repertoire of strategies for successfully navigating such assignments. An ambivalent deployment of literary techniques was an essential part of the affective compass of colonial order: colonized authors made use of literary techniques to perform their distance from older orders and their attachments to newer ones. In this way, para-literary authorship was a key terrain on which colonial modernity was enacted and measured.

After outlining the characteristics of para-literary authorship through a reading of the Ponty archive, I shift focus to studying this mode beyond the colonial classroom. Para-literary authorship was one of the most common registers of written expression in colonial French West Africa. We find it in studies of native life written by colonized schoolteachers, in debates on the cultural evolution of Africa among elites, and even in the ways that citizenship applications made by colonial subjects were evaluated. Most perplexingly, we find extensive traces of para-literary authorship in texts that are now widely considered to be literary. Many of the earliest novels written by Africans in French have a great deal in common with the more widespread mode of para-literary writing that I study here. Reconstructing this entanglement between literary and para-literary texts of the late colonial period also provides a backdrop for the larger study of the language question that animates this book. As I will show in later chapters, many vernacular writers seem to refract the complexities of authorship that existed in the colonial era.

I close this chapter by reflecting on how para-literary authorship recasts the terms in which literary history is imaginable. Literary scholars are used to thinking historically through categories such as aesthetic movements (negritude) or genres, styles, or forms (the novel or free indirect style). But to study para-literary authorship and its legacies, we need an approach that can track the reconfiguration of literary institutions and practices. Whereas in Chapter 1 I examined the consolidation of a certain understanding of textuality, this chapter explores the volatility of authorship.

Authorship is a variable in literary history, not a constant. What it means to be an author, who can claim that distinction, and what kinds of texts or performances can be inscribed with a proper name—all these qualities are flexible across different lifeworlds and discursive formations. While this has been widely accepted in literary studies at least since Foucault, we have yet to explore the consequences of this insight for the study of world literature.[11] If we are to study the consolidation of modern literary culture on a global scale, then authorship and its variability must be a viable and even necessary site of inquiry. In the para-literary modes that predominated in French West Africa, we see the emergence of a contingent form of authorship that flourished under colonial conditions.

Literature and Colonial Education

Scholars have long shown that literature was intertwined with imperialism in a variety of ways: from the role of literary texts in securing the "power to narrate" on which colonialism depended, to the consolidation and export of national literary canons, to the importance of literary history in producing ideologies of culture.[12] In the case of French West Africa, a different kind of entanglement also existed. Literary study was pressed into service as a way of cultivating proper performances of colonial modernity from colonized students, without these performances in turn appearing *too* literary. To understand this use of literature, we need situate it in the context of the immense anxiety that existed around teaching the French language to colonized students.

From the beginnings of the secular school system in 1903, colonial education in West Africa took place almost exclusively in French. Although the political and educational climate varied greatly over the nearly six decades of the system's existence, hand-wringing over how French was being taught was one of the most evergreen topics in colonial pedagogical discourse. An influential strain of thought argued for teaching simplified French to colonized students. Georges Hardy, the first director of the school system, suggested that colonial teachers ought to "eliminate with care from [their] lessons [any] abstract terms or figurative language" so "that [colonized students] always know exactly what they are saying and that their capacity of expression does not go further than their capacity of thought."[13] For Hardy and his followers, teaching literature was especially risky; Africans were thought to be racially predisposed to verbosity, and literary studies were suspected of aggravating that inclination. As André Davesne put it in a 1929 circular, "We have no desire to turn our students into poets or novelists; we simply want to give them the means to express themselves with clarity, simplicity, and precision."[14]

But mistrust of literature and the unruly expressivity it generated had its counterweight: colonial teachers were also terribly worried that students were merely repeating what they had read, that they were not adequately expressing themselves "in their own words." It became clear to many teachers and administrators that if studies in the French language were too rote, colonized students would produce suspect written results. To teach students to write properly in French, colonial teachers often found that they had to make use of extensive training in what we would otherwise describe as the literary arts. Davesne himself acknowledged as much a decade later in the preface to a widely used colonial school reader: "How does an author create a particular impression for the reader? This is what we must try to have them discover. . . . If we neglect to study the technique of writing, we are failing in the principle goal of our instruction. What would we say of a teacher of painting who scrupulously taught the composition of colors that an artist used but who was silent on the characteristics of his art?"[15] Throughout the first half of the twentieth century, a certain model

of literary studies would be an essential and deeply mistrusted pillar of colonial education, particularly at the highest levels. In compositions and
research assignments, students were expected to put their literary training to use and yet not appear too literary lest they be accused of simply
copying what they had read. To be recognized as speaking in their own
words, colonized students often had to draw on literary texts and yet not
appear to be cribbing from a model.

An undated composition by a colonized student captures this tension
well. The essay is a commentary on a citation from Montaigne, "savoir par
cœur n'est pas savoir" (to know by heart is not to know). The author of the
composition was the future Senegalese novelist Abdoulaye Sadji, who would
go on to write some of the earliest francophone novels, *Nini* (1953) and
Maïmouna (1954). The unpublished composition was likely written when
Sadji was still a student in the 1920s. Sadji writes approvingly of Montaigne's
maxim, arguing that a child who memorizes only "absorbs knowledge and
discoveries from elsewhere which he merely makes his own. In reality, he
is nothing but a repeating machine." Sadji writes that teachers ought not
to cultivate bookish memorization, but instead encourage their students
to be more attached to the idea than to the expression itself. Montaigne's
maxim condenses in a single phrase, Sadji argues, "the great principle of
pedagogy" that helps "guard against the abuse of memory and routine" and
contributes instead "to the formation of the scientific spirit, so indispensable
to progress."[16]

Sadji's reading of Montaigne puts into sharp relief the tensions that existed around authorship in the colonial classroom. At first the lesson he
derives from Montaigne seems to be about the disqualification of memory.
But while Montaigne may complain about overly bookish instruction, his
essay actually stages the impossibility of what it counsels. The full quotation from Montaigne reads: "To know by heart is not to know; it is simply
to retain what we have entrusted to our memory. That which we rightly
know we can deploy without looking back at the model, without turning
our eyes back toward the book."[17] Throughout the text, Montaigne's eyes
are constantly and knowingly wandering back to his own library, where
he lingers with Plato, Plutarch, and Seneca. Similarly, while Sadji advocates for a pedagogy that would focus only on the idea itself, he does so
cunningly, through a certain indebtedness to past models—notably the citation from Montaigne that spurs the essay. Rather than producing a
perfect replica of what has been read, both Sadji and Montaigne suggest
we ought to make use of our readings as inspiration for our own original
reflections.

But how are we to tell the difference between bookish memorization and true, original thought? This question, of course, is not unique to colonial education. As Mikhail Bakhtin observes, the teaching of rhetoric always separates into two categories—reciting by heart and retelling in one's own words. The latter must be a double-voiced narration to a certain extent, since retelling in "one's own words" should never completely dilute the quality that makes another's words unique.[18] But in colonial education, this pedagogical paradox unfurled into a racialized double bind: the imperative for colonized students to speak in their "own words" existed alongside a demand that they include a trace of how those words had become "theirs." Literary training afforded both students and teachers the space and the methods to negotiate a proper performance of authorship under these conditions.

The William Ponty School and the "Africanization" of Colonial Education

Abdoulaye Sadji's composition was likely produced at the Ecole Normale William Ponty, where he was a student from 1926 to 1929.[19] Ponty was a teacher-training college and widely considered to be the most elite educational institution in French West Africa. The school that would become Ponty was founded in Senegal in 1904, as an Ecole Normale specifically designed to train African teachers for the new secular school system. For more than 50 years, Ponty drew male students aged 17–22 from across the federation to its campus in Senegal.[20] The opportunity to become a teacher seems to have offered young African men a greater degree of social mobility in the colonial period; in addition to the prospect of a teacher's salary, Ponty was often seen as a prestigious gateway to other careers in administration and educational opportunities abroad.[21] The instructors at Ponty were almost always young French men who had recently arrived from the *métropole*, often with only the level of *instituteur* (graduates of Ecoles Normales themselves but not qualified to teach in such institutions in France).[22] Training African teachers apparently began as a cost-cutting strategy, since Africans could be part of a separate cadre of personnel and therefore be paid less than Europeans.[23]

Many Ponty graduates later became involved in politics, and there is a strong case to be made that the friendships and affinities that students developed at the school played an important role in shaping the post-independence trajectories of several francophone African countries.[24] After independence, a number of Ponty students went on to successful careers in a variety of fields. The school's notable alumni include several future presidents and prime ministers: Félix Houphouët-Boigny (first president of Côte d'Ivoire), Modibo Keïta (first president of Mali), Mamadou Dia (first prime minister of Senegal), and Abdoulaye Wade (third president of Senegal). They also include a number of writers and artists: the novelists Bernard Dadié, Abdoulaye Sadji, Ousmane Socé, and Paul Hazoumé and the poet and performer Fodéba Keïta. The school's alumni are so threaded through the politics and cultural production of twentieth-century francophone West Africa that nearly half the members of the first editorial board of the landmark journal *Présence Africaine* were Ponty graduates. But to trace the impact of Ponty as an institution, we must shift focus away from its production of exemplary individuals and toward its role in the emergence of the discipline of para-literary authorship that marked an entire generation of elite students.

Beginning in 1933, colonized students at Ponty completed their studies by writing monographs known as the *devoirs de vacances* (summer projects). In this assignment, students were required to research some aspect of their communities of origin during their summer vacation and then use the material they gathered to produce a formal study in their final year. The Ponty notebook assignment was a key condition of social mobility and access to educational advancement for several generations of male francophone African elites. The assignment lasted until about 1950. In the following sections, I explore the Ponty notebooks as a prime example of para-literary authorship. I begin by situating the emergence of the notebook assignment against the backdrop of a broader project to reshape colonial education. I then study how and why Ponty students made use of literary models in their notebooks, even though the assignment itself ostensibly forbade "false literary descriptions."[25] I unpack the major tropes and rhetorical strategies that students employed as well as the feedback from instructors that constrained their performances.

Senghor praised Ponty in 1947 for instilling "an African spirit" in its graduates and preparing them to "respectfully research black values."[26] This research-driven curriculum took hold fairly late at Ponty, during a period of intense political and educational transformation. Although Ponty stood at the apex of colonial education in French West Africa, it was not directly modeled on the French Ecoles Normales. From its early beginnings, it had had a curriculum all its own that was primarily focused on preparing African teachers to participate in spreading the French language.[27] As schooling came to be viewed as a primary vector of colonization, Ponty assumed an increasingly central role.[28] But in the late 1920s and early 1930s, a major shift in colonial rationality and policy reshaped the curriculum at Ponty and gave rise to the notebook assignment.

Although the production of anthropological knowledge about African lifeworlds was already widespread in the nineteenth century, ethnography became increasingly central to French colonial administration in the interwar period. Colonial policy and ethnography mutually reinforced each other in the works of administrator-ethnographers such as Robert Delavignette, Georges Hardy, and Maurice Delafosse.[29] As their writings found favor with a series of sympathetic governors general, a new political rationality coalesced around the position that replacing indigenous social structures with metropolitan ones was a mistake and that native policy could be successful only if it based itself on a methodical study of local populations and committed itself to maintaining indigenous societies in their authenticity.[30]

This ethnographic turn in colonial policy coincided with a major reorganization of the school system.[31] From its founding in 1903, the system had been organized in a pyramidal structure that reflected its priorities, with village schools at the bottom and elite institutions like Ponty at the top. Early on, the system recruited only a tiny percentage of school age children and was focused on training small numbers of educated Africans as functionaries for the colonial administration.[32] But after the First World War, there was a push to "Africanize" colonial education. This meant converting a system built to produce a few assimilated individuals into one that targeted the rural masses and was bent on simultaneously preserving and transforming African societies.[33]

The "Africanization" of schools in French West Africa was part of a much larger move toward "adapted education" that spread across the empire in the 1920s and 1930s. In principle, adapted education meant a move away from imposing a metropolitan system of education in the colonies and a push to develop pedagogies that were adapted to local societies and "mentalities."[34] In West Africa, adaptation meant reforms that emphasized decentralization; the importance of rural, village schools; and "cultural training" for elites that would reacquaint them with their African culture.[35] Although begun under Governor Jules Carde in 1924, adapted education found its most vocal advocates in the 1930s in Governor Jules Brevié and Inspector General of Schools Albert Charton (who would later formalize the notebook assignment at Ponty).[36] Charton bemoaned the older style of colonial education, which he faulted for having "practiced the politics of the tabula rasa and considered the young native like the statue of Condillac, apt to receive everything from the teacher who animates him with all his ideas, all his perceptions, all his thoughts." For Charton, what was needed was a new kind of education adapted to the "native mentality which must be known and analyzed in its diverse manifestations in order to transform it and orient it toward a new life."[37]

The centerpiece of this new style of education was the ecole rurale populaire, or rural popular school. Governor Brévié described these as "a farm and a workshop, a dispensary and an experimental field" that would be "liberated from ambitious academic curricula."[38] Academics were to be de-emphasized in favor of a curriculum focused on farming techniques and manual labor and the study of local history, art, music, and customs.[39] In short, such schools had "the paradoxical task of creating traditional Africans."[40]

The reorganization of the school system in French West Africa also came during a long-running political struggle between the colonial administration and the French-educated, urban African elite. The election of Blaise Diagne as the first African deputy to the French National Assembly in 1914 sent shockwaves through the colonial establishment. By the end of First World War, the colonial state was forced to confront the rising political power of urban African communities, some of whom had historically enjoyed French citizenship as *originaires* born in the four communes of Senegal.[41] The temporary stabilization of the *originaires'* citizenship status through the 1915 and 1916 Blaise Diagne Laws only deepened the antipathy.[42] In the period leading up to the school reforms of the early 1920s—which followed on the heels of Diagne's reelection—the colonial administration put in place a series of roadblocks to Africans ever becoming "French," no matter their level of culture.[43]

For its part, the colonial education system increasingly soured on policies that had formerly valorized assimilation, epitomized by elite institutions such as Ponty. Discourse on colonial pedagogy in this period became fixated on portraying the "*évolués*"—the "evolved" African elite—as dangerously uprooted from their own communities and worryingly attuned to political currents of the wider world.[44] Advocates of adapted education sought to transform the school system into one that would teach future elites to be properly, authentically African—and thus possibly incapable of acceding to citizenship, since in this period, an African applicant for French citizenship had to demonstrate not only French cultural competence but above all that he had adequately separated himself from his "native customs."[45] It was against this backdrop of mounting claims on French citizenship and demands for political representation that the school system began trying to teach Africans to be African again.

At the same time, however, the colonial administration carried on expanding the existing higher levels of education in the interwar period, with the aim of maintaining the elite it counted on as auxiliaries, collaborators, and intermediaries.[46] Located at the intersection of these competing priorities, the Ecole Normale at Ponty came under heavy scrutiny. Sitting at the top of the educational pyramid, Ponty had long been a focus of suspicion—particularly for its methods of teaching French. This had already come to a head in 1921 during the exit exams at Ponty, when 71 out of 71 candidates acquitted themselves satisfactorily and had to be given diplomas. The jury suspected that a large number of candidates had simply committed their lessons to memory and reproduced them during the exams. The supervisor of schools at the time, Aristide Prat, complained bitterly at having to pass so many mediocre candidates. In a special memo, he blamed the "meddling of memory, which gives, wrongly, the illusion of progress." He called on the teachers at Ponty and at all levels of instruction "to search for new methods of examination" such that they could "continually assure that the student has really understood, that the child knows what he is saying . . . to effectively verify his intellectual acquisitions."[47]

As the turn to adapted education intensified in the 1930s, the search for new methods of evaluation at Ponty developed into a significant shift in pedagogy. In the new educational dispensation, Ponty was simultaneously tasked with producing African teachers for the newly "adapted" schools, while also being obliged to train an ever-more mistrusted (because politically effective) local elite. Thus when the time came to reform Ponty in the 1930s, the curriculum was restructured around what was called "Franco-African culture."[48] This took hold in the 1930s under Charton and was greatly intensified under the directorship of Charles Béart from 1939 to 1945.[49] Charton defined Franco-African culture as a process by which French culture "must descend into the native mentality, to make it intelligible and to transform it." Charton added that it would be up to the "cultivated native to guide the way"; but that in so doing, the native must not break "the bond with his original environment, since that would put him at risk of becoming an errant and aberrant spirit."[50]

In practice, the Franco-African curriculum at Ponty often meant a simplified one, with less ambitious math and science instruction.[51] In their place was an increased emphasis on reacquainting students with their "African culture," or as one teacher put it, to "re-submerge these young men into their [own] milieu."[52] Experiments in Franco-African culture at Ponty took a variety of forms, including a short-lived attempt to teach the transcription of African languages.[53] But the best-known aspects of the Franco-African curriculum at Ponty were the notebook assignment and the theatrical productions in which Ponty students wrote and staged plays in French based on African source material. Begun at roughly the same time in the early 1930s, the notebooks and the plays were the heart of Franco-African culture at Ponty.

Of these two activities, the theater of Ponty has received far more scholarly attention.[54] The reasons for this are understandable, since the plays produced by Ponty students were some of the first francophone African theater productions. While the scholarship on the Ponty theater has been both productive and comprehensive, one unfortunate consequence of this line of research has been to sharply delineate the staged performances from the notebooks themselves. To the extent that the Ponty notebooks have been discussed at all relative to francophone African literature, it has been from a distance in terms of an assumed influence on this dramatic tradition. In this respect, the notebooks have largely been assumed to be just dusty source material. Nothing could be further from the case.[55]

The Ponty Notebook Assignment

In the notebook assignment, Ponty students were usually given a choice of topics and a prompt or a questionnaire to accompany each one.[56] The topics included foodways, folklore, agriculture, marriage, children's games, clothing, and animals—to name just a few. Students also wrote monographs on particular villages or regions as well as on individual social or ethnic groups. Given that these were teachers in training, the education of children in the students' communities of origin was also a favored topic. In light of the size of this archive, it is difficult to generalize, but there are some common features. All the notebooks are quite literally composition books, and the texts within them range anywhere from twenty-five to sixty pages—although some run considerably longer—and are often accompanied by illustrations and (more rarely) photographs.

In the original description of the assignment, Charton makes it clear that the notebook is to be for Ponty students a "discipline" with a threefold purpose. First, it is intended to be a self-modernizing project, with the imperative that the student recount a return to his origins. As Charton puts it, the idea is "to turn the gaze of our future schoolmasters toward the rational knowledge of their original environment. . . . In this sympathetic return to the facts of native life, our teachers will discover respect for living traditions as well as the feeling that transformations are necessary."[57]

As another description of the assignment put it, the Ponty student was supposed to "confront the ideas and opinions that he has encountered at school with those of his illiterate brothers who have remained in the village."[58] The second purpose of the assignment was to serve as a stylistic exercise. Charton hoped it would improve the students' written expression by regulating any unruly expressivity. The notebooks, he writes, will "oblige our students to use precise observation, and an exact description of known, familiar facts . . . to contain the verbal imagination, to avoid false literary descriptions."[59] Lastly, Charton envisioned a documentary function for the notebooks. "These modest works," he writes, "contain a certain documentary or even scientific value."[60] This was despite the fact that students had little if any formal training in ethnography, and in most cases, instructors would have had no way to verify the information that their students reported.[61] My research suggests that although the assignment varied over time, the three-part structure outlined by Charton was largely conserved.

Students were enjoined to translate their own lived experience into the terms of an ethnographic monograph in a Ponty notebook, to rewrite their own past and that of their community in a new perspective. Despite nominally being about given topics, the notebooks are often about the students' relationships to themselves. In their introductions and sometimes throughout their compositions, the students were often at pains to situate themselves with regard to the writing of the notebook. There was a double function to this assignment: to write an ethnography but also to provide the warrant for that ethnography's having been written, to tell the story of how the world came to be ethnograph-able the student. This is quite memorably captured by one student-author, Lokho Damey, who writes of former students like him "qui ne veulent plus répondre à l'appel du diable dans la forêt, qui n'entend plus dans le cri du hibou le passage d'un mauvais esprit" (who no longer want to respond to the devil's call in the forest, who no longer hear an evil spirit in the cry of the owl).[62] As Damey's vivid phrase suggests, the notebooks required not only descriptions of seeing the world in new ways but also a story about no longer seeing in older ways, about no longer hearing certain voices in the social world. We need to distinguish between these two requirements—the ethnographic and the performative—lest we collapse the two. A Ponty student was asked not only to see the world with new eyes but also to tell the story of how those eyes came to be theirs. The assignment demanded not only ethnography but a kind of justificatory self-writing in which the student demonstrated that he had come to be the modern-enough colonial subject who was himself the author of the testimony he was providing.

To accommodate this double function, the official assignment had to be stretched. While the use of "false literary descriptions" may have been explicitly discouraged, many of the notebooks themselves are structured on a deep level by a variety of literary techniques and practices. Some notebooks make extensive use of literary forms or styles; others provide literary translations of oral texts or use excerpts from literary works as prompts for cultural comparison. Far from being excluded from the notebooks, literature was an important space in which these student-authors negotiated the performance of self-making that the assignment obliquely demanded.

One of the more common literary tropes we find in the notebooks is a trace of the *bildungsroman*, or novel of formation.[63] Some students, particularly those writing about the socialization of children, write their notebook almost as if they were *éducations sentimentales*. Those who do this often employ a fictional double, most frequently a young boy from their community of origin who serves as the negative image of the author's own "modern" education that has culminated in Ponty. In his notebook on Fulani education, for example, Ibrahima Sow uses a character named Mamadou in a cautionary tale that parallels his own. Unlike Sow himself, Mamadou is sent to study with a Quranic teacher, where he acquires "aucune notion de sciences, d'histoire, de géographie" (not even the smallest idea of science, history nor geography) and ends up an itinerant practitioner of "maraboutage."[64] Another student, Amadou Sakhir Cissé, employs a similar foil in his study of the education of Gourou children in Côte d'Ivoire. Cissé invokes the character of young Oka to demonstrate the dangers of a traditional Gourou upbringing: "Cette vie fait d'Oka un méchant garçon, et plus tard un homme très dur, sans pitié, pour bien dire, un barbare." (This life has made of Oka a wicked boy, and later a hard man, pitiless, in other words, a barbarian.)[65]

In other notebooks, the fictive double is a child who was at one time on the same educational track as the author, but who for various reasons has slid "backward." Joseph Batiéno, writing about a Mossi community, contrasts his own personal story with the character of Manéguedo, who leaves primary school to return to his village. Upon crossing paths with Manéguedo later on in life, the author complains of the regression he observes in this young man: "[Manéguedo] était intelligent, sympathique et toujours gai. Qu'est-il devenu, cet ami aux yeux brillants qui suivait attentivement les leçons des maitres?" ([Manéguedo] was intelligent, kind and always gay.

What has become of this friend with the shining eyes who followed his teachers' lessons so attentively?) Batiéno continues, mournfully, "Parle-t-il encore français? On le dirait pas." (Does he still speak French? It would seem not.)[66] Students employ such narratives of failed formation to legibly enact their own socialization as modern subjects.[67]

A second kind of literary trace found in many notebooks is the use of free indirect style. Students often write about ritual experiences, lifeways, and traditions in which they themselves may have been participants at a younger age, but in their notebooks, they must write simultaneously from a "lived and observed" experience and inhabit a more pulled-back, "scientific" point of view.[68] This produces narrative volatility. Porous voicing styles that we would recognize as free indirect in a novel are a common outcome. For example, in a notebook on folklore a student named Cheikhou Tidiane Dieng writes on the existence of spirits:

> Nous sommes nés au milieu des parents superstitieux qui nous ont habitués à avoir peur des vents de sables . . . de bonne heure nos parents ont mis en nos têtes cette erreur: qu'il existe des esprits malfaisants et jaloux. Et je vous dirai en toute sincérité que quoique n'en ayant jamais eu une preuve, j'y crois, malgré moi, et je ne me sens pas encore la force de lutter contre ces traditions injustifiées.[69]

> We were born amidst superstitious relatives who accustomed us to being afraid of the sandy winds . . . early on our relatives put this error in our heads: that there exist evil and jealous spirits. And I will tell you, in all sincerity, that even though I have never had any proof, I believe, despite myself, and I do not yet feel the strength to fight against these unjustified traditions.

Three centers of enunciation are superimposed in this passage: there is a "we" that is located in the past and which speaks for an entire generation; there is an "I" that speaks in the present as the modernized, Ponty-educated narrator; and there is another "I" who still believes in spirits and who cannot be entirely untangled from the first two speakers. The effort to look upon the past from a skeptical remove places Dieng beside himself: in the phrase "I believe, despite myself" Dieng's "I" drifts away from "myself" without the two being entirely distinct. Such temporal and subjective dislocations are fairly common. The narrators of Ponty notebooks often seem at risk of splitting into two voices, one saying, "This is what I saw," and the other interrupting, "But this is what that must have *really* meant."

If Dieng's notebook were a novel, we would speak of free indirect style; there are statements that cannot be attributed to any one speaker, and yet

the personae are not entirely dissolved into each other. One could reason-
ably object that free indirect style is a hallmark of classic ethnographic
writing—think of the sweeping and yet intimate pronouncements anthropologists of a certain era could make about indigenous lifeworlds.[70] But
any omniscience the Ponty students derived from free indirect style was
usually fleeting. Instead, the students often use free indirect style to craft a
kind of doubled narrative consciousness that allows them to tack between
ethnographer and native informant.[71] But here we must remember that the
split consciousness that unfolds on the pages of a Ponty notebook is not
necessarily a trace of a subjective crisis experienced by the student-author so
much as an enactment of the requirements of the assignment itself. As Barbara Johnson reminds us, free indirect style reveals "a discourse learned, not
a person perceived."[72] It is this artifactual quality that is most useful in the
notebooks; free indirect modes allow students to perform themselves as subjects who have been sufficiently, but not completely, detached from their pasts.

A third trace of the literary that we find in the notebooks is an extensive and visible practice of translation. Translating material out of African
languages and into French was central to the Franco-African curriculum
at Ponty. The Ponty theater assignments, for example, were initially pitched
as exercises in translation.[73] The notebooks were similarly reliant on translation, since they involved students gathering material in African languages only to transform it into French. In more normative anthropological
work of this era, we might expect such dependence on translation to be
concealed in the final monograph. But in a successful Ponty notebook, students heavily thematize translation, an effect that serves to legitimize
their own position as authors.

Ponty notebooks on various topics overflow with translations and transcriptions from African languages. Some students sort the performance
traditions they collect into commensurably literary categories, categoriz-
ing them as folktales, fables, epics, or proverbs—a practice that harkens
back to David Boilat, studied in Chapter 1. Some students go further and
translate their collections into French verse. The notebooks that concen-
trate on oral traditions tend to have the largest anthologies, but even those
that focus on foodways, agriculture, or clothing sometimes include extensive appendices. In the notebooks, translation was important less for evi-
dentiary reasons than for the way it buttressed a claim to narrative authority.
For example, in a notebook on oral traditions, Kalifa Keïta writes that it
was "almost impossible" for him to adequately render Bambara sayings
into French, so instead he chose to "simplify" the speaking styles of his
informants.[74] What matters about this gesture is the way Keïta positions

himself as someone who can confidently serve as an intermediary and a spokesperson. The grader of a notebook was unlikely to care about how accurately Keïta had translated from Bambara. Most instructors at Ponty would have had only a limited ability to verify such translations, even from such a major language. We can therefore identify this tendency in the notebooks as a *performance* of translation. Such a performance was an integral part of the notebooks' self-justifying claims on colonial modernity.

A final trace of the literary in the notebooks is comparative: literary texts are used as a platform for discussions of African societies. Students at Ponty seem to have been asked to compare French literary texts to aspects of native life. This seems to have been particularly true of gender norms. A vivid example was the use of Molière's *Les Femmes savantes*, which was apparently taught to the all-male Ponty student body to provoke reflections on the education of women in their communities.[75] An echo of such an exercise is evident in at least one notebook, by Mamadi Diakité.[76] Citing extensively from Chrysale's monologue in act 2, scene 7, Diakité uses Molière to warn of the dangers of overeducating women. In the scene, Chrysale is complaining that his servant has been chased off by his *précieuses* female relatives, who have been offended at the servant's incorrect French. In the passage cited, Chrysale holds that:

> Il n'est pas bien honnête, et pour beaucoup de causes,
> Qu'une femme étudie et sache tant de choses.
> Former aux bonnes mœurs l'esprit de ses enfants,
> Faire aller son ménage, avoir l'œil sur ses gens,
> Et régler la dépense avec économie,
> Doit être son étude et sa philosophie.

> For a hundred reasons, it's neither meet nor right
> That a woman study and be erudite.
> To teach her children manners, overlook
> The household, train the servants and the cook,
> And keep a thrifty budget—these should be
> Her only study and philosophy.[77]

Chrysale's speech, Diakité observes, contains "general truths that concern our country."[78] Diakité seems mainly to mine from Molière a certain misogynistic critique of female intellectuals who foolishly "veulent écrire, et devenir auteurs" (wish to write, and become authors).[79] But the scene he quotes is also about a dangerous obsession with overly perfect French. The debate between Chrysale, Philaminte, and Bélise in the play itself revolves around what it means to be learned and literate, and how true learning can easily be mistaken for a careful deployment of rhetoric and citation. In the very scene Diakité quotes, Chrysale counsels Philaminte to burn her library, referring to books themselves as just useless furniture (a *"meuble inutile"*).

But in Diakité's uptake of *Les femmes savantes*, the *meuble* in question is Molière's text itself, which becomes the means by which this student demonstrates his own learned credentials. Diakité has to do a bit of furnishing, as it were, to show the success of his formation as a (implicitly masculine) modern colonial subject.[80] He does this with a citation from Molière, but other students use other literary referents and models. The proof of successful colonial self-making in the notebooks sometimes seems to be the literary trappings—these *meubles inutiles*—that become both the medium through which the formation is realized and the means by which it is recognized. This is not to say that Diakité misses the point of Molière, nor even that there cannot be something subversive in the way he quotes this particular scene; rather, his use of citation here animates a contradiction at the very heart of the para-literary mode he is working in. The literary is supposed to be the nearly invisible architecture of a certain disposition of a modern subject that is to unfold in the notebook. But whenever and wherever it appears, the use of a literary citation is always at risk of being rather too conspicuous.

No matter how closely some of the notebooks resemble literary texts at the level of form or style, they almost always follow altogether predictable trajectories at the level of structure: each notebook is divided into subsections that seem to have followed from the choice of topic itself. As part of the assignment, each topic came with a defined list of questions that students had to answer and around which they had to structure their notebooks. Thus any notebook on education, no matter how creative its emplotment, tends to follow the same arc. Students work through subsections, including the child's education in the family, moral education, physical education, social education—almost always in this exact order. Thus any room for inventiveness at a formal or stylistic level seems to have coexisted with some rather strict structural constraints that served to discipline these texts into something resembling works of social science. This dynamic produces some rather strange results, almost as if novelistic batter had been poured into an ethnography-shaped container.[81]

Incorporating literary techniques also affords the notebooks a greater repertoire of representational strategies. For instance, some students follow their protagonists into intimate situations and interior thoughts, which would be beyond the reach of an ethnographic observer. Edouard

Aquereburu, in his study of *évolués,* focuses his work around a character he calls François. "Nous allons voir François partout, chez lui, dans son ménage, dans sa petite famille, chez ses parents demeurés paysans. Nous allons le voir avec les Européens, nous allons le voir dans son village, nous allons le voir Instituteur à l'Ecole urbaine, fonctionnaire d'élite." (We will see François everywhere, at home, with his family, with his relatives who have remained peasants. We will see him with Europeans, we will see him in his village, we will see him as a teacher in an urban school, as an elite functionary.)[82] Allowing the reader to "see" François "everywhere" suggests a kind of surveillance function for these notebooks.

But gestures of representational license like Aquereburu's served a more practical purpose as well. Many students open their notebooks with a preface addressed directly to the reader/grader.[83] In these para-texts, some students comment on the difficulties they faced in gathering all the information that was required of them. Sometimes they report that they had no rights of access to topics that they were supposed to have studied.[84] This is often the case when dealing with the expertise of social groups other than their own—from bodies of knowledge belonging to secret societies and endogamous "castes" to practices associated with occult practitioners or gendered labor.[85]

Other students complain of even more elemental challenges—sometimes the basic demography of their home region is said to be elusive. Students report that individuals and family units withhold information about themselves for fear it could be used for purposes of taxation or military conscription—a detail that reminds us that inhabiting the position of the ethnographer may also have shifted the ways in which these newly nosy students were perceived by their own communities.[86] In such circumstances, fictional conventions for ventriloquizing other peoples' traditions and lived experiences became a strategy; students would avail themselves of fiction where sociological "information" could not be obtained.

But was this turn toward the literary always a pragmatic one on the part of the students? What were literary techniques doing in these notebooks after all, since they were never supposed to have been there in the first place? One theory might be that the students themselves initiated this turn and that the literary constituted a space for them to subvert the original assignment. This would be an attractive argument, but the literary dimensions of these notebooks are pervasive enough that it simply cannot be a case of overt resistance. Furthermore, an examination of the comments that survive in the margins—written by teachers at Ponty—tells a different story. While there may have been no official literary dimension to the assignment, in practice, graders' comments reveal that teachers would sometimes penalize students whose compositions fell flat stylistically. Amadou Arona Sy, for instance, received this tepid accolade for his work: "Documentation assez abondante mais sèchement présentée" (Adequate documentation but dryly presented).[87] In the very same year, Baffa Gaye was rather sharply criticized for a study that demonstrated the opposite tendency. His notebook was found to be too attached "aux apparences, aux faits extérieurs, au côté pittoresque du sujet" (to appearances, to exterior facts, to the picturesque side of the topic).[88] Such comments indicate how fine a line the students had to walk in their compositions.

But the push and pull of teachers' comments went well beyond a concern for style. Some students were called out for not having made more use of literary models, while others were chastised for going too far. Yapi Kouassi was condemned for not drawing more on "the good La Fontaine" in his study of animals.[89] But Lompolo Koné was raked over the coals for producing too literary a text in his remarkable notebook "L'Ancien tirailleur revenu au village." Koné's notebook follows a former soldier once he returns to his native village after fighting for France in the First World War. His notebook comes much closer to being an elegantly realized novella than most—there is a clear arc of character development for the protagonist and even a wonderfully cheeky narrator who gently mocks the ex-soldier's excessive vanity. But the grader at Ponty was unconvinced: "Malheureusement ce genre de travail à forme romancée incite au verbiage, au remplissage, aux développement filandreux: mieux vaut une étude précise qu'un sujet aussi flou." (Unfortunately this kind of work with a novelistic form seems to incite verbiage and overwrought development: a precise study is far better than such a formless topic.)[90] The marginal comments suggest that colonized students at Ponty were not to write novels, but nor were they permitted to entirely do away with a concern with style and literary expression. The slide toward the literary, then, appears to have been an unavowable but nevertheless tacitly understood requirement: students often actually *had* to use some literary techniques in their notebooks, though they could not appear to be writing literature.

An examination of how literature was taught at Ponty supports this reading. Some exposure to literary texts was seen as necessary, but activities resembling literary study were primarily undertaken to cultivate proper French expression. Despite its elite status in West Africa, a Ponty education was by and large intended to be a "just enough" education, aiming mainly for a certain level of French for these future teachers.[91] In a lengthy commentary on the place of literature in this educational model, one director declared that it was desirable (within limits) for Ponty students to "know the meaning of the works of major writers" such as Molière, Corneille, Shakespeare, Hugo, Flaubert, and Proust. Such familiarity provided "the literary references that are found these days in the speech and writings of average cultured people and which, by their human value, are like points of reference where sprits calibrate themselves." But there was, the director added, absolutely no question of teaching a "methodical" course in French literature along the lines of Gustave Lanson, the French scholar who helped popularize literary history in the early twentieth century. The goal of literary study at Ponty was to cultivate "better knowledge of French" through "a greater penetration of the 'genius' of the language."[92] As far as can be discerned from the archival record, literary studies existed in a piecemeal fashion primarily as a study of literary techniques and references. Literature was mainly useful as a space of "calibration" (*se réajuster*).[93]

Another place to look to understand the curious reliance on the literary in the notebooks is in the prompts for the assignments. A common prompt used in the notebooks on education from the 1940s begins with a citation from Hubert's *Traité de pédagogie générale*: "There is no human society, be it the most simple of all, without a pedagogical system; every society renews itself indefinitely by the accession of young members." The prompt itself continues by asking students to describe "the traditional education system of a society that you know well (education in the family, social rules concerning the adolescent, the initiation stage and the ceremonies that punctuate the physical and mental developmental phases of the child)." Students are then asked to show that the "traditional formation of the child 'has as its goal and function the maintenance of the constitutive type of the society under consideration.'"[94] There is little space in the prompt for articulating any alternative account of the socialization of children. This is because the prompt was not an invitation to open-ended research but rather an occasion for students to conclude that traditional education reproduced a given society's constitutive "type." The word "maintenance" (*maintien*) here is especially crucial, because in the dozens of notebooks that respond to this prompt, all manner of "traditional" socializations come to be reduced to the simple maintenance of a static, timeless African society.

Not surprisingly, the other side of this coin is a good deal of praise for French colonial education. A few representative examples of this binary will help clarify its terms. In a notebook on "traditional education," Ibrahima Ben Mady Cissé draws the contrast starkly: "la tradition est sacrée dans ce groupement. . . . La plus forte empreinte est la mécanisation qui attaque

tout, englobe tout et l'éducation semble être sa victime la plus éprouvée."
(Tradition is sacred in this group. . . . The strongest evidence is the mecha-
nization that infects everything, envelops everything and education seems
to be its most time-tested victim.)[95] Mahélor Diouf N'Doféne's notebook
provides another telling example: "Le dressage qui y est employé comme
méthode d'éducation noie l'individu dans la masse fabrique des enfants d'un
rouage de machine, tue la personnalité et la curiosité intellectuelle." (The
training [*dressage*] that they use as a method of education drowns the individual in a mass production of children as merely cogs in a machine, killing
their personality and intellectual curiosity.)[96] French education, on the
other hand, is usually lavishly praised. As Habibou Bâ writes, "Cette personnalité, cette souplesse d'esprit, cette plasticité, en un mot cette expansion
totale des virtualités et des facultés de l'enfant qui saurait mieux la favoriser
que l'Ecole française?" (This personality, this suppleness of spirit, this plas-
ticity, in a word this total expansion of the possibilities and faculties of the
child—who knows better how to promote it than the French school?)[97]

The educational contrast these notebooks (are seemingly obliged to)
draw can often be summed up by the opposition between a young mind
(*esprit*) that is merely furnished (*meublé*) with received ideas versus one that
is properly formed (*formé*) with critical faculties of its own. Whatever falls
under the banner of "traditional education" in the notebooks is most often
linked to mental furnishing and characterized as stasis, rigidity, the maintenance of a machine, and even *dressage*, a term generally reserved for the
training of animals. French education, by contrast, typically gets to be
about the formation of a student's personality, the unfurling of character
and *esprit critique*. A large number of notebooks reproduce this contrast—
and there is nothing especially surprising about this. It is exactly what one
might expect would have been required of colonized student-teachers. And
yet the critique of *dressage* and the ensuing praise for enlightened colonial
formation appears over and over again as regularly as clockwork. It appears
frequently in the prefaces or conclusions of notebooks on education but we
find similar comparisons across a broad sampling of the notebooks. In
other words, the trope itself is a sort of refrain. This suggests that it was
actually Ponty that was engaging in a certain mechanistic training of its
students: in this case eliciting very generic narrative accounts of their becoming modern, colonial subjects. And to produce such generic accounts,
a certain recycling of literary tropes appears to have been quite useful.

But while praise for the French school for cultivating the student's
critical faculties is common, in the rare instances when students actually
took a personal stand in a notebook, they were rather quickly tamped

down. One illustration of this is the extraordinary preface to Jacques-Marie Ndiaye's notebook, written in the late 1930s. The prompt Ndiaye appears to have been writing on was "Your Race" (*Votre race*). However, Ndiaye begins his notebook by explaining the difficulty of applying the concept of race to himself—he notes that his immediate ancestry is a mixture of Wolof, Sérère, Diola, and Portuguese. Furthermore, he points out, some of these groups trace filiation through patrilineal kin while others privilege the matrilineal line. Then Ndiaye states, "In my personal opinion, the theory of race is inexact. In this moment, it is almost impossible to find a pure race without any mixing of foreign blood." None of this goes over well with the grader, who underlines, crosses out, and even vents his annoyance in the margins. Here is a reproduction of the textual mise-en-scène that ensues:

Votre race???

Ma race!!!

Question à laquelle il m'est très difficile de répondre.

Mon aïeul maternel, Malamine Ndiaye, est originaire du Cayor. Il est donc Ouolof. Il fit "gadaye" c'est à dire qu'à la suite d'une querelle, ou d'un malentendu de famille, il laissa tous ses biens, abandonna ses par-
? On ne ents et s'exila. Il se fixa en Casamance, y fit fortune et épousa mon
comprend aïeule, M'Lomp Da Sylva, de *sang Diola et métisse portugaise. Quant à ma*
pas *mère, elle est de père Sérère d'où son nom N'Dour.*

Du côté paternel, mon aïeul est Ouolof et ma grand-mère Sérère.

Dire que je suis de telle race, plutôt que de telle autre serait une erreur. Car, si les Ouolofs acceptent la parenté par la voie paternelle, les Sérères, les Diolas et même les Lebous ne la reconnaissent que par la voie maternelle. Pour ceux-ci, le sang maternel est plus sûre [sic] que le sang paternel.

Je serais donc Ouolof dans le premier cas et Diola pour les autres.

En résumé, je suis un métissé qui a ~~encore~~ conservé les traits du quarteron, la taille petite du Diola, la fierté du Ouoloff et le caractère mystérieux et défiant du Sérère.

! A mon avis ~~personnel~~, <u>la théorie de race est inexacte</u>. Actuellement, il est presque impossible de trouver une race pure, sans aucun mélange de sang étranger.

Your racc???

My race!!!

A question that is very difficult for me to answer.

My maternal ancestor, Malamine Ndiaye, is originally from Cayor. He is therefore Wolof. He was *"gadaye"* which is to say that as the result of a quarrel, or a family misunderstanding, he left all of his belongings, abandoned his relatives and exiled himself. He settled in Casamance, made his fortune there and married my ancestor, M'Lomp Da Sylva, of *Diola blood and a Portuguese métisse. As for my mother, she is of a Sérère father from which she gets her name N'Dour.*

do not
~~derstand~~

On the paternal side, my ancestor is Wolof and my grandmother Sérère.

To say that I am of this race rather than that one would be an error. Because, if the Wolofs trace descent through the paternal line, the Sérère, the Diola and even the Lebou recognize it only through the maternal line. For these groups, the maternal blood is more certain than the paternal blood.

I am therefore Wolof in the first case and Diola for the others.

To sum up, I am mixed race boy [*un métissé*] who has ~~still~~ conserved the traits of the quarteroon, the small size of the Diola, the pride of the Wolof and the mysterious and defiant character of the Sérère.

In my ~~personal~~ opinion, <u>the theory of race is inexact</u>. In this moment, it is almost impossible to find a pure race, without any mixing of foreign blood.[98]

The student's assertion that it is his "personal opinion [that] the theory of race is inexact" is quite literally put under erasure by the grader. On the one hand, one can understand the grader's gesture here as a simple correction of a piece of awkward phrasing—the phrase "personal opinion" is clearly redundant. However, the rest of the marks on this page suggest another interpretation. The exclamation point in the margin beside this sentence seem to indicate surprise, possibly even outrage, and the underlining beneath the phrase "the theory of race is inexact" suggests that whatever the grader's sentiments were, they were not limited to Ndiaye's use of a redundant modifier. Furthermore, Ndiaye's mistake here is not a grammatical error but a stylistic blunder— and the Ponty graders do not typically intervene to correct every one of these. But above all, the larger context of the assignment itself must be taken into account if we are to understand the corrections that unfold. Ndiaye is dissenting from the very premise of his assignment ("Your Race"). He does so on the grounds of a lived, embodied history (his own and that of his family) that is felt to be incompatible with the reductiveness of the category of "race." Instead of a portrait of a timeless ethnic group,

Ndiaye opens with an account of his own origins (Wolof . . . Diola . . . Sérère . . . Portuguese) which, he explains, cannot be smoothly shoehorned into the prompt.[99] The grader appears to find this incomprehensible—*on ne comprend pas*. In this context, then, Ndiaye's use of a superfluous modifier is not merely redundant; it is also a question of added emphasis, with "personal" here serving as an extra layer of possessiveness attached to an opinion on race that the grader's comments suggest is out of place in this context.

Ndiaye's preface illustrates that there were limits to the notebooks as spaces in which an individual came to discover their own "critical spirit." It is precisely when the student makes subjective experience a warrant for the production of knowledge and critique that the corrector steps in. My claim here is not that the notebook assignment functioned to destroy or oppress individual expression. Quite the opposite—like many other colonial humanist initiatives of the period, the notebooks sought to "produce yet proscribe individuality."[100] Ponty students were *encouraged* to write as individuals, but they had to stage their self-making in a largely stereotypic way that would not exceed the parameters of the prompts nor trouble the ideological foundations of French colonialism.

I am not making the strongest possible version of this argument—that the notebooks and other compositions produced by colonized students necessarily accomplish the subjective transformations they enact. Inherent in para-literary authorship is a certain looseness of fit between the author and the account given. This looseness is sometimes performed in a dissident way, but more often it is not. In reading the Ponty notebooks, then, we ought then to insist on this distance between what the students perform on the page and what they may have really felt or thought. The notebooks are not an uncomplicated window onto subjectivity but rather scenes of subjection enacted in relation to the assignment itself.

That being said, we do need to remain open to the idea that not everything expressed in the notebooks is merely a performance from which the students would distance themselves if given the chance. As Gregory Mann helpfully points out, the problem with always reading the colonial archive against the grain is that it can lead us to dismiss sentiments that are genuine but ideologically compromised.[101] We must leave open the possibility that many Ponty students could have been quite sincere in their notebooks and that the intensely personal and sentimental aspects of seeing one's community "with new eyes" may have had a role in making the notebook assignment into such an enduring rite of passage.

Para-Literary Authorship Beyond Ponty

Although para-literary authorship appears in sharp relief in the notebook assignment that developed during the "Africanization" of the Ponty curriculum in the 1930s, the Ponty notebooks are not an origin point so much as a particularly concentrated example of a wider form of knowledge production. Para-literary authorship was widespread in the broader school system of French West Africa. Other schools elicited para-literary writings on tests and in compositions. In order to receive diplomas and access to higher education, colonized students across the federation were asked exam questions that interpolated them into the position of responding as an observer, looking back at their community of origin from a remove.[102] The pedagogical paradoxes that led to the notebook assignment—especially the question of what counted as a colonized student's "own words"— continued to be debated well into the 1940s and 1950s.[103] For the colonial school system, para-literary authorship spread because it was a useful means of performing and assessing a colonized subject's conscription to the colonial modern.

But para-literary authorship was not limited to pedagogical applications. From late 1920s on, similar research methods and composition techniques become an integral part of the broader print culture of French West Africa. As student-teachers graduated and dispersed across the federation, many continued to cultivate research practices and experiment with writing studies of the communities they had grown up in or worked around. For some, this was a means of career advancement. For others, these studies became a useful idiom for debating the modernization of African societies. And for a select few, they became a foundation for literary activity. While many of these writings have probably been lost, quite a large number found their way into print. Of those that did, a great many make use of the strange amalgam of social research and disavowed literary techniques that we see so clearly in the Ponty notebooks. This efflorescence of curiously literary studies of African life would become Senghor's "new literature," which he would acknowledge as the dominant strain of francophone writing by Africans.

One of the most important venues for the spread of para-literary authorship was *Education Africaine*. Initially known as the *Bulletin de l'Enseignement de l'Afrique Occidentale Francaise*, this was the official journal of the colonial school system. In the 1930s, the journal printed a series of surveys on aspects of "native life" that were circulated to teachers in Afrique Occidentale Francaise (AOF). The topics for these surveys overlapped

in many cases with the prompts for notebooks. They included the education of children, beliefs and customs, folklore, markets, local history,
foodways, and the suggestively titled "Enquête sur l'Enfant noir en AOF"
(Inquiry into the Black Child in AOF).[104] Beginning in 1930, for example,
the journal published a questionnaire for collecting folklore. Established
by Marcel Mauss at the Institut d'Ethnologie, the guide described how to
cultivate the "special attitude" required to collect oral traditions in a useful
manner. The practice was said to be especially useful for native teachers,
since it would teach them to "look with method" and "banish the imagination."[105] Quite a few African teachers wrote to the journal and contributed
studies of the regions to which they were assigned. Respondents included
future literary figures such as Paul Hazoumé (under a pseudonym), Alioune
Diop (the future founder of *Présence Africaine*), and Mamby Sidibé. The surveys waned a bit with the war, but the journal was still printing studies of
indigenous life written by schoolteachers well into the 1950s.[106]

But the venues for para-literary authorship also extended beyond educational channels. Journals of colonial social science such as *Outre Mer*, the
"General Review of Colonization" founded by Georges Hardy and affiliated with the Institut d'Ethnologie, regularly made appeals for knowledge
production about African societies. While their calls often seem addressed
more to French colonial administrator-ethnographers, some of the respondents were Africans, often schoolteachers.[107] Many local newspapers in
West Africa also circulated calls for original research. For example, in 1935
the *Cœur du Dahomey*, a government-associated daily, reprinted a call for
works on African history, calling on "cultivated natives, especially schoolteachers" to write down oral traditions in order to "save from oblivion and
destruction" these documents of great historical value.[108]

Para-literary authorship was also rewarded beyond the classroom. African writers who published studies of native life could find greater opportunities for career advancement and even sponsorship. Many of the most
successful para-literary authors seem to have developed patronage relationships with individual colonial administrators, who helped them publish
their works and wrote prefaces to accompany them.[109] Para-literary authorship could also bring other highly prized forms of recognition. At least
one author whom Senghor names as an example of his quasi-scientific "new
literature" found that his writings were useful when he applied for French
citizenship. This was Dim Delobson, a colonial clerk in Upper Volta who
would go on to write two ethnographic books in the 1930s—*L'Empire du
Mogho-Naba* and *Secrets des Sorciers Noirs*. In 1930, Delobson was just be-

ginning his ethnographic work when he applied to become a French citizen. For a colonial subject to become a French citizen was quite rare in this period, in part because the evaluation process was intentionally arduous. One of many conditions was that an applicant be "literate" in French. But what really mattered was a successful demonstration that the applicant had "approached French civilization" and was not "attached to native customs."[110] Delobson's dossier received a positive evaluation, and his research was singled out as fulfilling this crucial requirement: "Fils d'un chef indigène important, il s'est rapproché sensiblement de notre civilisation tant par sa manière de vivre que par ses occupations intellectuelles. C'est ainsi qu'il a pu écrire une étude intéressante et documentée sur les 'Conditions des Nienissés de Gourana.' "[111] (Son of an important native chief, he has clearly drawn nearer to our civilization as much through his manner of living as by his intellectual occupations. This is how he was able to write an interesting and well-researched study on the "Conditions of Nienissés of Gourana.") Rather than the scholarly merits of the study, what appears to count for the evaluation of the citizenship application is the mere fact of Delobson's authorship—that he "could have written" it (*qu'il a pu écrire*). Delobson's authorship proved him to be the type of subject who could be an author. This recursive structure of recognition is analogous to what we find in many notebooks. Both in the classroom and the wider world, para-literary authorship worked by joining together two temporalities—a first moment in the past, when the future writing subject was more of a participant in the lifeworld than an observer of it, and then a second moment in the present in which the subject is now capable of being the author. The para-literary narratives of this period involve a kind of shuttling back and forth between two perspectives and temporal frames to produce an account of the author's journey to becoming an author.

Para-literary authorship also became an important factor in debates about the modernization of African cultures among elites. As a greater variety of print venues opened to Africans writing in French, they played host to discussions about the past, present, and future of African societies. These print conversations did not often broach the idea of decolonization explicitly, but they did question both the legitimacy and methods of the French colonial project. They also frequently escalated into heated arguments about what a future political community ought to look like and how African cultures might need to be transformed. In such debates, the position of the native researcher was highly prized; participants could draw on research they had conducted to speak with authority about the

past and future of African societies. In this way, the techniques and constraints of para-literary authorship came into play in some of the earliest
debates about African cultural autonomy.

One of the fiercest of these intellectual print controversies in the late
colonial period was the debate on the "cultural evolution" of West Africa
that raged in the pages of the short-lived *Dakar-Jeunes*, a cultural supplement to the daily newspaper *Paris-Dakar* in the Vichy years. In Janu-
ary 1942, an article by the Ponty graduate and novelist Ousmane Socé in
Dakar-Jeunes solicited contributions on the present state of culture in
French West Africa.[112] For six months after, the pages of *Dakar-Jeunes*
played host to a lively exchange on this topic, a conversation that was largely
dominated by Ponty graduates.[113] But *Dakar-Jeunes* was not an entirely
open forum. The editors imposed some limits on the character and style
of these contributions and even ran an occasional small sidebar in which
the editorship would give informal grades or comments to the contributions of the former Pontins. This feedback is full of uncanny reminders of
the marginal comments from graders that these graduates once faced at
Ponty—contributions are declared unpublishable because they are too
"bookish" or "abstract." One such correction reads, "Too much abstraction, too many scholastic reminiscences. Here, we want only life." An essay that traces a portrait of a veteran is deemed "too particular for us"—an
eerie echo of the charge against Arqueburu's notebook.[114] The contributions of Ponty graduates to *Dakar-Jeunes* often strained against these
narrow guidelines. Over the short life of the series, Ponty graduates tried
to turn *Dakar-Jeunes* into a space for public debate but also had to contend
with attempts to make the publication into an extension of the colonial
classroom.

One of the most sensitive points in the cultural evolution debate was
the question of literature. In an essay entitled "Literature and Prejudice,"
a Ponty graduate named Hamidou Dia blames colonial education for failing to bring about a "black literary renaissance" in the region. Dia argues
for the legitimacy of literature written by Africans in French and criticizes
the idea that fables, epic theater, or translations are the only permissible
forms of literary writing. In a thinly veiled pastiche of the paternalism of
colonial schoolteachers, Dia criticizes those who would restrict African
writers to children's tales, landscape compositions, and comedy to keep
them away from more historical or dramatic material that would only "sur-
pass their understanding." Pushing back against the idea that his generation ought to confine itself only to certain limited forms, Dia crafts a
passionate defense of literature as a mirror that is held up to society.[115]

The claim Dia made on literature was provocative enough that it unleashed a polemic that eventually shut down the entire *Dakar-Jeunes* debate. In June, Charles Béart, Ponty's director at the time, wrote in to *Dakar-Jeunes* to scold all his former charges for their foolishness but above all to lambaste Dia for his presumption of African literary potentiality. Béart is incensed by the suggestion that the Ponty generation ought to become writers of literature. While he admits that these elite graduates are uniquely well suited to the task of gathering and translating oral traditions, he believes they will never produce literature worthy of the name, that all they are capable of is a library of folklore. In a comment that echoes one of the central motifs of para-literary authorship, Béart writes, "It is not he who thinks he saw a man transform into a hyena who will transform this myth into a symbol. . . . You have the material [but] not the means." He goes on to suggest that this incapacity is due to the temporal dislocation that the Ponty students have experienced: "You have aged ten centuries in only a few years." Béart adds, "I imagine you feel this, I do not believe you are capable of expressing it."[116]

Béart gives one further reason for foreclosing on the literary aspirations of an entire generation: he believes the Ponty graduates will never find an audience for their writings. With breathtaking condescension, he tells former charges that while he could teach them how to write a sonnet, they "would still not find a publisher." Of Dia's call for a "native literature" in French, Béart writes:

> C'est vraiment un bébé qui pleure parce que les grandes personnes ne veulent pas le laisser jouer comme il l'entend avec la machine à écrire. "Je veux faire une tragédie . . ." Ecrivez votre tragédie, mon enfant, mais comme vous ne trouverez point de public, ni même de lecteurs, vous resterez avec votre œuvre sur le cœur, incompris.[117]

> This is really like listening to a baby cry because the grown-ups will not let him play with the typewriter like he wants to. "I want to write a tragedy . . ." Write your tragedy, my child, but since you will find no public nor even any readers, you will remain there with your work pressed against your heart, unheard.

As young African writers laid claim to literary production in French in the colonial era, they often ran up against pushback like this, which sought to limit them to more para-literary modes. Despite such dismissals, a great many writers of Dia's generation proved Béart wrong—they did find publishers and went on to work in a variety of literary genres. This raises a question. What happened to the complex ambivalence around literary techniques when Africans (many of them graduates of colonial schools) began writing literary texts in French? It would be tempting to tell that story as the gradual emancipation of a literary field from the restrictions of the colonial period. But a comparison of para-literary and literary texts from the colonial period suggests a more complicated picture.

Para-literary Authorship and Early Francophone African Literature

The themes, motifs, and techniques that were the stock in trade of para-literary writers all spill over into early francophone African literature. For the playwrights, the connection was direct—the first francophone productions were written and produced at the Ecole Normale at Ponty. But we find traces in other genres as well. Senghor's early poetry adopts a complex ventriloquism of the rural past; his speakers "collect," "respeak," or even "sing" the voices of the ancestors "in a new voice."[118] There are also suggestive connections among the anthologists of folk traditions. In Birago Diop's preface to his celebrated collection of literary translations of Wolof tales by the *griot* Ahmadou Koumba, Diop describes himself as "gathering up the crumbs of [Koumba's] knowledge and wisdom."[119]

But the blur between literary and para-literary is most striking among the novelists of this generation. Many of the techniques that we see at work in para-literary compositions were themselves drawn from novels, which may explain why prose writers so often straddled the divide. At first there seems to be an obvious explanation for this overlap: many early African novelists were schoolteachers, and quite a few of them actually attended Ponty—notably Abdoulaye Sadji, Paul Hazoumé, Ousmane Socé, and Bernard Dadié. But there are also strong hints of para-literary authorship in texts by writers who never studied at Ponty. Indeed, some authors who had no direct connection to Ponty wrote works that have truly striking resonances with the Ponty notebooks. This is notably the case with Camara Laye's *L'Enfant noir*.

One could produce a large catalogue of the echoes of para-literary writing that abound in early francophone African novels. Ultimately, though, such a compendium would be of limited interest, since it would tell us little about the nature of the echoes themselves. In this section, I take a different approach. I briefly explore what authorship meant for several of the earliest francophone African novelists—Hazoumé, Sadji, Dadié, and Laye. My focus is on what can be uncovered about their practices of literary authorship and how these practices respond to and recast para-literary education. As more normative modes of literary writing emerged and solidified in francophone West Africa, literary authorship continued to bear the imprint of the earlier and more widespread modes of para-literary writing. For some writers, literary and para-literary modes remained so closely aligned as to be almost indistinguishable. For others, literary authorship came to be a way to adapt, rework, and satirize the clichés and limitations of para-literary writing. In the following pages, I explore a sampling of this spectrum before reflecting on how this entanglement reframes our understanding of literary history in francophone West Africa and beyond.

Some early novelists took their first forays into print through genres closely associated with para-literary authorship, especially through social-scientific research on African cultures. Paul Hazoumé is a clear example of this path. A Ponty graduate, Hazoumé worked in a para-literary mode essentially throughout his career. He conducted extensive research in Dahomey (present-day Benin) and published his first para-literary sketches in the 1920s in the periodical *Reconaissance Africaine*, an early venue for research-driven studies of African culture.[120] His research culminated in 1937 in a formal anthropological monograph, *Le Pacte de Sang au Dahomey* (*The Blood Pact in Dahomey*). But Hazoumé also drew on his studies of history and customs for the fictional *Doguicimi*, usually identified as the earliest African historical novel in French. The voluminous *Doguicimi* centers on court intrigues and bloody conflicts in nineteenth-century, precolonial Dahomey, and its early pages bristle with clarifying footnotes.[121] The text offers both highly detailed glosses of local customs and a large-scale historical narrative, leading subsequent scholarship to detect traces of both Flaubert's *Salammbô* and Michelet's *Histoire de la revolution française*.[122] When *Doguicimi* was published as a novel in 1938, it was accompanied by a preface by Georges Hardy, the early architect of the colonial school system and director of the Ecole Coloniale, who cautioned readers against being misled by "the novelistic form" of Hazoumé's work. Although *Doguicimi* would go on to win a prize from the Académie française for its style, Hardy tells us that the novel form is just an "appearance" that Hazoumé adopts to conceal his true methods, which are history and collective psychology. Throughout his preface, Hardy is at pains to defend Hazoumé against any suspicion of literariness, as if all of the text's elaborate plotting and character development were merely a work of misdirection.[123]

We do not know what Hazoumé thought of Hardy's preface, but we do know that he understood himself as working on the boundary between historical research and literary practice. In an unpublished lecture given in 1942, Hazoumé outlined the tenets of his research practice to a group

of African schoolteachers. For Hazoumé, it was the responsibility of educated African elites like his audience members to properly collect and
modernize oral traditions—to "translate all [these] forms of thought."
Drawing on his own experience working on both *Doguicimi* and *Le Pacte de
Sang* as examples, he suggested that African schoolteachers ought to
gather raw information from the communities they worked in to transform this into scholarship. His preferred metaphor was of bees gathering
honey before returning to the hive:

> A l'exemple des abeilles qui butinent inlassablement et activement
> toutes les fleurs et en tirent le nectar qu'elles transforment en miel,
> étudions les coutumes et l'histoire de ces populations afin d'en tirer
> des enseignements non seulement pour la formation de la jeunesse
> dahoméenne qui nous est confiée, mais aussi pour faire avancer la
> science de la connaissance de l'âme humaine et pour faciliter au
> Gouvernement son administration.[124]

> Using the example of those bees that tirelessly and energetically visit
> all the flowers and extract the nectar which they transform into honey,
> let us study the customs and history of these populations in order to
> obtain teachings that will contribute not only to educating the
> Dahoméen youth, who are our charges, but also to advancing our
> knowledge of the human soul and to facilitating the work of the
> Government in its administration.

Hazoumé advised the schoolteachers to resign themselves to the "slow work
of transcription, translation and transformation." In a version of a classic
para-literary gesture, he warned them that they had to set aside any purely
literary ambitions and should "exclude the novelistic imagination." Only
in this way could they hope one day to "attach [their] name to a book."[125]
This was Hazoumé's vision of authorship—historical, research driven, and
only ambivalently literary. But while the stated goal of Hazoumé's program
was to produce research rather than literature, his own writings strayed
back and forth across such an imaginary line. Africans writing in French
in this period often found themselves in a similar position; to publish, they
had to alloy anything resembling literature with other methods of research
and presentation.

The novelist Abdoulaye Sadji is an emblematic figure for a second type
of trajectory—early novelists who began their careers collecting and translating oral traditions. After graduating from Ponty in the late 1920s, Sadji
went on to become a primary schoolteacher at a variety of establishments
in Senegal. By the mid-1930s, he had broken into print by writing com-

mentaries on African performance traditions. In these early essays, which appeared in *Education Africaine* and *Paris-Dakar*, we see Sadji lay claim to the position of author through a practice of translation—his essays consist of translations of songs intermingled with his own extensive commentaries.[126] In a version of the Soundiata story that appeared in *Education Africaine*, Sadji breaks frame to lament an inability to translate the kora music that accompanied the performance:

> S'il m'était possible de mettre en notes la musique qui conserve la mémoire de Soundiata-Keïta, je le ferais pour disposer le lecteur à aimer ce souverain puissant entre tous, qui était venu de Sankaran dans le ventre de sa mère, laquelle avait nom Soungloung-Koudouma: je le ferais pour donner une idée de la musique la plus ancienne du monde donné par le premier instrument de la terre; je le ferais pour montrer qu'elle caractérise bien le chaos primitif qui précéda immédiatement les événements de Ouagadougou et duquel tous les êtres vivants sont issus.[127]

> If it were possible for me to put into notes the music that conserves the memory of Soundiata-Keïta, I would do so to persuade the reader to love this sovereign who is more powerful than all, who came from Sankaran in the belly of his mother, who was herself named Soungloung-Koudouma: I would do so to give an idea of the most ancient music in the world made by the first instrument on earth; I would do so to show how well this music captures the primitive chaos which immediately precedes the events of Ouagadougou and out of which all living beings spring forth.

In this passage, we no longer have a clear sense of whether this is Sadji speaking or the *diali* (oral performer) he is quoting. The reflexive use of the conditional mood and the knowing nod to the "reader" (as opposed to the audience) point to Sadji. But the use of formulae that are more characteristic of an oral performer suggest a *diali*'s voice. Such interplay between translation and double-voiced narration is consistent with para-literary authorship and yet also points to a significant departure. Sadji is employing one of the most widely used para-literary techniques: translation as a way of establishing oneself as a spokesperson. But the double-voicing puts this practice into question. Sadji's translations keep interrupting themselves, insistently reminding the reader that the communication is mediated and that a translation is taking place. In this way, Sadji's approach to translation in these essays anticipates by several decades the counterpoetics used by the vernacular writers whom I study in Chapter 5.

Sadji also explored translation as a mode of authorless critique in these early essays. In a series that appeared in *Paris-Dakar* in 1938, he translated and analyzed an unusual corpus of Wolof songs. Often when oral traditions were gathered and translated in this era, they were presented as artifacts of an ancient past, but the songs Sadji translated were of more recent origin. They were apparently sung by Senegalese women who were watching their conscripted husbands leave to fight for France in World War I. In a complex exercise in gendered ventriloquism, Sadji both quotes the original Wolof songs and provides his own translations. One of the most striking texts he translates is a song that encourages the conscripted Senegalese soldiers to uphold the honorable reputation of their community as they go off to fight:

Bou lène dimi tour,	Bu leen demi-tour
Tam ma n'guen a nàne n'gour	Tàmm ngéen a nànd ngor
Va quat commine	Waa quatre communes
Ne faites pas demi-tour	Do not turn back,
Vous êtes habitués aux honneurs	For you, honor is a habit
Vous ceux des quatres communes.	You, people of the four communes.[128]

Can we call this a translation? Sadji is not moving a text from one language into another, since the Wolof song is already calqued with French expressions (*dimi tour*). One of the Wolofized French phrases in particular stands out, because it makes an important political claim: the identity of the conscripted soldiers is described as *waa quatres communes* (people of the four communes). This is a reference to the unique political status of the *originaires* in Senegal—the African inhabitants of the four communes of Saint-Louis, Dakar, Gorée, and Rufisque in Senegal, who were not colonial subjects and had enjoyed a birthright claim to some of the privileges of French citizenship since 1848. The political circumstances of this translation are important. Sadji's commentary on these songs appeared in the major newspaper of French West Africa in the late 1930s, in the midst of new debates over whether to extend citizenship to all African veterans of the Great War.[129] The phrase *waa quat commine* is a dense, interlingual knot that indexes the long and entangled history of imperial citizenship. Translating these songs at this particular moment was a way for Sadji to interject a reminder of the history of the *originaires'* service and status into contemporary debates. The commentaries Sadji wrote on music in the 1930s show how early francophone African writers learned to appropriate the modes of writing that were widely permissible for African schoolteachers—here, the collection and translation of oral traditions—to exploit them for the purposes of subtle political critique.[130]

Another overlap between literary and para-literary practices of authorship in this era was the use of citation. Colonial education imparted an arsenal of literary references to its elite students. These continued to surface in the works of novelists for many years, while also creating the conditions for satire. As a student at Ponty, the playwright and novelist Bernard Dadié wrote exquisite compositions. In an essay written in the 1930s, Dadié responded to a para-literary prompt that asked him to describe a return to his home region and the feelings it inspired in him. The essay he produced is stunning: a novelistic depiction of a voyage home by boat from Ponty to his native Bassam. And yet despite the highly personal nature of the composition, Dadié studiously avoids the first person. His memories are presented as the observations of a distant narrator, who nevertheless has a clear connection to the scenes being described. But at a crucial juncture, Dadié must fulfill the obligatory performance of self-reflection that characterizes a para-literary assignment. But words appear to fail him. He writes, "L'amour et l'attachement que j'ai pour Bassam sont si grands et je serais bien embarrassé s'il me fallait analyser ses sentiments." (The love and the attachment that I have for Bassam are so great that I would be very troubled indeed if I were to have to analyze these sentiments.) Rather than analyze his own feelings about the past, as many other para-literary writers did, Dadié turns to a citation from a literary text: "Objets inanimés, avez-vous donc une âme / qui s'attache à notre âme et la force d'aimer?" (Inanimate objects, have you then a soul / that attaches itself to our soul and the force to love?)[131] This line from the poet Alphonse de Lamartine works as a kind of shorthand—it authorizes Dadié as an author by signaling that he is someone who can deploy just the right line of poetry. As often happened at Ponty, a literary reference serves as a space of calibration between student-author and reader-grader.

But in his first novel, *Climbié* (1956), a much older Dadié found ways to cast doubt on the usefulness of the trove of literary references that elite colonial education cultivated. Like many other African novels of its era, *Climbié* is a narrative of formation. The novel charts its eponymous hero's progress from his village school to Ponty (where he encounters the Franco-African curriculum) and beyond. But the text concludes on a more ambivalent note. Although Ponty prepared Climbié for a glorious life as a colonized elite, by the end things have not quite worked out that way.

Climbié has been reduced to selling his personal library on the street. He describes the indifference of the urban crowds to his cherished collection of books:

> Matin et soir, devant mon éventaire, les hommes passaient, emportés par le rythme tumultueux de leur existence. Les livres s'ouvraient d'eux-mêmes comme pour mettre un frein à l'indifférence générale . . . Un à un, les bouquins s'ouvraient, mais les gens passaient, semblant dire: "Te voilà vaincu! Quelle richesse expose-t-on de la sorte au public?" Les livres se recroquevillaient au soleil. Le vent les feuilletait, comme s'il eût été à la recherche d'une référence. Je me contentais de lire et d'attendre. . . . J'avais devant moi, pêle-mêle, de vénérables patriarches: Cicéron, Racine, Chamfort, Goethe, Hugo, Chateaubriand, Schiller, Gautier, Maupassant, Flaubert. . . . Les hommes maintenant passaient sans même me regarder.

> Morning and evening, in front of my tray on the pavement, men passed by, swept up in the riotous rhythm of their lives. The books opened by themselves, as if to bridle everybody's indifference to them. . . . One by one the old books were opened; then people would pass on, seeming to say: "I see you've given up! What sort of wealth is that to display in public?" The books shriveled up in the sun. The wind leafed through them, as if searching for a reference. I contented myself with reading and waiting. . . . I had in front of me, all mixed up, reverend patriarchs: Cicero, Racine, Chamfort, Goethe, Hugo, Chateaubriand, Schiller, Gautier, Maupassant, Flaubert. . . . The men passed by now without even looking at me.[132]

Literary references may have been an important currency in the late colonial era, but this suggests they are no longer the coin of the realm. "What good are old books and references in a city where only bank notes talk?" Climbié asks. The scene is a pointed reversal of the cultivation of literary citation that took place in elite schools. Climbié's library overflows with the right references, but these books have become useless—*meubles inutiles*, to recall that phrase from Molière that found its way into a Ponty notebook.

Perhaps the most puzzling case of an entanglement between paraliterary authorship and literary writing is Camara Laye's celebrated 1953 novel, *L'Enfant noir* (*The African Child*). Laye's novel has understandably been called a *bildungsroman*, since it traces the growth of a young Malinke boy from his infancy to early adolescence.[133] But Laye's narrator often struggles to inhabit a cohesive first-person narrative. In a manner reminiscent of many para-literary writings, the narrator quarrels with himself over the terms with which to understand his own past, particularly with how he can account for ritual or magical events he witnessed in childhood. "These unbelievable things," he writes of his own mother's occult powers, "I have seen them." He wonders, "Can I doubt the testimony of my own eyes?"[134] The struggle to reconcile what he saw *then* with what can *now* be believed leads to a split in the narrator's role, which appears divided between documenting what he has seen and being the subject who is now able to look back on the past. This seems to inaugurate a new kind of temporality, which comes into sharp relief in the following passage:

> Je ne veux rien dire de plus et je n'ai relaté que ce que mes yeux ont vu. Ces prodiges . . . j'y songe aujourd'hui comme aux événements fabuleux d'un lointain passé. Ce passé pourtant est tout proche: il date d'hier. Mais le monde bouge, le monde change, et le mien plus rapidement peut-être que tout autre, et si bien qu'il semble que nous cessons d'être ce que nous étions, qu'au vrai nous ne sommes plus ce que nous étions, et que déjà nous n'étions plus exactement nous-mêmes dans le moment où ces prodiges s'accomplissaient sous nos yeux. Oui, le monde bouge, le monde change.[135]

> I don't want to say any more and I have told only what my eyes have seen. These miracles . . . I think back to them today like the fantastic happenings of a distant past. Yet that past is very close; it dates from yesterday. But the world moves, the world changes, and mine perhaps more rapidly than all the others, and so much so that it seems that we cease to be what we were, that truly we are no longer what we were, and that we were already no longer exactly ourselves in the moments in which these miracles were occurring before our eyes. Yes, the world moves, the world changes.

The penultimate sentence introduces a dizzying play of tenses and a dense superimposition of both temporality and subjectivity: "We cease to be what we were" becomes "we are no longer what we were" and finally transforms into "we were *already no longer* exactly ourselves" (emphasis mine). As the narrator strives to rework lived experience in terms of believability, it is his relationship to himself that appears dislocated—"we were already no longer exactly ourselves." With this phrase, the narrator arrives in a complex, conflicted temporality. He seems to retroject his transformation ever further back into his past (*already*) without ever being able to totally erase the mark that there was once a moment when that transformation had not yet taken place (*no longer*). Sometimes the clearest shadow of para-literary authorship appears in novels of this era at moments like this—when it becomes a question of speaking in one's own words *and* being sure that those words are one's own.

In noting that a certain commonality exists between Laye's first novel and the Ponty notebooks, I am not arguing that *L'Enfant noir* is merely a colonial classroom exercise, as Mongo Beti once claimed.[136] Camara Laye never attended Ponty, nor did he write a Ponty notebook. To understand his text's affinities with that archive, we must take seriously the ways in which para-literary modes functioned as commonplace discursive strategies in the late colonial period.

Reading *L'Enfant noir* in this way suggests a new way to think through Laye's practice of authorship, which has since become the subject of some controversy. In 2003, Adele King's *Rereading Camara Laye* cast doubt on Laye's sole authorship of his novels. King suggested that the manuscript of *L'Enfant* was partially ghostwritten by several Europeans and that it was promoted by the French Overseas Ministry as an example of the success of colonial education.[137] King's allegations were vehemently contested by prominent scholars of African literatures.[138]

We can approach the issue of Laye's authorship differently through the optic of the para-literary. Instead of trying to establish definitively whether Laye wrote his first novel by himself, perhaps we ought to be asking where our own expectations of the author function come from and why we are so intent on applying them to francophone African writing of the late colonial period, when so many texts of this era have a vexed relationship with authorship *and* literariness. Laye is far from the only writer of his era to have produced texts in collaboration with others (if indeed he did so) or to have published texts with the support of the colonial educational apparatus (which it seems likely he did).

What makes Laye's text exceptional is that it is still widely read, analyzed, and translated as a work of literature, rather than as a para-literary text. Lest I be misunderstood, I am not making a value judgment about Laye's writing. I am arguing instead that his text appears to be caught up in a broader instability around the limits of authorship and literariness that extends well beyond literary texts alone. Part of the trouble here is that whenever we question whether a text or a tradition is "literature," this gesture is automatically understood to be a denigration. This reaction is understandable, particularly in and around African literatures. In face of the very long (and ongoing) history of denying the full worth and even existence of African expressive cultures, asserting and documenting African literary traditions has been one way pushing back. But our attachment to "literature" as a universal criterion of cultural value ought to remain open to continued examination, not least because it fares very poorly as a descriptive and analytical tool when we look at the earliest creative writings of West Africans working in French. The privilege and distinction we assign to the literary is *our* norm, and it was not necessarily a relevant (or even available) one to the many West Africans writing creatively in French from the 1930s to the 1950s. In this period, a great many complicated, challenging texts were written, but most of them do not sit comfortably either inside or outside the frontiers of the literary. Once we start to grasp this, we also begin to see that many of the texts of this era that we do recognize as literary actually seem to have quite a bit in common with the texts that we might prefer to keep at arm's length.

Rethinking Literary History

To study the persistence of para-literary authorship into literary works, we need to think more expansively about literary history. We need to move away from a version that privileges literary texts (odd as that might at first seem) and toward an analysis of the more hidden ways that literature and literary culture circulate: as models of expression or the wayposts through which one passes if one has to give a certain kind of account of oneself and one's community. Para-literary authorship offered new ways of quoting the social world and speaking for the collective past. It offered representational strategies for enacting colonial modernity in terms that were sufficiently familiar without appearing to be borrowed. While it was elicited and rewarded by a variety of institutions and forces in French West Africa, para-literary authorship never rose to the level of a literary genre, because its very functioning depended on not being recognized as such. It is more productive to think of para-literary authorship as a discipline, one through which many future writers had to pass. If we study literary and para-literary authorship together in this way, we also arrive at a different perspective both on the region's literary history and the broader terms in which global literary history becomes legible to us.

The 1930s through 1950s in French West Africa have long been something of a puzzle for literary scholars. Although these decades arguably see the emergence of francophone African literature, literary texts are quite thin on the ground and account for a tiny fraction of the textual output of Africans writing in French during these decades. Many more generically indeterminate, research-driven, and ideological texts are produced than recognizably literary ones. This initially led some scholars to simply bracket away whole swaths of this problematic era in order to arrive at histories that began with the texts that clearly pointed the way toward literary modernity, usually associated with the negritude poets. For example, in a foundational early survey of Africans writing in French, Lilyan Kesteloot located the beginnings of an "authentic literary movement" in French by African writers in the 1932 *Légitime défense* manifesto, since it contained, for her, the first stirrings of negritude.[139] Kesteloot allowed that the more ethnographically inclined works by Hazoumé, Delobson, and Quenum (all of whom Senghor groups under the rubric of his "new literature") were "interesting," but they were "trop peu littéraire" (not literary enough) to be included.[140]

Such exclusions were challenged by later critics—notably by Christopher Miller, who charted a far more inclusive approach based on a broader understanding of the literary. "If we take as 'literature' simply everything that is written," Miller observed, "we will be freer to examine writing as it happened, in whatever form it took."[141] Through this sensible approach, Miller unfurled a series of perceptive analyses of early francophone writings by African authors who did not find favor in Kesteloot's negritude-focused canon—figures such as Amadou Mapaté Diagne, Bakary Diallo, and Lamine Senghor. Miller's interventions served a valuable corrective function, and it is in large measure thanks to his work that we read these writers today. And yet Miller's suggestion that we take "everything that is written" as literature is worth pausing over.

Analyzing every text as if it were literature allows critics to nimbly tease out multiple meanings in texts that present themselves as having just one—something Miller does insightfully and persuasively. But it also risks sidestepping the problem of literariness as it is posed in and around many francophone African texts of this period. Miller's avoidance of any debate about the nature of literariness is very much intentional: he wants to "short circuit aesthetic definitions of the literary" in favor of a "material position" that would dissolve literariness into the "broader history of discourse."[142] I share Miller's suspicion about the usefulness of embarking on any attempt to arrive at a universal definition of the literary. And yet there is a compelling reason for not setting aside the problem of literariness entirely. Simply put, the question of whether texts were sufficiently literary, not literary enough, or too literary was frequently at issue in this body of writing as a whole. More than this, literariness—as a problem, a question, and a limit—seems to have spurred the establishment of a field of francophone African textual production in this period. Working through the para-literary allows us to sharpen our approach to the more expansive archive that Miller traced. By supplementing our readings of literary texts with attention to the problem of para-literary authorship, we can study the contingency of literariness itself.

Para-literary authorship further challenges us to reconsider our frameworks for thinking about the globalization of literary culture, a field of inquiry that has in recent decades been pulled into the orbit of discussions of world literature. In his "Conjectures on World Literature," Franco Moretti famously advanced a hypothesis: in cultures at the periphery of the modern literary system, the modern novel appears as a compromise between a western formal influence, "local material," and "local form."[143] If we run the emergence of the francophone African novel through Moretti's thesis, something strange happens. On the one hand, we *do* see an abundance of writers making use of familiar European forms—novels of formation, free indirect style—which would seem to confirm his point. But when we note that the "rise of the novel" in French West Africa coincides with the height of para-literary authorship, then the neatness of the conclusion seems suspect. What might appear to a scholar of world literature as a case of African writers employing familiar European forms and styles starts to look very different when we understand that learning to subtly repurpose and perform certain literary techniques was an important discipline in the colonial education system and that the production of narratives that were not altogether unlike novels was a key condition of social mobility.

Moretti's synthesis of existing scholarship on the "rise of the novel" points to another pattern: what precedes the eventual rise of the novel form is usually a wave of translations, most often of French and English novels, into a vernacular. But, as Moretti himself notes, West Africa does not fit the pattern; there were relatively few translations of modern European novels into African languages in the colonial period, and yet the novel arose anyway.[144] The trouble here is that Moretti is looking for translations in a very narrow sense—literary texts moving from one language to another. But if we adopt a more capacious view of translation that includes transformations of literary institutions such as authorship, then the late colonial era in French West Africa appears to be overflowing with translation. Literary techniques, cultivated in elite colonial schools, circulate widely as a set of conventions and norms for giving an account of oneself as a colonial subject, for relating differently to collectivity and history, and for debating colonial modernity.

The kind of analysis we do depends a great deal on what we take to be our objects of study. If we want to tell the story of the rise of a particular genre—such as the novel—then it seems understandable that we would go in search of novels. But knowing what one is looking for can have the unfortunate effect of deciding the outcome of the inquiry in advance. If we build our hypothetical study of the beginnings of the novel in French West Africa around novels alone, then we get a very skewed picture indeed, since the majority of Africans writing in French during this period had a complicated relationship to literary form and more often than not produced texts that are not easily recognizable to us as novels. For Moretti's hypothesis, the para-literary writers—and the institutions, assignments, publications, and prizes that sustained them—can only appear as a liminal stage in a story we all already know: eventually the novel rises in French West Africa, and it looks like the novel elsewhere, albeit with a colonial difference. But when we consider how the problem of literariness extends throughout the textual production of the late colonial era, then our rise of the novel story starts to seem inadequate.

If we broaden our inquiry to include para-literary authorship, a different comparative approach to literary history becomes possible. Instead of a history of genres, or movements, or aesthetic categories, we can study how literary institutions and practices are put to use far beyond the production of literary texts that are consumed in recognizably literary ways. Literary history can be expanded to examine the ways in which conventions such as authorship fluctuate across different circumstances.

The Refusal of Translation

Reconstructing the volatile nature of authorship in the late colonial era also helps us to propose a different genealogy for the politics of language. At the heart of para-literary authorship was the demand that colonized authors speak in French "in their own words" and yet also demonstrate how those words had come to be theirs. This often took the form of a performance of translation. For its part, francophone African literature broke with para-literary writing in many ways, but for quite a few early writers the connection between translation and authorship endured. Writing in *Présence Africaine* in 1956, the Senegalese poet David Diop observed that an African writer working in French "cannot truly translate the deep song of his country" but that he or she could "nonetheless contribute to the renaissance of our national cultures."[145] Senghor, writing two years later in his preface to Birago Diop's second collection of Wolof folktales, noted that modern African writers who wished to "manifest" their literary traditions had to present themselves "most often as translators."[146] Senghor saw francophone writers' reliance on translation as salutary, whereas for Diop it was a limitation. But both intellectuals agreed that translation was the condition of emergence for African literature in French.

The language question began as an attempt to unwind this entanglement of literature with translation. If early francophone African writing was premised on translation, as David Diop and Senghor suggested, then the politics of language can be understood as an explicit rejection of such dependence—in other words, as a refusal of translation. The language debates began in part as an attempt to cast off the complicated admixture of authorship, literature, and translation that had predominated for African writers in the colonial era. In a curious reversal, however, the language debates actually conserved the colonial injunction for African writers to speak "in their own words." But the polarity of this demand was reversed. For para-literary writers, these words were assumed be in French. But in the language debates of the 1960s and 1970s, some would go so far as to argue that only writers working in African languages were speaking "in their own words." In this way, the postcolonial turn toward vernacular writing can be understood in part as an attempt to unravel the inheritances of para-literary authorship.

In Senegal, the many attempts to explore African languages as vehicles for modern literary expression have not often led to a complete break with French. As I show in Parts II and III of this book, Wolof-language writers produced not rejections of translation but a variety of creative approaches that worked *through* translation—from Ousmane Sembène's and Cheikh Aliou Ndao's counterpoetics, to Maam Yunus Dieng's reworking of Mariama Bâ, to the many versions of Boubacar Boris Diop's *Doomi Golo* project (Chapters 5, 6 and 7, respectively). In these more recent projects that stretch across languages, we can still detect the echoes, faint and changed, of the paradoxes of authorship in the late colonial era.

CHAPTER 3

Toward the Future Reader: Print Networks and the Question of the Audience

Je dédie ce livre à ma mère, bien qu'elle ne sache pas lire. Penser qu'elle y promènera les doigts suffit à mon bonheur.

I dedicate this to book to my mother, even though she does not know how to read. Thinking that she will move her fingers across these pages is enough to make me happy.

—SEMBÈNE OUSMANE, *Le Docker noir* (1956)

So goes the extraordinary epigraph to Ousmane Sembène's first novel. Sembène dedicated his text to someone who could not read it—his own mother. Nevertheless, the book presents itself as being *for* her. Here we detect the outline of another legacy of colonial literary modernity in West Africa: the question of the audience. How can African literature address a public that cannot read it? Sembène was hardly the first and certainly not the last West African writer to invoke this dilemma, but his epigraph to *Le Docker noir* is noteworthy for the way it poses the problem. Unlike Charles Béart, the Ponty headmaster who caustically dismissed the first generation of francophone African writers—*you will never write literature, much less find a public*—Sembène's epigraph engages with the question of the missing reader by reimagining the separation between text and audience. In the image of the mother who "reads" the novel with her fingertips, the novelist explores whether there might be other ways of relating to a literary text. Can literature be for a public of nonreaders or not-yet-readers? How can a writer circumvent silent, private reading as a privileged means of relating to a literary text?

We must immediately acknowledge, however, that the novel that Sembène wrote was far less concerned with alternative ways of reaching its audience than this epigraph would lead us to believe. The epigraph envisions the mother reading with her fingertips, but in the novel itself Sembène did not explore what it meant to try to write for such a reader. This is indeed broadly true of most francophone African literature written in the colonial period. It is rare for literary texts composed in this era to refer to the distance between themselves and their audiences, and rarer still for them to engage with it. When such a distance is invoked at all, it tends to be thematized but little more. Unease over literature's distance from its audience would become more acute with the intervention of the language question, which made the question of the public a central concern. And yet we would be quite wrong to conclude from this admittedly reductive schema that the question of the audience was altogether absent from the colonial period. In fact, the colonial era was full of creative explorations of the nature of reading and the possibilities and limits of audience. But to reconstruct this history, we once more need to look beyond literary texts alone and toward the entanglements of the literary with a broader spectrum of print that includes newspapers, journals, and political pamphlets as well as other more ephemeral textual media.

In this chapter, I explore how the figure of the future reader was deeply interwoven into the print cultures of French West Africa. By a future reader, I mean a figure like Sembène's mother in the epigraph to *Docker*—not just any addressee, but an elusive one who is located just beyond the margins of existing print publics. As print expanded rapidly in French West Africa, newspapers and other periodicals often had to ask themselves: What does it mean to be a reader? Who counts as a reader? And are there ways for a printed text to produce the readers it does not yet have? We sometimes think that writers working in African languages are uniquely burdened by a chasm of illiteracy that supposedly separates them from the publics they hope to reach. But the challenge of creating the readers one needs or hopes for has a far longer history in West Africa.

From 1930 to 1960, francophone West Africa was the site of an extraordinary wellspring of creative writing. In this era, the vast majority of printed textual production, both literary and para-literary, appeared in periodicals.[1] This period saw the development of a network of newspapers that were written, edited, and printed in West Africa and connected to the wider world. It was in these networks that the figure of the future reader became a consuming issue. Printed periodicals in French West Africa developed a rich repertoire of strategies for exploring the nature of their audiences, cultivating readerships, and reflexively testing the limits of their own textual medium.[2] These concerns would become central features of the politics of language and the vernacular literature movements they helped spark. To understand how the question of the audience became central to the postcolonial period, we need to trace its roots in the era of colonial literary modernity.

Print Networks

Neither books nor paper were new in much of West Africa in the modern period. The region had been an important site of Islamic learning and libraries for centuries.[3] West Africa had also been importing paper since at least the fifteenth century, first from Northern Algeria and Spain and then later from Europe. The region had been part of a global supply chain of papermaking as a source of gum arabic, a commodity that was essential to the textile, printmaking, and bookbinding industries well into the nineteenth century.[4] The rise of printing, however, was a new development. Newspapers appeared across the African continent at different times during the nineteenth and twentieth centuries. In what was to become French West Africa, the first locally published newspapers were produced in French in Senegal in the nineteenth century, but it would be the twentieth century that would see an explosion of print.[5]

In their helpful synthesis of scholarship on print culture in colonial Africa, Derek Peterson, Emma Hunter, and Stephanie Newell provide an overview of many of the main characteristics of African newspapers in the first half of the twentieth century: newspapers rarely confined themselves to "news" in a narrow sense. Instead, they ran a heady mix of content that included selections from wire services alongside advice columns, travel writing, political commentary, essays on traditional values, and many more ephemeral genres. Across these many formats, newspapers experimented with the ways that print allowed them to edit discourse, from citation and juxtaposition to summarization and cutting and pasting. Through these forms, newspapers introduced a variety of ways of convening and addressing publics as well as new models of sociability. Newspapers were also hotbeds for collecting, translating, and editing what was then called traditional wisdom or oral literature. Since the material infrastructure of printing was often precarious and the periodicity of serials was new to many readers, editors often had to try to produce new kinds of audiences, to fashion not just customers but new ways of relating to texts. Many newspapers did this by opening themselves to readers' letters and contributions. In many sites across Africa, this generated a fascinating interplay between editors, columnists, and readers, who experimented together with new forms of address, new modes of reading, and even new genres.[6]

By the last decades of colonial rule, a great variety of print circulated in French West Africa, with a smaller subset being published locally. There were newspapers produced in the region on a monthly, weekly, and eventually daily basis. At the upper end of professionalization, this included outfits such as *Paris-Dakar* that used wire services and were quite close in appearance to metropolitan dailies, while at the other end we see hand-lettered and roneographed papers produced by single individuals with extremely limited print runs. There were newspapers published by political parties, unions, trade groups, and religious organizations. Also in circulation were metropolitan-based periodicals produced in France by citizens and colonial subjects (from radical Left papers such as *Le Cri des nègres* to the reformist *La Dépêche Africaine* to internationalist outfits such as the *Revue du Monde Noire*) as well as academic journals and administrative bulletins for various cadres of colonial personnel. Quite a bit of printed material from outside "Greater France" also seems to have circulated, from missionary books on moral education to glossy magazines, *romans roses*, and pornography. The francophone press of this era overlapped and existed alongside a healthy and much older trade in Arabic-language books as well as a steady circulation of texts in 'Ajami—modified Arabic scripts used for writing African languages.

Scholars have long recognized that print cultures tend to project an audience. In literary studies, we have tended to think about this work of projection through the framework of nationalism. Benedict Anderson's pioneering *Imagined Communities* helped us see the ways in which both novels and newspapers can provide the technical means for "re-presenting" the kind of imagined community that is the nation.[7] As useful as Anderson's model can be, it can also lead us to assume that newspapers and novels necessarily tend toward the homogeneity and simultaneity of nationalism. The print cultures of French West Africa suggest otherwise. In the 1930s through 1950s, there were many ways of imagining and figuring a print readership, but relatively few of them aimed at the production of national consciousness or the consolidation of a vernacular as national patrimony. In French West Africa, national sovereignty was by far the least advocated vision of political decolonization.[8] Although print was linked to political imagination throughout the period, the orientations of newspapers toward their audiences and their uses of language were far more diverse than a nationalist model would predict. As Karin Barber writes of anglophone West Africa, "In contrast with Benedict Anderson's narrative of the role of the press in the consolidation of a single national language, early African newspapers and books reveal a complex relativism—a sense of the relationships between languages, even when only one is being deployed—and an ability to adopt shifting frameworks, convoking audiences that tended to be either far larger than a linguistically-defined nation state, or far smaller."[9] To attend to the shifting nature of audience in the print cultures of colonial French West Africa, a similar reorientation will be necessary. Once we remove the nation as the presumptive outcome of efforts to produce an audience in print, a host of other strategies, experiments, and struggles start to become visible.

Instead of sifting through a complex print ecosystem for traces of a proto-"Senegalese" national consciousness, I suggest that we can better approach the print cultures of French West Africa through the figure of the network.[10] The print periodicals of this era can be thought of as a series of overlapping networks with each node or cluster of nodes existing under markedly different circumstances. I use the term *network* here in contradistinction to both a literary field and a public sphere, which tend to presume autonomy and enclosure even just as regulative ideals. Neither a literary field nor a public sphere existed in French West Africa.[11] Rather than looking for wholeness and sovereignty where they were in short supply, it will be more useful for us to look at the contingent and shifting discursive and material practices that actually thrived under these conditions.

Thinking through the network helps us in at least three ways. First, the network allows us to conceptualize the great unevenness of the print cultures that spanned French West Africa. Nodes and clusters of nodes varied in terms of the legal regime they were under, the degree of capitalization they had, and the levels of infrastructure for printing and distribution on which they could rely. Second, the network lets us recognize that this unevenness coexisted with interconnectedness. Despite the widely different conditions of their editing and publication, print publications managed to circulate texts and ideas among themselves, even where there were legal impediments to doing so. The network allows us to appreciate the links between periodicals operating in geographically far-flung areas—from West Africa to metropolitan France to further afield. The third and final advantage of the network is to allow us to recognize that print meant and did different things across West Africa. Although newspapers may have made it their business to project their audiences as if reading and print were the same everywhere, not all readers had equivalent practices of reading. Much as Trish Loughran observes of the print cultures of the United States in the late eighteenth century, there was no monolithic print ideology.[12] Neither reading nor print nor textuality necessarily meant or did the same things in rural and urban areas. Newspapers found ways of reckoning with this diversity and making it a part of their editorial practice.

Above all, the form of the network helps us track how the question of the audience varied widely across clusters of periodicals. For example, looser press and libel laws allowed a vocal group of anticolonial newspapers to exist in the 1920s and 1930s in metropolitan France but not in colonized territories. Periodicals could be prosecuted for libel anywhere, but this power was wielded very differently in the *métropole* and in the colonies. Although the laws on press freedoms changed over time, the censorship and libel powers of the colonial administration remained quite strong with regard to papers published in French West Africa, whatever language they were printed in. But papers published in France, even those produced by colonial subjects, theoretically enjoyed the same set of press freedoms as any others appearing in France. In turn, these metropolitan papers could be regulated in West Africa only at the point of sale and in their distribution.[13] In practice, the most anticolonial and outspoken of these papers were relentlessly harassed and surveilled. But they nevertheless enjoyed far greater freedom of expression than any print periodical published in West Africa.

This legal differential was one factor of many that led papers in West Africa and metropolitan France to project their audiences differently. The metropolitan papers produced by colonial subjects in France were situated around what we might call a central node—they were more directly connected with other, larger print networks that linked France, West Africa, the Caribbean, and the United States.[14] For papers in the metropolitan cluster, the question of the audience tended to appear as a concern with circulation more so than with reading. While metropolitan papers were aware that they had to hail an audience, they rarely saw this as a question of training an audience to read or engage differently with print. They usually had a high degree of interest in increasing the range of their circulation but relatively little concern with reflexively shaping the practices of reading they might encounter. Instead, the metropolitan papers tended to envision discourse in print as a one-directional affair, with their opinions and information radiating outward toward the colonies.

We can see this orientation most clearly in the communist publications, such as *La Voix des nègres*, *La Race nègre*, and *Le Cri des nègres*, that existed in the 1920s and 1930s.[15] In theory, any individual in French West Africa, citizen or subject, was free to receive a copy of these papers from France by mail and read it but could not then resell it or even pass it along to a friend or comrade. Under the 1928 press law, these papers could be read but not circulated. Of the papers in this cluster, the later *Le Cri des nègres* especially seems to have made a crusade of engaging with this limitation. *Le Cri* was constantly asking its subscribers never to tear up the paper but rather to "wrap it up again and send it to another comrade."[16] Every worker who received *Le Cri* was enjoined to "not be content with simply reading it" but to "fulfill their duty" by spreading it.[17] *Le Cri*'s visions of its audiences tended toward scenes of centrifugal circulation on a massive scale. "Our *Cri* penetrates more and more wherever there are *nègres* who work and who suffer; in all of French Africa, in America, in the Caribbean, in South Africa, in the Belgian Congo, in Oceania. Our paper is found in Marseilles, in London, in Vladivostok, in California, in New Zealand, between the hands of black sailors who transport and diffuse it in every corner of the world."[18] This picture may seem grandiose, but reports from the 1930s do confirm that police in West African ports at least would seize shipments of *Le Cri* and other communist papers brought in by sailors who likely acquired them in union circles in Marseilles, Le Havre, and other French ports.[19]

Le Cri's focus on circulation had another side: there was very little reflexivity to the way the paper addressed its readers. It imagined itself spreading a message outward into the world but did not reflect much on the different types of readers or readings it might encounter.[20] In addition to the cluster of communist periodicals, there were many other papers, journals, and shorter-lived publications based in the *métropole* that circulated in West Africa, from *La Dépêche africaine* to *La Revue du monde noir* to *L'Etudiant noir*. Each of these conceived of their relationships to an audience differently, and they cannot be equated with their more radical peers.[21] Nevertheless, the many publications operating within France but connected to French West Africa do seem to have been more concerned with circulation and less with the ways in which they would be read.

The question of the audience resonated differently for print publications within West Africa, whose circumstances included different legal frameworks, publishing infrastructure, and horizons of circulation. With some exceptions, West African periodicals tended to be less focused on extending the reach of their circulation than their metropolitan counterparts. Instead, they tended to be more concerned with eluding colonial censorship and with developing forms of engagement with more local audiences. We can find an example of the first dynamic in the papers of the Dahomey cluster, where a local press appeared in the 1920s. Like many other West African papers, the Dahomey cluster had to contend with libel charges for defaming the reputations of colonial administrators. This was the most common way that censorship was achieved in French West Africa. But because of the existence of multitiered legal regimes across much of French West Africa, the legal personhood of the author of a libelous text often came into play, especially outside the four communes of Senegal. In French West Africa, it mattered a great deal whether the signed author of a text was a citizen or a subject. A citizen had recourse, in theory, to the same legal system as any other French citizen, while a colonial subject was under the *indigénat* and could be tried in customary courts.[22] This distinction was a major issue in the 1930s in Dahomey, where the prosecution of libelous texts ran up against the issue of an author's standing. If the offenders were not French citizens, they could be prosecuted in customary courts—even if libel was not a transgression that had heretofore existed in whatever "custom" meant. This led to many hybrid legal quandaries and a wide set of strategies for eluding prosecution in the first place. Like other papers across West Africa, the Dahoméan periodicals made use of pseudonyms as well as citation to elude prosecution, although not always successfully.[23]

The Dahomey cluster in particular seems to have developed complex strategies for circulating discourse around censorship. In July 1934, the *Voix du Dahomey* published accusations of bribery against a French administrator. After declining to comply with an order to print a retraction, the paper saw its offices raided.[24] The police discovered a trove of supposedly stolen government documents and memos. The lead investigator theorized that there existed a network designed to collect and "mine" official documents for the purposes of finding material with which to criticize the administration.[25] We should avoid giving too much credence to the conspiracy theories around this shadowy network, but the correspondence of the *Voix*'s staff reproduced in the police report do give an indication of some of the strategic uses of the author function that the paper employed. In one such letter, the editor of the *Voix* is shown to be colluding with a correspondent. He promises to introduce his correspondents' articles into the *Voix*'s columns through a subterfuge he describes as "melting and remaking them."[26] In this image, the columns of the newspaper serve as molds where the ore of opinion can be melted down and smuggled across the federation—under any name that is convenient.

The Bamako-based paper *L'Essor* illustrates some even more reflexive strategies for circulating texts and projecting an audience. *L'Essor* was affiliated with Rassemblement Démocratique Africain (RDA), an increasingly potent political party that in 1946 had succeeded in merging many of the more territorial parties from across French West and East Africa.[27] *L'Essor* was the RDA mouthpiece for what was then called the Sudan, but in reality the paper had an absolutely tiny circulation that was limited to Bamako. Despite its seemingly narrow reach, *L'Essor* had a high degree of connection to other points of the network and a great deal of investment in producing and engaging with a hyper-local public. One particular episode helps us see these factors at work together. In September 1950, *L'Essor* reprinted an excerpt of Aimé Césaire's *Discours sur le colonialisme* (*Discourse on Colonialism*). The appearance of Césaire's text in *L'Essor* shows the interconnectedness of the networks spanning West Africa—a text by the deputy of Martinique appears in the Sudan just months after it first appeared in France in *Réclame*. But the reprint would spark a campaign of reprisals against the paper. In a confidential memo, the governor general of French West Africa fumed over Césaire's text with its "tendentious character," "extremely violent" tone, and "racist inspiration," all of which were likely to constitute an attack on "the maintenance of public order." The governor wondered if any "judicial action" might be taken against Césaire.[28] There was little that could be done about Césaire, but *L'Essor* was another matter. Just months after the Césaire complaint, the publisher of *L'Essor*, Abdoulaye Sangare, was arrested. But his crime was not reprinting the *Discourse*. Instead, the charges were libel claims against colonial administrators related to a very different set of articles in *L'Essor*. Some of these charges approached the absurd. The arrest warrant targeted one article that was said to "damage the reputation" of local magistrates and the police. The article in question suggested "that the local police are requiring cyclists to have bells and brakes at the behest of a local bicycle shop."[29] The crime was literally a bad joke, but the consequences for Sangare as the presumed author were potentially serious. As virtuosic as Césaire's text might have been in its indictment of colonialism, it was more difficult to prosecute than a very "local" satire of corruption.

The texts that actually led to Sangare's arrest help illustrate *L'Essor*'s complex relationship with its readers. The articles come from a series called Bobards, which was one of the more extraordinary minor textual forms that sprang up in French West Africa. The name itself means a false rumor, a fib, or a lie. Each edition of Bobards is a small dialogue, usually between two characters, typically staged as a phone call. The dialogues combine elements of a play, an open letter, and a blind item from a gossip column. The characters in Bobards are not named individuals, but pseudonyms—such as "Diablotin" (little devil), François-Michel, Luc, and "Mr. Mayor." The characters call each other to talk nonsense and complain. The topics they discuss are a mix of the banal and the serious. They gripe about minor inconveniences: an absence of trees around a monument to the abolitionist Victor Schoelcher and the presence of too many dogs and showing of too many cowboy films in local movie theatres. But they also explore more serious issues: corruption, mismanagement, and poor living conditions in Bamako.[30] These complaints are usually hyperlocal and reference particular neighborhoods if not individual streets.

The Bobards series drew on its complaints to elicit a dialogue with *L'Essor*'s readers. The characters often called on their audience to complete their work of satire and confirm the rumors they spread.[31] Readers wrote back and seemed to treat the Bobards (as the characters were collectively called) fairly seriously.[32] Many readers offered corrections to some of the more outlandish claims, sometimes sparking a back-and-forth. Although the Bobards proclaimed that "mockery is not fatal," they were operating in a legal grey area, as Sangare's arrest showed.[33] The series often features the irascible Diablotin calling up Mr. Mayor to harangue him and demand that he address some problem. The satire and criticism are put in the mouth of Diablotin for a reason—pseudonymity allowed Bobards to skate dangerously close to the limits of signed criticism of named colonial administrators.[34] For printed discourse to be punishable as libel, it needed to have a signed author who had a legal persona under a given regime. The pseudonymity of the Bobards ended up offering Sangare some protection; it proved impossible to prosecute him for the series without knowing for sure that he wrote it.[35] Given the extremely limited circulation of the paper (just five hundred copies) and the local nature of the complaints, it seems unlikely that "Diablotin" was ever a true form of pseudonymity—the audience may well have known who was responsible for these microplays, but in their exchanges with the Bobards, the readers nevertheless maintained the fiction, always addressing the characters as Diablotin or François-Michel.

The relationship between Bobards and its audience was not an expansive one—there was no outward push here toward a broader national public. Instead, the series imagined its scenes of circulation through the figure of rumor—limited in reach but difficult to contain. "Rumors circulate," Diablotin says. "One hears things. Some believe them. Others do not. They contradict each other—doubts hover where truth and lies cannot be distinguished."[36] The rumors that were the series' stock in trade did produce a certain collectivity, but it had a pointedly local rather than a national

character. We must not confuse this local focus for a lack of political critique or creativity. By including the Mayor of Bamako as a character who
could be reached by telephone in 1951, Bobards was performing a work of
fiction. It was not until 1955 that Bamako would become a *commune de pleine exercice*, that is, a municipality with an entirely democratically elected
local government. In the early 1950s when Bobards was appearing, the post
of administrator-mayor was still a position appointed directly by the colonial government. Once the post of mayor became open to elections in the
mid-1950s, the RDA won handily and Modibo Keïta, the political director of *L'Essor* (and a Ponty graduate), was elected mayor.[37]

Print periodicals in French West Africa frequently imagined their audiences at the extremes of scale—sometimes hyperlocal like Bobards but
at other times regional, imperial, or even humanity itself. Sometimes
we see such vertiginous shifts within the very same article. To appreciate
the work that newspapers did toward fashioning publics in this period, we
cannot compare every address to an audience to the normative ideal of a
national public. Working through the network rather than the nation allows us to think about the many nonnationalist ways of addressing and
constituting an audience that existed in the late colonial period.

Newspapers in West Africa often could not lay claim to the abstract,
disembodied forms of address that we associate with print, except as en-
abling fictions. Periodicals responded to the challenging circumstances of
their production by taking advantage of the porousness of print. Print
makes it possible to rework texts and opinions, to copy and paste the words
of others, and to express oneself under the cover of a pseudonym. Experiments with creating an audience were a consistent feature across the print
networks of French West Africa. Such experiments went well beyond what
we would understand as marketing in a contemporary sense. Newspapers
were not necessarily trying to carve out a share of an existing market for
themselves. They were often in the position of trying to produce a readership, to teach their readers how to be readers of newspapers. And if they
wanted to be successful, this process could not be one-directional—
newspapers had to solicit reader engagement, and they had to respond to
and be changed by that engagement.

"Dancing on One Foot": Reading and Its Doubles in Ousmane Socé's Karim

One of the most potent sites for experiments with audience was at the intersection of literary and print cultures, specifically in the publication of

literary texts as serials. We sometimes have a tendency to project backward into the colonial era a literary field full of books and book publishers, but relatively few works appeared as bound volumes. The vast majority of printed texts, literary and para-literary, appeared in newspapers.[38] The centrality of periodicals had a profound impact on literary production. From the earliest works of prose fiction to the first novels, many literary texts appeared not just in newspapers but as serials.[39] Seriality is crucial to understanding the development of the question of the audience. Serials foreground a sense of an audience's involvement differently than books do. A serial often has to depend on reader engagement for its continued existence in a way that a bounded text usually does not. The serialization of literary texts in West Africa contributed to the development of reflexivity around the question of the audience. When texts were serialized, the nature of the encounter with the reader came to be altered. In some cases, seriality spurred writers to reflect further on their relationship with their readers.

One of the most visible cases is Ousmane Socé's novel *Karim*, which appeared in several versions in the 1930s and 1940s. *Karim* was published in a book format by Les Nouvelles Editions Latines in 1935 but was serialized nearly simultaneously in the largest paper in French West Africa, *Paris-Dakar*.[40] The serialized version of the text diverges from its book counterpart in significant ways. Socé would also return to the Karim character years later, when he wrote a short, serialized sequel, entitled "Karim 1942." This later work ran serially in *Paris-Dakar*'s cultural supplement, *Dakar-Jeunes*, but it was never collected as a bound volume.

The original novel of *Karim* focuses on an eponymous urban African protagonist in the 1930s who is caught between competing pressures to return to his "native culture" or become more "modern." (As this schema suggests, Socé was a Ponty graduate.) Karim's attachment to his culture of origin is often represented by thick descriptions of proverbs and folktales (which Socé was collecting at the time), while the more modernizing direction is associated with a Ponty graduate named Abdoulaye. Karim eventually synthesizes these two directions. The conclusion of the novel, staged as a marriage plot, makes Karim appear as the realization of Socé's ideal of a *civilisation métisse*. The scholarship on Socé has more fully explored his second novel, *Mirages de Paris*, which presents a far more sophisticated treatment of the "cultural problem" of the late colonial period.[41] *Karim* seems by contrast to be a rather more simplistic *roman à thèse*. But when we closely examine the ways in which the figure of the reader shifts across the several versions of the *Karim* story, the series emerges as a rather more complex work than it first appears.

The idea of being a modern reader starts to become very important toward the middle of the 1935 novel *Karim*, at a moment when the protagonist is in a deep crisis. Originally from Saint-Louis, Karim has relocated to Dakar and ever since has been sinking into debt and vice. Just as he threatens to hit rock bottom, Karim at long last listens to the counsel of his friend Abdoulaye, the Ponty graduate who represents the novel's Eurocentric pole. Abdoulaye agrees to lend Karim money to pay his debts, but he also gives him a moralistic lecture about the value of reading. "Have you noticed that many Senegalese never open a newspaper or a serious book? They believe that instruction should end on the bench of the classroom. . . . We cannot not risk confining ourselves merely to ways of being, thinking or acting that are only compatible with the framework of a native society that no longer exists; or at least one that is decomposing and in full evolution." Karim agrees and resolves henceforth to live "an orderly life."[42] This resolution takes the form of a renewed dedication to reading:

> Ses loisirs étaient consacrés à l'étude. [Karim] reprit, pendant quelque temps, sa grammaire française et son arithmétique. Bientôt il s'adonna à des lectures—plus distrayantes. Abdoulaye, le maître d'école, lui prêta des romans intéressants qui parlaient d'un pays qu'il connaissait et de personnages qu'il voyait autour de lui: "La Randonnée de Samba Diouf", "Le Roman d'un Spahi", "Batouala" . . . Karim regretta de ne pouvoir lire beaucoup de romans semblables. Elle était pauvre la littérature africaine, la plus susceptible, cependant, de plaire au lecteur indigène moyen. Il se tourna, sur les conseils de son ami, vers une littérature européenne dont il pouvait saisir l'état d'âme des personnages, sinon les détails de costume et de décor. Il relit avec enthousiasme: "Les Trois Mousquetaires". "Le Capitan" de Zévaco lui procura des minutes d'émotions indicibles. En poésie il ne comprit pas toujours les sentiments qu'il jugeait trop artificiels. Il fut admirateur de Victor Hugo et apprit, par cœur, "Waterloo", "Les Soldats de l'An II", "Ultima Verba". Toutes ces pensées épiques correspondaient bien à son fond guerrier de sénégalais. Puis, ce fut Corneille et toutes ses tragédies héroïques. Ce changement moral se doublait d'un autre purement vestimentaire. Les boubous et le fez musulman, d'autrefois, servirent disgraciés et remplacés par un complet veston, par un casque colonial. Il acquit dans les magasins élégants de Dakar des souliers acajou et des cravates aux belles couleurs bleu, marron, argent. Dans ses nouvelles fréquentations ç'aurait été se singulariser que de vouloir conserver le costume sénégalais: "Kou dem tchi deuk bou niep di fethié ben tank, nga féthie ben tank."

His free time was devoted to study. [Karim] took up, for a certain time, his French grammar and his arithmetic books. Soon he indulged in more distracting readings. Abdoulaye, the school master, loaned him interesting novels that spoke to him of a country that he knew and characters that he saw around himself: "La Randonnée de Samba Diouf," "Le Roman d'un Spahi," "Batouala." . . . Karim was sorry that he could not read more similar novels. How poor was African litera- ture, and yet the most likely, at the same time, to please the average native reader. On the advice of his friend, he turned toward a Euro- pean literature in which he could grasp the emotional states of the characters if not the details of costume and décor. He reread with enthusiasm "Les Trois Mousquetaires." "Le Capitan" by Zévaco gave him minutes of glorious emotions. In poetry he did not always understand the sentiments which he felt were too artificial. He was an admirer of Victor Hugo and learned "Waterloo," "Les Soldats de l'An II," "Ultima Verba" by heart. All these epic thoughts corresponded well with his spirit of a Senegalese warrior. Then, it was on to Cor- neille and all his heroic tragedies. His moral change doubled itself in another that was purely sartorial. His old boubous and the Muslim fez were dismissed and replaced with a suit jacket and a colonial helmet. From the elegant stores in Dakar he acquired mahogany shoes and ties in beautiful colors like blue, brown, and silver. In the new company he was keeping, wearing his Senegalese outfit would have only made him stick out: "Kou dem tchi deuk bou niep di fethié ben tank, nga féthie ben tank. "[43]

Karim's rediscovery of reading is depicted as a commitment to a new ethi- cal practice, a way of fashioning a more perfect self that will eventually lead to a "moral transformation." As Karim reads, the outside of his per- son starts to reflect the change inside: he starts to dress in suits and ties rather than a boubou and even dons a colonial pith helmet. By the end of the novel, Karim will abandon the pith helmet for the boubou once more, but his rediscovery of reading is presented as a decisive step toward "an- other form of life" (*une autre forme de vie*).[44]

But to arrive at this new state, Karim must acquire a new "*savoir-vivre*." His reading habit becomes the cultivation of what Bourdieu would call a new *habitus*. However, Karim's successful acquisition of this new subjec- tive capacity is expressed not through a citation from his beloved Victor Hugo but through a Wolof *léebu*, or proverb: *Kou dem tchi deuk bou niep di fethié ben tank, nga féthie ben tank. (Ku demm ci dëkk bu ñepp di fecc benn tank, nga fecc benn tank.)* A literal translation would be, "If you should go to a country where everyone dances on one leg, you must also dance on one leg." At the moment when Karim is supposed to have attained a new westernized form of life through reading, the text captures his achievement with a Wolof proverb that indexes a very different body of knowledge as well as a different audience. The proverb is about a guest's obligation to adapt upon arriving in a new place of dwelling (*dëkk*)—a conscious effort to adapt your own way of being to a norm that has preceded you. This accommodation is figured as a dance, a performance which attenuates the guest's otherness and allows the guest to be recognized as belonging in some sense—or at least acting as such. The proverb makes Karim's habit of reading into a kind of dance. For all its transformative powers, then, reading is not imagined as natural but as a performance. Becoming a modern reader is something that one has to work at. It is an acquired capacity, a way of training an embodied self to take up a new habit in order to *be* in a new way. The proverb suggests that becoming a modern reader may be experienced as an awkward limitation at first—like dancing on one foot will be to one who is accustomed to using both.

This passage is one of many points at which the novel *Karim* differs from its serialized version. The proverb appears in the printed novel published by Les Nouvelles Editions Latines but not in the serialization in *Paris-Dakar*.[45] It is not possible for us to assign these changes to Socé's hand alone, since they could be the work of an editor. But the ways in which the two versions of *Karim* differ can still help us see how texts could be transformed as they circulated for different readerships. First, we need to situate the proverb's disappearance as one among many edits. The edits to the serial of *Karim* have an overall pattern: the serialized version is in general much leaner, while the book version is far baggier. The opening pages of the novel provide a good example. As a book, *Karim* opens with a rather dreamy invocation of the city of Saint-Louis at sunset, as Karim looks on. At this magic hour, all seems to melt into an "ether," giving the inhabitants of the city a certain fluidity.[46] But the serialized version skips all this and snaps the reader right into place with a rather more factual beginning: "Saint-Louis du Sénégal, est une vielle ville française, un centre d'élégance et de bon goût Sénégalais. Il a joué ce rôle durant tout le dix-neuvième siècle. De nos jours, avec la concurrence des villes jeunes, comme Dakar, Saint-Louis dépérit." (Saint-Louis of Senegal, an old French city, a center of elegance and Senegalese good taste. It played this role throughout the nineteenth century. These days, with the competition of younger cities, like Dakar, Saint-Louis is in decline.)[47] This reads almost like a newspaper dateline or the beginning of a history lesson, situating the reader in a particular time and place. In the book version of the novel, it is not until page two that we learn we are in Saint-Louis. Instead of a temporal and spatial fluidity, the reader of the serial is immediately placed into a shared present of "these days" (*de nos jours*).

This is one of many changes, large and small, that separate the versions. The serialized *Karim* seems on the whole to be more concerned with holding its readers' attention. On the pages of *Paris-Dakar*, *Karim* ran episodically beside a wide variety of other print content, including global and local news items, photos from wire services, advertisements, beauty tips, and health advice. As a serial, *Karim* had to hold an audience, mobilize a readership, and compete amid a much noisier discursive landscape. The changes to the novel tend toward tightening the text, removing exposition, and focusing on the plot.

These changes do not neatly map onto a divide between an African vs. a European audience. The readership for both versions would likely have been mixed. The novel published in France might have had the potential to reach not only French readers but also an African student community, while the readership of *Paris-Dakar* would have been rather diverse as well. What the differential between the versions does track is a variation between fields of circulation and presumed practices of reading. Here we start to see the shadow cast by the differential print networks of French West Africa. As texts move, they shift not in relation to the presumed identity of their audience but rather in relation to the practices of reading they presume they may encounter.

The proverb helps us conceptualize this. If we think of the novel *Karim* as a kind of guest in the various circumstances in which the text finds itself, then we can see its transformations as attempts to adapt it to a new *dëkk*, or dwelling place. Although at first this will seem counterintuitive, the absence of the proverb is actually the realization of the accommodation it advocates—the text dances on one foot by streamlining itself for a serialized readership. Through its very absence, the proverb teaches us something about the way in which text and audience are engaged in a complicated negotiation. A text is in a kind of dance with the audience it expects or hopes to find. But this is always a dance with a future, even virtual audience. A text never gets to invent this audience entirely, but nor is it completely constrained by the circumstances it finds itself in. Instead, a text tries to enter into and become a part of a performance that has preceded it, which it may well be able to remake but only by virtue of its participation.

Socé's dance with his readership would continue in the later sequel, which ran briefly in *Dakar-Jeunes* but was never republished. In "Karim

1942," Socé created new, metafictional episodes in which Socé the author joins Karim the character on adventures. In one episode, Karim and Socé are on their way to a wrestling match when they meet a farmer named Massaër, with whom they have a frank dialogue about educational policy. The farmer has heard about Socé: "Ah! You're Ousmane Socé: you recently wrote that we should all become white people [*toubabs*]."[48] Socé is stunned into silence as he processes this mischaracterization of what he had written. Eventually he responds: "Massaër, they did not accurately report my words to you. The Arabs say that speech is a stone. One is the master of it only so long as one has it in one's hand. Once it is thrown, all it takes is a ricochet . . . and *voilà* the stone receives a destination that was not in our intentions."[49] It is unclear whether Massaër is referring to Socé's novels or his essay on the "cultural evolution" of West Africa that had initiated the debate among Pontins in *Dakar-Jeunes*. Socé goes on to make his case to Massaër for what sounds like his version of adapted education, advising Massaër that in the educational reforms he foresees, elite schools will still produce elites, but everyone else will be urged to learn a traditional trade, and the "*déracinés*" (uprooted) will return to the earth.[50]

The premise of this scene is a misreading—or a misunderstanding, since Massaër seems not to have actually read what Socé wrote (and perhaps cannot read French). The scene is a dialogue with a person who is not a member of the text's public, but whom the text nonetheless tries to reach and convince. Socé figures this through the image of a ricochet. The image is an ambivalent one—a printed address can indeed travel far, but like a stone that has been thrown, where it goes and what it does are no longer under the author's control (if indeed they ever were). There are some audiences, the image suggests, who can be reached by print only indirectly, by a ricochet, but who may still lay claim to having been implicated in what has been written.

The figure of Massaër the nonreader projects, in a negative image, a vision of what the text assumes to be its own proper reader. Massaër has not read Socé but still has opinions about what he has written. A "true" reader, the text implies, would engage with Socé's texts rather than with hearsay and also be sophisticated enough to navigate this metafiction. The problem for "Karim 1942," though, is that it can only stage a replacement of a "bad" reading with a "good" one. It does this in a densely self-reflexive gesture: to correct misinterpretations of his work, Socé, the author, has to step into the discursive world of his earlier novel. But in the metafiction, the character Socé overcomes the farmer's misunderstanding in direct conversation, not in print. The printed text can represent the overcoming of a "misreading," but it can never fully vanquish the potential for one; it re-mains a printed text in a newspaper, written in French. Socé's text cannot wall itself off from its own ability to ricochet, to find new "readers" where it does not expect them or perhaps even want them to be.[51] Even though "Karim 1942" stages the successful conversion of Massaër to the author's point of view, it cannot bridge through representation alone the fissures that separate address, circulation, and audience. The limits of a reading public cannot be overcome heroically by the author and must instead be discussed and negotiated between the characters, in dialogue across dif-ferent modes of reading and nonreading.

Literacy and Politics

After the Second World War, the French Union nominally replaced the empire. In this shifting political climate and alongside advances in infra-structure and distribution channels, the print landscape of West Africa be-gan to open up to a variety of periodicals with new kinds of aims and ambitions. In what would become Senegal, the question of the audience took a new turn as two *littérateurs*-turned-politicians began publishing newspapers to help them build competing party networks and personal brands. In the early 1950s, Léopold Senghor and Ousmane Socé were not just competing politicians in search of votes, they were also rival newspaper editors. Senghor's foray into publishing took the form of his newspaper *Condition Humaine*, which was the mouthpiece of his Bloc Démocratique Sénégalais (BDS) party. Socé, who was politically affiliated with the So-cialist Party of Lamine Guèye, was the publisher of the avowedly apolitical illustrated magazine *Bingo*. Through these two publications, Senghor and Socé explored very different strategies for cultivating their readerships.

In the venerable tradition of political newspapers in Senegal, Senghor's *Condition Humaine* was a political organ that aimed to shape opinion and mobilize readers as voters. Senghor was the political director of the paper, with Alioune M'bengue the editor-in-chief. Its motto reflected a reform-ist political program: "We say revolution . . . but not revolt." Unlike ear-lier political papers in the region, *Condition Humaine* was also concerned with fashioning its audience's sensibilities as readers of literary texts. This is signaled clearly in the October 1948 issue in which Senghor announces his break with the Socialist Party and the formation of the BDS. In the same issue, *Condition Humaine* began a serialization of Jean-Paul Sartre's essay "Orphée noir" ("Black Orpheus"), the preface to the *Anthologie de la nouvelle poésie nègre et malgache de langue française* that Senghor had edited earlier that same year. These two texts—Senghor's open letter announcing his new party and Sartre's literary preface—are juxtaposed on the same page. This gesture makes Sartre's introduction into ballast for the founding of Senghor's party by making it appear as if the radical new black voice that Sartre was announcing was somehow Senghor's alone.[52] This impression is deepened in later issues as the serialization of "Orphée noir" continues and Sartre's text is misleadingly proclaimed to be a "preface to a work by L. S. Senghor" rather than to an anthology of work by multiple writers.[53] But the serialization of "Orphée noir" did far more than lend prestige to Senghor's political maneuvering. It also signaled the beginning of the paper's experiment in producing literary readers.

Sartre's "Orphée noir" is usually remembered as the essay that inaugurates *negritude* as a literary critical term, to such an extent that later writers complained about the way Sartre had eclipsed the volume of poems he had been asked to introduce.[54] But the essay's nearly simultaneous serialization in Senghor's newspaper suggests a very different interpretation, centered around the question of the audience. What is often forgotten about "Orphée noir" is that it also includes Sartre's attempts both to define the language issue for African writers and to propose a kind of solution. Sartre argues that national and linguistic independence are one and the same, since the traits of any given society correspond exactly "to the untranslatable locutions of its language." Because of this natural correspondence between language and nation, Sartre thinks that Africans and African-descended writers working in French will be "betrayed" by the French language itself. French is the "thinking-apparatus of the enemy." Its syntax and vocabulary were "forged in a different time," and they will be "unsuitable" for the black writer to speak of himself. The only response to this situation, Sartre thinks, must be a rejection of prose for modernist poetry. "Only through poetry," he writes, "can the blacks of Tananarive and Cayenne, the blacks of Port-au-Prince and Saint-Louis communicate between themselves without witnesses." Poetry can overcome the language question by "short circuiting" language itself (he seems to have in mind a kind of Mallarméan explosion of signification here). "Because the oppressor is present even in the language that they speak," Sartre suggests, black poets "will speak that language to destroy it."[55]

Sartre's interpretation of the language issue anticipates some of the positions taken in later debates. But what interests me here is the way he casts modernist poetry as a way of responding to and even overcoming the question of the audience. This move is crucial to understanding why poetry became central to the political project of *Condition Humaine*. The serialization of Sartre's preface marks the beginning of a years-long effort by *Condition Humaine* to teach its audience to be readers of negritude poetry. We see the overlap from the very beginning in the October 5, 1948, issue— the same reader that Senghor addresses as his "fellow citizen" in his open letter is also advised of the "capital importance" of having the *Anthologie* in their library. As if to head off the possibility that a reader might not follow this advice, *Condition Humaine* would over the next eight years obligingly serialize a good portion of the *Anthologie* in its pages. From 1948 to the mid 1950s, roughly half the poets who appear in the *Anthologie* were published in Senghor's paper. In each case, the poems selected were the very same ones that appear in the *Anthologie*.

In a series called "Chronique littéraire" or "Les Lettres noires," each poem from the *Anthologie* was accompanied by a short framing note that described the life and career of the author and his place in literary history. These were often written by Lamine Diakhaté and sometimes by Senghor himself. A principal aim of the series seems to have been teaching the readers of *Condition Humaine* about the poetry of negritude—and above all how to read such poetry. In an introduction to a poem by Damas, for example, Diakhaté describes the effect the text ought to produce on the reader: "And the reader starts to tremble with the hammering of the words; he separates from his own self, rather he integrates himself in the Other and follows the invisible threads that links all men sweating and suffering throughout the world."[56] This image of the reader trembling at the empathetic force of Damas's words suggests that the serializations were not just about appropriating the *Anthologie*'s prestige for Senghor's political career nor even providing a roadmap to the emerging literary history of African literature in French. The introductions to these poems were glosses on *how* to read these texts.

When critics or writers today discuss Senghor's *Anthologie*, they probably have in mind a landmark edited volume of modernist poetry with a famous preface. But the poems and essay that make up the *Anthologie* were serialized almost concurrently with their first publication as a book. In the process, the contents of the *Anthologie* were separated and put to use in different ways. In the serialization of the *Anthologie* in Senghor's newspaper, we see a sustained effort to prepare an audience for these poems. What *Condition Humaine* proposed was an ongoing guide on how to be properly moved by negritude poetry. Not unlike the protagonist's transformation in *Karim*, the aim of this serialization was the cultivation of a certain of readerly disposition, which *Condition Humaine* regularly modeled for its audience. When we reframe the *Anthologie* as a collection that was broken up and recontextualized for different audiences as it circulated across the print networks of French West Africa, we start to see how the shadow of the future reader extended across some of the most celebrated monuments in African literary history.

Ousmane Socé's magazine *Bingo* appeared at roughly the same time, but it developed a very different approach to the question of its future audience. In contrast to many other colonial-era print publications produced in French for an African audience, *Bingo* defined itself as "apolitical" and consciously sought to cultivate a mass audience—both in West Africa and among African students in Europe. Socé laid out his vision for the periodical in an editorial in the first issue entitled "What Our . . . Future Readers Think. . . ."[57] *Bingo* would include a far greater variety of content than many of the more intellectual journals or political papers. In any given issue of *Bingo*, a reader would encounter profiles of African intellectuals and writers such as Camara Laye, Bernard Dadié, and Cheikh Anta Diop alongside articles and photospreads on sports, celebrities, fashion, and world news. Essays on African art exist alongside comic strip versions of Socé's own novels. *Bingo* appears to have been supported by an advertising department that was rather more successful than many other periodicals in francophone West Africa—the pages are sprinkled with ads for a wide variety of consumer products, from cars, refrigerators, and clothing to alcohol, radios, and razors.[58] In the magazine's early years, *Bingo* adopted a unique strategy to position itself as the magazine for a mass readership that was not necessarily literate.

These attempts crystallized in a recurring feature of reader-submitted photo portraits. The feature was called Our Readers (*Nos Lecteurs*) early on and then became the Page of Bingo. It consisted of a page, sometimes two, on which we see a collage of portraits of *Bingo*'s readers (Figures 9 and 10). The feature seems to have been very popular. The editors described themselves at times as being inundated with images sent in from all over the federation and abroad. The letters to the editor also testify to the feature's popularity; as one reader put it, "We love *Bingo* because it shows us the photos of our friends and relatives."[59] The Page of Bingo documented different kinds of interactions between the magazine and its readers. Some readers are pictured posing with copies of *Bingo* (Figure 11, *top left* and *bottom right*). One reader cut up his collection and made a homemade album of *Bingos* (Figure 9, *top left*). A crucial element of the feature is the title given to these collages: "Tous lecteurs de l'illustré africain!"

Figure 9. La Page de Bingo, Bingo N°13, February 1954.

(Figures 10 and 11). All those pictured are declared "readers" of *Bingo*, regardless of how they interact with the magazine or whether they are literate in the narrow sense. To be a "reader" of *Bingo* did not mean being literate in French. It meant participating in the new modes of identification and publicness that the magazine was opening to its audiences.

Not every one of Bingo's "readers" saw it this way. Some letters to the editor objected to the recurring feature. An unsatisfied schoolteacher wrote in, "*Bingo*! *Bingo*! Everywhere the enthusiastic cheers of our populations. But what is *Bingo*? A photo album of individuals, a newspaper for illiterates."[60] Socé himself replied, "We hope to give satisfaction to our *évolués* and intellectual readers in the near future. The goal of *Bingo* is to reach the great mass of Africans."[61] These exchanges depict a tug-of-war between self-identified *évolués* who wanted a magazine of critique and culture and those whom the schoolteacher dismissively identifies as *illettrés* (illiterates) who were seeking from *Bingo* other forms of representation, correspondence, and affiliation.[62] The struggle was over what it meant to be a "reader" of *Bingo*. The collages were an attempt to visualize and realize a public and to invite that public to constitute itself in the work of representation. So although *Bingo* strove to remain "apolitical," its attempt to invite a mass public to constitute itself ended up creating space for politics to happen—namely, a fierce debate about what it meant to be a reader.

Figure 10. La Page de Bingo, Bingo N°9,   Figure 11. La Page de Bingo, Bingo N°11,
October 1953.   December 1953.

What kinds of readers can print cultures accommodate? What would it look like for a printed text to open itself to an audience that may not be able to or may not wish to read it in the way a printed text is usually expected to be read? Both *Condition Humaine* and *Bingo* were concerned with fashioning their audiences, but they adopted markedly different strategies for approaching and producing their readerships. Senghor's paper wanted to teach its readers what and especially how to read, while Socé's magazine was, for a short while, an effort to fashion a print public that did not depend on reading in a narrow sense. In these contrasting strategies, we see how the figure of the future reader came to be enmeshed in African print cultures of the late colonial period.

Toward the Future Reader

The wide spectrum of reflexive strategies that flourished in West African print networks in the colonial period began to shift in the later 1950s and especially the early 1960s. The most likely explanation is the rise of nationalism. The interest of editors in experimenting with different modes of addressivity starts to yield to the task of projecting new nations. There is perhaps no clearer example of this than *L'Essor*. In the late 1950s, the paper Sangare edited was an extremely local periodical. By the early 1960s, it had become the official newspaper of the new nation of Mali. The look, feel, content, and especially the attitude toward the readership would drastically change. Microgenres with high audience implication such as Bobards gave way to a more conventional party newspaper, focused around the person of the new president, Modibo Keïta. But while we do start to see the outlines of a more conventional story of the rise of print in these decades, the reorientation of newspapers around national publics and politics never succeeded in completely eradicating the earlier models that had sustained newspapers during the political and economic hardships of the colonial era.[63] One space where the late-colonial interest in reflexively fashioning a future audience clearly did survive was in vernacular language writing, publishing, and activism.

Like the nature of textuality and the limits of authorship studied in Chapters 1 and 2, the figure of the future reader would pass from colonial literary modernity into the postcolonial era in debates around writing in vernacular languages. When Sembène was publicly challenged by Birago Diop in 1963 to repeat his critique in Wolof, Sembène's response turned around the question of the audience. "If I had taken the time," Sembène replied to Diop, "I could have written *Le Docker noir* in Wolof. But then who would have read it? How many people know how to read the language? And if I had not taken the trouble at least to learn the grammar, even if only phonetically, I should not be in a position to write it; but then, who is going to read me?"[64] While he figured this separation from an audience as an impasse at the conference in 1963, in the decades that followed, Sembène and other writers would start to engage more extensively and creatively with such contradictions. As they did, they inherited one of the central concerns of colonial literary modernity: how does one not just address but *produce* a readership?

When Sembène started a Wolof magazine called *Kaddu* in the 1970s, he began each issue with a kind of acknowledgment that a potential reader might face some difficulties. The first page of every issue of *Kaddu* is a guide to the periodical's orthography—a kind of paratext that we still see in many Wolof texts published to this day. In the Editor's Note (*Ubbi*) to the second issue of *Kaddu*, Sembène and his coeditor Pathé Diagne explained their use of this simple phonetic guide by framing it as a provisional answer to the question of readership. Writing under the pseudonym *"boroom yoon,"* Sembène and Diagne asked their readers to think of *Kaddu* and its orthography guide as a broader instrument for learning (*jangukaay*) to read and write Wolof. Sembène and Diagne urged their readers to create new readers, especially among those who could not read for themselves.[65] *Kaddu* addressed itself to a public that might not yet be able to read it, and in so doing, it tried to make the process of producing its own reader into an integral aspect of its relationship to the wider world.

If we consider *Kaddu* in isolation, then this separation from a future readership appears like a cruel fate that awaits publications in African languages that do not yet have mass readerships. But *Kaddu* is not an isolated case at all; the experiments of vernacular writers and editors exist in dialogue with a long tradition of producing an audience, a tradition that extends back to the print networks of the late colonial era. *Kaddu* and other postcolonial vernacular writing projects were certainly not alone in striving to address virtual readers. *Kaddu*'s sense that it had to concern itself with the production of and care for its future public links it to the long tradition of reflexive address that I have studied throughout this chapter. The figure of the future reader that we see in the print networks of French West Africa was not about trying to reach already-existing modern readers. It was above all a way of experimenting with the very nature of reading itself. During decolonization, however, the figure of the future reader would start to become politicized in new and different ways. As we will see in the following chapter, *Kaddu*'s seemingly innocuous phonetic guide would become the spark that ignited a new phase in the development of a politics of language: a fierce struggle over the alphabet itself.

PART II

Decolonization and the Language Question

CHAPTER 4

Senghor's Grammatology: The Political Imaginaries of Writing African Languages

We often picture the language question as an argument between writers over what languages to use. But in the first few decades of a newly independent Senegal, the most intense conflicts focused on the very means of writing. When a recognizable politics of language erupted in Senegal in 1960s and 1970s, one form it took was a fierce argument over how to write Wolof and other African languages. The conflict pitted writers, linguists, and filmmakers against the state. This episode culminated in the extraordinary censorship of Ousmane Sembène's film *Ceddo*, which was banned for its use of a double letter *d* in its title. This chapter examines how writing African languages came to be a site of conflict in the Senegalese postcolony. To reconstruct this story, we need to provisionally leave behind what we think is at stake in the politics of language—identity, commitment, cultural rootedness. While each of these were aspects of the language question in Senegal, the most vehement arguments of the early independence era were over the alphabet itself. In the first decades of independence, debates over writing systems for African languages came to represent the stakes of decolonization—who was authorized to speak for the past and who would shape the terms in which the future would be imagined.

In 1960, the poet Léopold Sédar Senghor became Senegal's first president, and French became the official language of the independent nation. Article 1 of the first constitution made clear that "the official language of Senegal is French."[1] No mention was made of any other language. French was to be used in education, government, the judiciary, and state-sponsored media. Senghor's administration would also make an effort to consecrate French as the language of national culture and, further, to develop a patronage system that supported artists who worked in French and who were amenable to Senghor's vision of negritude.[2] In 1971, the constitution was amended, and Jola, Soninké, Pulaar, Malinké, Sérère, and Wolof were formally recognized as "national languages" (*langues nationales*), but the official language would remain French. This peculiar linguistic status—national but not official—was contested by writers who declared for the importance of working in African languages.

The language debates of the 1960s and 1970s took many guises, but some of the most heated were arguments around a series of presidential decrees made in the 1970s that sought to tightly regulate any writing in African languages intended for the public sphere. These conflicts over phonetics in the 1970s were a high-water mark of postcolonial linguistic politics in Senegal. Although these debates seem almost absurd to many today, the stakes at the time were felt to be high indeed. How did writing systems for African languages come to assume such a capital importance in the context of decolonization, both for artists and for the state? This chapter traces the roots of the conflict back to the late colonial era, when young African students in France became deeply invested in conducting research on African languages.

In the final decades of the colonial system, linguistic research was a way in which some of the most elite African students asserted the value of African languages and cultures. As they reached the highest levels of the French educational system and confronted deeply ingrained racism, African students pushed back against imperialist scholarship that had often denied that African languages had any worth or even any grammar. African students used linguistic research to make the case, in the most academically unassailable terms they knew, of the cultural worth of African civilizations. Linguistic research also served a second purpose. It allowed African students to sketch the outlines of decolonization. These took the form of discussions over how African languages would be written in the future. A discussion of writing systems at first appears completely separate from any discussion of politics. And yet this very separation was what allowed such conversations to become highly charged and productive spaces for thought experiments: Did African languages needed to be modernized? If they did, should new writing systems be developed? Who or what would be responsible for producing such systems? In these discussions about writing African languages, young intellectuals explored many of the central issues that would confront decolonization: What should a future polity look like? How should it be governed? What should its institutions look like, and for whom would they work? What should be the role of language, culture, and literature? Such questions would later be articulated in more explicitly political terms, but many of them were first rehearsed in discussions over how to write African languages. Before linguistic research and debates over writing systems became contested ground in the postcolonial period, they were generative spaces for imagining what decolonization might look like. To discuss the future of writing African languages was necessarily to risk imagining a different temporality.

This decolonial linguistic turn was epitomized in the work of two young Senegalese intellectuals whose thinking would come to dominate the first several decades of Senegalese independence: Léopold Senghor and Cheikh Anta Diop. Although they articulated divergent intellectual and political projects, both Senghor and Diop built the foundations of their theoretical edifices on research on African languages. As a student, Senghor researched and published on the grammar of several Senegalese languages, including Wolof and his native Sérère. Many of the central claims in Senghor's thought are derived and staged in part through his research on African languages. And Senghor would continue to draw on his linguistic research throughout his career as a public intellectual, a poet, and a politician. Cheikh Anta Diop was Senghor's great intellectual and political rival. Diop also undertook extensive linguistic research on Wolof as a graduate student. And like Senghor, he used his research to ground some very broad claims about the nature of African civilizations and the direction of decolonization. Diop also dedicated himself to creating a modern writing system for Wolof, a project that would prove highly influential in Senegal and later inspire the earliest versions of what has become the standard orthography system for Wolof. Although Senghor and Diop were both heavily invested in linguistic research, they arrived at different positions on nearly everything: they disagreed on the essential qualities and capacities of African languages, whether African languages needed to be modernized, and even the very nature of alphabetic writing. The postcolonial struggle over writing African languages was in many ways the direct outcome of Senghor and Diop's competing approaches. When the debates over spelling broke out in the 1970s, they pitted the administration of President Senghor against the intellectual heirs of Cheikh Anta Diop.

Grammatology, Writing, and Wolof

Grammatology—the study of writing systems and their impact on culture and thought—offers us a helpful optic through which to understand what was at stake in Senghor's and Diop's linguistic research as well as the later struggles over orthography that their works helped spawn. Senghor's and Diop's projects were grammatological because their concerns over *how* to write African languages became explorations of the very nature of writing and what writing could do *to* and *for* African languages. While at times Senghor and Diop appeared to be interested in only the particulars of phonetics and grammar, more often than not their research became an exploration of the intersection of language and writing—what writing is, where it comes from, and what it brings.

My sense of grammatology will be familiar to many from the early work of Jacques Derrida. In *De la grammatologie* (*Of Grammatology*), Derrida shows how the seemingly inconsequential problem of writing radically unsettles the transcendental truth claims of philosophy and the social sciences.[3] My own exploration of grammatology in this chapter both narrows and extends Derrida's focus. I will not be following the problem of writing into an exploration of *différance* as Derrida does. However, I will explore further an aspect of grammatology that Derrida leaves somewhat implicit—that any science of writing has both poetic and institutionalizing aspects. Grasping this dimension of grammatology is crucial for understanding why debates about writing systems became so intertwined with decolonization.

In Senghor's and Diop's linguistic work, we find a series of claims, gestures, and performative declarations that are deeply poetic. These include translations of literary texts into African languages, attempts to create new writing systems or even new words, and proclamations of the necessity of building modern literatures in African languages. These gestures are poetic because they attempt to do radically new things to and with words. But Senghor and Diop also had to confront the institutionality of writing—the simple fact that no one can implement a new writing system or declare a literature on their own. Writing is a social phenomenon, and writing systems inevitably force us to confront the fact of other people. Grammatology becomes a privileged space for decolonial thinking precisely because it brings together the poetic and the institutional—projecting a radically new future is fundamentally a poetic act, but such a projection must also grapple with the fact that it has to be realized collectively with others.

Before we can explore Senghor's and Diop's grammatologies more closely, we need to situate them against a broader history of writing *and* Wolof. I say "writing and" rather than "writing in" because I have no intention of answering the question, When did Wolof begin to be written down? While the motive behind such a question is understandable, the framing assumes in advance that we know what we mean by both writing and Wolof and that these are stable entities that met at some point in the distant past that we might still be able to uncover. Derrida warned us long ago against the notion that any society is ever entirely without writing. We can only sustain this dangerous fantasy, Derrida argued, if we persist in thinking of writing in what he calls "son sens étroit" (its narrow sense)— as strictly linear and phonetic notation. This familiar view of writing was for Derrida a very limited understanding, an ethnocentric misconception. If instead we understand writing in a broader sense—as what he called the capability to "jouer de la différence classificatoire" (bring classificatory difference into play)—then there is not and indeed never has been a society completely without writing.[4]

Derrida's critique of "writing in the narrow sense" can be sharpened by complementary work done in African literary studies. Karin Barber notes the ways that many oral traditions make discourse concrete without recourse to linear, phonetic notation. Barber convincingly argues that many of the qualities we associate with alphabetic writing—making discourse durable, object-like, and "out-there"—have analogues in what we think of as oral traditions. For Barber, the passage from orality "into" writing is not nearly as radical as the advent of the technology of printing, which does manifestly transform configurations of address and publicness.[5] To heed Derrida's warning and Barber's corrective, we have to set aside our initial question—when did Wolof begin to be written?—to ask a more grammatological one: When did the ways in which Wolof could be written come to matter, and why? This grammatological question will help reorient our brief history of writing away from a positivist quest for the earliest traces of alphabetic transcription and toward a history of the ways in which writing Wolof has come to matter.

Three traditions in particular are part of the backdrop of Senghor's and Diop's grammatologies: the 'Ajami tradition of Wolofal, which uses an Arabic-derived script; the tradition of missionary linguistics; and the colonial history of transcribing African languages. A history of writing and Wolof could, of course, touch on many more points than just these three, but for the twentieth-century grammatologists, these would be the precedents that mattered most.

The first extensive linear and phonetic writing of a language like Wolof probably occurred centuries ago in 'Ajami. We do not know when modified Arabic scripts were first used to write a language like modern Wolof, but 'Ajami appears to have been in diplomatic use in Senegambia in the early nineteenth century, and the multiscript petition that Boilat collected further testifies to its importance in Saint-Louis in the middle of the same century. This is the great irony of the postcolonial debates over how to write Wolof in a Latin script—the grammatologists were relative latecomers. A poetic tradition emerged in Wolofal (Wolof written in a modified Arabic script; *Wolofal* literally means "to make Wolof") in the late nineteenth century around the rise of the Muridiyya Sufi brotherhood.[6] Literacy in Wolofal is still fairly widespread to this day, although the long history of not counting 'Ajami readers as literate makes statistics somewhat unreliable.[7] The debates over the modernization of Wolof in the twentieth century have a complicated relationship with this longer history. Although Senghor and Diop were aware of the 'Ajami traditions, neither one of them would see Wolofal as a possible foundation for a *modern* writing system or literary tradition. Here the question of script was decisive.[8] For the modernizers, the Arabic script itself seems to have been associated with religiosity, and thus 'Ajami traditions were framed (incorrectly) as inherently "religious." This likely had more to do with the space in which 'Ajami literacy was learned—Quran schools—and less to do with the wide variety of writings in these scripts. But for the mid-century grammatologists, it would be the Latin script that came to be associated with modernity.

The second tradition of writing that matters for Senghor and Diop was that of the Catholic missionaries of the nineteenth century. As happened elsewhere across the continent and indeed the globe, missionary activity in what would become Senegal involved transcription, translation, and linguistic study. David Boilat's work is a perfect example. The Catholic missionaries who predominated in Senegal wrote grammars and translated religious texts into local languages. In Senegal as in so many other places, missionary linguistics is also inseparable from the history of languages themselves. As Judith Irvine and Susan Gal show, the nineteenth-century grammars of Wolof and Sérère by Aloys Kobès and Père Lamoise, respectively, "highlight—perhaps even maximize" differences between the two languages and "erase variation and overlap." In other words, missionary grammars helped produce Wolof and Sérère as two languages and two speech communities that were distinct and different.[9] The Catholic missionaries preferred to distinguish between Wolof and Sérère along ethno-religious lines—they wanted to keep the "animist" Sérère separate from the "Muslim" Wolof. We can no longer reconstruct where Wolof ended and Sérère began in the nineteenth century. This puts us in the position of recognizing that missionary dictionaries and grammars, on which both Senghor and Diop relied, themselves played a role in producing the languages they purported to describe.

The last tradition of writing that matters for the grammatologists is that of the colonial state. Contrary to stereotype, colonial governance in French West Africa was intermittently invested in attempting to develop writing systems for indigenous languages. There is no question that French colonialism on the whole sought to marginalize every language other than French, but this existed alongside a good many attempts to study and manage vernaculars. First, there was a tradition of early colonial administrators who styled themselves as linguists and produced grammars and dictionaries—this includes Baron Jacques-François Roger, patron to Boilat.[10] But the interest in indigenous languages really became acute in the twentieth century with the rise of the colonial humanist social sciences studied in Chapter 2. In the 1930s, the colonial administration became interested in creating systems for reliably transcribing local languages. This emerged not from any benevolent concern for the languages themselves but rather from a need to find a reliable way to inscribe colonial subjects into the *état civil*, or civil registry, of French West Africa. The *état civil* recorded births, deaths, and marriages, but as the project took shape, it became apparent that "native" names were being inconsistently spelled.[11] There were several efforts to develop a unified system of writing "native" names (none of them ultimately successful).[12] While it is unlikely that either Diop or Senghor were aware of these efforts, this precedent is important in a different way. It shows us that the association of writing African languages with "modernization" and the outward reach of a state was already present in efforts to inscribe colonial subjects into the civil registry. In other words, the colonial state's ambitions to gather and standardize its subjects' language use would survive into its postcolonial successor.

A Tale of Two Grammatologists:
Léopold Sédar Senghor and Cheikh Anta Diop

Senghor's interest in languages began early and lasted throughout his decorated scholarly career. Senghor was born into a Sérère community in Joal in 1906 and sent to study at the mission school at Ngasobil in 1914. At

Ngasobil, biblical study took place in both French and Wolof, and by the end of his eight years there, Senghor had learned both languages.[13] In 1922 he briefly went to seminary in Dakar before attending the Lycée Van Vollenhoven. After arriving in France on a partial scholarship in 1928, he enrolled in the prestigious Lycée Louis-le-Grand, where he met Aimé Césaire and Léon Damas.[14] After twice failing the Ecole Normale Supérieure entrance exam, Senghor studied French, Latin, and Greek at the Sorbonne, where he obtained his *license ès lettres* in 1931. The following year, he received his *diplôme d'études supérieures*, with a thesis on exoticism in Baudelaire, and obtained French citizenship. As a student in Paris in the early 1930s, Senghor also studied at the Institute d'Ethnologie and the École Pratique des Hautes Études. During visits back to Senegal in these years, he began conducting research on Senegalese languages for a planned doctoral thesis. He researched verbal forms in Wolof, Sérère, Pular, and Diola and returned to Joal to conduct research on Sérère oral traditions.[15] It was in this same period that Senghor began writing poetry. After obtaining an *agrégation* in grammar in 1935, he became a professor of Latin and Greek in Tours. He continued to explore his linguistic interest in African languages and published several articles on the grammar of Wolof and Sérère in the 1940s. As he began to further articulate his political and aesthetic philosophy in the postwar period, he returned time and again to his earlier linguistic research to round out his theories.

Like Senghor, Cheikh Anta Diop was a gifted student and something of a polymath. Born in 1923 in Céytu, Diop is said to have developed an interest in transcribing African languages as a high school student when he created the beginnings of a writing system for Wolof.[16] But his fascination with linguistics seems to have become a passion when he was a graduate student. For his doctoral thesis, he undertook research on what he saw as the linguistic and cultural similarities between Wolof and ancient Egyptian. Diop was unable to constitute a jury for a doctoral defense of his interdisciplinary project and ended up having to write a different thesis to obtain his degree.[17] Nevertheless, he published his research as a series of articles in the 1940s and eventually developed the work into his best-known book, *Nations nègres et culture*. Published in 1954, *Nations* argues that the ancient Egyptian and modern Wolof languages are related. This linguistic comparison serves as the basis of a sweeping assessment of the similarities between "traditional" African and ancient Egyptian cultures, which Diop uses to argue that African peoples and civilizations are directly descended from ancient Egypt. This filiation would in turn allow Diop to argue that Egypt's considerable cultural heritage could serve as the basis for a new approach to African humanities and the patrimony of a new, federal African state.

In conjunction with his attempts to establish this civilizational pedigree, Diop was equally concerned in *Nations* with the revalorization and modernization of African languages. Anticipating the postcolonial challenge to "say it in Wolof," he translated a variety of French texts into the language, including Einstein's theory of relativity, the *Marseillaise*, and excerpts of Pierre Corneille's play *Horace*. Diop also created long lists of new Wolof words to express scientific and mathematical concepts. Although Diop went on to write many more works besides *Nations*, the origins of his intellectual project lay unmistakably in the linguistic research and writing systems he began developing as a student.

Though they were born seventeen years apart, both Senghor and Diop were icons for their peers. Senghor was the first African student to receive the prestigious *agrégation* in 1935, while the younger Diop's thesis defense in 1960 was a major event for the African student community in Paris. Besides being intellectual rivals, Senghor and Diop would later become political adversaries. Senghor founded the Bloc Démocratique Sénégalais in 1948, while Diop was active in the more radical Rassemblement Démocratique Africaine. Before national sovereignty emerged as the model of decolonization that France would pursue, both Senghor and Diop supported federalizing approaches, albeit in very different ways. Senghor favored a commonwealth-style approach that included France; while for Diop, only a pan-continental federation could guarantee economic and political autonomy for Africa.[18] After independence, their political ambitions became more national in focus. During Senghor's presidency, Diop was an important, if never very successful, opposition figure. After being briefly imprisoned by Senghor's regime and eventually excluded from politics, Diop devoted his life to scientific and archeological research in support of his Afrocentric theses. Diop's confinement to his laboratory and prohibition from formal politics would make him an icon for a generation of Senegalese intellectuals.

Though Senghor's and Diop's projects once seemed closely intertwined, the connection between them has faded for scholarship conducted outside Senegal. Senghor's imposing body of poetic and critical writing is more likely to be studied today in terms of negritude. Recent scholarship especially has reopened a variety of new approaches to Senghor's work through this optic, considering negritude's links to vitalist philosophy, decolonization, and aesthetic philosophy.[19] While drawing from this revival of interest in negritude, my own engagement with Senghor will be more indirect.

Negritude is in many ways the royal road into Senghor's thought—it takes us on a well-trodden path through his major interventions. When we approach Senghor through the more winding pathways of his fascination with languages and writing, as well as his intellectual rivalry with Diop, a different and more oblique approach opens up. Instead of Senghor the pioneer of negritude, we start to see Senghor the grammatologist.

Diop's work has had a different afterlife. His influence was considerable in the 1950s through the 1970s. His books, especially *Nations*, were widely read and cited—both Aimé Césaire and Frantz Fanon were admirers—but scholarly memory of his thought has become clouded in recent decades.[20] Diop certainly remains a touchstone in Senegal, but the racializing framework of *Nations* has since come under a lot of criticism and scrutiny, particularly in the North American academy. Even among Senegalese scholars, as Mamadou Diouf and Mohamed Mbodj point out, his scholarly oeuvre is a foundational and yet curiously forsaken intellectual edifice—it casts a long shadow, but it is rarely engaged with directly.[21] When we reconsider Diop's project in terms of the concerns he shared with Senghor, we begin to appreciate a different, grammatological aspect of this thought. This in turn opens up new ways to consider his relationship to the Wolof-language writers who followed in his footsteps.

"Under Each Rock, A Nest of Words": Senghor's Vitalist Grammatology

As a poet and a linguist, Senghor felt that language was an incomplete but necessary way of intuiting the vital force of experience and existence. Senghor's conception of language was vitalist and owed much to the work of Henri Bergson. But Senghor went beyond Bergson in thinking that different languages had different capacities of manifesting the *élan vital*, or vital force. In Senghor's early writings, African languages are described as naturally poetic and surrealistic. European languages (usually Senghor was speaking of French) are described as having a natural technicity that makes them better suited for expressing the modern world. This contrast will appear familiar to anyone acquainted with the broad contours of Senghor's thought, but the distinctions he drew between languages take surprising turns when we look further into them.

In the early 1950s, Senghor wrote extensively about the nature of African languages. In many cases, he grounded his claims in his doctoral research. In a speech he gave in 1953 in Yaoundé, Senghor argued that "Negro-African" languages were "essentially concrete." They expressed "a synthetic thought in a syntax of juxtaposition and not coordination." In African languages, words themselves were always "pregnant with images" while abstract words were very rare. The very syntax of African languages was "surrealistic," according to Senghor. The syntax of French was the opposite. French was an "analytic language" with a "syntax of subordination, and consequently of logic."[22] Senghor further elaborated on these claims in a 1955 essay on "Language and Negro-African Poetry." He argued that not only could a poet take advantage of different resources in African languages but that meaning itself worked differently in them—a phrase in an African language did not need to rely on syntax to be meaningful. Instead of using "word-tools" (which is how Senghor described the smaller, prepositional parts of speech that connect phrases), African languages could rely on the "word-images" that were both sign and sensation at once. Since African languages had a syntax of juxtaposition rather than subordination, they could do without the logical bonds of syntax. Thought could move intuitively by leaps and bounds.[23]

Senghor's contrast between African languages and French turns on this distinction over syntax. African languages were inherently surrealistic for him in a very specific sense; it was not that they had no grammar, it was rather that the *way* they meant anything relied not on syntax but on intuition. As Souleymane Bachir Diagne points out, the key concept for Senghor was parataxis, "the replacement of syntax by juxtaposition or coordination."[24] Senghor drew the concept from the Dadaist poet Tristan Tzara. He cited Tzara directly, as if Tzara were speaking of African languages, when he writes, "Under each stone, there is a nest of words, and it is from their rapid swirling that the substance of the world is formed."[25] In this image, we get a glimpse of the seething vision of signification that undergirds Senghor's theory of African languages. Parataxis could not be further from the clean, tree-like structure of signifier/signified that we find in Ferdinand de Saussure. Here the meaning that lies beneath the signifier is not the signified but a scintillating, pulsating, even living substance. This natural surrealism, Senghor thinks, never entirely leaves words in African language. He describes it as clinging to the very words themselves, like a patina of oxidization one finds on certain metals. There has been an understandable tendency in scholarship to focus on the essentialism of Senghor's broad claims. His thinking on language clearly made such moves. But to understand Senghor as a grammatologist, we also have to explore how his philosophy of languages was articulated with a theory of writing.

Since African languages are naturally poetic in Senghor's schema, writing them down risks a kind of loss. For Senghor, African languages need to be preserved, but this usually means translating from them, studying them properly, and above all using them as poetic inspiration. In his view, the point of studying African languages often seems to be oriented toward translating their natural vitality into French.[26] But the poetic ontology that Senghor assigns to African languages should not be confused with an argument that these languages are incapable of abstraction per se. Rather, Senghor seemed to think that African languages expressed abstraction in an image-rich, poetic way. Although we need to be careful in assuming too much of a continuity between Senghor's early writings and his later political career, his concerns about what writing would do to African languages can help us grasp the background of his later projects to regulate spelling. Senghor was mistrustful of efforts to rapidly modernize African languages as vehicles of science and technicity—French, for Senghor, was better suited for that purpose. At his most grammatological, Senghor suggested that writing is that which crystallizes and therefore impoverishes a language. Before he became president, the future he often preferred to imagine for African languages was one of conservation, not necessarily codification—a kind of museumization of African speech.[27]

Senghor's understanding of African languages as naturally surrealistic led him to endorse further analysis of them (he was, after all, an *agrégé* in grammar), the better to understand their unique properties (which he always seemed to already know). But in his view, more extensive analysis had to precede any attempt at creating new systems of transcription. He had little patience for those who wanted to transcribe African languages without proper analysis or training. The Ngasobil school of his childhood and its grammars of Wolof and Sérère seemed to represent an ideal of how to properly study and write African languages. The Ngasobil translation of the *Imitation of Christ* into Wolof was a "masterpiece" for Senghor. Just a few years into his presidency, he would complain of "contemporary translators and transcribers" who more often than not did not know how to analyze languages and produced transcriptions that "lacked precision."[28]

The writing of African languages is a point at which Senghor's early thought connects with his later practice of governance—though not in the sense that his views did not change or evolve nor that what he said earlier in his life committed him to a particular strategy as president. The connection is subtler. In the younger Senghor's concern that writing systems for African languages were being developed too quickly, we start to see the limits of his grammatology. What Senghor stumbled into in his early writings was the simple fact that having a theory of language and writing is one thing, but implementing a vision of how writing will take place in the world is a very different proposition, since it inevitably raises the fact that writing systems involve other people. In the late colonial era, Senghor articulated a complex account of what he saw as the special nature of African languages and warned of the dangers of writing them too rapidly or carelessly. But the futurity of writing in African languages would ultimately elude his direct control—even after he became president.

WE NEED NEW WORDS: DIOP'S NATURALIST GRAMMATOLOGY

Diop's views on writing developed from a very different philosophy of language. Diop was a linguistic naturalist; he thought that there ought to be a natural correspondence between words and things. Unlike in earlier linguistic naturalisms, in which such correspondence was often divinely ordained, Diop saw the connection between language and the world as being at least partly the product of human endeavor.[29] Although Diop was trained in the wake of Saussure and was familiar with the arbitrariness of the sign, his linguistic ideal was a kind of connection between the abstraction of language and what he understood to be the real world. This was in part what led him to object so strenuously to French as a language of education and to try to "modernize" Wolof.

Beginning from this standpoint, Diop approached the question of writing African languages very differently from Senghor. Whereas Senghor worried that writing would instrumentalize African languages and make them lose their natural vitality, Diop considered writing to be a stabilizing intervention.[30] The aim of his linguistic work was to modernize the Wolof language and in so doing set a precedent for other African languages.[31] In addition to his translations and his comparisons of Wolof with ancient Egyptian, Diop believed it was necessary to invent new words so that Wolof would be able to express the fundamental concepts of modern science. He usually did this by creating portmanteaus and modifying roots; for example, his new term *mbari-koin*, or "many corners," is supposed to translate *polygon*.[32]

For Diop, the stakes of inventing new words were quite high, since he was convinced that there had to be a link between abstract concepts and the language of everyday life. Diop knew, of course, that the words for scientific and mathematical concepts in European languages were at best vestigially indexical—*polygon* may have meant many corners to the ancient Greeks, but certainly no French schoolchild would enter a classroom with that knowledge already. But the fact that such terms were once indexical seems to have been rather important for him. His word lists are attempts to produce a kind of rudimentary indexicality between the language of conceptuality and the language of everyday life. If there was no such connection, Diop worried, then it would be needlessly difficult for an African child to learn the concepts of math and science. When an African child was mainly educated in a foreign language, Diop argued, it was as if reality were "covered by a thick membrane that separates it [from the child's] spirit." In such a situation, Diop wrote, the child's mind "becomes only attached to formulas, to declarations, taken for magical recipes that constitute in themselves knowledge . . . memory comes to be substituted for reason [and] . . . the intellectual faculties do not have the same occasion to be tested."[33] For Diop, modernizing Wolof meant overcoming this membrane between the world and the spirit. He sought to do this by extending the words that were already there, to make them touch the concepts that the modern world seemed to him to require. Whatever one thinks of the account of conceptuality that underlies Diop's theory of language, his gesture of creating new words was quite remarkable. Although the aim of the word lists was scientific, the gesture of extending, bending, and recombining existing terms to accommodate new concepts was also deeply poetic. Diop was in a sense trying to create a new dictionary—but rather than a catalogue of words in current use, his lists consist of future words.

As poetic as they are, Diop's word lists are also a strangely solitary, even vanguard, project. They seem to proceed from the assumption that the substance of scientific concepts comes from dictionary definitions, rather than the social life of language. To put that more simply, creating new words does not in itself create the institutions that will use them. Much as we saw with Senghor, the grammatological corners of Diop's thought exist in a tug-of-war between a pressing need to create new ways of using of language and a desire to dictate the terms in which new things will be done with words.

The (Un)Translatability of Beauty

Despite their apparent differences, Senghor's and Diop's philosophies of language converge in a shared reliance on translation as method. For both Senghor and Diop, a translation was a preferred proof for demonstrating the nature of a language and then scaling that observation to make a larger claim. We can draw this method out further by examining how they both discussed a single Wolof word: *rafet*, or "beautiful." Senghor used what he thought of as the *untranslatability* of this word to help him make a case that African languages and civilizations had a distinctive aesthetics and ontology. Diop used what he considered the *translatability* of this same word to help him ground a very different argument about the origins of African languages and civilization in Egyptian antiquity.

The word *rafet* comes up in Senghor's essay "The Negro-African Aesthetic," which was originally delivered at the First Congress of Black Writers and Artists in 1956 and later republished in *Présence Africaine* and *Liberté*. In this essay, Senghor develops some of his broadest claims about the nature of African civilization. As is often the case, Senghor's claims are based partly on his own linguistic research. At a key moment in the text, Senghor argues that African civilizations have a functional rather than a mimetic understanding of beauty. His central example is the difficulty of translating *beauty* or *beautiful* from French into Wolof. Where French would use *beauté* or *beau*, a Wolof translation would have to choose between a variety of different terms. Senghor observes that terms such as *tar* and *rafet* are primarily used to describe the beauty of humans, while for aestheticized objects a Wolof speaker might prefer *jekk*, *yem*, or *mat*. Senghor thought the impossibility of a neat translation between French and Wolof terms for *beauty* was evidence of the special nature of the beautiful in African civilizations. Drawing on this reading, Senghor goes on to argue that the African understanding of beauty is necessarily surreal and participatory, not an imitation of nature, as it is in a Western tradition. Senghor's principal aim here is to rescue beauty from any contamination with abstraction or mimesis. Emancipating the beautiful from mimesis allows it to become a kind of vitalist intuition of the world.[34]

But Senghor's argument for the special nature of the beautiful in African civilizations draws not only on linguistic analysis but above all on a reading of the poetic features of various performance genres. When he wants to demonstrate the "existential" ontology of the negro-African in this essay, he cites the call-and-response formula that initiates a Wolof *léeb*. When he wants to illustrate the special sense of rhythm that he sees in the negro-African aesthetic, he provides the scansion of two Wolof poems. Senghor also marvels over the poetic possibilities of Wolof verbs, which are conjugated in terms of aspect rather than tense.[35] Senghor's argument for the negro-African aesthetic is derived in part from his very keen and close reading of certain poetic effects, especially (though not exclusively) those found in Wolof performance genres. A metonymic chain then serves to scale up these readings: he observes a poetic technique keenly and brilliantly, only to then make it into the truth of the language, and then from there the nature of African languages or styles of expression more generally, and further still, the essence of African civilization.[36]

This is a recurrent move for Senghor's larger arguments—from a reading of a poetic feature to a broader claim. We see this occur in an equally striking fashion in the essay "Language and Negro-African Poetry," in which Senghor wants to demonstrate the essence of African poetic style. He focuses on readings of several songs he gathered during his own research, some of which he gives in Wolof, while others he keeps in translation. Senghor focuses on these songs' tendency to rapidly shift focus and aspect and to create meaning more through parataxis than syntax. These quick transitions become the "verbal alchemy" by which we are meant to recognize the "essential" nature of African poetic style.[37] The examples Senghor gives are indeed full of rapid, short phrases that move in leaps and bounds. But there is another interpretation of the features he identifies. Senghor collected and transcribed several *woy* (songs) and *bàkk* (songs performed by wrestlers), and these are genres that are typically performed for a crowd. The staccato bursts that he recognizes as evidence of a naturally juxtaposing style common to all African poetics might instead be understood as part of the registers of certain performance genres. Senghor selects texts that already have rather "naturally surrealistic" qualities. This allows the techniques of more declamatory performance styles to stand in for the nature of African languages and poetics more generally.

Diop also employs the Wolof word *rafet* in a claim about the nature of African civilization—in his case, as part of a demonstration of how words from ancient Egyptian are supposed to have been transformed in predictable ways as they moved into modern Wolof. Diop takes *rafet* as an example of how the roots and gender of ancient Egyptian words have morphed in distinctive patterns. His claim is that the Egyptian word for *beautiful, nofert*, becomes *rafet* in Wolof. While this is by no means Diop's primary example, it illustrates how he uses linguistic evidence. Diop is not making an explicit claim about the beautiful in general, but his example works by presuming that "beauty" is an entirely translatable concept across time and space, between the languages and lifeworlds of ancient Egypt and contemporary Senegal. Diop proceeds to examine two phrases, one in Egyptian using *nofret* and one in Wolof using *rafet*. He marvels at the sonic similarities of his examples: "At times, you would think you were speaking the same language."[38] At this point, Diop is offering more than a linguistic argument. Although he began by talking about a pattern of transformation in linguistic roots, his evidence is now the sounds of the words themselves. The auditory echo Diop that detects in *rafet* feels to him like a trace of ancient Egyptian. Diop is asking the reader to just listen, to hear with him a kind of rhyme between *nofret* and *rafet*.

The translation of a single word—*rafet*—draws out contrasting methodologies and unexpected affinities. Senghor and Diop arrived at sweeping and competing claims about the nature of African languages and civilization, but they both constructed those arguments through translation. Both Senghor and Diop based their linguistic work on attending to very minute shifts in language. Beyond their studies of grammar and phonetics, this mode of attention seems to have developed out of the practice of translation.

Some of Senghor's most important insights are staged through his difficulties in translating into French the speech and performances genres in Sérère and Wolof that he had collected over the years. Such translation work often provided him with the footing he needed to scale up his arguments. Once we see this aspect of the genesis of Senghor's thought, it becomes clearer that his thinking on African languages and civilizations does not emerge fully formed. Rather, these arguments seem to take shape gradually, often first as intuitions that acquire their decisive formulations through an attempt at translation. Senghor's most sweeping statements take shape through his repeated discovery that certain stylistic, grammatical, and rhetorical features that he finds in Sérère or Wolof texts are challenging to translate into French. Noticing this helps us de-monumentalize Senghor's thought. By this I do not mean minimizing its importance but rather finding other lines of approach. Instead of considering Senghor's claims about the essential nature of African languages and civilizations as the axioms they became, we can approach his works more obliquely when we see how these points tend to emerge from translations, especially failed ones. Frustrated translations are where Senghor seems to work out his sense that each language works differently and contains only a piece of a larger, human truth. Even his understanding of negritude is not infrequently staged through his own creative failures of translation.[39] In this sense, Senghor actually had more in common with the later movement that developed around Wolof than he may have realized. Although as president Senghor frequently found himself in an adversarial relationship with writers and filmmakers advocating a turn to Wolof, they were in a sense both departing from failures of translation. Much like Senghor's theories seem to have taken shape around the untranslatability he detected in certain poetic features in African languages, the counterpoetics of Ousmane Sembène and Cheikh Aliou Ndao (studied in the next chapter) developed out of the difficulty of rendering into French certain aspects of communication in Wolof.

Diop's intellectual project also presents itself in a monolithic manner—as a comprehensive demonstration of the Egyptian origins of African civilization. But much of the force of Diop's argument derives from moments like his translation of *nofert*, where it is a question of an aesthetic judgment, not just a scientific one. Diop clearly wanted to prove his thesis in a purely scientific manner, but he often asks his reader to recognize the kinship he hopes to demonstrate by appealing to the reader's senses, to a shared aesthetic experience of the evidence. "Do you hear it too," he seems to ask us, "that echo of Egyptian in Wolof? It's *right there*." Diop needs his reader to join him in experiencing the word *rafet* as a linguistic trace that has to be felt as much as observed and analyzed.

African Languages and the Literature Question

Senghor's and Diop's research on African languages also led them to the question of literature: what a literature was, who it was for, how a collectivity could "possess" it, and which languages were suited to literary expression. Well before the politics of language emerged as such and posed these questions with a vengeance, Senghor and Diop reflected on what literature in African languages ought to be.

Given his eventual concern over the effects of writing African languages, it may be surprising to note that Senghor was also one of the first francophone African intellectuals to publically call for a modern, written literature in African languages. This occurred in his very first published essay, a speech that was delivered to a capacity crowd at the chamber of commerce in Dakar in 1937. The speech was also quickly reprinted serially in *Paris-Dakar*. In the speech, Senghor focused on the "cultural problem" in French West Africa. He argued against a purely metropolitan curriculum in colonial schools and proposed educational reforms that would teach colonized students about France and the wider world and yet immerse them in their own cultures—what Senghor called "bicephalism." Senghor's proposals both harmonized with and revised the broader move toward adapted education in colonial reformist circles in the 1930s, precisely the turn that led to the rise of para-literary authorship.[40] Most importantly, though, Senghor insisted that instruction ought to take place in African languages as well as French—still a somewhat radical idea at the time, and one that neither the colonial government nor his own future administration was ever prepared to adopt. Educating students in African languages would prepare for the coming of a "native" literature (*littérature indigène*) that would be the work of intellectuals who would "restore black values" and awaken the people. A written literature was necessary for this purpose: "There is no civilization without a literature that expresses and illustrates its values, much like a jeweller who fashions the jewels of a crown. And without a written literature, there is no civilization that goes beyond the level of a simple ethnographic curiosity."[41] Contrary to the image we may have of him as the consummate francophile, Senghor argued that French alone would never be able to capture the essential qualities of the African experience, that a "native" literature had to be written in a "native" language. Although this seems directly at odds with other aspects of his theories, the statement is not as much a departure as it seems. Senghor foresaw the rise of a "native" literature taking place in a bilingual context, in which different languages would have different specializations: scientific works would be produced in French, while African languages would become literary by producing written works in the genres that were most proper to them—poetry, theater, and tales. These genres, he argued, best expressed "the genius of the race."[42]

This call for a written literature in African languages was also the moment at which Senghor's speech was interrupted. "I hear whispers over there [*on chuchote là-bas*]," Senghor says, before wondering aloud whether some of his peers (*congénères*) were disappointed by what he had to say and had hoped for a more policy-focused speech.[43] This trace of an interruption (or the staging of one) occurs directly after Senghor argues that African languages need only proper cultivation to become literary languages. We have no way of knowing whether a murmur really did run through the crowd in Dakar on that evening in 1937. Senghor may have written this piece of banter ahead of time, anticipating a moment when he would begin to lose his listeners, or he might have improvised the line as he spoke, only to add it later to the text of the speech. Either way, the fact that he conserved this aside whenever the text was reprinted is striking. It serves as a reminder that Senghor's diagnosis of the "cultural problem" and his call for a written, "native" literature were not proclamations made to the ether. They were appeals to and for an audience. In this aside, Senghor seems to acknowledge that his listeners' participation and even attention were not guaranteed and that the success of what he was asking for depended on others. This trace of Senghor losing—or staging the possible loss of—his audience at the moment at which he declares the need for a written, "native" literature foreshadows some of the difficulties he would later face in instituting as law his vision of the way African languages would be written.

Diop also argued passionately for the development of a written literature in African languages, which he saw as a precondition for what he called an African cultural renaissance. Diop, however, was more concerned with how a collectivity could be said to "possess" a literary tradition, and above all for whom a written tradition was intended. "Why and for whom do we write?" he asked in an early essay.[44] His initial response to this question was starkly nativist. Early in his career, Diop believed that the language of a text indexes not only the audience but also the community that can claim ownership over the work itself. "Every literary work," he wrote, "belongs necessarily to the language in which it is written."[45] Thus Diop dismissed the writers of his generation who worked in French. He argued that they had to be classified by the language they used, so their works could therefore never be considered "monuments of African literature."[46] Diop's position anticipates by more than a decade the identitarian tack that the language question would take in the early 1960s. But Diop also softened his stance on language somewhat, perhaps realizing, as Birago Diop would later point out to Sembène, that there was a certain irony to denouncing others for writing in French when your own critique was expressed in that language. "We cannot reproach [our contemporaries] for [writing in French]," Cheikh Anta Diop wrote, "because there does not currently exist an expression adequate to their thought. This is the dramatic problem of our culture: because we are obliged to employ a foreign expression or shut up; and we know how impossible this is for someone with the need to express themselves."[47] In this vivid formulation, Diop too anticipated the counterpoetics that would develop in the first Wolof novel and film. Early in his career, though, Diop envisioned a clear way out of this "dramatic problem"—by preparing for a modern African literature through the modernization of African languages.

Diop's linguistic work was an effort to lay the groundwork of a "complete, modern literature" in Wolof and other African languages that would be "endowed with monuments in prose as well as poetry."[48] But there was an additional precondition. Diop acknowledged that to truly modernize African languages there had to be a certain shift in "mentalities." What was needed above all was the acquisition of an "intellectual discipline" that would bring speakers to "acceptance of the necessary neologisms with less and less resistance."[49] This small aside points again to the curious fragility of Diop's word lists and translations. It also speaks volumes about the stakes and limits of his overall project. For all his work creating new writing systems, translating literary and scientific texts, and coining new words, Diop at times had to admit that this would never be sufficient on its own. Much as Senghor seems to have intermittently realized, Diop saw that his ambitious project was also completely dependent on other people. Without an audience for his new words, his goal of a modernized language and literary monuments would elude him.

In the late colonial era, both Senghor and Diop wrote extensively on African languages and what their relationships to writing ought to be. They both developed grammatologies that would play an outsize role in shaping the intellectual and political terrain of postcolonial Senegal. Their projects were highly attuned to and reliant on both poetics and translation—the meaning of particular rhythmic techniques, what the translation of a word did or did not show, and whether one could fashion new concepts out of old words. Senghor and Diop drew on the poetic to imagine new, future trajectories for African languages, but neither one of their projects could be simply projected outward into the future. Their proclamations of a new linguistic future also had to be invitations, attempts to get others to join in. In this tension between the poetic and institutional, we start to see the outlines of the coming conflict over the writing of national languages in postcolonial Senegal. Once the framework became national, the grammatological question became who or what had the authority and the sovereignty to shape new ways of writing language.

The Ceddo *Affair*

The first rumblings of a postcolonial battle over orthography began in 1971, when President Senghor fired off a detailed letter to his prime minister, Abdou Diouf. Senghor informed Diouf that he had just read "with stupefaction" the second issue of Ousmane Sembène and Pathé Diagne's Wolof periodical *Kaddu*.[50] The issue contained a bit of political critique and appeared during Senegal's tenure as a one-party state under Senghor (1963–76). But the ostensible problem was not politics, but phonetics. Senghor was infuriated by the way in which *Kaddu* was writing the Wolof language. In his letter to Diouf, Senghor notes that he believes it is his duty to react to what he sees as the many grammatical and spelling errors in the magazine. He goes on to correct them with precision. But the larger problem for Senghor was the fact that *Kaddu* was using an unsanctioned transcription system. As we saw in the last chapter, Sembène and Diagne's magazine always began with a one-page guide explaining its system of orthography. This single page on Wolof phonetics would touch off years of controversy.

At the moment Senghor wrote to Diouf, their administration was in the process of attempting to standardize writing systems for each of the newly "national" languages. Beginning in 1968, a series of presidential decrees created a new regulatory framework for orthography, transcription, and word separation in African languages. But by 1971, Senghor was already lamenting to Diouf that literacy classes, textbooks, and even periodicals were starting to appear in the national languages, with each one using "its *own* orthography and its *own* separation system." The appearance of *Kaddu* seemed to confirm Senghor's worst fears. "Now we are in a royal mess [*en pleine pagaille*]," he wrote, "that is really the only word for it."[51] Senghor's 1971 letter concluded by instructing Diouf to convene a commission to study further the possibilities of formalizing writing systems for Senegal's African languages. This would eventually lead to an even more strident series of presidential decrees, which would make it illegal to publish anything in the national languages that did not conform to their official standards of transcription.

That these standards were adopted by presidential decree was no accident. Senghor was deeply and personally invested in this topic. For the second of the decrees, published in 1972, Senghor himself wrote a long essay defending his government's linguistic policies. He began by noting that the initial 1968 laws had caused many suggestions to be sent his way; some of them were from "amateur grammarians," while others were from "real linguists." Rather than respond to the criticisms individually, Senghor reflected at length on the spirit behind his reforms, and in the process, he revisited and revised some of his earlier positions on writing and African languages. Senghor reminded his critics that he had been, in his 1937 speech, the first of his generation to publicly call for education to take place in African languages. He also tied his government's linguistic policy to a defense of multilingualism. Senghor urged his critics to see that "every language, like every civilization, contains only a part of the wealth of humanity; every language, like every civilization, has emphasized certain traits of the human face, has cultivated certain values of human civilization and neglected the others." But to those who called on him to replace French altogether, Senghor made it clear that there would be no change in the state's official language or its language of education. Revising his earlier positions, he noted that an African language could absolutely become "an instrument for instruction in science and technology" but that it would take "two generations" and require experts who were "qualified enough." In the second half of the twentieth century, Senghor observed, Senegal simply did not have fifty years to spare.[52]

The attempts of Senghor's government to regulate writing in African languages were in direct competition with other, less state-centered projects. For Wolof, these were initiated by the followers of Cheikh Anta Diop, who had been busy developing transcription systems of their own. These began to take shape just before independence, when the Association des Etudiants Sénégalais en France met in Grenoble. According to one of its members, the future novelist Cheikh Aliou Ndao, the group was inspired by Diop's work in *Nations*. Together they published *Ijjib Volof*, usually identified as the first systematic attempt at a standardized orthography for the Wolof language using a Latin script.[53] *Ijjib* is a small booklet that includes simple phonetic lessons and a transcription of a *léeb*, as well as two short prefatory essays. In its two prefaces, the *Ijjib* group makes it clear that it sees writing systems much as Diop did, as a means to modernize and "stabilize" African languages.[54] *Ijjib* saw modernization through a pan-Africanist rather than a nationalist lens; the project is framed not as a system to be adopted by a sovereign state but as a model for anyone interested in writing African languages. The *Ijjib* group was rather modest and framed its work as preparatory and open to adaptation. It noted that the system it had created was merely "sufficiently exact" and "an example to be considered as such." The group wrote, "There is no doubt that the system could be smoothed out, amended, as it is used. We count on your suggestions in order to make modifications in a new edition."[55] Although there was never a second edition to *Ijjib*, this call for further participation and innovation was clearly heard. *Ijjib* would help spark interest in writing and publishing in the romanized script for Wolof. The provisional and open-ended nature of the *Ijjib* project contrasts sharply with Senghor's legislation a decade later. For Senghor, the "modernization" of a language had to be rigorously and properly prepared by accredited grammarians before the first step could be taken. *Ijjib* suggested that writing systems had to start somewhere and that even an imperfect beginning would be better than any further delay.

In 1975 and 1977, two more presidential decrees set the stage for a direct confrontation with those interested in adopting *Ijjib*'s system. The new decrees stipulated that all Senegalese languages were to be transcribed without doubling any letters. But an increasing number of linguists recognized that Wolof employs long consonant phonemes called geminates (*dd* or *kk* for example). Doubling letters was seen as necessary to avoid confusion in written Wolof, since the difference between long and short consonants (*dd* vs. *d*) could matter greatly. The writings of Cheikh Anta Diop, the *Ijjib* group, and Sembène's *Kaddu* all made use of geminates.

Senghor's decrees ruled geminates out altogether and imposed stiff penalties on anyone who used them to write African languages. "At the moment when a literature and press written in our national languages are developing," Law N° 77–55 read, "it is impossible for public power to tolerate the establishment of anarchy and confusion in this domain, which is what we are witnessing with the hatching and profusion of 'unauthorized' [*sauvage*] systems of transcription for the national languages which are marked by nothing so much as the improvisation and individualism of their authors."[56] Along with previous decrees, the law required that every piece of writing in a national language that was intended for the public sphere be approved by a commission, which would, in theory, only be allowed to regulate the correctness of the writing, rather than the content. Being in violation of the law carried a one- to three-month minimum prison term and fines of anywhere from twenty thousand to one million CFA. The first casualties of the decree were the opposition publications *Siggi* and *And Soppi*, which were routinely critical of the government. Although both journals were actually written in French, they used Wolof titles and thus were subject to the decree. Both *Siggi* and *And Soppi* were forced to change their names (to *Taxaw* and *Andë Soppi*, respectively) or face steep fines.[57]

The most famous target of the decree regulating the writing of African languages was not a piece of writing at all. In 1977, Ousmane Sembène released his film *Ceddo*, a two-hour historical epic about indigenous resistance to religious conversion in a seventeenth- or eighteenth-century Senegambian kingdom. Distribution of the film was held up when a governmental commission insisted that Sembène had to change the title of the film from *CEDDO* to *CEDO*. Sembène refused, and the film was forbidden to be shown in Senegal. In the months that followed, a war of words ensued in the opposition press sympathetic to Sembène and the government daily *Le Soleil*.[58] Sembène fired the opening salvo: "Ceddo cannot be written otherwise," he declared in an open letter to Senghor and the Senegalese people. "We know the cost, in Wolof and Pulaar in particular, of neglecting geminates. We would end up in total incoherence. If the authorities want to prohibit writing in Wolof, they should just go ahead and do so."[59]

Sembène's letter generated a swift response from the minister of education, Abd'el Kader Fall. Writing on the government's behalf, he lambasted Sembène and his supporters in a full-page editorial. The article, entitled "A chacun son métier" ("To Each His Profession"), scolded Sembène and his sympathizers for trying to turn what was a "scientific" debate into a "political" one. Fall emphasized the "rigorously scientific process" that the government had gone through to arrive at its decision regarding the use of geminates. He pointed out that the president—himself an *agrégé* in grammar—had said that one would have to wait for "six or seven doctoral theses on the question [of geminates]" to be published before being "more or less" sure about the orthography. To make a good argument in this case, one had to try to convince "scientifically" and not "subjectively." Otherwise, Senegal's national languages could "never become effective instruments of our culture if every citizen set themselves up as a linguist and a grammarian." As Fall put it, "one can be a good writer without having been to university" but "no matter what the quality or level of one's studies, one can never improvise oneself as a grammarian." In this way, Fall positioned Senghor as schoolmaster to the entire nation. As for the linguists who had dared side with Sembène in the quarrel, "What are their university and scientific titles?" Fall thundered, "Where are their works? Where are their theses? What scientific study, or even article, proves that one must write *ceddo* and not *cedo*?"[60]

Fall's intervention did little to quell the uproar. A flurry of commentaries and polemics followed. In a lengthy piece entitled "Defense and Illustration of the Senegalese Languages," Pathé Diagne, the coeditor of *Kaddu*, opined that "Senegalese citizens, with diplomas or not, are free to reflect and reason on what is proposed or imposed on them."[61] Arame Fal, the linguist who was to eventually codify what has become the standard transcription of Wolof in Latin characters (which includes geminates), argued that the government was taking its cue on Wolof orthography from several dictionaries and grammars written during the missionary and colonial period. As she pointed out, it was not until the Prague School in the 1920s and 1930s that phonology developed as a sub-discipline of linguistics, resulting in generations of linguists trained to both hear and record as significant the difference between *d* and *dd*.[62] The most wry commentary of all, though, was Ibrahima Gaye's "Un contre-décret du peuple" ("A Counter Decree of the People") in which the author writes a letter of complaint to Senghor in French but applies the decree to the written French, which results in a royal linguistic mess.[63]

And yet none of these arguments were successful in reversing the government's decision. Sembène steadfastly refused to change his title, and so *Ceddo* would remain unseen in Senegal until Senghor's resignation some three years later. But the struggle to define what, precisely, was being censored and why continued to unfold. As late as 1979, Senghor himself wrote in to the French daily *Le Monde* to complain when an article described *Ceddo* as being "banned" in Senegal. Senghor pointed out that it was not banned outright but simply could not be shown in its current format because "M. Ousmane Sembène does not wish to obey Senegalese law."[64]

The conventional wisdom on the *Ceddo* controversy is that the linguistic debate was merely a smokescreen. For many, it seems obvious that the real reason the film was censored was that it was deemed offensive to many religious sensibilities in Senegal. In this interpretation, the problem with the title was just a convenient way to make a potentially troublesome film— which the government had, to its embarrassment, helped bankroll—go away. But when we reread the spelling debates themselves, this explanation appears insufficient. The vehemence of the disagreements over geminates is simply undeniable. Both sides seem to have felt that something very serious was at stake in this battle over orthography. A closer look at the etymology of the word *ceddo* can help us understand why.

Ceddo is a loaded word that evokes specific associations with the precolonial past. The *ceddo* were originally a category of royal slaves who served as warriors to the crown in the precolonial Wolof kingdoms. Most contemporary historians of Senegal would agree that sometime in the eighteenth century, the rulers of some of these kingdoms were overthrown by their *ceddo*, who in turn established dynasties of their own.[65] During this period, Senegambian society was ravaged by the instability of these military regimes, which survived in part by capturing and selling slaves. In the nineteenth century, resistance to these *ceddo* kingdoms crystallized around Muslim teachers and charismatic leaders, and the term *ceddo* became an epithet that was used to refer to all the non-Islamic Wolof aristocratic kingdoms, including the original ones the *ceddo* had overthrown.[66] Through this trajectory, the word *ceddo* has come to mean "unbeliever" or "pagan" in Wolof.[67]

In Sembène's film, though, the *ceddo* are the heroes. They revolt against their king when they believe he is allowing his realm to be overtaken by Islam and Christianity. But their rebellion is crushed by a scheming imam, a Catholic priest, and a slave trader. (One can well understand, from this rough plot summary alone, why many believe that religious sensibilities were the real reason for the film's censorship.) Outside Senegal, the film *Ceddo* was sometimes received as a historical epic that glorified indigenous African resistance to monotheistic conversion.[68] The trouble with this reading is that both written records and oral traditions suggest that conversion in Senegambia was actually a gradual process of accommodation. More astute viewers of the film suggest that far from having made an historical epic, Sembène was actually rewriting precolonial Senegalese history to comment on the contemporary entanglement of institutionalized religion and state power.[69]

Ceddo is a term from another age that Sembène seemed to be trying re-
claim in order to unsettle the postcolonial present. Although the word
evokes the precolonial past, Sembène flatly refused to give a clear answer
on when his film was actually set—even in which century. He would say
only that "these events occurred in the eighteenth and nineteenth century
and are still occurring" and that even though Wolof is spoken in the film,
"it could take place in any part of Africa, at any time."[70] The authorities
seemed to grasp this gambit; the only other condition imposed on the film
being shown in Senegal was that Sembène agree to distribute flyers before
each screening informing viewers of the "historicity" of the film.

In interviews, Sembène seemed to be working toward a different etymology for the word *ceddo*. *Ceddo* can also mean something like "tradition-
alist," and Sembène tended to gravitate toward this usage when he was
asked what his title meant. But he almost never gave quite the same definition twice. He described the *ceddo* as "those who resist slavery," "those
who conserve the tradition," and "the people of refusal." He described being *ceddo* as "being jealous of one's absolute liberty" and a "manner of being with rules" (*être avec des règles*).[71] Sembène seems to be trying to make
this term speak to an ethical position in the present that would not be totally synonymous with the historical *ceddo*. But unlike many of Cheikh Anta
Diop's neologisms, *ceddo* was a word that already had a certain etymology.
The term's potent associations in collective memory are inseparable from
the spelling debate that ensued. Far from being a diversion, the quarrel
over how to spell *ceddo* was a struggle over who could claim the authority
to define the *ceddo*—Sembène or the state. How else can we understand
why Sembène preferred to let his film go unseen in Senegal rather than
change a single letter of its title? The stakes were no more or less than who
or what was authorized to speak for the past and what kinds of futures doing
so might make possible.

Grammatology and the Decolonial Imagination

One of the great mysteries of the *Ceddo* affair is that, despite all the words
spilled over how to spell this one word, it is still not entirely clear where
Sembène's crime was supposed to have taken place. To belabor the obvious, *Ceddo* is a film. The law regulated written expression in the national
languages, but the only place that the word *ceddo* appears in writing in the
film is on a title card that exists for a few seconds every time the film is
viewed.[72] Of course, it could be argued that any screening of the film in

Senegal would have involved the word appearing in public on a theater marquee, poster, or newspaper advertisement, but it is hard to see how that would have been under Sembène's control.

The struggle over the word *ceddo* was about whether the state could claim sovereignty over language. But curiously, only writing and writing systems ever became an issue. How the actors in the film or indeed anyone else pronounced *ceddo* was never legislated on. Forcing publications with Wolof titles to change their names seems equally strange from this perspective. In neither case was the law being applied to extensive written discourse in African languages but rather to single words. Some might take this as evidence that the orthography debate was really cover for Senghor's persecution of his critics, and it surely was in some respects. But we must also look more closely at what the law sought to regulate to understand why a single letter could assume such importance.

During the decades of Senghor's presidency, it was only the domain of the printed word that was so obsessively made subject to the law of the state. These decrees sought to regulate not writing in general but the *future* of writing in African languages. There was no suggestion that the laws applied retroactively. They were clearly aimed at the unfolding of "a literature and press written in our national languages," as the 1977 decree put it. The battle over postcolonial grammatology was a struggle over the shape of a future reading public.

This is why the writing of African languages came to represent the stakes of decolonization—not just for Senghor but also his critics. For the critics, the postponement of "modernized" writing systems for African languages became an indication of all the state was not doing fast enough: it was not breaking with French, it was becoming neocolonial, it was stalling on true decolonization. For Senghor, though, writing systems were also about decolonization—but in his version of decolonization, which put heavy emphasis on ensuring that everyone was on the same page before the first step could be taken, so as to ensure that the remaking of institutions happened in a deliberate rather than anarchic fashion.

Grammatology came to epitomize the stakes of decolonization, because writing systems represented dominion over the past and the capacity to dictate possible futures.[73] Creating a new writing system was both a poetic and institutionalizing gesture—poetic because no matter how dry it appears, producing a writing system necessarily involves inventing new ways of doing things with words. But as Derrida observed, any grammatology also confronts the fact that writing is for someone else, even or especially if that other is the subject relating back to the written trace as if it were the work of another. In other words, a grammatologist—even one who is a president—needs others. To create or proclaim a new way of writing is simply no guarantee that others will follow your lead.

Producing "modern" writing systems for African languages became a privileged site for political imagination in the first decades of independence, because it captured the poetic and institutional dimensions of decolonization. Decolonization hovers between what might be and what must be, between imagining a future that is not yet here as if it were just around the corner *and* needing to institute that future collectively. Writing systems capture this tension: they too are attempts to give shape to a certain futurity, to balance a desire to imagine a radically new future use of language with a need to establish control over the unfolding of that same process.

The *ceddo* debate proved to be a curiously Pyrrhic victory for both sides. The Senghorian state succeeded in preventing the distribution of Sembène's film, but it failed to comprehensively institute its vision for writing African languages. Sembène and his allies lost the battle over geminates but won the war. Geminates have come to be a standard feature of the official transcription schemes for Wolof and other languages that use them. But the official transcription systems that emerged after these decades are still not hegemonic. And the large scale educational reforms that Senghor's critics called for have never manifested themselves. French is still the official language and the language of education. Wolof today is written widely across a variety of media in a mixture of different orthographies and scripts. The official romanized orthography is used in most modern literary texts, but the vast majority of the writing in Wolof that occurs in the wider world takes place outside the standard writing system. What emerged from these first two decades of independence was the triumph of the "unauthorized" systems of transcription that Senghor feared, albeit without the chaos he predicted.

CHAPTER 5

Counterpoetics: Translation as Aesthetic Constraint in Sembène's *Mandabi* and Ndao's *Buur Tilleen*

We often think of the language question as a separatist gesture that leads to a rejection of the language of the colonizer and an embrace of a vernacular—an act of defiance that we may find to be heroic, quixotic, or a bit of both, depending on our point of view. But the language question seldom produces such a rupture. Writers usually continue to produce work in both languages, often through their own translations. The most famous case is the Kenyan novelist and playwright Ngũgĩ wa Thiong'o, whose turn toward Gikuyu in the 1980s did not signal a complete retreat from English. Ngũgĩ's subsequent creative works would appear in English in translations, sometimes made by the author himself. Practices of autotranslation are a hallmark of many vernacular literature projects that erupted around the globe in the wake of decolonization. Rather than causing writers to abandon one language altogether, the language question more often spurs writers to produce texts that exist in more than one language at once.

This was the trajectory of modern Wolof literature and film as well. The first Wolof film and novel—Ousmane Sembène's *Mandabi* and Cheikh Aliou Ndao's *Buur Tilleen*, respectively—exist in both Wolof and French.

Although Sembène and Ndao very much set out to break with French in the 1960s, they found for various reasons that it was impossible to do so. Both Sembène and Ndao ended up being obliged to make francophone versions of artworks they had already made in Wolof. When we closely examine the multiple versions of these projects that now exist, we see the outlines of a unique poetic strategy that confounds our expectations of the language question. The rejection of a colonizing language for a vernacular has sometimes been associated with a retreat into an essentialized vision of the precolonial past. Conversely, scholarship has tended to celebrate the subversion of a former colonial language as an act of cosmopolitan appropriation.[1] But the first Wolof film and novel conform to neither of these typologies. Nor did the practices of auto-translation that produced these works lead to a "secure, unequivocal position" in which "two separate texts emerge."[2] What emerged in *Mandabi* and *Buur Tilleen* was a more complicated entanglement between the two versions, a situation that produced a reflection on translation as a mediating condition of expression itself.

After being challenged to "say it in Wolof" in 1963, Ousmane Sembène would go on to adapt his own novella *Le Mandat* into 1968's *Mandabi* (*The Money Order*). *Mandabi* was the first feature film shot in an African language, but any hope Sembène might have had of leaving French behind entirely would prove short-lived. As a condition of his funding, Sembène had to make a version of his film in French as well. Sembène complied with this requirement in a rather remarkable way; he shot two versions of *Mandabi* simultaneously, with his actors performing first in Wolof and then in French. The Wolof version actually went on to be the one in wide release, while the French version was shelved and never screened publically. But this practice of nearly-simultaneous translation exerted a powerful influence on the films themselves.

Cheikh Aliou Ndao's 1967 *Buur Tilleen* (*King of Tilleen*) evinces a similar dynamic. The young poet and playwright Ndao was in the audience in 1963 for Sembène's confrontation with Birago Diop and months later wrote admiringly of Sembène's defiance in a student journal.[3] Ndao too dreamed of "saying it in Wolof" and began work on *Buur Tilleen*, the first novel written in Wolof. But Ndao also found that producing an artwork in Wolof in this era meant still having to deal with French. Ndao tried for ten years to find a publisher for his Wolof manuscript before giving up. In the meantime, he rewrote the novel in French, and an adaptation entitled *Buur Tilleen: Roi de la Medina* (*Buur Tilleen: King of the Medina*) was published by Présence Africaine in 1972. The Wolof "original" was finally published only in the late 1990s—nearly thirty years after it was first written.

In the late 1960s, both Sembène and Ndao tried in different ways to reply to the language question, only to discover that it was not so easy to break with French. Their dilemma brings us to another facet of the language question: the intersection of translation and poetics. In this chapter, I explore the creative strategies that develop where writers wish to express themselves in a vernacular language rather than a dominant one but are confronted with the structural impossibility of making a radical break. To chart these strategies, I work across the multiple versions of these two artworks. I compare the wide-release Wolof version of *Mandabi* with its unreleased, French double, which I located in an archive in France after years of research.[4] I also draw on the now out-of-print Wolof version of *Buur Tilleen* to explore its entanglements with Ndao's French adaptation. Working through this comparative perspective, I demonstrate that the Wolof versions refer to and comment on their French-language counterparts. When we look closely at the affinities and intertextualities that exist between the Wolof and French versions of *Mandabi* and *Buur Tilleen*, we uncover neither a rejection of the dominant language nor a nativist assertion of absolute difference. Instead, we find that Sembène and Ndao have refashioned the obligation to work simultaneously in two languages from an imposition into a multilingual and self-referential poetics of linguistic constraint. This is a strategy that I will call *counterpoetics*.

Counterpoetics

The concept of counterpoetics was first developed by the Martinican theorist Édouard Glissant in *Le discours antillais*. Glissant articulated counterpoetics (*contre-poétique*) as creative responses to an opposition between a desire to express something and the language that is available for doing so. He uses the term to describe the ways in which speech genres in Martinique find complex ways of pointing to the hierarchical relationship between French and Créole as a mediating condition of expression. Glissant first tells us that counterpoetics can exist wherever "a need for expression confronts an inability to achieve expression." They emerge when a "collective yearning" (*tension collective*) for expression is stifled by a blockage at the level of expression itself, because of an opposition between "the content to be expressed and the language suggested or imposed." In the case of the French-speaking Caribbean, counterpoetics arise because of the "constraining presence of French as the linguistic background and the deliberate wish to renounce French." This situation leads to an awareness, in Glissant's words, of the opposition between a language one uses and a form of expression that one truly needs. Glissant believes that this dynamic is not confined to a dominated language; counterpoetics may develop from a consciousness of French as a constraint, but he insists that the styles of expression that result can exist in Créole or in French.[5]

Glissant's conception of counterpoetics is not a generic description of language use in any situation of linguistic domination. It refers to certain kinds of responses to such a situation—a kind of second-order creativity that takes a situation of linguistic constraint as its own condition of possibility. Counterpoetics involve an awareness of an imposed language as a constraint and a poetic engagement with this very situation. Glissant also refers to counterpoetics as forced poetics (*poétique forcée*) and constrained poetics (*poétique contrainte*). In a revealing turn of phrase, he writes, "The constrained character of a forced poetics gives it all of its force."[6] Counterpoetics are then a poeticization *of* a linguistic constraint: they transform a linguistic situation one would wish otherwise into an aesthetic possibility. In counterpoetics, the suggested or imposed language is both constraining and productive—a limitation and the grounds of a second-order poetics. Glissant's work does not so much define counterpoetics as illustrate them iteratively. While this makes it difficult to arrive at a stable definition, this same labile quality also allows his account to be highly flexible—which in turn helps us extend counterpoetics to describe the strategies of *Mandabi* and *Buur Tilleen*.

The Two Versions of Mandabi

Between 1966 and 1971, Sembène moved away from literature and toward filmmaking, producing four films in a five-year span but no literary texts. Although he later returned to work in prose as well, this turn toward cinema in the early postcolonial period is usually understood as a response to the question of audience.[7] Sembène himself presented his filmmaking as a way of circumventing the barrier that literacy raised to the circulation of texts written in French. Although Sembène's interest in exploring alternative channels for artistic address became acute after his return from France in 1960, the figure of the inaccessible audience had already been present in his work from the beginning—as we saw in the dedication of his first novel. Sembène's move toward cinema was part of an effort to develop other ways of engaging with a public that was beyond the reach of a printed text written in French. In this sense, his filmmaking can be thought of as a response to the language question. But instead of producing a move from one language to another, Sembène began a shift of medium.

Sembène's turn toward film did not, however, result in unfettered access to the audiences he hoped to reach. Filmmaking instead introduced Sembène to a space of new possibilities and constraints. The challenges he faced were financial, technical, legal, and linguistic. But his response to these difficulties was rather remarkable. Sembène is often thought of as a neo-realist and sometimes even as a ploddingly didactic filmmaker. But as I argue elsewhere, his 1960s films are in fact quite experimental in a specific sense. They employ a distinctive, self-referential strategy of finding ways to index within a film the difficulties that were faced in making the film.[8] Throughout the 1960s, Sembène explores ways to incorporate the heavily mediated circumstances of his films' production into the viewing experience of the films themselves. We see this approach developing across the early films of *La Noire de . . .* and *Borom Sarret*, but the strategy became truly acute in the counterpoetics of *Mandabi/Le Mandat*.

To uncover the creative genealogy of Sembène's approach in *Mandabi*, we need to reconstruct the strange status of the voice in early francophone African cinema. The question of what was to be done with the voice had been a central issue in the development of filmmaking in French West Africa. As Manthia Diawara has pointed out, France became interested in regulating cinematic production and distribution in its African colonies only after the advent of sound technology. During the silent film era, the colonial authorities had been relatively uninvolved in the development of film. But in 1934, the government issued the Laval decree, which gave the administration the right to examine both the scripts and the credentials of anyone wanting "to make cinematographic images or sound recordings" in the colonies. Applicants had to describe the legal regime they fell under, provide proof of their professional credentials, and include the script for the film. The law was rarely applied to French filmmakers, but it was often used to restrict the activities of a burgeoning generation of African filmmakers.[9] In the early postcolonial period, the strategy and the infrastructure changed. In the interest of forming "binding economic, political, and cultural relations with its former colonies," France partially financed the installation of "partial production units" in francophone capitals. This meant films produced in the former colonies—primarily newsreels and documentaries—had to be sent for postproduction in Paris.[10]

All of Sembène's 1960s films—leading up to *Mandabi*—bear the traces of this postproduction structure. Most of them were shot silently, and it was sometimes impossible—for financial or bureaucratic reasons—to bring the actors who had performed in the films to the postproduction studio to complete the sound editing. Quite often, this meant that the characters in

Sembène's early films were performed and voiced by different actors. The clearest example of this is Sembène's breakthrough film, *La Noire de . . .* (*Black Girl*) (1966). The film was shot silently. The main character, Diouana, is played onscreen by the Senegalese actress Thérèse M'Bissine Diop, but the voicing of the character in the soundtrack is done by the Haitian actress and singer Toto Bissainthe. Bissainthe voices the thoughts of Diouana in French, although the character is not supposed to be fluent in that language. Sembène was apparently unable to pay for Diop to travel to Paris to record her voiceover, since the script for *La Noire de . . .* had been rejected by the French Ministry of Cooperation, which was the principal way francophone African film was funded at this time.[11] As I argue elsewhere, voices in these films are estranged from the scenes and the bodies they accompany.[12]

The production of *Mandabi* (1967) must have seemed auspicious in comparison. Sembène had funding and distribution from the outset this time from the French Centre National du Cinema (CNC). André Malraux, then French minister of culture, had given Sembène special permission to apply for CNC funding, which had previously been granted only to French nationals such as Jean-Luc Godard and François Truffaut. But with this new source of funding came new kinds of strings. The most irritating of these came in the form of the French producer Sembène was required to work with, Robert Nesle. Nesle wanted Sembène to film in color, which Sembène argued against because he thought it would give the film a "folkloric" quality. Sembène eventually conceded this point, but some of Nesle's other suggestions were impossible to stomach. Specifically, Nesle saw the film as more of a madcap comedy and also wanted it to include more nudity; he thought these changes would make it more palatable to French audiences, which might not appreciate a rather slow-burning but devastating satire of the stifling bureaucracy and rampant desperation of the early independence period. Sembène flatly and successfully refused these changes, though he had to go to court do so.[13] But the final and most fateful condition of funding was that Sembène had to make a French version of his film as well as a Wolof one. This meant, in practice, that Sembène had to shoot two versions of *Mandabi* at the same time, one in French and one in Wolof.

The arduous production history of *Mandabi* is more than a little ironic, since the film itself is about how a gift of money sent from France transforms itself into a burden of endless bureaucratic wrangling for the recipient. *Mandabi* was adapted from Sembène's novella *Le Mandat* (*The Money Order*), published in 1965 by Présence Africaine.[14] The story—which conserved the same basic structure in the transition from fiction

to film—follows the futile efforts of Ibrahima Dieng, an unemployed patriarch in Dakar, to cash a money order sent by a nephew who is working in
France. Dieng needs an identity card to cash the money order, but he has
only his voting card and a tax receipt. In order to get an identity card, he
needs a copy of his birth certificate, which in turn he cannot get because he
does not know and cannot prove the date he was born. The resulting plot
follows Dieng, the hapless petitioner who cannot prove who he is, from bank
to post office to police station to city hall in a vain attempt to acquire the
proper authorizing documents. Along the way, Dieng is fleeced by a variety
of shady characters and, when word gets out about his newfound "wealth,"
his friends and neighbors descend on him to ask for loans or extend him
credit. He is finally ensnared in a web of obligation that he cannot escape.

Unlike Sembène's earlier films, *Mandabi* was shot with sound. Sembène
had with him a full sound unit on location in Dakar, which he used to capture both his actors' performances and the ambient soundscape around
them.[15] Whereas his earlier films have an eerie sonic mix of dubbed speech,
sound effects, and music, *Mandabi* has a far richer soundtrack. Not only
do the actors voice their own lines, they do so against a sonic backdrop
that actually sounds like Dakar with all its noise and hustle. While this
would seem like a step forward, the "disembodied" voices of Sembène's
early films have not been entirely banished in *Mandabi*. There is still a
strangely uncanny fit between voices, bodies, and the larger social world
but in a new way. To understand the nature of this, we have to explore the
way in which *Mandabi* was shot twice—once in Wolof and once in French.

Accounts vary on how Sembène shot two versions. What is clear from
all available sources is that Sembène produced the film with a cast composed of mostly nonprofessional actors. The rehearsal process was intensive and took two and a half months (compared to just five weeks of
shooting). Paulin Vieyra, the director of production on the film, later re-
counted some of the complexities of these rehearsals. Vieyra claims that
the nonprofessional actors were hired in part based on their ability to read
the script.

> "To facilitate the passage from one language to another, Ousmane
> Sembène had written the screenplay for the film in literary French,
> and he had tried to make it so that the dialogue was a literal transla-
> tion of the Wolof into French so that the actors, by learning the
> French text . . . could turn it back into Wolof without difficulty."[16]

According to Vieyra, this led to a unique rehearsal practice, in which Sembène had to discuss the script with his actors in order to settle on how to

"adapt their gestures to the Wolof text translated into French." The description Vieyra gives of this process is extraordinary and worth quoting at length.

> In people's everyday speech there is an interaction of language and gesture. Naturally, *certain expressions call for certain gestures* that are the same from one individual to the next. The differences in the amplitude of the gestures indicate differences in temperament. But in the film *Le Mandat*, because they began with dialogue written in terms of the action and in strict conformity with the sentiments evoked, *they had to abbreviate certain gestures in order to maintain the logic of the story that needed to be told.* It was not the case that these were artificial gestures recreated in light of a particular aesthetic, but rather what we call "functional gestures." The author [Sembène] *reduced certain gestures here and there, and elsewhere eliminated them entirely. . . . Without taking anything away from the genius of the language, in this particular case, cinema disciplined it.* It is not the case in *Le Mandat*, as it has often been said, of *cinema verité. . . .* Ousmane Sembène thought that it was necessary to keep the language in the dramatic context that he had established beforehand in order to avoid watching the film get away from him. Because *Wolof speech, liberated from any constraint, demands frills, coquetry and hyperbole that could have risked stretching the film or denaturing its spirit.*[17] (emphasis mine)

Part of the rehearsal process, then, consisted of editing the gestural aspects of the Wolof speech styles that the cast brought with them. This apparently was done in rehearsal by moving the "text" of the film from Wolof into literal French and then back again. This iterative translation worked to shear the text, as it were, of some of the pragmatic and gestural elements that had attached themselves to it. As Vieyra rightly points out, certain expressions in Wolof call for certain gestures, and unlearning (or, as Vieyra puts it, disciplining) these aspects of everyday speech would take a lot of practice. In Vieyra's account, certain aspects of the script—its referential meaning—became the basis of the performance and thus the final work. Vieyra's characterization of Wolof speech styles as being filled with "frills" and "coquetry" seems judgmental, but he is really just ventriloquizing a basic assumption about the process of translation Sembène had to settle for: the rehearsal process had to proceed as if, in practice, it was possible to separate content from what appeared to be ornament.

For Wolof speech to take place in the film, then, it had to be put in a relation with its French translation, against which it would have to be measured and, if necessary, in whose image it might have to be adjusted. In addition to the obvious power imbalance, a certain language ideology underlies this imposition.[18] The assumption inherent in the obligation to produce two versions simultaneously was that nothing of substance could possibly be lost in such a transfer. But, as we can see from Vieyra's account, the need to keep the two versions equivalent did have an effect: it reoriented the criteria of the performances around the "logic of the story" and "the sentiments evoked" such that "certain gestures were abbreviated." The iterative performance of *Mandabi/Le Mandat* was not a case of a translation of a given, bounded work, but rather a series of renegotiations, within a set of constraints, of what in a given scene was going to be meaningful. The question then is not, "What was lost in translation?" but rather, "How might the requirement to translate have framed in advance which aspects of the script would be translatable and which could be lost?"

The results of this remarkable rehearsal and shooting process become clear when we compare the French and Wolof versions of the film. Watching the French-language version alongside its more well-known Wolof counterpart is an uncanny experience. With the exception of a few scenes, the French version is nearly a shot-for-shot duplicate of the Wolof. The actors and scenes are practically all the same, except that everyone speaks in French. The film also sticks very close to the French script Sembène produced for his actors. The French version is not a remnant—it is a complete, edited version of the film, ready for wide release with front and end titles and a full soundtrack.[19]

The French version feels most like a continuation of the style of voicing that prevailed in Sembène's earlier films. The speech of the principal actors had to be transposed into French, but instead of this occurring in a postproduction studio in Paris, the actors had to overdub themselves, as it were. This produces some very strange results. The actors are comfortable speaking in French to varying degrees, and the differences between their abilities introduces new qualities into film itself. In certain scenes, a switch from Wolof to French was supposed to be meaningful, but this is completely scrambled by the French version.[20]

Another complication in the French version is the relationship between the actors' dialogue and the incidentally recorded ambient surround. One of the innovations of *Mandabi* was not only that the actors performed in Wolof, but that Sembène was able to record the sounds of the urban world around them. The sounds of Dakar—traffic noise, the hum of crowds, and most importantly, its speech ecology—are everywhere in *Mandabi*. In the Wolof version especially, the sound of public space is an important factor in the film. Rumor plays a central role in the story, and the abundance of incidental noise is anything but window dressing. The murmurs and cries of outrage from Dieng's neighbors, the grumbling of customers waiting in line behind Dieng at the bank—all of these are captured by the microphone in *Mandabi*.

The soundtrack of the French version includes these recordings of the world around the characters, but the multilingual sounds of Dakarois public space contrast sharply from the stiff French dialogue. In the French version, a viewer can still hear traces of Dakar Wolof in the background, such as "*Comprend nga?*" in the bank scene. But the sound of public space seems oddly extra-diegetic in relation to the stilted dialogue of the principal actors. This makes the performances feel even more out of place, very much at odds with the social world depicted around them.

Written language is another important, albeit less obvious, dimension of the linguistic scrambling that occurs in the French version. Writing is ubiquitous in African cities; walls, signs, billboards, clothing, and vehicles are all often inscribed with a riotous mix of scripts and languages. In *Mandabi*, Sembène's camera captures traces of this linguistic abundance, what Ato Quayson calls the urban scriptural economy of African cities.[21] Establishing and tracking shots collect some of the many scripts of urban Dakar: the sober signage of a post office is set against more informal advertisements, prayers, and sayings that adorn blank walls, small business, and *car rapides*. This iconic, scriptural dimension of language use is often forgotten in discussions of the language question. But it is an important aspect of the linguistic ecology of Sembène's film.

Although *Mandabi* is often called the first feature film shot "in" an African language, what the camera and microphone actually capture is a linguistic environment that exceeds any one language, in terms of both speech and writing. Whether or not Sembène intended it to be this way, his film makes it possible to notice the complexity of language use in urban Dakar without making that complexity its main focus. Part of the strangeness of the French version, then, is precisely that the complexity of the linguistic backdrop *does* become something of the main focus, since the main actors' performances now contrast so sharply with the world around them. The actors' dialogue in the French version becomes curiously like the rigid, official lettering of the Hôtel de ville, which stands in splendid isolation from the city all around it.

Perhaps the most striking difference between the two versions is what goes unsaid. The French version is full of strange, awkward silences. Scenes that should be filled with greetings and goodbyes are performed with a minimum of talking, with little improvisation or chatter on the part of the actors. The actors perform as if they are reading the French script, rather than as persons embedded in a social world.[22] Vieyra describes the way in which Sembène rehearsed and negotiated with his nonprofessional actors over how to include or edit aspects of everyday speech that were too "ornate." One of the most obvious examples of such ornate speech styles in Wolof are the lengthy and often seemingly repetitious exchanges of greetings that some speakers use when encountering acquaintances they have not seen in some time. In a late interview, Sembène described how he often had to try to negotiate with his amateur actors to adjust their tendency to break into greetings in order to "reproduce the language of real life" in his films without "destroy[ing] anything of the original atmosphere nor . . . their personality."

> Take for example the question of greeting. People will greet each
> other and go into some other matter, and in the middle of the other
> matter they would suddenly start greeting each other out of the blue.
> The cinema is rational, therefore, you have to suppress the repetition
> of greetings, but if you tell non-professional actors this, they can't
> grasp it. The roundabout way of thinking, the ins and outs of thought,
> it is very difficult to get people to change them. So when you are
> rehearsing the actors, you have to rehearse the language, gesture, and
> look, to make sure that there is no dead space.[23]

Nuyu, or greetings, are a complex and fine-grained genre of speech in Wolof. As Judith Irvine demonstrates in a classic study, Wolof speakers use the set of questions and answers that form the greeting to negotiate their status with regard to each other. A particular positionality in the standard exchange (the question-asker) is associated with a lower-status position. Irvine argues that a speaker who launches back into asking after the other person's well-being after the conversation has shifted (as Sembène describes his actors doing) is doing so to position himself or herself as lower-status, possibly to curry favor.[24]

There is an example of precisely this kind of negotiation in *Mandabi*. The scene exists in both the Wolof and French versions, and the "sense" of the scene is nearly identical. The neighborhood imam stops by to try to borrow money from Dieng and discovers his host eating breakfast. Dieng invites the imam to join him, and after a brief pause, they talk about money. In the Wolof version, the imam and Dieng exchange *nuyu*, begin their conversation, then break back into *nuyu*, giving the viewer a sense of the tense calibration of politeness going on. Dieng wants to be polite to the imam, but the imam also wants to be polite to Dieng. In the French, though, there is no *nuyu*, and the entire scene is filled with a suffocating silence. "Come in, have a seat," Dieng tells the imam, and the imam does just this. They eat, saying nothing. Total silence reigns as Dieng pours the imam tea and breaks bread. When the conversation eventually starts up, it emerges out of nowhere. The dialogue spoken in French in this scene is identical to what is in the script produced for the French version—nothing more, nothing less.[25] The effect is bizarre: it is unthinkable—or at the least incredibly rude—for characters of this generation to enter into someone's house like this, sit down, and begin eating, without so much as a word exchanged about each other's family, their health, and so on. The deafening silence comes down to the absence of *nuyu*.

How to accommodate in cinema the language of everyday life in all its roundaboutness? The differences between the two versions of *Mandabi* suggest an answer: while the pragmatic and gestural features of Wolof speech may have been "disciplined" in the filmmaking process, they were not entirely suppressed. Without ever naming the constraint directly, the performances of the principal actors are marked by an obligation to translate, an obligation that existed not just between different languages but between different media and different sets of conventions for embodied speech. Counterpoetics in the case of *Mandabi* took the form of a negotiation around this constraint that included both the director and the actors.

As the director, though, Sembène did have a certain privileged authority to decide on what in these performances would count as dead space and what would be meaningful interaction. Rather than dissimulate the power to mediate between different languages, registers, and media Sembène found ways to obliquely draw viewers' attention to it. One of the recurring images in early Sembène films is of the director himself. In both *La Noire de . . .* and *Mandabi*, Sembène plays the role of the *écrivain public* (Figure 12). An *écrivain public* is a scribe, a writer/reader for hire whose role is to serve as a middleman of the written word for a community with limited access to it. A scribe both writes and reads letters for people who cannot do this for themselves. Sembène playing the *écrivain public* draws awareness to the mediation of his films through a regime of enforced translation, from dubbing to simultaneous performance. By taking on this role in his own films, Sembène suggests that what he is engaged in is not *auteur* cinema, but *écrivain public* cinema, which would heighten awareness of the director's role as a mediator.

Of course, Sembène flatly denied that these cameos were intentional. "There are times," he said, "when actors who've promised to come—because often certain actors aren't paid, they just promise me they'll come—don't show up. . . . I have to be ready in case of an absence." He went so far as to say that the cameos he or his crew made were "never planned . . . a priori."[26] Although these statements seem to deflate my interpretation, they are not as troublesome as they first appear. Sembène seems to have been aware of the mythology that was accumulating around him as the father of African cinema. Beneath his occasionally irascible demeanor, Sembène seems to have been adept at stage-managing his own self-presentation in interviews. At times he is happy to play the role of the father of African cinema, but he also seems to enjoy turning the tables on his interviewer, deflating the myth of his *auteur*-ship even as it is being built. One way of understanding his denials about his cameos ("I never meant to play any of the roles I played in my films") is to see that they serve to direct attention away from Sembène's agency as the director and back onto the social web of personal and economic contingency in which his production was embedded. To put that another way, by repudiating the idea that he meant to draw attention to himself in these early films, Sembène is actually continuing the performance. He is refusing to take authorship of the very gesture that could be interpreted as the work of a self-conscious *auteur*, rather than that of an *écrivain public* director at the mercy of contingency.[27]

To understand what kind of a position Sembène might have been trying to create for himself, we can contrast the idea of the *écrivain public* with a certain conception of the public intellectual. There were many moments in his life when Sembène was called on to speak in the genres of a public intellectual—at the conference in Dakar, for instance—but his strategy was often to respond as the *écrivain public*. He would agree to perform the mediating function required of him but refuse to take total authorship and insist on the legibility of a certain double-voicing in what he had to say. In situations where he was called on to be a public intellectual, Sembène tended to try to redirect the focus of the conversation to the context in which this demand was being made and the terms it set for him. This helps explain why he was such a difficult person to interview. To read his interviews is to read a set of conversations with someone who seems impatient with the genre of the interview itself. Occasionally, if an interviewer did not rub him the wrong way, Sembène would comment on (rather than perform) his discomfort with the genres of public speech.

Figure 12. Sembène (right) playing the role of the écrivain public (scribe) in Mandabi/Le Mandat (1967). Mandabi, Ousmane Sembène, 1968, Collection Cinémathèque Française.

GADJIGO: In 1975, at the University of Indiana at Bloomington, you gave a lecture entitled "Man Is Culture." During that whole week that I worked with you, you were always searching for, I would say, the "right word" to express what is, for you, African culture.

SEMBÈNE: *But I was speaking to whom?* In this area there are those who speak Mandingue, but there are also people who don't speak Mandingue but that also speak French. It's by that exact word that I am going to be able to situate them and show them what's going on. Here, it's not about academic French, academic English . . . it's about language used in everyday life. *It could be also that this worry about the exact word comes to me through literature; the worry of being heard well, understood properly.*[28] (emphasis mine)

As Sembène describes it, his search for "the right word" is not only a struggle to say what he means; it is rather a struggle to be heard well, to situate both himself and his interlocutor. This intersubjective dimension of speaking, rather than language "choice," seems to be the aspect of the language issue that Sembène wrestled with most throughout his initial turn to filmmaking. The position he seemed to reach was this: if the terms in which he spoke, artistically or as a lecturer or interviewee, were not entirely up to him, what he could do about it was to draw attention to this mediation. This is the sense of the role of the *écrivain public*. If the terms of the encounter were already given in a way that was unfortunate but at that moment uncontestable, Sembène sought to contextualize his reply in a way that made explicit the givenness of the terms in which he could speak.

Discourse Arrested: The Two Versions of Buur Tilleen

In the domain of the printed word, the struggle to "say it in Wolof" in the early independence period followed a similar trajectory—writers often found they had to "say it in French" as well, but for different reasons. Although filmmaking required a far greater amount of capitalization than publishing a novel, publishing literary texts in Wolof was for a very long time far more difficult. Sembène had his share of funding and censorship troubles throughout the 1960s and 1970s, but he nevertheless found ways to make films in Wolof and then—government willing—have them distributed. But Cheikh Aliou Ndao's *Buur Tilleen* didn't appear until some thirty years after it was initially written.

Ndao is best known as a playwright, especially for his 1967 play *L'Exil d'Alboury*. Since *Buur Tilleen* finally appeared, he has had a very prolific writing career in Wolof and has published works of poetry, short stories, novels, and essays. Ndao began writing poetry in Wolof while completing his secondary education in Swansea in the 1950s. Later, in Grenoble, he was part of the *Ijjib Volof* group.[29] Upon his return to Senegal after completing his secondary education, Ndao began work on a novel in Wolof, *Buur Tilleen*, which he finished in 1967. The French version appeared as *Buur Tilleen: Roi de la Medina*, published by Présence Africaine in 1972. *Buur Tilleen* was finally published in Wolof in 1988 by the elite research center Institut Fondamental d'Afrique Noire under the direction of the linguist Arame Fal.

Buur Tilleen is, like *Mandabi*, the tragedy of a traditional patriarch out of step with the changing urban world around him. It is also set in the early independence period. The drama of the novel unfolds when Gorgui Mbodj is informed by his wife Maram that their daughter, Rakki, has become pregnant by Gorgui's best friend's son. Because Rakki is unmarried and because the father is of a lower caste, Gorgui banishes his daughter rather than suffer the shame of having her continue to live under his roof. Maram continues to visit and care for their daughter behind Gorgui's back, but when Rakki goes into labor, neither parent is able to get to the hospital before she and the baby die in childbirth. The novel appears to condemn Gorgui's intransigence and stubborn pride and could be read as a "crisis of traditional values" novel.

The two versions of *Buur Tilleen* are quite different. Ndao maintains that the French version is not a translation at all, but rather an adaptation.[30] The French edition is considerably longer; it develops certain plotlines and characters further, and scenes that take place in francophone social spaces that were marginal in the Wolof version are stretched out over several chapters. But the differences go beyond the level of the plot. With respect to the narrative, Ndao's adaptation of his Wolof novel into French did more than amplify certain aspects. Through subtle shifts in narrative voicing at key junctures of the text, the two works together produce a complex reflection on the difficulties of publishing in a vernacular and the obligation to adapt one's work into a former colonial language to reach an audience. By working across the two versions of the *Buur Tilleen* text, we can trace the contours of a literary mode of counterpoetics that has strong affinities with Sembène's filmic approach in *Mandabi*.

The site that I want to focus on will at first appear to be just a ripple in the current of the larger plot. The scene in question is a long monologue by Gorgui, and it is handled quite differently in the two versions. After Maram reveals their daughter's pregnancy, Gorgui leaves the house in distress to be alone with his thoughts. In the pages that follow, he drifts through the streets of Dakar at night. In both versions, Gorgui's physical wandering eventually spills over into the narration as well. The story leaves the present and delves into his past, where we learn of Gorgui's childhood, education, past glories, and eventually the downfall that brought him to his present, sorry state. As the narrator and the character's voices become conjoined, the narrative is able to leave the particular and reflect on a larger, collective past of which Gorgui's story is merely the token. But this reverie stops abruptly when a policeman appears, demanding to see Gorgui's papers. In his haste, Gorgui has left the house without his identity card, so he is arrested and taken to the police station. This scene serves a very minor function in the plot—it conveniently ends Gorgui's foray into his past and brings the focus back to the present and its unfolding drama. Although embarrassed, Gorgui is quickly released. But as trivial as the episode seems, the policeman's demand for identification has a rather striking effect on the narration itself. In both the Wolof and French versions of the novel, the mode of narration before and after the demand for identification changes rather dramatically. In Wolof, *Buur Tilleen* is narrated mainly in indirect discourse. Here, for example, is the beginning of the novel:

Maram gën a teel a tëdd! Mu ngi walbatiku di walbatikuwaat. Mënul fexe ba nelaw. Te nag dafa mel ni guddi tey la fel yi ak màtt yi doon nég. Lee-léeg baraag bi jaayu, ngelaw li di ko yëngal, muy kox-koxi ni ku ànd ak jàngoroy sëqët. Ci biti, lépp a ngi ne tekk; kenn du dégg lu dul dàllu nit ñi mujje ci mbedd yi ñuy karaas-karaasi di ñibbi. Xelu Maram yépp a ngi ci Góorgi Mbóoj, jëkkër ji. Ndaw saa ngi naan, man de, xawma fu sëriñ bi war a ne ba waxtu wii.[31]

Maram is in bed very early! She tosses and turns. She cannot find a way to sleep. The fleas and bedbugs are so bad that night is like day. From time to time, the shack trembles as the wind shakes it, wheezing like someone with a cough. Outside, all is still; all one can hear are the sounds of people in the street shuffling their way home. Maram is thinking of Góorgi Mbóoj, her husband. Where could that man could be at this hour, she asks herself.

The alignment of the narrator with the pathos of the scene at hand is typically modeled with such interjections as *Ndeysaan!* (Alas, poor man!/Le pauvre!)[32] For the most part, the voices of narrator and character are easily distinguished. In the passages before the identity check, however, the narration in Wolof slides further into free indirect discourse, to the point where the difference between the narrating consciousness and the individual character's voice is no longer clear.[33] This slide into the past occurs gradually, through framing clauses. Here is how the reverie begins.

Góorgi génn kër gi, topp Tilleen, di dox, ndeysaan, te xamul fu mu jëm. Mu ñëw-a-ñëw ba Kër Alkaati yi taxaw, ba yàgg mu jàdd ci ndeyjooram, jublu sëg yi; bi mu ca yegsee romb leen. Li muy dox lépp xalaatul dara, saagawul, sikkul kenn; newul Maram nii mbaa Ràkki naa, xanaa di dem rekk te xamul lu tax. Yegsi na jawu Gëltàppe jàddati, dem ba buntu kër sëriñ Abdu mu taxaw. Góorgi daal dox naa dox ba ne jaas postu Tilleen te xamul na mu fa yegsee. Ndeysaan, mu sonn, faf toog ci eskale yi. *Fi Góorgi gi déju xelam yépp a ngi jublu démb, muy gis dundam, di gis ba muy gone ba léegi ak fi mu masa jaar yépp.*[34]

Góorgi left the house, heading toward Tilleen, walking—poor man!—and not knowing where he was going. He kept walking all the way to the Cité Police, paused for a while, then turned to his right, heading toward the cemetery; when he reached it, he kept going. As he walked, he thought of nothing, did not blame or reproach anyone, not even Maramm nor Rakki, just kept walking and not knowing why. He arrived at the bridge of Geule Tappé, turned again, went as far as the gate of Serigne Abdou and stopped. Góorgi walked and walked till he suddenly found himself in front of the Tilleen post office and he had no idea how he had got there. Poor man, he was tired, and sat down, exhausted, on the steps. *As Góorgi sat there, his whole mind rushed back to the past, and he could see his life, from childhood to the present, and every single thing he had been through.* (emphasis mine)

Note the final sentence, where the narration signals that it is about to switch into a more free indirect mode. Immediately after, the speaking voice will start to advance statements that are somewhere between the more distant narrator the reader has encountered before and Gorgui's own strong views. As the reverie continues to take hold, the framing drops further away and the narration no longer signals that it is speaking for Gorgui's lived experience. In the final passages before the policeman appears, the reader encounters phrases from which it is difficult to say who or what is being voiced:

> Ndekete goney tey, ñoom, seen yoon nekkatul ci loolu. Moo fu àddina jëm su fekkee ne li fi maam ya ba woon lépp jox nañ ko gannaaw? Waay waay ku xam fu ñuy teere?[35]

> Ah, but look at today's children, they will have none of this. Oh, but where is the world heading when they toss everything that mattered for the elders behind them. Oh god, who knows where we are heading?

In the Wolof version of *Buur Tilleen*, Gorgui's monologue represents a retreat into an idealized vision of the past. But the free indirect mode complicates this nostalgia. One of the features of free indirect style is what D. A. Miller calls its "impossible identification."[36] Or, as Lauren Berlant puts it, glossing Barbara Johnson, "Free indirect discourse performs the impossibility of locating an observational intelligence in one or any body, and therefore forces the reader to transact a different, more open relation of unfolding to what she is reading, judging, being, and thinking she understands. In Johnson's work such a transformative transaction through reading/speaking "unfolds" the subject in a good way, despite whatever desires she may have not to become significantly different."[37] In the nighttime excursion scene in *Buur Tilleen*, free indirect discourse unfolds Gorgui's consciousness and the narrator's relation to it, situating the reader slightly askance from the reverie in which these two are engaged. The openness created by this gesture of triangulating the reader, the character, and the narrator has an ethical quality to it: the vanishing "world of the elders" evoked here is an idealized vision of a rural, Wolof past, seen

partially through Gorgui's eyes and his twin rose-colored glasses of patriarchy and caste privilege. The passage mourns the value system that existed "back then" for Gorgui and which seems to be in the process of
disintegrating all around him in an urban Dakar of the early 1960s. But
through the use of free indirect discourse, the passage actually performs
the opposite of what it romanticizes, creating space for different sorts of
alignments to this nostalgic vision.

By unwinding any possibility of a stable, observational consciousness
that could exist either in the narrator or the character, the passage proposes instead a more open and diffuse perspective on this evocation of the
world of the elders and prevents any easy identification with the value system that is being memorialized. In other words, the narration makes it so
that the reader is not commanded to participate in this sense that "things
were better" back then. Instead, the fluidity of the voicing invites the reader
to reflect on and even respond critically to the predominating affect of nostalgia: Were things really better back then? Better for whom? Whose past
and whose value system are standing in for the communal past? The novel
conjures a vision of vanishing cultural unity, making it present to the reader
through the very act of mourning it. But by placing the reverie in free indirect discourse, the text prevents the reader from completely entering
into Gorgui's nostalgia.

This remarkable overlay of memory, identification, and affect ceases
completely when the policeman interrupts it. Seeing Gorgui sitting for-
lornly on the steps lost in thought, the cop demands, "Ey, sa waay, looy
def fii ba waxtu wii?" (Hey buddy, what are *you* doing *here* at *this* hour?)
Through demonstrative pronouns and an inflected verb, this question in-
terpolates the narrative into a more clearly delineated deictic frame in
which the referents of *you*, *here*, and *this hour* are more rigid and less open
to the errancy and interplay that occurred during the nighttime excursion.
After the policeman appears, the voices of the narrator and the characters
become more sharply distinguished. The narration still includes occasional moments of free indirect discourse, but these tend to be used for
framed and limited glimpses of present, interior sentiments rather than
long stretches of discourse that propose an image of a collective past.[38]

Let me put the stakes of this shift as concisely as I can: the first example of novelistic free indirect discourse in Wolof is, literally, arrested. The
Wolof narrative responds to the policeman's request for identification and
permission to circulate by distinguishing between the unnamed, narrating voice and the individual, named characters. Their collusion with each
other or the reader no longer seems possible.[39]

In the French adaptation, the overall effect of the intervention of the cop on the unique narrative mood of the reverie is both preserved and completely transformed. To understand how this can be, I must briefly sketch the differences between the two versions. *Buur Tilleen: Roi de la medina* is also written mainly in indirect discourse. For example, here is the beginning of the novel in French:

> Tôt couchée, Maram se tourne, se retourne, ne pouvant dormir. Les puces, les punaises, s'acharnent sur son échine, parcourent sa nuque, envahissent ses cheveux. Les insectes évitent ses tapes maladroites, se moquent de son énervement, de son impuissance. La vieille baraque, faite de planches disjointes, bouge, grince, beugle, miaule, fouettée par le vent. De temps à autre, Maram l'entend gémir comme un homme rongé par les ans, un malade pris d'une violente quinte de toux. Du dehors ne parvient que l'écho des pas des derniers passants attardés, leurs voix de noctambules se perdant au loin. Maram pense à Gorgui Mbodj, son mari. Elle prépare son accueil, essaie toutes sortes de phrases, se surprend à murmurer des sentences, des proverbes, des mots à moitié articulé, comme pour conjurer la colère éventuelle de son époux. "Je me demande où est-ce qu'il se trouve."[40]

> In bed early, Maram tosses, turns, unable to sleep. Fleas and bedbugs nibble on her back, roam over her neck, invading her hair. The bugs avoid her clumsy slaps at them, mocking her annoyance, her powerlessness. The old shack, made of loose boards, moves, squeaks, moans, mews, whipped by the wind. Sometimes, Maram hears it moan like an old man, or an invalid overcome with a violent coughing fit. Only the echoes of the final, late passersby reach her ears, their nocturnal voices losing themselves from afar. Maram thinks of Gorgui Mbodj, her husband. She prepares for his arrival, trying out all sorts of phrases, surprising herself mumbling sentences, proverbs and half-articulated words as if to conjure the eventual anger of her husband. "I wonder where he could be."

But when the narrative arrives at Gorgui's nighttime reverie, the French text switches into a different narrative mode that allows it to speak for the past. And when the cop appears, the voices of narrator and character become more clearly identifiable, and their ability to move freely in time and space splinters into a more static, third-person narration.[41] After the intervention, the voices are free to remain private, interior voices of psychology, but nothing more.[42] There is, however, a very important difference between the two versions of the novel in terms of how Gorgui's nighttime excursion is narrated. In Wolof, the text uses a free indirect mode that intermingles the narrator and the character. In French, the text employs a first-person singular within quotation marks, making Gorgui speak directly to the reader about *his* past:

> Gorgui longe les murs de la rue 6, s'arrête de temps à autre, puis reprend son errance. A la cité des policiers, il bifurque sur la droite en direction du cimetière musulman. Il ne maugrée pas; n'en veut à personne. Sur le pont de la Gueule Tapée, il hésite quelque peu, laisse le marché sur sa gauche, se trouve devant le Repos Mandel, lui tourne le dos, dirige ses pas vers la poste de la Medina. Parvenu au bâtiment, fatigué, il s'effondre sur la dernière marche. Gorgui Mbodj, la tête dans les mains, plonge dans les ténèbres de son village ancestral, en quête de forces nouvelles dans sa lutte contre un sort cruel.
>
> "Je n'ai pas dévié de l'enseignement de mes pères; sur le chemin de l'honneur, je me suis conduit en homme bien né. Ma devise: ne pas déchoir aux yeux de mes pairs. Je m'en suis tenu à la vérité, refusant le rôle de brandon de discorde, la tête haute quoi qu'il advienne. Les voisins savent que j'ai respecté ma règle de vie. Par stricte obéissance à ma morale, je ne milite dans aucun clan politique. Las de ne pouvoir m'attirer dans leur sordides intrigues, les gens m'ont donné ce surnom 'Buur Tilleen'—'Roi de la Medina.'"[43]

Gorgui follows the walls of sixth street, stopping from time to time, then begins his wandering again. At the Cité Police, he heads right toward the Muslim cemetery. He doesn't grumble, is not angry at anyone. On the bridge of Gueule Tapée, he hesitates a bit, leaves the market to his left and finds himself in front of the Repos Mandel, turns back the other way, directs his steps toward the Medina post office. Reaching the building, exhausted, he collapses on the last step. Gorgui Mbodj, head in his hands, plunges into the darkness of his ancestral village in search of reinforcements in his fight against a cruel fate.

"I have not strayed from what my fathers taught me; on the path of honor, I conducted myself as a well-born man. My motto: never disgrace myself in front of my peers. I limited myself to the truth, refusing to be anyone's troublemaker, head held high no matter what happens. My neighbors know how I respected my principles. Through strict adherence to my moral code, I am not a part of any political clan. Tired of not being able to lure me into their sordid intrigues, people gave me the nickname 'Buur Tilleen'—'King of Medina.'"

In Wolof, the narrator signaled to the reader with framing clauses that a shift to free indirect style was coming, but in French, the narrator vanishes and the character speaks directly. The content of what is spoken is rather similar between French and Wolof: Gorgui's reverie is a ventrilo-quization of the character's deeply patriarchal, *géer* point of view and his sentimental attachments to the way things were "back then."

> La génération actuelle ignore le respect du sang . . . Si nous tournons le dos à la cohésion du groupe, si nous perturbons le cercle ancien, nous aboutirons à l'abîme. Vers quel rivage? . . . Quel horizon de ténèbres, d'émiettement des valeurs, de dispersion de notre pérennité?[44]

> The current generation ignores the respect of blood. . . . If we turn our back on the cohesion of the group, if we disrupt the ancient circle, we will find ourselves hurtling into the abyss. Toward what distant shore? . . . What horizon of darkness, disintegration of values, scattering of our future?

The passage above communicates Gorgui's commitment to his sense of honor and his obsession with the waning societal respect for "blood." But whereas free indirect discourse in *Buur Tilleen* created space for at least the possibility of ambivalence toward Gorgui's particular vision of the past, here that same past speaks only through his voice, definitively localized in his person and walled off from the reader by quotation marks.

At first, we might be tempted to conclude that a transposition from in-direct to direct speech must make the French version *less* mediated than its Wolof counterpart. But while the character can say "I" in the French version, this is a first person that exists only within quotation marks. To illustrate this, I have reproduced below how the passages actually appear on the page in the two versions.[45]

Beyond the difference in narrative mode (indirect vs. direct), the most striking modification is actually typographic. The French version uses the guillemet («), which runs down the left side of the entirety of Gorgui's monologue. This use of the guillemet is a typographic tradition typically used for large stretches of reported discourse. While this formatting is un-common in the English-speaking world, it does appear occasionally in texts in French. What makes this typographic feature unique is that it clearly indicates at all times that a given passage is reported speech. In other words, the guillemets here make us aware at every moment that the voice that says "I" is a reported one. Because of the guillemet, we are constantly reminded that this reverie is being quoted.

When Gorgui's monologue is transposed in this way into direct speech, the omnipresent quotation marks do some of the work that free indirect

Ndekete gone tey, ñoom, seen
yoon nekkatul ci loolu. Moo fu
àddina jëm su fekkee ne li fi
maam ya ba woon lépp jox nañ ko
gannaw? Waay waay ku xam
fu ñuy teere?
Fi Góorgi Mbóoj toog ci postu
Tilleen xalaat naa xalaat ba faf
nelaw. Mu ngi sëngéem, jël bopp
bi teg ci kow óom yi. Fa la ne ba
benn alkaati fekk ko fa.

« Pourtant chacun de nous est
« conscient de l'origine de l'autre.
« La génération actuelle ignore le
« respect du sang . . . Si nous
« tournons le dos à la cohésion du
« groupe, si nous perturbons le
« cercle ancien, nous aboutirons à
« l'abîme. Vers quel rivage? . . .
« Quel horizon de ténèbres,
« d'émiettement des valeurs, de
« dispersion de notre pérennité? »

Ey, sa waay, looy def fii ba
waxtu wii?
—Uu!

Perdu dans ses pensées, Gorgui
    finit par s'assoupir, la tête sur
    les genoux. Survient un alkati:
—Ey, mon bonhomme?

discourse did in the Wolof, reminding the reader that this vision of the past is a particular one. But the guillemets also have an added, counterpoetic valence, which relates to the obligation to translate itself: the use of the quotation marks in the French indexes a certain degree of distance in the alignment of the narrator and the subjectivity the narrator is quoting. The capacity of Gorgui's monologue to voice a certain relationship to history and to circulate more freely in time and space in French are subject to his voice being made quotable, to its being, in several senses, *reported*. The quotation marks also shift the frame in which memory is expressed from one that exists within discourse itself ("he remembered") to the meta-discursive, typographic level. This has the effect of making the frame in which memory is reported more visible. The quotation marks indicate that something is being passed along, across a certain boundary. They represent a frontier across which the character's subjectivity can cross only by being translated into a set of given terms. The way in which Ndao's novel shifts as it is adapted into French points obliquely to a policing mechanism of a different order—it points to the impossibility of getting literary work in Wolof published in this period and thus, the imposition of having to translate one's work into French to have it circulate. Like Sembène's cameos as the *écrivain public*, the quotation marks in Ndao's text serve to both to heighten the reader's awareness that an obligation to translate exists and to transform this mediation into an aestheticized constraint.

The Texture of Translation

By comparing the shifts that occur across the multiple versions of *Mandabi* and *Buur Tilleen*, a clearer understanding of counterpoetics starts to emerge. Both works respond to the urgency of making a break with French and speaking "in one's own words." In this sense, they exist in a line of development from the paradoxes of authorship under colonial conditions that were studied in Chapter 2. But rather than achieving a clear break with French, both Sembène and Ndao find themselves grappling with the persistence of a requirement to translate. Counterpoetics, then, name a mode of response to an obligation to translate as a condition of expression; rather than accepting such an obligation only as a limitation, counterpoetics turn this constraint into a site of experimentation.

In counterpoetic works such as these, the voices of characters and performers often have a certain porosity to them—they belong to a given someone who is embedded in the world of the artwork, and yet these voices are also inflected by a demand to translate that saturates the entirety of the work. This permeability of voice in counterpoetic works often resembles the techniques of free indirect style. The connection is simple enough; free indirect style tends to raise questions about who or what is speaking.[46] But while free indirect style does suggest a helpful analogue, our usual understanding of that mode is too narrow to accommodate the complex play of voices that we find in counterpoetics. Whether in prose or in film, free indirect style typically is reserved for a merging of the voice or vantage of a character with that of the narrator, the filmmaker, or common wisdom. There is a partial dissolution of the distinction between these two centers of enunciation, without the difference between them being completely erased.

But in counterpoetics, translation itself becomes free indirect. An obligation to translate partially dissolves itself into the voices of characters or performers, much like the voice of a reporting narrator does in free indirect style. In other words, the linguistic circumstances that condition and constrain expression can be heard in the work itself, in a play of permeable voicing. We see the suggestion of this phenomenon in Glissant's original formulation: if counterpoetics describe an opposition between a language one uses and a form of expression that one truly needs, then its manifestations will necessarily tend toward modes of voicing that are able to encode and comment on the existence of a requirement to translate as a condition of their possibility.

But how exactly? How might an obligation to translate be heard in a work, if it is neither described nor named explicitly? Counterpoetics take place at a level of language that I will call *texture*. Here I am drawing on the work of the Russian linguist and literary theorist V. N. Volosinov, whose thinking on texture emerges from his discussions of direct and indirect speech forms. Volosinov understands free indirect style, as many others do, as a fluid mode: in a free indirect passage, the author and the character's intonations flood into each other, and yet the distinction between them is not entirely dissolved.[47] But what sets Volosinov's approach apart is that he has no interest in defining free indirect discourse as such. Instead, he conceives of direct and indirect speech as a spectrum of possible modes, with free indirect discourse being a portion of the indirect side of the spectrum.[48] Such flexibility allows Volosinov to pay close attention to the smallest of ways a message is transformed as it moves from direct to indirect speech. One important type of shift occurs at the level of what he calls *texture*.

For Volosinov, linguistic texture is not part of the semantic content of a speaker's message, and yet the message would not be the same without it. For example, a speaker might emphasize a particular word in a sentence, or a speaker's accent might communicate something. His key insight is that indirect discursive modes do especially interesting things with texture. As a speaker's message is displaced into an indirect mode, the texture of the original message can be preserved and made noticeable through a variety of creative means. In the simpler modes of indirect discourse, a speaker's accent might be highlighted through quotation marks or italics. In more complex modes such as free indirect discourse, that accent might be analyzed by a reporting narrator. In other words, as a message is passed from direct discourse into indirect speech, its form or texture becomes content. In free indirect discourse especially, a message's original texture—what Volosinoiv calls its "subjective and stylistic physiognomy"—can be made strange for a variety of ends, from amusement to analysis to critique.[49]

Volosinov's thinking on texture resonates with what contemporary linguistic anthropologists call the pragmatic features of communication. Pragmatics as a field studies the way in which context contributes to meaning. Register, emphasis, and pronoun use are all examples of pragmatic features. They may not be directly implicated in the semantic meaning of a given message, but they do contribute—sometimes decisively—to the overall meaning of a message as part of its emergent context. Thinking about Sembène and Ndao's translations in terms of texture or pragmatics will help us move toward a more dynamic understanding of a work and its context than we typically encounter in literary studies.[50]

Rather than thinking of a work as having a static or given context that it merely reflects, pragmatics draws our attention to the ways in which the meaningful aspects of context are constantly being renegotiated. Once again, the Wolof *nuyu*, or greeting, that we saw at work in *Mandabi* helps us grasp how such renegotiations of context can function. When Wolof speakers repeatedly break back into greetings, there is no further semantic meaning in their exchanges, but their repeated inquiries about their conversation partner's family, health, and so on *do* serve important pragmatic functions. They can help subtly reconfigure the relationship between speakers and recontextualize the entire exchange.[51] So when Gorgui and the imam try to out *nuyu* each other in *Mandabi*, they are each trying to shift the terrain of an ongoing conversation. This negotiation happens without either one of them referring explicitly to what is going on. For the pragmatics of the *nuyu* to work, the participants must share some kind of awareness of what they are doing, even if they do not share it identically or entirely understand it themselves. This space of shared, secondary-level consciousness of pragmatics is called, in the work of Michael Silverstein, *metapragmatic awareness.*[52] This refers to speakers' recognition of the pragmatic dimensions of their communication. In other words, metapragmatics is a terrain of negotiation and renegotiation over what about the context of a particular utterance is going to be meaningful.

To connect this back to Ndao's and Sembène's work, we can observe that a second-order awareness of pragmatics or texture is precisely what is at issue in the counterpoetics of *Mandabi* and *Buur Tilleen*. In *Buur Tilleen*, the shifting features of the passage analyzed above—the register of Gorgui's speaking voice, the pronoun the passage speaks in, the guillemets that set it off on the page—these are all at the level of what Volosinov calls *texture*. Similarly, in the two *Mandabi* films, it is the texture of the actors' performances and their relationship to the soundscape of urban Dakar that shifts, rather than the semantic content of the script.

Counterpoetics draw attention to the ways in which a work's texture has changed because of an obligation to translate. In Silverstein's terms, we could say that counterpoetics are an aestheticization of a metapragmatic awareness of translation as a condition of expression. To put that in Volosinov's only slightly less jargony terms: counterpoetics occur at the level of texture. Counterpoetics invite a viewer or a reader to become aware that an obligation to translate is part of the work's relevant, meaningful context, that it has shaped the texture of what can be said. Both *Mandabi* and *Buur Tilleen* strive to point out such an obligation without ever directly naming it as such.

In the early 1960s in Senegal, struggling to "say it in Wolof" often meant doing so within the contours of what was sayable in French. Although we may associate the language question with a dramatic break with one language for another, in this chapter I have argued that the first modern film and novel in Wolof tell a very different story. Both Sembène and Ndao find ways to aestheticize the difficulties they faced, by taking the challenge of producing and sharing work in Wolof and making this into an aspect of the work of art itself. Rather than a nativist return to "pure" indigenous sources, the language question led them to a poetics that attended to its own complicated and multilingual conditions of possibility. While these two works were attempts to turn away from French, what they ended up generating were meditations on the difficulty—even the impossibility— of such a rupture. What emerged instead was a mode of counterpoetics that drew attention to the linguistically mediated character of an artwork, while also doing far more than merely highlighting the continued hegemony of French. *Mandabi* and *Buur Tilleen* linger over what happens when the obligation to translate becomes a condition of expression in its own right. This is the terrain of counterpoetics, and for Ndao and Sembène, it sparks profound questions about the subtle possibilities and limitations of such a situation: Is it possible to translate embodied, pragmatic, and non-referential aspects of communication, such as the *nuyu* exchange or the gestural repertoires that amateur actors bring with them? Is it possible to translate the affective and haptic dimensions of a soundscape, the way a particular urban space feels to the ear and the body? Is it possible to translate the textural dimensions of the first novelistic free indirect monologue in Wolof? Counterpoetics in these two works are not about what is lost in translation. They are rather a negotiation of the contours of the sayable.

PART III

World Literature, Neoliberalism

CHAPTER 6

How Mariama Bâ Became World Literature: Translation and the Legibility of Feminist Critique

Just a few years after it was first published in 1979, Mariama Bâ's novel *Une si longue lettre* (*So Long a Letter*) existed in more than half a dozen translations, from English and German to Japanese and Norwegian. Although Bâ did not live to see the full extent of her first novel's success, *Letter* would go on to become one of the most widely translated African novels of the twentieth century, also appearing on countless syllabi.[1] Along the way, prize committees, translators, editors, and critics all shaped how the Senegalese author's work became recognizable to a global audience.

In this chapter, I retrace the path *Letter* took to become world literature. I begin by showing how Bâ's success came to be bound up with two interpretations of her work: first, that her novel is a broadside against the institution of polygamy in Senegal, and second, that it is a celebration of the self-fashioning powers of literary culture.[2] I reject both of these standard accounts, arguing instead that the widespread investment in framing the novel in these ways is deeply revealing of the terms through which postcolonial literatures become legible to a world literary public. Although I do engage with individual readings of the novel throughout this chapter, my intention is not to personalize the argument or to enter into a polemic with any single critic's analysis. My engagement is with what I take to be two durable trends in the critical reception that were also wrapped up with *Letter*'s success as world literature.[3]

I show how an obsession with reading *Letter* as a denunciation of polygamy has eclipsed the novel's critique of a very modern effort to reform the legal framework of marriage in Senegal. I also examine how the acclaim for *Letter* as a story about the emancipatory powers of writing and book culture overshadows the text's rather more ambivalent relationship toward the print public sphere it conjures.

After setting aside these interpretations, I reconsider Bâ's feminism—a term around which Bâ herself circled without always claiming. I contend that the feminism of *Une si longue lettre* takes the form of a struggle over what alternative forms of social value may still be possible. But rather than supplying an answer in advance, Bâ leaves this question open—as if asking without being certain of an answer had a value in and of itself.

I conclude by comparing the original French text of *Letter* with two of its translations: the English edition that helped catalyze its success as world literature and a more recent translation into Wolof by the contemporary Senegalese writer Maam Yunus Dieng. Dieng not only collaborated on translating *Lettre*, she also adapted aspects of Bâ's text into her own novel, *Aawo bi (The First Wife)*. By reading *Letter* back through Dieng's two engagements with it, we can appreciate Bâ as a very different sort of writer than the version we have come to know.

Bâ probably never expected the level of acclaim her work has received. Instead, her *Letter* is saturated by an uncertainty about how it will circulate in the world. As one of the very first francophone African novels written by a woman, *Letter* is consumed by the question of its audience—whether it will be read, by whom, and in what ways.[4] This emerges most clearly when the text is read back through its translations, as though there is something about translation that dislodges and illuminates the novel's presuppositions about its own conditions of circulation and intelligibility. Although Bâ's approach to the question of her audience is quite exceptional, it also resonates deeply with many of the fault lines that I have been tracing throughout this book. Bâ's work takes up and extends the questions of how one can write for a future reader and what it means speak in one's own words.

This chapter also deepens my inquiry into the ability of translation to uncover the contingency of literary worlds. The distortions of translation are a familiar motif in discussions of world literature, but this chapter offers a different approach. Rather than weighing what is lost or gained or insisting on a kernel of untranslatability, I argue that the reception of Mariama Bâ raises some equally fundamental methodological questions: How do literary texts take for granted certain interpretative conditions about the world in which they will be received? And how does this feature of a text's "worldedness" become altered, loosened, or otherwise reshaped in the circulation of texts that we call world literature?[5] Working in the interstices between world literature and vernacular poetics, this chapter repositions Bâ's novel as a text that foregrounds the contingency of its own literary address and transforms this into an animating contradiction.

Mariama Bâ in Frankfurt

One can rarely pinpoint a single moment when a writer and her works become world literature. But for Mariama Bâ, that transformation clearly began at the 1980 Frankfurt Book Fair, where she accepted the inaugural Noma Prize for Publishing in Africa. Although Pascale Casanova's world republic of letters orbits around centers of literary capital like Paris, London, or New York, there is a contrarian's case to be made for prosaic Frankfurt as a hub of world literature in its own right, since by some accounts close to 80 percent of all the translations that appeared in the early 1980s were negotiated there.[6]

Frankfurt's role as a capital of the translation market played a significant part in the flurry of interest that arose around Bâ's debut novel. The Noma Award choreographed an introduction of Bâ onto the world literary stage, including a series of receptions and a carefully edited press packet, which led in turn to the first eight translations of her novel in 1981 and 1982—into English, German, Japanese, Italian, Swedish, Norwegian, Dutch, and Finnish. This first wave of interest in Bâ's work also set in motion the rapid adoption of her novel onto literature syllabi and helped cement *Letter*'s reputation as a classic of modern African literature.

During the presentation in Frankfurt, the Noma Award also offered Bâ a venue to make a speech. She spoke on the political dimension of African literature, and her speech has since acquired a life of its own, persisting past the author's untimely death in 1981 as a privileged touchstone for critical readings of her work. The speech balances a portrait of the African writer as a social critic with a sense of unease about the limitations such a writer may face when working in a "borrowed language":

"The [African] writer must echo the aspirations of all social classes, especially the most disadvantaged ones. He must denounce the ills and pains that afflict our society and hold back its full blossoming, he must strike out at the archaic practices, customs and mores that have nothing to do with our precious cultural heritage. This is his sacred mission, to be accomplished against all odds, with faith and tenacity. . . . The language the writer uses is understood and spoken only by a tiny minority of the population. The writer thus runs the heavy risk of failing in his political mission, because his message has a limited reach and is heard outside the people whom he addresses."[7]

Given Bâ's cautious tone, it is curious that only one aspect of this speech tends to be remembered: the suggestion that the writer's job description includes "striking out at archaic practices." Bâ's worry that the African writer might be at a linguistic distance from her audience tends to be forgotten. By 1989, a small excerpt of this speech was being included as part of a short, anonymous preface to the second edition of *So Long a Letter* in Heinemann's prestigious African Writers Series.[8] The preface reads: "[Mariama Bâ] promoted the crucial role of the writer in a developing country. *She believed that the 'sacred mission' of the writer was to strike out 'at the archaic practices, traditions and customs that are not a real part of our precious cultural heritage.' So Long a Letter* succeeds admirably in its mission."[9] [emphasis mine] Something curious has occurred here. Bâ's speech has been subtly transformed into a frame story that explains the objective of her novel, but her concern with how she would be heard has faded away. For an anglophone audience, then, the mission of the novel has been identified as striking out at archaic traditions, even before the reader reaches page one.[10]

Bâ did not, in her speech, elaborate on which traditions she had in mind, but many of Bâ's readers have not been nearly so circumspect. From very early on, Bâ's *Letter* was presented, marketed and celebrated as a full-throated condemnation of the institution of polygamy. Indeed, it would be very difficult to disentangle the impression that *Letter* is a book "about" polygamy from the terms in which it became internationally acclaimed. The press release announcing the Noma Award gives an indication of just how intertwined these were:

Mariama Bâ won the Noma Award for her remarkable and compelling first novel *Une si longue lettre*, published by Les Nouvelles Editions Africaines of Dakar in 1979, which deals with the theme of women's emancipation in Africa, specifically, though not exclusively, in the context of polygamy. It portrays the isolation of married women who reject polygamy in a society where it is taken for granted, and the plight of articulate women living in a social milieu dominated by attitudes and values that tend to deny women a proper social personality. In making the award, the Committee that has been entrusted with the selection of the annual prize winner, was impressed by the social significance of a work written from the point of view of a Muslim woman in a society in transition.[11]

This commendation distills many elements of what have come to be a widespread framing of the novel: Bâ's *Letter* as the story of a self-making female subject who painfully emancipates herself from tradition and religion through the power of the very practice of writing that forms her narrative. And yet the Noma Award announcement is itself the product of a certain amount of editing: the phrases that compose it are drawn from three anonymous readers' reports that were prepared for the Noma committee as part of the process of selecting and awarding the prize.

In those reports, the readers voiced varying assessments and even harsh criticism of Bâ's novel, but Hans Zell, editor of the *African Book Publishing Record*, which administered the award, appears to have stitched together phrases from each reader to assemble this commendation, sometimes knitting two separate thoughts into a single sentence.[12] While the press release gives the impression that it is merely reproducing the award committee's preexisting consensus on the novel, in fact it is producing just such a consensus. There is nothing particularly scandalous about this, since committees of all kinds produce edited joint statements all the time. But this particular work of synthesis is notable for the way in which it takes divergent readings of Bâ's novel and manages to arrive at the terms through which her work would be acclaimed as world literature. It is as if there were a centripetal force to the reception of Mariama Bâ, whereby both the novel and the authorial persona tend to consolidate into a certain mold. While this shift may have begun in Frankfurt, it cannot be attributed to any one individual or institution.

Specters of Tradition and Custom

The Noma Award's framing of *So Long a Letter* seems to have much to recommend it. The overall plot of the novel appears at first to supply all the evidence necessary to support a claim that this is a book about how the development of Senegalese women's "proper social personality" is

hindered by polygamy. Both the main characters—Ramatoulaye and her
friend Aïssatou—are shocked when their husbands secretly take second
wives. Aïssatou chooses to divorce her husband, while Ramatoulaye remains married to hers, even though he subsequently abandons her and
their children. The novel opens with Ramatoulaye's husband's death, and
while she mourns him in seclusion, she composes the "novel" as a long,
sprawling missive addressed to Aïssatou.[13] In addition to the plot, a specific passage does seem to lend support to readings of the novel that take it
to be a book about polygamy. In this passage, Ramatoulaye reflects back
on the education she and her childhood friend Aïssatou received at a colonial all-girls school.

> *Nous sortir de l'enlisement des traditions, superstitions et moeurs*; nous faire
> apprécier de multiples civilisations sans reniement de la nôtre; élever
> notre vision du monde, cultiver notre personnalité, renforcer nos
> qualités, mater nos défauts; faire fructifier en nous les valeurs de la
> morale universelle; voilà la tâche que s'était assignée l'admirable
> directrice.

> *To lift us out of the bog of tradition, superstition and custom*, to make us
> appreciate a multitude of civilizations without renouncing our own, to
> raise our vision of the world, cultivate our personalities, strengthen
> our qualities, to make up for our inadequacies, to develop universal
> moral values in us: these were the aims of our admirable headmis-
> tress.[14] (emphasis mine)

The school described here is modeled on the Ecole des jeunes filles de Rufisque, a real, elite institution that drew students from all over French
West Africa. Rufisque was the all-girls sister school to the Ecole Normale
William Ponty, whose writing assignments and Franco-African culture
were studied in Chapter 2. Mariama Bâ was a Rufisque graduate, and her
biographer (and daughter) Mame Coumba Ndiaye has suggested that the
heroic headmistress here was based on Bâ's headmistress.[15] By bringing together students from all across the federation, elite schools like Rufisque
and Ponty created space for new forms of solidarity and helped generate
intellectual resistance to colonialism. But they were also closely associated
with imperialism's humanist alibis—which is in part what this passage
evokes. Ramatoulaye's description of her headmistress's pedagogy is a note-
perfect replica of the ideology of "adapted education," which became central to elite schools like Rufisque in the late colonial period. As I discussed
in Chapter 2, adapted education saw itself as a program for teaching future
elites to be both modern and properly, authentically African. The girls'

studies at Rufisque are presented in this light: as a new kind of self-fashioning that can rescue women from the "bog" (*enlisement*—"to be stuck or stalled, as in quicksand") of tradition, superstition, and custom without uprooting them culturally.

So Long a Letter is often understood as a condemnation of the ways political independence in Senegal did little to address gender-based inequality. This is clearly its aim on one level, but in responding to this dilemma, some of Bâ's readers have been very quick to return to this passage on colonial education as proposing a sort of answer.[16] In a discussion of models of female empowerment in Bâ's novels, Rebecca Wilcox writes approvingly of the "admirable feminist tendencies" of the education the two main characters receive, which prepares them to resist the "pressures of tradition."[17] I agree with Wilcox in certain respects. A certain feminism *does* seem to derive from Ramatoulaye's education. But the question could also be, What are the stakes of reading *So Long a Letter* only in terms of *this* particular feminism? Furthermore, what is authorized if we equate the goal of feminism with producing stable subjects who can "resist" tradition? Do we not risk trying to accomplish, in criticism, what colonial education purportedly set out to do?

Some readers of Mariama Bâ go very far in this direction. For instance, in a comparison of Bâ's *Letter* with Toni Morrison's *Beloved*, Kathryn Fleming writes nearly interchangeably of "the controlling forces of Islam," "the powerful machinations of tradition," "the insidious lure of polygamy," "the looming specter of Islam," and finally, "the looming specter of polygamy." With this collection of figures, Fleming perhaps personifies "tradition, superstition and custom."[18] But how does this trio then become "polygamy and Islam"? I ask this because polygamy is indeed something of a specter in *So Long a Letter*, but not in the way Fleming intends.

Polygamy is a motivating engine of the plot; it touches every character's life in the novel; and yet actual examples of polygamy are always staged just outside the narrative frame. As Obioma Nnaemeka points out, "It is puzzling that a book . . . in which the word 'la polygamie/polygamy' *never* appears and polygamy (the institution) *never* functions . . . has been debated and analyzed *ad nauseam* in literary criticism . . . as a book *about the institution of polygamy*." Nnaemeka suggests that one possible reason the book has been read in this way is the English translation. Bâ's English translator, Modupé Bodé-Thomas, renders the phrase *le problème polygamique* as "the problem of polygamy." As Nnaemeka wryly observes, this is like translating *le problème politique* (the political problem) as "the problem of politics."[19]

One can avoid singling out Bodé-Thomas through a quick survey of the other seven translations that appeared in 1981–82. From German and Japanese to Italian and Norwegian, all of them follow roughly the pattern that Nnaemeka identifies, transforming an adjective into an institution.[20] A curious consensus thus appears in the text's translation into world literature, as if what Ramatoulaye really ought to have said was "the problem of polygamy." In the Wolof version by Maam Yunus Dieng and Arame Fal, however, this phrase becomes *"mbirum jabar yu bari"* (the matter of many wives), because there is not a word for polygamy qua institution that could be distinguished from the institution of marriage itself.

Other readers of Mariama Bâ go beyond the "specter of polygamy" and take the novel as an injunction to denounce what polygamy is understood to be like in Senegal. In an otherwise insightful comparison of Bâ's *Letter* with Ousmane Sembène's *Xala*, Keith Walker grounds his analysis with a definition: "African Muslim polygamous societies are, by definition, relationships of permanent Koran-sanctioned social inequality in which the power of the husband reinforces the domination, subordination, and submission of women. This power is rationalized by the elders and their Koranic explications of what 'ought, should, and better' be and of what is 'right, good, and bad.'"[21] This definition locates the origin of social inequality in a scene of "bad reading," specifically the naive or cunning reliance on the sanction of a sacred text. Defined in this way, polygamy becomes something static and purely exterior to particular women and men who might practice it. But if this is what African Muslim polygamous societies are like, by definition, should we not expect to find an abundance of elders citing the Quran in *So Long a Letter*? In fact, nowhere in the novel is the Quran invoked to justify polygamy, nor even are any of the *hadith* to which Bâ's characters could very well have referred. What is cited to explain polygamy? Fate, God's will, filial duty, the materialism of the poor— but perhaps the most frequent explanations are secular, even biological, accounts of human nature.[22] Nevertheless, I believe that this definition demonstrates something fundamental about the reception of *So Long a Letter*. It offers a version of polygamy in the novel *as it should have been*. In a sense, this account corrects the picture of polygamy by adding a supplemental definition in which a scene of overly literal reading comes to explain social inequality.

Walker's scene of "bad reading" seems eerily like the mirror image of another well-known passage in the novel. In this scene, Ramatoulaye lauds her friend Aïssatou's decision to leave her husband after he secretly takes a second wife. In response to this duplicity, Aïssatou divorces him, continues her education, and eventually becomes a translator in New York. Famously, the novel ascends here into a paean to book culture:

> Tu t'assignas un but difficile; et plus que ma présence, mes encouragements, les livres te sauvèrent. Devenus ton refuge, ils te soutinrent. Puissance des livres, invention merveilleuse de l'astucieuse intelligence humaine. Signes divers, associés en sons; sons différents qui moulent le mot. Agencement de mots d'où jaillissent l'Idée, la Pensée, l'Histoire, la Science, la Vie. Instrument unique de relation et de culture, moyen inégalé de donner et de recevoir. Les livres soudent des générations au même labeur continu qui fait progresser. Ils te permirent de te hisser. Ce que la société te refusait, ils te l'accordèrent.

> You set yourself a difficult task; and more than just my presence and my encouragements, books saved you. Having become your refuge, they sustained you. The power of books, this marvelous invention of astute human intelligence. Various signs associated with sound: different sounds that form the word. Juxtaposition of words from which springs the idea, Thought, History, Science, Life. Sole instrument of interrelationships and culture, unparalleled means of giving and receiving. Books knot generations together in the same continuing effort that leads to progress. They enabled you to better yourself. What society refused you, they granted.[23]

This account of reading and sociality seems like the polar opposite of Walker's "African Muslim polygamous societies." In those, everyone is beholden to a holy text that reinforces the subordination of women. In this account of a society organized around a reading public, books join together generations in a "progressive labor" as a privileged instrument of culture and a force outside of society.

Ramatoulaye's praise of books can easily be taken to be the novel's articulation of its own ideal reading public.[24] Other scenes that might demonstrate the limitations of this model are sometimes considered largely in relation to this idealized vision. This has been especially true of a certain key moment in the narrative in which Ramatoulaye tries to decide whether she should leave her husband. After learning of his betrayal, Ramatoulaye agonizes over what to do but does not divorce him. At the very moment when we as readers have been prepared to see Ramatoulaye assert her independence, she appears to do nothing of the kind.

This scene generates enormous frustration for many of Bâ's readers. It is not difficult to see why; this is a particularly opaque moment in a text in which the narrator's thoughts, feelings, and opinions are usually at center stage. While there is no consensus in the criticism over how to read this scene, two argumentative threads stand out. First, critics debate whether this scene means that Ramatoulaye "accepts polygamy."[25] Another persistent trend is critics' attempts to resolve this scene's troubling opacity by "fleshing out" the psychology of Ramatoulaye. There is a great diversity in these latter attempts to make sense of this moment (although Islam and polygamy are frequently cited as reasons for Ramatoulaye's inaction).[26] My interest is not so much in the psychological portraits critics have provided but rather in why this moment in the text provokes this genre of response. The move to offer a psychological account of Ramatoulaye's inaction works to restore a clear sense of the protagonist's individuality at the moment when it seems most in peril. Perhaps it is because this moment is left open to interpretation that critics are tempted to complete what Mariama Bâ left, as it were, unfinished. It is as if some readers are able to understand Ramatoulaye's choice only as a deviation from what she should have chosen, as a sign of incomplete self-liberation.

Another way of approaching this moment would be to suggest that it does not need to be explained away. Perhaps the dissonance is precisely the point. Indeed, when Ramatoulaye is debating whether she should stay or go, she does so through the image of a book. "Leave!" she writes, "Draw a clean line through the past. Turn over a page on which not everything was bright, certainly, but at least all was clear."[27] At the moment when, in the eyes of many of her readers, Ramatoulaye should have acted as if her life were a novel, she does not do so. She tries but fails to conceive of her self as a text here—or to put it more accurately, *as that kind of a text*, the one where you can just turn the page.

Even more strikingly, as Ramatoulaye weighs what she will do, she continues to try out other ways of seeing, besides the reading of books. Just after discarding the possibility of turning the page, Ramatoulaye recalls her mother's warning: that the gap between her husband's teeth was a sign of his appetite for pleasure. Ramatoulaye had ignored this advice because it was superstitious. And yet in this moment, she cannot help but recall how right her mother was. In a study of social marginality in Bâ's novels, Igolima Amachree points to this reaction as evidence that Ramatoulaye's story is ultimately the tragedy of not being modern enough. Amachree bemoans the way Ramatoulaye "rejects the custom of polygyny and wants to be lifted out of it and yet she accepts the superstition of reading a person's character by the shape of the teeth. . . . Thus we see her enmeshed in those same 'traditions, superstitions and customs' while thinking that she has been lifted from the 'bog' of them."[28] Amachree appears to be correcting

Ramatoulaye here for not resembling more closely the ideal subject that her education was supposed to produce. What does it tell us about the terms through which we, as critics, apprehend world literature that it is at the moment when the image of selfhood as a book is found to be problematic, that a world literary public has often intervened to adjust the picture, to restore an emancipatory account of reading and subjectivity?[29]

Amachree's suggestion that the novel stages a conflict between modernity and tradition is also a common interpretative frame for *So Long a Letter*.[30] In a foundational study of choice and ambivalence in Bâ's fiction, Irène Assiba d'Almeida also invokes this binary. "What Ramatoulaye really wants," d'Almeida writes, "is to be a modern woman, conscious of her rights as an individual and determined to fight for these rights. However, being a modern woman is at once seductive and threatening. Seductive because it opens up to the possibility for freedom and change, threatening because potentially, it has the power to destabilize the ground on which she stands. And so, Ramatoulaye is always torn between modernity and tradition."[31] Elsewhere, d'Almeida offers a nuanced appraisal of the ambiguities of Ramatoulaye's choices, but here she risks framing tradition as something static, even unchanging. D'Almeida describes it as the "ground" on which Ramatoulaye stands. But the applicability of "tradition and custom" to the institution of marriage in Senegal has a complicated legal history, which is an aspect of the novel that critics have overlooked.[32]

So Long a Letter stages a complex dialogue with the struggles over women's civil rights in Senegal that took place in the 1970s and 1980s. Specifically, *Letter* is deeply intertextual with a set of legal reforms introduced in 1973, known collectively as the Family Code. The code marked a significant shift in the Senegalese legal system. Before its introduction in 1973, legal issues related to marriage, divorce, and inheritance were ostensibly governed by religious or customary law in certain regions. This distinction was a legacy of colonial jurisprudence. During the era of French West Africa, there were essentially two legal systems—one for citizens (to whom French law applied) and another for colonial subjects (who were in theory under religious or customary courts).[33] Most pertinently for Bâ's novel, what came to be enforced as "religious and customary law" was itself partially the product of an effort to standardize and make permanent a diverse set of practices. Before instituting the customary tribunals that would govern subjects, the colonial administration deployed anthropologists to study and formalize local customs, which were then given the force of law.[34] "Tradition and custom," then, did not refer to unchanging, indigenous practices but rather to new, negotiated legal formations, to which individuals and institutions responded strategically. So the idea—very common in readings of Mariama Bâ—that there exists a simple binary here between modernity and tradition needs to be set aside, especially when it comes to questions of family law and family form. Far from being a "bog" in which women had been stuck since time immemorial, tradition and custom were hybrid socio-legal spaces in full transformation.

In the early 1960s, after Senegal's independence, a committee was convened to resolve this complicated legal history by reforming and unifying family law. After more than ten years of debate, the Family Code introduced a number of reforms, including making repudiation illegal, making signed consent mandatory, making dowries optional, and changing inheritance laws. Most relevantly for *So Long a Letter*, the code made it mandatory that husbands declare their intent to be either polygamous or monogamous at the time of marriage—with polygamy being the default option. The code generated significant debate about marriage in Senegal throughout the 1970s and 1980s, the period during which Bâ's novel was written and published.[35] The code actually comes up in passing in the novel, but it is also present in another, more structural sense.[36] The betrayals that the two main female characters suffer in the novel—in which their husbands take second wives without their knowledge—would have, in theory, been illegal under the Family Code. In this sense, there is a very close resemblance between the family dramas the novel stages and the family forms the law sought to regulate.[37]

I want to propose that literature and the law continue to be intertwined in the reception of the novel as well. When the committee that produced the Family Code tried to reform polygamy, the solution they reached was to stipulate a choice for or against it. One objection to this solution has been that, in its effort to offer a choice in the matter of polygamy, the committee imagined both men and women as abstract subjects who could either say yes or no. But in practice such a choice might be more of a negotiation that would take place in a whole matrix of competing commitments, affiliations, dispositions, and constraints.[38] This legal persona who could say a simple yes or no to polygamy is not what we find in Bâ's narrator, Ramatoulaye. Yet it *is* what we often find in the reception of Bâ as world literature, in which Ramatoulaye is frequently recast as she should have been, namely as someone who simply says no to polygamy. What can we make of this curious convergence? Or of the way the terms of legal intelligibility seem to parallel those of literary legibility? Perhaps both world literature and modern, positive law cannot do without categories such as tradition, religion, and custom, which serve as screens onto which narratives of the development of secular, modern individuality are projected.

Criteria of Value

If we can see *Letter*'s feminism as more than an attack on tradition and custom, a host of other approaches and problematics come into view. Among them are two questions that hang over the entire work. In one of Ramatoulaye's apostrophes, in which she seems to be addressing some indeterminate, larger audience, she asks, "When will educated society reach the point at which it determines itself not by virtue of sex, but rather criteria of value?" In response to this demand, her exasperated interlocutor blurts out, "Whom are you addressing, Ramatoulaye?"[39] It is difficult to answer either one of these questions. Ramatoulaye's demand for a new form of social value encapsulates the mode of feminist contestation for which the novel is rightly famous. And yet it is not clear from the immediate context quite what she has in mind. An answer to the second query—"Whom are you addressing"—also appears elusive, since the implied audience here and elsewhere is incredibly elastic. At times, Ramatoulaye seems to be writing to herself as much as to Aïssatou, while at other times she seems to address a public that is much, much larger.[40] In this section, I will argue that, far from being an aporia, this unresolvability of both value and address is what grounds Bâ's distinctive mode of critique.[41]

One of the most persistent, and indeed anguished, questions in *Letter* is what *other* kinds of value might be possible. What could be an adequate, alternative source of value with which to transform society in the context of rapid urbanization; the extension of the market into countless new areas of social life; and the persistence of caste privilege, patriarchy, and colonial structures of social inequality? The source of value the novel seems to advocate for most often is an interior, individual space which houses faculties of sentiment, reason, and agency. What goes on in this space of interiority is usually presented as what others *should* value in a person, rather than caste, wealth, gender, and so on. Ramatoulaye sums this up neatly as she chastises her brother-in-law for offering to take her as a second wife after her husband's death: "You forget that I have a heart, reason, that I am not an object to be passed from one hand to another."[42]

The dramatic progression of *Letter* is principally driven by the many ways in which Ramatoulaye's individuality is under constant threat from other criteria of value. These include the demands of an "antiquated, traditional morality" and the "imperious laws" associated with "desires, in-stincts and drives."[43] Ramatoulaye seems on occasion to be subject to both of these in complicated ways, and some of the moments that are taken to define her progress toward becoming a free, independent individual seem curiously superimposed onto these other forms of valuation.[44]

There is, however, another form of value in the novel that is neither moral nor instinctual—namely, exchange value. Despite (or perhaps because of) how often Ramatoulaye asserts that the individual's interior-ity is what should count, she worries that it is at risk of becoming some-thing that is merely countable. At the funeral of her husband, as the gifts of condolence pour in, Ramatoulaye bemoans the fact that expressions of sympathy are now all made in bank notes: "Troubling exteriorization of invaluable interior sentiment, counted in francs."[45] *Letter*'s fundamental crisis turns around the ways in which Ramatoulaye's life might be measured—but also risks being mismeasured. The language of quantifi-cation suffuses the prose at the most intimate of moments. Ramatoulaye worries, "I *gave without counting*, gave more than I received [in her mar-riage]." She tells herself, "It's *the sum* of all the lost or seized seconds that make for successful or failed lives." Even her most reflective and outraged moments are often inflected with measurement: "I *measured* myself against the shadows," "I *measured*, in front of stunned eyes, how thin was the lib-erty accorded to women."[46]

How could one account for a life? The need to do so spurs Bâ's *Letter*, and yet the novel seems riven by the impossibility and the inevitability of recounting in a given set of terms. While the individual's agency, reason, and sentiment often seem to be what Ramatoulaye means by her new "cri-teria of value," the novel complicates this progressive teleology and ulti-mately leaves the question of value open. It is as if *Letter* cannot do without the individual's interiority (to ground its critique of actually existing so-cial values), but it also cannot make do with it either. The generative force of this paradox drives *Letter* to pose the possibility of a new form of value while refraining from identifying it with any preexisting category. I pro-pose that we might find this gesture to be valuable in itself, as a mode of critique.

The demand for a new form of social value is also intimately bound up with the elasticity of *Letter*'s address. For the novel to demand another val-uation without determining it in advance, it must *necessarily* refuse to limit its address to any already-achieved form or genre. This is what accounts for its famous generic indeterminacy: the novel resembles a letter, a diary, and a *bildungsroman* without quite assimilating itself to any of these.

The instability of the novel's addressivity echoes Bâ's own anxieties of audience. Her worry in Frankfurt over how and where her work would be read could, of course, be understood to refer only to the material conditions in which her address was situated—the fact that she could not take for granted widespread French literacy in Senegal or a local economy that could sustain a book publishing market. But Bâ's concern with address is at least as much about *how she can be heard.* The capacity to be heard depends on what modes of address one is authorized to make, whether one can make others listen if they would prefer not to, whom one can speak for, what can be spoken about—not to mention the stylistics, sensibilities, and expectations of a given audience.[47] In *So Long a Letter,* the struggle to give shape to a new form of social value is fundamentally a struggle over how one might be heard—and in what terms.

Imagined Assemblies

Part of what makes *So Long a Letter* so appealing to readers and teachers of literature is clearly the convergence it proposes between letter-writing and self-writing. That Ramatoulaye fashions her self through a practice of writing has tended to confirm our idealizations of what kind of sociality print culture makes possible. In the redemptive vision of books and writing as gateways to agency and autonomy that the text appears to offer, we recognize our own deeply felt and often implicit convictions. What is at issue in the reception of *Letter* as world literature, then, is a certain reflexive recognition occurring on the part of the international audience.

To draw out the limits of this form of recognition, I want to look again at that celebrated passage on the power of books. But this time I will complicate matters by comparing the English translation linked with the text's status as world literature with an examination of the Wolof version by Maam Yunus Dieng (the Senegalese writer who has staged a long-running dialogue with Bâ's work) and her collaborator Arame Fal. Here is the same passage in French, in English, in Wolof, and in my translation of the Wolof (emphasis mine throughout):

Puissance des livres, invention merveilleuse de l'astucieuse intelligence humaine. Signes divers, associés en sons; sons différents qui moulent le mot. *Agencement de mots d'où jaillissent*	The power of books, this marvelous invention of astute human intelligence. Various signs associated with sound: different sounds that form the word. *Juxtaposition of words from*

l'Idée, la Pensée, l'Histoire,
la Science, la Vie. Instrument
unique de relation et de culture,
moyen inégalé de donner
et de recevoir. Les livres soudent
des générations au même labeur
continu qui fait progresser.

which springs the idea, Thought,
History, Science, Life. Sole
instrument of interrelationships and
culture, unparalleled means of giving
and receiving. Books knot generations
together in the same continuing
effort that leads to progress.

•

Dooley téere, doy na waar;
kéemaan la ci kéemaan yi xelum
doom-aadama sàkk: ay rëdd nga
boole muy baat; *nga booley baat,*
xel nàcc, indi xalaat, nettali taarix,
génne xam-xam, wone àddina.
Téere mooy jumtukaay yu yéeme,
ci jàllale caada ak weccentey xalaat.
Ñooy boole ñu bokkul jamono,
tënk leen ci benn gëstu, ba ñu
génne ci lu jariñ mbindeef yi.

The power of books is quite
extraordinary. They are a marvel
amongst all the mysteries of the spirit
of the children of Adam. Lines that
you combine until they are words.
You join together words and intelligence
flows forth, bringing thought, narrating
history, leaving knowledge in its wake,
revealing the world. Books are astonishing
tools for the transmission of culture and
the mutual exchange of ideas. Books
bring together those who are not of
the same generation, tying them into
the same inquiry, whose goal is that
which is useful to all creatures.[48]

In the French original, books are presented as powerful assemblages
(*agencements*) of words that serve as the glue of social relation in an idealized public sphere (*instrument unique . . . moyen inégalé*). Books are cred-
ited with summoning up ideals such as Thought, History, Science, even
Life, all of which appear in their capitalized, allegorical forms.[49]

What must be translated is not only the semantic content, but also the
way in which this passage makes assumptions about what it is that books
do and how they exist for a public. The English and Wolof versions differ
markedly in how they approach this. In English, books continue to be a
"juxtaposition" of words from which flow History, Life, etc. But in Wolof,
Dieng and Fal approximate these grandiose concepts in lowercase, shear-
ing them of allegorical status. They also shift key sentences from third to
second person; instead of having books themselves give rise to knowledge,
intelligence, etc., these qualities result from the actions of an impersonal
"you" who joins together words (*nga booley baat*).

A more striking departure appears in the way the translators handle the pronouncement that books are an "instrument unique de relation et de culture." *Unique* in French can mean "only" but also "exceptional" or "special." Opting for the former sense, the English translation makes books the "sole instrument of interrelationships and culture," thereby amplifying the status claimed for them in the original. In Wolof, books are still called an "astonishing" (*yéeme*) technology, but their privileged power seems to have been diminished.[50]

The translators are encountering a moment in which the novel imagines what it means for it to address an audience in print—and this is something that is *not* the same in Wolof, English, and French. As the passage warps across languages, the publics and contexts of use that these translations can envision for themselves come into focus. Both versions remain close to the meaning of the original, and yet they recreate the way in which this passage imagines its own field of circulation. The English version intensifies a belief in the special powers of print culture, whereas the Wolof translation dampens this same aspect of the original. Dieng and Fal are transposing this praise of books' unique power into a literary context that is, at present, not very amenable to such idealization. Although there is an abundance of written discourse in Wolof across media and scripts, to romanticize the printed book as *the* privileged medium of knowledge and culture is to dismiss other modes of relation; more concretely, it is to ignore the many challenges faced by book publishing in vernacular languages in Senegal.[51]

The divergence between the translations records the difference between what a printed literary address can take for granted in these three languages.[52] The English version, closely associated with the text's success as world literature, augments the heroic account; Dieng and Fal recalibrate it for a very different anticipated audience for whom the power of books cannot be presumed in quite the same way.

The drift brings to mind Walter Benjamin's famous claim that in a translation, content adheres only loosely to language, like the "ample folds of a royal robe." What makes us experience language and meaning as tightly bound together in the original—like "a fruit and its skin," in Benjamin's image—is, I think, precisely what is nonlinguistic about how we "mean" anything at all.[53] Our capacity to be meaningful *and* to be heard is conditioned by what we can presume about the terms in which our utterance might become intelligible to another. The subtle differences that emerge among the translations suggest that this dimension of language— what we presume we can presume on—has a tendency to become ill fitting (or, following Benjamin, more capacious) in translation.

A text's public is not a function of books nor even of readers, but rather of being presumable and reflexive—of being able to presume both that readers exist and that they will identify themselves as your addressees.[54] Through small but significant shifts, Dieng and Fal's Wolof translation introduces what the original French and the English version seem not to include—a sense that the projected reading public imagined in this passage is, indeed, a *projection* and not an inherent, almost magical feature of books themselves.[55]

But perhaps here my comparison risks flattening the complexities of the original passage. While one could indeed read this praise of books as a moment in which the novel sketches its own field of circulation, we ought to recall that Ramatoulaye's text is not included in the public sphere described here. The series of letters that form the novel are not self-described as literature, nor are they even sent within the text itself. Instead, Ramatoulaye concludes her *Letter* with a promise to hand deliver the manuscript to Aïssatou the next day. While Ramatoulaye's paean to books clearly celebrates the transformative social power of a reading public, we ought to recall that within its own narrative frame, this is a text that has not (yet) circulated.

Bâ presents Ramatoulaye's letter as something intended for but *not yet* offered to a public. With this paradox in mind, the drift that the Wolof translation registers appears not to be an intervention on the translators' part at all but rather an echo of a mode of address that already saturates the original work. Working through Dieng and Fal's translation, then, we see the internal complexity of *Letter*'s address. The novel seems to oscillate between an idealization of a reading public on the one hand and a deep concern that the terms in which one might address such a public *and be heard* are all already predetermined. If we read Mariama Bâ only in English—as is sometimes the case—we risk missing this aspect of her poetics entirely. Reading *Letter* back through its Wolof translation corrects this tendency but not by recovering a more relevant "local" interpretation. Instead, it lets us see how each version of the novel projects a public for itself, posing anew the question of its own audience.

For the Public Yet to Come

Long before she translated *Letter*, Maam Yunus Dieng faced a crisis of audience herself, as one of the earliest novelists working in Wolof. Dieng could not take for granted widespread literacy in the recently standardized orthography when she composed her 1992 novel *Aawo bi* (*The First Wife*).[56] Like Mariama Bâ, Dieng was worried about how she would be read, but she was equally concerned with being read at all. Dieng responded to this crisis in part by appropriating and transforming aspects of Bâ's *Letter*.[57]

Dieng's novel is, in its own way, also a translation of *Letter*, but the case for reading *Aawo bi* as a response to Bâ requires a short explanation. On the face of it, the plot seems suggestive of a connection. The novel follows the story of Ndeela Diop in her marriage and charts her survival of her in-laws' awful treatment of her. Ndeela perseveres through their abuse and is relieved when her husband takes a second wife—with whom she forges a lifelong friendship. In the face of all the scorn and abuse her in-laws heap on her, Ndeela refuses to be driven away and indeed defies her tormenters by enacting the conduct of a virtuous wife in the face of their harassment. The strength of her character is eventually publicly celebrated, and she is rewarded with a plane ticket to Mecca. Ndeela's story is told by Penda (a *géwél*, or a female griot/griotte)[58] to another listening woman, Fama, whose hair she is braiding. The novel by and large conserves this conversational frame.[59]

From this story arc alone, it would be easy to identify Dieng as a rural defender of polygamy, as opposed to Bâ, its urban opponent. But just as it was inadequate to read Bâ only as a critic of tradition and custom, such a reading of *Aawo bi* would be equally reductive and lead to a superficial account of Dieng's dialogue with Bâ. Both of these novels are certainly intertwined with polemics about family form and feminism that took place in Senegal in the 1970s and 1980s (and continue to this day). But Dieng's work, like Bâ's, is not reducible to a statement for or against any one institution.

If we look beyond the overlapping subject matter, Dieng's *The First Wife* appears as a response to Bâ's *Letter* in a rather more subtle way: both novels are concerned with how a particular narrative practice makes possible a certain formation of the self. Dieng takes up the central conceit of *So Long a Letter*, namely, that the novel's main narrative device is also a form self-making. But rather than letter writing, Dieng works through another narrative practice. In *Aawo bi*, the virtuous conduct of the main character Ndeela is "inscribed" in praise by the *géwél*-narrator, Penda, who verbally composes the story for the woman whose hair she is braiding. Just as in *Letter*, one woman's story is passed along to another, but in *Aawo bi*, letter writing has been replaced with the voice of the *géwél*. Ndeela's self is "written" here through her being spoken about by someone else.

Aawo bi is structured as a conversation between Penda the *géwél* and the woman whose hair she is braiding. As one might expect of a *géwél* narrator, Penda makes a strong claim to her own narrative authority: "Man maa teewee cocc ba coset, dara umpu ma ci; déglul tey ma wax la fi Ndeela jaar ba agsi fii." (I was there from beginning to end, nothing in this escaped me; listen, today I'll tell you what Ndeela went through to get here.)[60] But Penda's narrative frequently stretches beyond this frame and includes scenes for which she was clearly not present. Thus *Aawo bi* resembles a conversation between two women without quite limiting itself to this format, much as *Letter* presents itself as a letter to be exchanged between two women, while still taking license to bend the story toward literary conventions. But unlike Ramatoulaye in *Letter*, Penda does not focus on the thoughts and sentiments of the main characters in her story. Instead, her narrative is centered on their deeds—both virtuous and blameworthy.

In Dieng's reply novel, the self-writing that takes place is the protagonist's enactment of a certain ideal of virtuous conduct, which then makes her quotable by the storyteller. Ndeela "authors" a public persona for herself. Ndeela is a *géer*, a noble or non-casted person, and thus a subject to whom public praise can accrue. She "writes" the story of her self by enacting ideals of feminine virtue in a way that is legible and can be circulated for others. But someone else (the *géwél*) must do the "writing." This is done toward the end of realizing a very different ideal of subjectivity than the one we encountered in *Letter*.

If the focus of Bâ's novel is Ramatoulaye's interior space of sentiment, reason, and agency, in Dieng it is her heroine's *jikko* (character/nature/*comportement*) that takes center stage. The valances of this particular term of Wolof ethical vocabulary are difficult to render into English, but Jean-Leopold Diouf's standard Wolof dictionary translates *jikko* as a person's "character" or "nature."[61] Detailing and recognizing the exemplary qualities of Ndeela's *jikko* is the principal aim of Penda's narrative: "Wallaay jikkoo jeet wurus la." (By god! Her *jikko* is also gold.)[62] And indeed, the voice of the *géwél* is particularly well suited to this task, since one historic function of a *géwél* was to publicly perform the honor and glory of noble subjects and bloodlines, much as one function of a letter is to communicate the intimate thoughts and feelings of an individual subject. The *géwél*'s speech is to Dieng's *Aawo bi* what the epistolary form is to Bâ's *Letter*.

In *Aawo bi*, Ndeela's *jikko* becomes a text, by virtue of its capacity to become object-like, to become quotable. To do this, her *jikko* must bear some resemblance to established expectations of feminine virtue and conduct. To celebrate the virtue of its main character, the novel depends on certain expectations of pious subjectivity and ethical behavior that are neither wholly interior nor exterior to the character herself. It is this tension—between Ndeela's pursuit of virtue and the socially determined categories in which that pursuit is enacted—that generates much of the friction that animates *Aawo bi*. But just as individual interiority in Bâ's *Letter* turns out not to be the intrinsic truth of subjectivity but rather a certain capacity that must be cultivated by the protagonist, so too are the virtues of Ndeela's *jikko* presented not as natural in and of themselves but rather as achievements in process that might in turn inspire others to the cultivation of virtue.[63]

Dieng's novel sketches a very different formation of the self, but one that is also enacted through a certain textual practice. Instead of private reading and correspondence, though, we have public praise and public reputation. And just as Ramatoulaye's letter never arrives in the course of the narrative, so too the narrator of *Aawo bi* never actually breaks into the public praise we expect of her as a *géwél*. Instead, Penda's narration is presented as a private conversation between the two women. Both novels absorb genres (letter writing, the *géwél*'s public praise) of self-writing, and yet neither work fully commits to how these genres typically exist for an audience. Much as Bâ wrote an epistolary novel in which letters are not actually exchanged, *Aawo bi* is narrated in the *géwél*'s speech without it ever becoming public praise before an assembled audience.

In the absorption of these genres into novelistic form, a drift of a different order is introduced between the formations of subjectivity these genres of self-making appear to promise and the novelistic use to which they are put. Bâ's *Letter* appears to consolidate an individual self, while the *géwél*'s praise in Dieng's *The First Wife* appears to record the heroine's virtuous nature. And yet both novels withhold the closure promised by their own central narrative devices. In her reply to *Letter*, Dieng echoed and reworked Bâ's distinctive mode of address.

Dieng also responds to Bâ in the preface to *Aawo bi*, where she ruminates on the possibilities and contradictions of writing a novel for an uncertain public. Dieng begins by hailing her reader as a friend and assuring her that, while the task of reading will be difficult at first, "there is nothing in this book that you don't already know":

> Kon, xarit, nanu jëli démb *boolek* tey, yaatal sunu xam-xam, jottali ko sunuy moroom, nu waajal ëllëg. . . . boo jàngee sama Aawo bi ba noppi, daldi may fey, te bu ko waaj. Bindal te bul tiit, bul taxaw; noonu la ñépp tàmbalee. . . . Aywa, jëlal sa xalima nu bind.

> So, friend, let us go and get the past and *join it* with the present, broaden our knowledge, convey it to our peers, and prepare for tomorrow. . . . When you have read my *Aawo bi* through to the end,

now you can repay me, without hesitation. Write without fear, without stopping. This is how everyone begins. . . . Come, take up your pen and let us write.[64] (emphasis mine)

This preface imagines an audience for whom the reading of literature will present some difficulties. But Dieng positions her novel as a gift to her reader, a gift that puts the reader in the author's debt. The repayment Dieng expects is quite extraordinary—she calls on the reader to become a writer in turn. The action of the reading public Dieng envisions is that of bringing the past and the future together, and the verb she chooses is *boole*, which means "to join together, to assemble." An assembly of people or a public, *mboolo mi*, is derived from this same verb, *boole*.

For both Bâ and Dieng, then, books are indeed an "astonishing technology" that permits one to *assemble* a public. And while they are attuned to the transformative possibilities of such assemblies, each writer's work remains askance from any idealization of them. There are no guarantees of where, how, or whether one will be understood. These novels raise the prospect of closure with an intended public—of being heard—even as they suspend it in the realm of potentiality. The as-yet undelivered letter is the figure of this potentiality of address for Mariama Bâ. For Maam Yunus Dieng, it is the author's gift of writing, which the reader is invited to return. In different circumstances and in different ways, both Bâ and Dieng address themselves to publics the shape of which is not given yet.

CHAPTER 7

Aesthetics After Austerity: Boubacar Boris Diop and the Work of Literature in Neoliberal Senegal

Vernacular literary movements are avant-gardes, but the futures that animate them are not static. In 2003, after a career of writing in French, the contemporary Senegalese writer Boubacar Boris Diop published his first literary text in Wolof, a lengthy and ambitious prose work entitled *Doomi Golo* (*The Monkey's Offspring*). Diop has since been asked many times to justify his decision. Why, he is asked, would he want to write in Wolof, given the supposed lack of an audience for literature in that language? "The history of all human literatures," he once replied, "shows that it is always the texts that precede the public and not the reverse—sometimes by several centuries."[1] Struggling with how to write for a public that is yet to come has been a common thread in the writers I have studied so far, from Ousmane Sembène to Mariama Bâ to Maam Yunus Dieng. But Diop's reply greatly expands the temporal frame. In the 1960s and 1970s, there was a feeling that a public for vernacular literatures might take decades to emerge. But Diop now suggests that it may take *centuries*. How did this happen?

Since the 1980s in Senegal, there have been dramatic shifts in the politics of language. It has become more difficult for vernacular writers to summon the sense of imminent institutional transformations that sustained them in the first few decades of decolonization. This stems in part from the neoliberal restructuring of Senegal's economy in the 1980s and 1990s. Around 1980, Senegal became one of the first countries forced to accept a series of "structural adjustment" loans from the International Monetary Fund (IMF) and the World Bank, in an attempt to balance its disastrous debt-to-GDP ratio. As with the austerity policies of today, these loans were contingent on a variety of economic restructuring measures. But instead of stabilizing Senegal's debt, structural adjustment had the opposite effect—sovereign debt increased, inequality spiked, economic growth slowed, and the government was obliged to withdraw from many of its developmental and cultural functions.[2]

Any discussion of neoliberalism at this point is likely to be overdetermined, and we can wonder about the continued usefulness of a single term to designate varied forces, rationalities, and policies.[3] My own working definition in this chapter will be more narrowly focused on the legacies of structural adjustment policies. In Senegal after 1980, a period of deregulation, privatization, and economic disembedding of the state had significant repercussions on the cultural field. For the politics of language, three transformations in particular stand out: first, structural adjustment changed the nature of the relationship between the state and culture; second, it shifted the framework of mass literacy campaigns away from a vocabulary of decolonization and toward NGO-administered development; and third, it curtailed some of the most extreme attempts by the state to control language use and created space for the rise of private media, many of which were Wolof speaking. All these developments together have exercised a profound influence on the kinds of audiences that vernacular literary movements can envision and their relationship to time.

As I explored in Chapter 4, during the first twenty years of its independence, the Senegalese state was an active player in cultural politics. When writers and filmmakers such as Sembène and Cheikh Aliou Ndao began to work in Wolof, they were doing so partly to contest the state's stringently francophone policies and its aspirations to cultural hegemony. But in the age of austerity that began in the 1980s, the state was obliged to partially retreat from the cultural domain and abandon many of its attempts to dictate the terms of linguistic and cultural politics. This turned out not to be a victory for intellectuals who wished to promote literary production in Wolof and other African languages, since the state was less willing and able to engage in the kinds of institutional transformations that activists had long seen as necessary to intellectual decolonization—the promotion of mass literacy, changes to the largely francophone educational system, and so on. Mass literacy projects were gradually ceded to NGOs. As the Senegalese state retreated from cultural politics and literacy promotion, the horizon of political action in which vernacular literatures were embedded shifted as well. With the state no longer a credible addressee of linguistic politics, many writers and filmmakers who had advocated turning to Wolof had to reimagine the future of their projects. Since structural adjustment, writers working in vernaculars have been faced with a dilemma: What *now*? What happens to the oppositional stance of African-language literatures after the heyday of state-centered cultural nationalism?

Tracking once more between literary texts and the futures they envision for themselves, this chapter examines how literary imaginaries have been transformed in this neoliberal era. I begin by situating the new politics of language that has emerged in Senegal since structural adjustment in a comparative perspective. Here I focus on whether Pascale Casanova's influential framework for understanding vernacular literary movements can account for Senegal's age of austerity. To test Casanova's claim that all modern vernacular revivals are essentially nationalist and modeled after the German Romantics, I compare two works of Wolof literary activism from before and after 1980—Pathé Diagne's anthology of world literature in Wolof and Cheikh Aliou Ndao's Wolof aesthetics. I chart how the publics these authors picture for themselves have changed, an evolution that I argue throws into question Casanova's assertion of the fundamental equivalence of all literary language politics.

This chapter concludes with an extended reading of the many iterations of Boubacar Boris Diop's *Doomi Golo* project. After the text first appeared in 2003 in Wolof, Diop went on to adapt it into French, resulting in a 2009 novel entitled *Les Petits de la guenon*. In addition to the two printed novels, Diop also recorded an audio version of the Wolof text that was broadcast weekly on the radio in and around Dakar in the fall of 2014. I trace *Doomi Golo*'s movements across languages and media to explore how this mutating project engages with the new temporal horizon of audience for vernacular language literatures. My argument is that *Doomi Golo* is an ongoing experiment with the poesis, or creation, of audience, an attempt to develop new strategies that can satirize, query, and critique the precarious work of vernacular literatures in neoliberal Senegal. My reading of *Doomi Golo* also unfolds into a reflection on the possibilities and challenges that scholars face as they compare vernacular literary movements across time and space.

The Senegalese case has broad implications for thinking about the fate of aesthetics after austerity more globally. The loans imposed on African nations in the 1980s are in many ways the prototype of the politics of austerity in the Global North. If, as Jean and John Comaroff have argued, Euro-America and the Global South are entangled in the same world-historical processes, it is now the South that tends to feel the effects of these processes first.[4] If this is so, then the ways in which Senegalese writers such as Diop have engaged with structural adjustment can be a bellwether for the possible futures of literature, vernacular and otherwise, under neoliberal economic conditions. In addition to raising far-reaching questions about transformations of artistic labor in our current global moment, the Senegalese case shows how a situation of crisis may also unfold novel aesthetic engagements and new possibilities of critique.

Revisiting the Herder Effect

Although the idea of a writer waiting centuries for their public seems dire, Diop was clearly right to suggest that this situation is not uncommon. Global literary history is full of texts and writers preceding the publics they want to address. This occurs often when the dominant language of literary expression does not align with the languages of everyday life. In *The World Republic of Letters*, Pascale Casanova argues that a single mode of nationalist linguistic politics has been the rule in global literary culture since the late eighteenth century. She traces this strategy back to Johann Herder's attempt to revitalize German. In her account, Herder and the German Romantics crafted a novel and influential response to a situation of linguistic domination: namely, a politics of language in which writers, linguists, and anthologists seek to revitalize and institutionalize a vernacular by returning to its folk sources in order to then transform it into a recognized language of literary expression. In such a nationalist iteration of language politics, the people become the source of literary inspiration, and language is the means through which the people are accessed and imagined. So to study the vernacular and to recover it as a source of literature becomes by extension a way to care for, preserve, and (eventually) modernize the people and the nation.[5]

According to Casanova, the "Herder Effect" has been the dominant strategy by which authors who work in vernacular languages stake a claim on cultural autonomy and literary recognition. In her account, the linguistic activism of the German Romantics became the prototype that continues to organize every single instance of literary language politics since the nineteenth century. Casanova writes that the wave of vernacular movements that erupted in the twentieth century during the period of decolonization were in a sense "que la continuation et l'extension de la révolution herderienne: les nouvelles nations indépendantes, *obéissant aux mêmes mécanismes politico-culturels*, vont, elles aussi, formuler des revendications linguistiques, culturelles et littéraires" (only the continuation and extension of the revolution inaugurated by Herder: the newly independent nations of Africa, Asia and Latin America, *obeying the same political and cultural mechanisms*, moved to assert linguistic and literary claims of their own) (emphasis mine).[6] Casanova expresses this relationship of sameness in a variety of ways. Postcolonial vernacular movements are said to be "dans la continuité" (of a piece with) the linguistic nationalism of the European nineteenth century. The Herderian revolution "se poursuit" (carries on) in new forms in the literatures that emerge from decolonization, whose writers are said to be acting according to "la même logique" (the same logic) and to have begun "le même processus" (the same process). The postcolonial language question—especially in Africa—is also supposed to operate "dans des termes très semblables" (in very similar terms) to its nineteenth-century European predecessor.[7] Taking Herder as a template allows Casanova to construct an analytical framework for language politics that is stunning in its reach and scope. This understanding of vernacular revivals as fundamentally transferable also plays an important role in supporting the picture she gives of a world republic of letters. If we conclude that language politics have indeed remained the same since Herder, then it becomes possible to treat every attempt at a vernacular literary revolution as equivalent—a unique but at the same time entirely comparable occurrence that works to both produce and suture the literatures of new nations into world literary space.

But can this model explain literary language politics so globally and so completely? Part of what makes a model desirable in this case is that many scholars would readily acknowledge that a demonstrable affinity exists between modern projects to revitalize a vernacular, with writers as far flung as Brazil, Ireland, India, and Kenya seeming to make the same moves. But to call such affinities the result of one and the same mechanism is to overlook crucial questions: What is it that allows a vernacular literary movement to emerge in nationalist terms in the first place? And what happens to such a movement when these conditions are no longer present?

The Herder Effect depends on a certain horizon of futurity, in which a vernacular literary movement can project outward its own realization and imagine a kind of closure with a future public. Whether this public is the people, the nation, or some other collectivity, this distant-but-attainable figure is what animates the model. In other words, a nationalist politics of language always involves a politics of temporality, a struggle over possible futures. The sought-after tightness of fit between literary production and a future readership works as a kind of regulative ideal, generating further energy and investment toward its realization even if closure with this future public appears to be far off. Without this temporal framework of projection and longing, there is no Herder "mechanism" to speak of.

Such an imminent future was indeed broadly imaginable around 1960, when a wave of decolonizations took the mold of national independence. The trajectory of national sovereignty, combined with the diffusion of print capitalism studied by Anderson and others, helps account for the affinity that Casanova rightly detects between the postcolonial language issue of the 1960s and that of the European nineteenth century. But in the decades since midcentury, the modes of time-reckoning that once sustained nationalist narratives of linguistic politics have become increasingly difficult to conjure or sustain. Here I am interested in interrogating how "the decline of the near future" in public culture has scrambled the coordinates that once sustained the Herder Effect.[8] My argument is that there has been a collapse in the horizon of possible futures for vernacular nationalisms, and instead of the palpable, future-oriented linearity of national culture that flickered once more at decolonization, contemporary vernacular writers and activists are increasingly faced with a more uncertain temporality. While nationalism is clearly again on the rise across the globe, the Herder Effect is not what it used to be.

The experience of vernacular literary movements in Senegal in recent decades helps illustrate these larger claims. The climate that once animated Senegal's contentious language politics has changed dramatically. Although there is something arbitrary about any periodization, 1980 may be seen as the pivotal year for several reasons. First, Senegal accepted the first of a series of loans from the IMF and the World Bank that inaugurated decades of economic and social turbulence. As the "adjusted" Senegalese state withdrew from cultural politics and ceded mass literacy programs to NGO-organized private/public partnerships, the imaginable publics of African-language literatures began to be transformed. Since 1980, it has been less and less possible, even for the most ardent activist, to envision a tight fit between literary work in vernacular languages and a reading public that is imminently on its way, at least not in the same way that it once was during the heady early decades of independence. As Mamadou Diouf

and Rosalind Fredericks warn, though, we ought to be careful about giving neoliberalism an internal coherence and an analytic privilege that it
may not warrant.[9] So to characterize the post-1980 cultural landscape, it is
imperative to also take note of the other important shifts of the last few
decades that have changed the terrain of vernacular literary projects.

In 1980 a second important event occurred: Léopold Sédar Senghor re-
tired after serving as president for twenty years, much of it as the leader of
a one-party state. Senghor's departure coincided with a reconceptualiza-
tion of the role of the state with regard to culture but also more broadly.
Senghor's "African Socialism" had sought to make the state a spearhead of
modernization, but the economic crisis of the 1970s put into question this
providential model.[10] The 1980s and 1990s saw a further diminishment of
the state's field of action, particularly in the realm of culture, as President
Abdou Diouf, Senghor's handpicked successor, broke with the ideology of
negritude as a governing project of knowledge. Although Diouf made no
public declaration of de-Senghorisation, his project of *sursaut national*
(national leap forward) elevated technocratic expertise at the expense of
negritude.[11]

The 1980s and 1990s were also a period of great changes in the nature
and scope of education in Senegal. This period saw a deep crisis for the
formal education system, characterized by campus unrest and student
strikes.[12] The relationship between the state and mass literacy projects
changed as well. The adjusted Senegalese state shifted efforts to promote
mass literacy onto decentralized campaigns that partnered with NGOs and
private providers. Gradually, the discourse around literacy activism shifted
from a vocabulary of decolonization to one of development. As the state
shed direct control over basic literacy campaigns in rural areas, funders
such as the World Bank stepped in. Although the NGO-driven model appears to have generated some successes, the World Bank has also been criticized for promoting an entrepreneurial approach to mass literacy, in
which private literacy providers proliferate and compete with each other
to earn as much as possible, as easily as possible.[13]

The rise of NGO-driven literacy programs also created a new market
for books in African languages, which in turn has had an impact on the
production of literature in these languages. Beginning in the 1990s, literary texts in Wolof began to be published directly for the literacy market.
A key example here is Organisation Sénégalaise d'Appui au Développement
(OSAD), a nonprofit publisher founded by the linguist Arame Fal in the
early 1990s. Part of the impetus behind the founding of OSAD was the

relatively small emphasis placed on literature in basic literacy programs.[14] OSAD's catalogue is illustrative of the ways in which the public for Wolof literature now overlaps with a developmental imaginary—OSAD publishes literary texts by Maam Yunus Dieng and Cheikh Aliou Ndao, as well as more instructional texts on basic hygiene, human rights, the Senegalese constitution, and Ebola. According to Fal, OSAD's print runs are about one thousand copies, many of which are bought by NGOs involved in literacy programs.[15]

Alongside the rise of an NGO-mediated audience for African-language texts, the overall prestige of print culture in Senegal has declined sharply since the 1960s and 1970s. For a variety of reasons, literary discourse (in French and in the national languages) now finds itself in a far less privileged position than it was early on, and the claim of writers to unveil possible aesthetic and political futures has been diminished. Whereas writing and the book exemplified the capacity of a generation of nationalist intellectuals to represent the people, in the contemporary moment there is a "desertion of scriptural space," writes Mamadou Diouf, especially for young people who no longer see the formal educational system as a guarantee of access to bureaucratic careers. It is, of course, not the case that book culture has evaporated in contemporary Senegal, but Diouf argues that urban cultural forms such as hip-hop and *mbalax*, iconography, and fashion have all eclipsed print imaginaries as privileged terrains of self-fashioning, mass mobilization, and political critique.[16]

Writers working in Wolof especially have also found themselves in an increasingly paradoxical situation with regard to their language of expression. Senegal has become ever more Wolof speaking, without being officially Wolof speaking. The Wolofization of the Senegalese public sphere has largely taken place not through the direct action of the state but from below.[17] With the explosion of private radio and television stations, discourse in Wolof is more and more hegemonic but without the advent of a mass reading public in the manner of earlier vernacularizations.

The Senegalese case demonstrates the limitations of taking Herder as a universal model. Instead of confirming that all postcolonial language politics fit within coordinates derived from nineteenth-century European nationalisms, the situation points to a rupture between the possible futures that animated the independence-era literary imaginaries studied in Part II and the stalled futures of the neoliberal present. While nationalist discourses of literary-cultural revitalization do certainly persist in Senegal, the terrain for their realization has been altered. In their place, we find in-

stead a variety of strategies for engaging with the precarity of contemporary literary address.

Vernacular Futures Before 1980:
Pathé Diagne's World Literature Anthology

Pathé Diagne's *Teerebtanu ladab ci wàlàf* (*Anthology of Literature in Wolof*)
captures what a vernacular literary future could look like in Senegal before the era of structural adjustment. The 1971 anthology collects works
by writers of Wolof expression and puts them alongside Wolof translations
of excerpts from a wide variety of authors, from Goethe, Neruda, Sappho,
and Lao Tzu to Claude McKay and Amos Tutuola. Diagne's *Teerebtanu* is
essentially an anthology of world literature in Wolof, anticipating by several decades the recent resurgence of interest in this term. But instead of
a canon of global classics read in English translation, Diagne traces a
vision of world literature that is defiantly vernacular yet still planetary in
its scope.

Diagne's anthology sorts the literatures of the world into an alternate
and Afrocentric mapping of world literary space. This begins with ancient
Egypt and precedes directly into "traditional negro-African literature" (in-
dicating Diagne's allegiance to Cheikh Anta Diop). From there, it seeks to
document and translate the literary heritage of entities that are sometimes
national but also frequently racial or linguistic. These include categories
such as Black America, India, China, Arabic, Turkey, Greco-Latin, Italian, Spanish, Chilean, German, English (including America and England),
and finally Russia.[18] As the linguistic breadth of this project suggests,
Diagne's anthology is itself a reworking of other existing literary anthologies and translations. His Wolof version of *The Palm-Wine Drinkard*, for
example, is translated from Raymond Queneau's French translation of
Tutuola, *L'Ivrogne dans la brousse*.[19]

Diagne freely acknowledges this recombining approach to the anthology form and indeed thematizes it as the work's central purpose. He hopes
the anthology will make known to "wolophones and africophones" classic
texts of both ancient and modern literature that possess "an incontestable
dimension of universality." The result will be an "initiation into the essential techniques and frames through which writers of other epochs, languages and cultures make works of imagination." Diagne's stated goal in
all this is to "transform Wolof and other African idioms into modern languages." But to do this, he believes, the Wolof language needs to "find

echoes in works and creators of every epoch, in order to renew and enlarge its horizons." The anthology "borrows its substance," he says, "from Lingala, from Chinese, from Douala, from French, from Russian or from Greek, indifferently." Only in this way can Wolof speakers realize a literature that is "totally open to the world."[20]

Although this is a Wolof anthology of literature, Diagne's framework does not understand itself as overtly nationalist or ethnically bound.[21] Diagne notes that he has given African literature and Wolof literature in particular a smaller place in the anthology than he might otherwise have done. He hopes that this will break with "nationalist and chauvinist tendencies" that too often characterize literary culture and offer up instead "possibilities of comparison."[22]

So far, so Herder—or so it would seem. Although the anthology offers a provocative vision of a vernacular world literature, we have to admit that its strategies of anthologizing vernacular texts and translating established classics are time-honored approaches to modernizing a literary tradition. The *Teerebtanu* succeeds in provincializing Europe in its alternative vision of world literary space, but it cannot do without the literary equivalencies on which the anthology form depends. However, the *Teerebtanu* may yet help us reveal the shortcomings of an understanding based on the Herder model—not so much through the text's own strategies but rather in the way in which the world has changed around this 1971 volume. Diagne wrote his anthology partly in the hopes of its becoming an institutional text. It emerged out of a seminar at the Institut Fondamental d'Afrique Noire in Dakar on the adaptation of African languages, which studied ways to make vernaculars into languages of modern education and communication. The seminar was a continuation of the long-running but loosely defined movement, studied in Chapters 4 and 5, that aimed to modernize the Wolof language and lay the groundwork for a modern literature. This movement picked up momentum in the 1960s and 1970s, in part because of the resistance it encountered from the Senegalese state under Senghor. In many ways, though, this tumultuous era of language politics now appears as a kind of high water mark of state concern over (or obsession with) vernacular languages.

Forty plus years on, it is difficult to imagine new, statist interventions in language politics and policy on the level of Senghor's decrees. For one thing, the Senegalese state is no longer as invested as it once was in promoting a unified vision of national culture—there is no contemporary equivalent for the role of negritude as the foundation of Senghor's African Socialism. Although widespread literacy in national languages remains a political goal, there is little sense that it will be achieved through direct state action. An organized, statist approach to vernacular literacy was precisely what was being fought over in the 1970s. A large-scale project in which the state promoted education in national languages was the future that Senghor promised his opponents in theory, while postponing it in practice.

There is another reason a statist language politics is difficult to envision today: the Wolofization of the Senegalese public sphere is such that it seems almost quaint that the state once believed it had the power and the imperative to regulate spelling. Wolof written in a romanized script is more ubiquitous than ever, but it is being written in a variety of nonstandard orthographies across a plethora of media, from billboards to text messages to internet comments. The orthography system for Wolof that Arame Fal pioneered in the 1970s is now the official one, but few speakers use it exclusively.

Vernacular Futures After 1980: Cheikh Aliou Ndao's Aesthetic Theory

If Diagne's anthology illustrates the sense of possibility that existed around Wolof literature before 1980, Cheikh Aliou Ndao's 1995 treatise *Taaral ak ladab ci lammiñu wolof* (*Aesthetics and Literature of the Wolof Language*) offers a glimpse of how vernacular imaginaries have shifted after structural adjustment. Like Diagne's anthology, Ndao's treatise is an aesthetic project that doubles as a work of Wolof literary activism. Ndao's text has two functions: first, it is an anthology of Wolof literary expression, albeit in a less structured and formal manner than Diagne's collection. Ndao discusses various oral and written genres, from the aphorisms of Kocc Barma (a Wolof sage of the late sixteenth and early seventeenth centuries) and Wolofal poetry to the *bàkk* performed by wrestlers and the works of contemporary authors. This canon-gathering impulse provides material for the essay's second aim, which is to develop a more general aesthetic theory founded on an account of Wolof poetics in particular.

For Ndao, aesthetics—*taaral*, or "to make beautiful," in his usage—is to be understood as active poetics, as *liggéey* (work) on language. Ndao compares the work of poetics to the way in which a traditional artisan such as the *tëgg*, or smith, labors over a piece of gold. Another comparison he offers to help us understand what he means by aesthetics is that of the Lawbe carving a piece of wood into a sculpture. For Ndao, aestheticized speech is language that has been worked on and transformed. As I understand his argument, this is to differentiate from what he will call *àddu* (communication that is mere sound) from *wax* (speech, and specifically words that have the intention of reaching a listener and being understood). Ndao's aim seems to be to produce a materialist account of poetics as fashioned speech. It is in this respect that the two-part function of Ndao's treatise is important; the essay is both an account of verbal aesthetics in general and a collection and celebration of a specifically Wolof poetics. The two tendencies reinforce each other. Ndao's examples of fashioned speech at its best also tend to be examples of the excellence of Wolof poetics.[23]

Like Diagne's anthology, Ndao's treatise seems to be written for a future classroom. But attempting this in 1995 is not the same as doing so in 1971. Even though discourse in Wolof was more pervasive than ever by the time Ndao was writing, an institutional future for national languages, especially a comprehensive educational future, was already a project that was at risk of receding past the horizon of the imaginable. Ndao invokes this very tension in his conclusion, in which he urges his readers not to give up on the project of formalizing education in Wolof and other national languages:

> Amerikeñ beek Frànse bi ak Sàppone bi ñoo yem xam-xam bu ñu jàng, waaye ku ci nekk bàyyiwoo làmmiñ wi nga nàmp. Kii ci àngle la jaar ba defar Ford mbaa Cadillac. Kee jaar ci frànse ba defar Renault, Sàppone bi yit jaar ciw làmmiñam ba génne Toyota.[24]

> The Americans, the French, and the Japanese are all at the same level of knowledge, yet not one of them turns their back on their mother tongue. One goes through English to make a Ford or Cadillac. Another goes through French to make a Renault, and the Japanese go through their language to put out a Toyota.

Ndao's final turn here feels familiar. Versions of this plea to revitalize the vernacular have been made ever since the German Romantics (and, further back, by Joachim du Bellay): look to other nations not to imitate their works but rather for examples of what can be achieved when a people rededicates itself to its language/culture. Ndao rehearses this move with a crucial difference; the organic imaginary that usually pervades language politics in a Herderian vein has vanished, replaced with a very different vocabulary. Instead of a language-nation-people unity, Ndao makes car manufacturing an example of what can be achieved when a mother tongue (literally here "the language that nurses you" [*làmmiñ wi nga nàmp*]) is harnessed as a technology. This is very much an update on Herder, with the production of cars replacing the production of national culture—a vernacular nationalism that is more Volkswagen than Volk.

Ndao's gesture raises the question of whether literature is now just another complex commodity in a globalized world order, with texts being produced elsewhere for consumption in Senegal and literature that is produced domestically in raw form being exported to be finished elsewhere for other markets. The particular brands Ndao mentions certainly suggest this might be the case. The choice of Ford, Toyota, and Cadillac is not without a certain irony—these brands may still be identified with particular nations, but they are all now multinational corporations, and even Renault was privatized in 1996. In other words, the cars that bear the labels of Ford, Toyota, Cadillac, and Renault are no longer the work of any individual nation. Ndao began his *Taaral* by comparing Wolof poetics to artisanal, casted labor, but the example that he concludes with ends up illustrating a certain anachronism in fetishizing that earlier conception of work as a model of poetics.

Cadillacs and Toyotas raise a tough question: Has it become every bit as difficult to envision a thriving, mass public for African-language literature in Senegal as it is to imagine a domestically built and nationalized auto industry? Ndao's shift from the work of the smith to the multinational automobile points to what James Ferguson has called the difficulty of constructing "national culture and nationalist discourses of legitimation under conditions of neoliberalism."[25] Ferguson's claim is not that neoliberalism has done away with nationalism (it has not), but rather that the cultural nationalism that flourished in many newly independent nations in the 1960s and 1970s has become increasingly hollowed out. Cultural nationalist discourses persist under neoliberal conditions, even as the means toward their realization become scattered. In the wake of austerity, it becomes difficult to see literature as a privileged means of assembling and addressing the nation, if indeed it ever was.

Diagne's *Teerebtanu* and Ndao's *Taaral* are both plans for preserving and institutionalizing Wolof literature, one in the form of a world literature anthology and the other through a theory of Wolof poetics. These works are not narrowly nationalist, but they both share a drive to study, categorize, preserve, and thereby revitalize Wolof as a literary language. They seem intended for a future classroom, and yet neither text has come to be widely adopted in schools—to the best of my knowledge—nor does this seem likely at this time. Both texts are, in a sense, artifacts of a time when the institutional changes they envisioned seemed closer at hand. Since 1980 it has become more difficult to conceive of the near-term realization of many of the large-scale projects that were dreamed of by vernacular writers and activists like Diagne and Ndao in the 1960s and 1970s. As David

Scott argues, the sense of the post-socialist, neoliberal present as time stalled is a pervasive one.[26]

But another interpretation of vernacular writing after 1980 is also possible. Despite structural adjustment's apparent foreclosure of certain possibilities, neither the language question nor vernacular language writing have been extinguished. The revolution that the language debates anticipated has apparently failed to appear, but how we think about this situation depends on our understanding of time. If we locate vernacular writing within a linear notion of time, then the present conjuncture appears as stasis, even crisis. But if we think of time in a less unidirectional fashion, noticing its fluidity and its fractures, then we start to see how an apparent failure in the past can also become a source of inspiration and investment for contemporary writers. Jennifer Wenzel's work on the afterlives of unsuccessful anticolonial struggles invites us to rethink "failed resistance," in order to recognize how an ostensible failure in the past can still generate new conditions of possibility. In the case of the language question in Senegal after structural adjustment, we can recast Wenzel's intervention to ask how the politics of language survives its apparent failure to produce the kind of decolonization that it had hoped for, only to live on as a source of aspiration for later writers.[27] This is precisely the kind of untimely temporality that seems to animate Boubacar Boris Diop's *Doomi Golo* project.

Boubacar Boris Diop's Doomi Golo

Boubacar Boris Diop was exploring the anxieties of audience well before he began publishing in Wolof. His 1997 novel *Le Cavalier et son ombre* (*The Knight and His Shadow*) features a character called Khadidja, who faces a particularly evocative crisis of audience. Khadidja is hired to be a storyteller but made to tell her stories to an open but darkened doorway. Every night, Khadidja narrates fictions for a listener whom she cannot see and who may not actually exist. Since she cannot see her interlocutor, she invents one, picturing her invisible listener as a young child and envisioning an entire life for him. Here we see Khadidja trying to initiate the exchange that traditionally signals the opening to a *léeb*, or tale.

> Quand elle lança: "*Leebòòn*," seul lui répondit le silence. Au bout de quelques secondes, elle répéta le mot "*Leebòòn*" et le silence lui parut encore plus lourd. Elle fut prise de peur en s'apercevant qu'elle était condamnée à être à la fois la conteuse et le public. Elle commença à délirer un peu, contrefaisant sa propre voix pour répondre aux ques-

tions qu'elle se posait à elle-même . . . Elle n'obtint jamais le moindre écho et cela finit par la mettre dans une rage folle contre la personne qui se trouvait de l'autre côté de la porte. Mais sa colère ressemblait beaucoup à du dépit amoureux.[28]

"*Leebòòn*," she began. But only the silence replied to her. After several seconds, she repeated the word—*leebòòn*—and the silence seemed even heavier than before. Fear seized her as she realized that she was condemned to be both the storyteller and the public. She started to babble, disguising her own voice in order to reply to the questions she herself was asking. . . . There was never the slightest echo. This ended up putting her in a mad rage against the person who was on the other side of the door. But her anger very much resembled unrequited love.

As I discussed in Chapter 1, the call of *leebòòn* and the reply of *lëpoon* constitutes the storyteller and the audience into their respective roles and frames the coming narrative as a tale. But Khadidja's *leebòòn* meets only with stony silence. She therefore has to play both parts. Inventing a missing call-and-response structure becomes part of the work of fiction itself. But in *The Knight and His Shadow*, Khadidja's approach to her missing audience eventually contributes to driving her mad. This seemingly unbridgeable distance between storyteller and audience resonates with many of the uncertain publics that I have traced so far. Eileen Julien observes that Khadidja's dilemma might be read as a representation of Diop's own position as an author working in a former colonial language.[29] Although *The Knight* was already Diop's fourth novel in French, he was publicly questioning his use of that language. In a 2001 interview, Diop declared, "No writer, whether African, American, or Australian, knows anything of his public. But it's even worse for an author like me: I write in a language my public doesn't understand, putting out books that my public can't afford to buy." In the same conversation, he referred to French merely as his "instrument."[30] In the six years after *The Knight*, Diop underwent a period of "self-exile," temporarily abandoning francophone literature to go in search of an "uncertain public" of a different kind.[31]

Diop's return took the form of the 2003 text *Doomi Golo* (*The Monkey's Offspring*), his first in Wolof. *Doomi Golo* is a sprawling prose work whose main narrative frequently splinters into a dazzling array of subplots, digressions into local history, references to oral traditions, and even dreams and hallucinations. The central narrative, if indeed there is only one, recounts the story of the Senegalese town of Ñarelaa alongside the life of the text's octogenarian narrator, Ngiraan Faay. Ngiraan is writing the novel in a series of notebooks for his grandson Badu, who has emigrated and lost touch. *Doomi Golo* is expansive, challenging fiction, a narrative stretched to the breaking point of coherence as it strains to incorporate a panoply of stories. Diop waited a further six years before adapting *Doomi Golo* into French, resulting in 2009's *Les Petits de la guenon*. The French version can be quite different; it amplifies certain sections and adds glosses to others, and the two versions have distinct narrative styles. At the same time, the central narratives and characters are consistent across versions, and even many of the departures from the main story are also broadly similar.[32] In addition to these two printed texts, Diop recorded an audio version of the Wolof text that became a weekly radio broadcast in Dakar in 2014.

Doomi Golo is a work that exists in several iterations—it began its "life" as a Wolof text but has since been rewritten in French and remade as radio broadcasts. In the pages that follow, I explore the project's trajectories across versions and languages. I argue that Diop's *Doomi Golo* project challenges our expectations of vernacular literatures in at least three ways. First, instead of a commitment to anthologizing and preserving earlier vernacular traditions, the project distorts and reshapes these in surprising ways. Second, instead of vernacular literature attempting to call forth and give rise to "the people," this project addresses itself to an absent reader, a distant and virtual audience whom the text invites into a disorienting process of mutual invention. And third, the *Doomi Golo* project generates a profound meditation on the practice of comparison itself. It produces a theory of nonreflective semblance and invites the reader to consider it as a principle of literary relation. In these three ways, the project upends any sense that vernacular literary movements are fundamentally equivalent across space and time. I examine these three dynamics successively, before turning to the *Doomi Golo* project's afterlife.

Doomi Golo 1: The Folk Anthology in Ruins

In both the French and Wolof versions of Diop's text, the first few pages signal that the coming narrative will have a complex relationship to Wolof literary tradition. The works' narrator, Ngiraan, begins by reflecting on what led him to write a series of notebooks for Badu, his absent grandson. In these musings, Ngiraan situates his own writing with regard to earlier Wolof authors, mentioning by name the poet Musaa Ka as well as Cheikh Aliou Ndao. But instead of this being a self-glorifying gesture, Ngiraan's invocation of these precursors serves to indicate the great inferiority of his own efforts.[33] Rather than counting himself in the company of these great writers who have, Ngiraan says, touched the soul of the people, he explains that he is merely an amateur, an old man scribbling away as his health is failing. Ngiraan cautions Badu not to expect great literature from these notebooks. Instead, Ngiraan warns Badu that the notebooks will confront him with great obscurity and difficult enigmas, but if he can persist through these, he may yet discover lessons that will be useful to him.

Both versions deliver amply on this early warning of density and chaos. In both *Doomi Golo* and *Les Petits*, stories pile up, reality is difficult to distinguish from dreams, and scenes of everyday life threaten to crowd the central narrative out of the frame. In the Wolof version, as Cullen Goldblatt shows, the text figures its own obscurity as a kind of darkness, or *lëndëm*. Ngiraan memorably describes his fictions for Badu as "léeb yu lëndëm" (obscure stories). Goldblatt convincingly argues that the Wolof version privileges a mode of reading that is like *lëndëmtu*—groping along in the dark or moving through what one cannot see.[34] The French version confronts the reader with opacity in different ways. Early on in *Les Petits*, Ngiraan warns Badu that, because of his inexperience as a writer, he has allowed his notebooks to be overtaken by other stories that demanded to be told. He describes these stories as banging on his door and trying to jump over the borders of his notebooks. Ngiraan acknowledges that these other stories have worn him down and that he has let them have the last word.[35]

The many stories that push their way into the pages of Ngiraan's notebooks include a variety of Wolof speech genres and written accounts thereof. For example, Ngiraan quotes one of the four maxims attributed to the Wolof sage Kocc Barma, "Mag mat naa bayyi cim réew." We might translate this as "elders are valuable to a community" or, more figuratively in *Les Petits*, "Malheur au peuple qui ne sait plus écouter ses vieillards."[36] This is one of the most recognizable proverbs for many Wolof speakers and is often understood to evoke the importance of the presence of older generations to the health of a community. But the narrators of Diop's text suggest a couple of revisions that question who or what ought to be valuable to a body politic: "Gone mat naa bâyyi cim réew" and "Dof mat naa bàyyi cim réew."[37] (Respectively, children and the insane should be valuable to the community.) Rather than being dismissive of the proverb, Diop's narrators seem ambivalent; they carefully announce their veneration of Kocc Barma, even as they recast his vision of political community. Similar reworkings of Wolof discursive traditions abound in these texts, which include rewritings of episodes from oral tradition, interpolations of the poetry of the Wolofal writer Musaa Ka, and snatches of *bàkk*.[38]

In the emerging commentary around *Doomi Golo*, there are two kinds of interpretations of its dense intertextuality with Wolof oral and written traditions. The first interpretation argues that these incorporations serve a restorative, preservationist function. Critics who read the novel in this way claim that the rewritings and references anchor the novel in Wolof tradition, preserve elements of Wolof culture for future generations, or establish Diop's bona fides as a vernacular literary activist.[39] Other scholars point out that Diop's incorporations seem not to be preserving tradition so much as rewriting it—these texts swallow up proverbs, stories, and historical narratives only to reinvent and critique them. For this second interpretation, *Doomi Golo* and *Les Petits* inaugurate a new kind of literary project in Wolof that lays the foundations of a different aesthetic posture toward tradition.[40]

My own reading tacks between these two positions, both of which are useful but insufficient. Diop's work clearly participates in the long history of Senegalese literary works absorbing earlier traditions in text and performance, and there is an undeniable canon-building impulse to this project. But Diop's texts also seem to unsettle their own capacity to ventriloquize a literary past and often put their own privileged power of "literarization" into question. But is such a revisionist strategy really a radically new departure in Senegalese or African literature? If we situate Diop's practice in a longer history of authorship, translation, and collection that stretches back at least to the colonial period, then his approach to the literary past seems not quite so novel. Practices of collecting and rewriting proverbs and other performance and scriptural genres were a near-constant feature of West African print cultures throughout the twentieth century, from the colonial classroom to African-run newspapers and magazines. What is distinctive about Diop's project is its heightened degree of self-reflexivity toward its own place in an unfolding literary history. This is a text that seems acutely self-conscious that a vernacular writer often faces a kind of imperative to collect and document a vernacular literary past. Diop's project remains committed to honoring that imperative and engaging with earlier performance and scriptural traditions, but it also seems not to be entirely at ease with its own capacity to answer that call. Instead of preserving a literary past, these texts relativize theirs without ever dismissing the seriousness of their own responsibilities.

The *Doomi Golo/Les Petits* project does read as an effort toward a vernacular literary revival but not in the same manner as either Diagne's anthology or Ndao's aesthetics. While there is no question that Diop himself is a vocal promoter of vernacular languages, *Doomi Golo* is not a work of

Wolof literary activism in any kind of self-evident or transparent way. But nor is it a completely radical departure that abandons the attachments that animated earlier iterations of vernacular activism in Wolof. In *Doomi Golo/ Les Petits*, the transformation of earlier traditions into literary ones is oriented toward visibly distorting and finally reinventing them. But this is done alongside a slightly melancholy refusal to transcend the attachments of earlier generations. The imperative to collect and produce a literary past persists but in an almost ghostly manner.

Doomi Golo 2: Haunted by an Audience

Far from resolving the question of audience that hovered over Diop's francophone fiction, the turn to Wolof appears to have amplified it. But *Doomi Golo/Les Petits* organizes its own separation from its audience in rather surprising ways. The occasion for Ngiraan's taking up a pen is the absence of his emigrated grandson, Badu. The narrative springs from a grandfather's desire to pass something along to a grandson he does not really know anymore and is not sure he can even reach. Although Ngiraan does not know where Badu is or whether he is even alive, he fervently hopes for Badu's return while correctly suspecting that he himself will not live to see it. Badu's return does not occur within the texts' frame, and yet the notebooks are intended only for Badu—not for the community and not for "the people"—only for the one who has left, to recount the past and capture what has become of the community in his absence.[41] The narrative takes its very shape from the ghostly figure of Badu, the transnational migrant.

Ngiraan's writing for the absent Badu has echoes of other virtual interlocutors, from Sembène's epigraph to *The Black Docker* to the structure of address in Mariama Bâ's *So Long a Letter*.[42] But the nature of Badu's absence is quite different from these earlier absent readers or listeners. In Bâ's novel, a friendship between two women of the same generation forms the basis of the work—even if Ramatoulaye's address must cross a distance, the novel concludes with a promise that the narrative will be delivered "tomorrow." Sembène's dedication of his first novel to his illiterate mother also imagines some form of definite, imminent closure in the way that the mother may "run her hands" across the pages. But in Diop's story, the distance between Ngiraan and Badu is far greater and approaches the absolute. Badu is *gone* in this narrative—remembered but gone—and while the possibility of his coming back is the occasion for the story, such a return is conjectural to the point of vanishing into the realm of the hypothetical.

And yet both *Doomi Golo* and *Les Petits* do conclude with a promise of closure with a future reader, but the nature of this promise is extraordinary. The occasion for it is the narrator's own funeral. By the end of the text, Ngiraan has succumbed to an illness, and the storytelling duties and custody of the notebooks have been passed on to the madman Aali Këbóoy (Ali Kaboye, in the French version), who narrates the final quarter of the book. It is Aali who promises that the notebooks will someday reach Badu, no matter how long it takes:

> Soo nibbisee fii ak juróom-ñetti xarnu it, dinga ma fi fekk, man Aali Këbóoy, ma lay xaar.

> Even if you return seven generations from now, you will find me here: me, Aali Këbóoy, I am waiting for you.

> Peu importe l'année où tu reviendras: moi, Aali Këbóoy, je serai toujours là à t'attendre et je te remettrai les mots patiemment écrits pour toi par ton grand-père.

> It does not matter the year you return: I, Aali Këbóoy, I will be always there waiting for you, and I will give you the words patiently written by your grandfather for you.[43]

The texts imagine closure with a future reader here, but this is a promise that can exist only within the strange temporality of the character of Aali Këbóoy. Aali is both a local madman and a kind of supernatural being who seems to exist out of time. He appears to be murdered during the portion of the book that Ngiraan narrates, only to somehow return. In the sections of the book that Aali narrates after Ngiraan's death, he is a ghostly figure who wanders with the reader widely across time and space. Whatever Aali's nature is in these texts, his relationship with temporality is clearly unique. It is only Aali who can make the texts' final promise to Badu. The closure that the texts envision with their intended reader extends the temporality of textual reception so far that it seems to approach something like the vanishing point of a horizon. There is no guarantee of Badu's return, but Aali declares that he will be waiting to deliver the notebooks, no matter how long it takes. The responsibility that Aali assumes is truly vast: his promise is impossible within the confines of any familiar, linear conception of time. In French, Aali says it makes no difference the year Badu returns; the Wolof is even more elliptical, as he declares that he will wait seven ages or generations. In either case, the promise is made both to Badu and not to Badu—since one mortal being cannot promise another that a period of waiting can be indefinite. Aali's responsibility is to a future reader of these notebooks, but it is a responsibility that extends beyond life and death, beyond any human scale of time and connection. It is a responsibility to the one who is both no longer and not yet here, made in the understanding that this return may take a form that we cannot yet imagine.

Aali's impossible and yet necessary promise to Badu captures something of Diop's own sense that his text may have to wait "centuries" for its public. But rather than thinking of this promise to Badu as a tidy allegory of Diop's own situation, we can more productively think of the promise as a point at which the *Doomi Golo/Les Petits* texts collide with the limits of their own address and then recoil backward into themselves, figuring their own grasping for an audience within the work of fiction itself. If Pathé Diagne's and Cheikh Aliou Ndao's anthologies were addressed to a classroom that has yet to adopt them, Ngiraan's notebooks in *Doomi Golo/Les Petits* offer themselves up for a more elusive public, whose creation seems to become part of the work of fiction itself.

Doomi Golo 3: Reflection and Comparison

The *Doomi Golo/Les Petits* project layers stories upon stories, encrusts them with riddles, and burrows these amid songs, histories, and allegories. The form of these texts is karstic—there are unexpected fissures in the works' texture where the central narrative collapses, allowing other tales, genres, and forms to flow into the hollows and find expression there. This makes for a disorienting reading experience, made all the more so because these many tributaries seem often to flow into one another. Tropes, phrases, even styles that appear in one section often recur in a slightly different way "later" in the work. This creates a challenge for the reader: how does one approach these texts when their many pieces are constantly collapsing into and refracting each other? Instead of isolating individual elements, the project invites us to engage with its own shifting form—to notice something about the ways it patterns the many elements it absorbs, the ways in which its many pieces seem to interlock and rhyme.

One way of understanding this patterning is through a figure that is dear to *Doomi Golo/Les Petits*: the mirror. Mirrors are everywhere in these texts. They play key roles in many of the major and minor narratives, producing shame, deception, and even transformation. Aali Këbóoy uses a large imaginary mirror to chasten the community of Ñarelaa, making the townspeople believe that the imaginary reflection he displays in the street can reveal all their sins and hypocrisies.[44] In a digression that takes place in the colonial era, an outsize mirror tricks two gorillas who have been sabotaging the construction of the Dakar-Thiès railroad; the gorillas mistake their reflections for interlopers and end up killing themselves as they attack the mirror.[45] In an episode that sparks the novel's conclusion, a young woman named Yacine Ndiaye wants to become French, so she visits a *marabout* who uses a mirror to transform her into a white French woman—but the occult practitioner also changes Yacine's children into monkeys, and she is forever separated from them.[46] The texts' obsession with reflection also extends beyond the thematic. These works describe their relationship with their implied reader through the figure of the mirror. In both versions, Ngiraan compares his text to a mirror. In the Wolof, Ngiraan tells Badu not to fear the mirror he is extending to him, while in the French he warns Badu not to deny the truth that the mirror shows.[47] As this self-reflexive dimension suggests, figuring out what mirrors mean to these texts starts to seem rather important indeed.

The way we read *Doomi Golo/Les Petits* is likely to turn on how we understand mirrors to work in the text writ large. One way of interpreting the abundance of mirrors is as a warning, specifically one about the dangers of cultural alienation. For such an interpretation, the many mirror scenes would represent moments when an alienated subject or community is supposed to look at its reflection and be cured back into a more authentic relationship with itself through the shame of coming face to face with its reflection. Mirrors would then reveal that which one really is, forcing one to see past mimicry and hypocrisy to the truth, even if one chooses to deny it. In cases where the truth continues to be denied, the mirrors exact a terrible revenge.

Such a reading would help us develop an account of *Doomi Golo/Les Petits* as a particular kind of vernacular literary activism. After all, the novel tells us that it is like a mirror, so perhaps then it is a kind of mirror held up to a community to shock it into self-recognition and expose its alienation and hypocrisy to itself? The text does at times appear to invite this type of reading. But it is impossible to sustain this interpretation across the work as a whole. The problem is quite simple; mirrors in the *Doomi Golo/Les Petits* project work differently.

Rather than reflecting back a faithful image of that which we already are, what we ought to be, or what we want to be, mirrors in these two texts produce a kind of nonmimetic reflection. These mirrors seem to have three principal properties: they unsettle a subject's sense of itself; they reject any neat original-copy relationship; and they throw into question the viewing subject's place in time. A young Ngiraan gets an example of the first effect when he is warned that the only mirror in which he can truly read his own soul will be found in the eyes of others.[48] But such a "mirror," he learns, will reveal not his own true image but rather a mode of intersubjective relation that is far stranger. What a mirror says to Ngiraan is this: "You are me, I am you." ("Yaay man. Maay yow." / "Tu es moi, je suis toi. Il en est de chaque collectivité comme de chaque être humain.")[49] For these texts, a mirror seems to destroy the possibility of bounded, autonomous selfhood. Instead, mirrors reveal a web of interdependence and relationality. Another mirror is vividly described as sending back not a reflection but rather "a forest of interlaced and twisted bodies, like the branches of a baobab."[50] The distorted visions of interconnection that mirrors offer can take on positive or negative valences at different moments, but reflections almost always produce opacity instead of clarity.

The second effect of mirrors in these texts is to undermine the viewers' certainty that they can distinguish themselves from their reflections. The mirrors produce fractal reflections that tend to make off with the original. A clear example of this can be found in the Yacine Ndiaye story. By looking into an occult mirror, Yacine is transformed into a white woman as she seems to have desired, but the transformation does not stop there. The last quarter of the novel is devoted to the havoc wrought by a series of ghostly and nonhuman copies of both Yacine and her children. The mirror that transforms Yacine is itself described as a kind of in-between space—the Wolof text calls the space of the mirror *foofe* (over there), while the French version calls it *ailleurs* (elsewhere). Mirrors in these texts are not spaces of likeness so much as a kind of unmasterable elsewhere.[51] As Yacine looks into the mirror and watches herself be replaced with a reflection that is not her own, the *marabout* repeats a version of the same idea that Ngiraan heard before: "Yaay moom, mooy yow." / "Tu es elle. Elle est toi."[52]

Reflections in *Doomi Golo/Les Petits* also seem to snap the viewing subject out of linear time altogether. Diop once proclaimed his mistrust of sequential temporalities in an interview: "Time doesn't advance in a straight line, time goes in loops, it's circular. You can't understand the present until you give your mind over to the past."[53] Mirrors in *Doomi Golo* sometimes produce this disorienting effect. When a young Ngiraan goes in search of one of his ancestors, a figurative mirror suggests a paradox: the ancestor he has gone in search of is actually not yet born—it will be the duty of Ngiraan's grandson Badu to bring the ancestor into the world.[54] Rather than reflecting a particular moment in time, mirrors in these texts produce elusive copies that defamiliarize the present and call into question any separation of past and future.

One could fairly object, though, that this second interpretation of reflection is merely privileging a different aspect of the mirrors in these texts.

I suspect that there is no way to settle on just one reading. So instead of favoring one interpretation over the other, it will be more useful for us to think of the figure of the mirror as consisting of at least two tendencies. In other words, the first interpretation of mirrors is correct: *Doomi Golo* and *Les Petits* do manifest a fierce desire to think of themselves as holding up a mirror to a reader or a community, to cure alienation and hypocrisy through an encounter with a reflection. But the second reading of mirrors is also correct: the texts seem to constantly undercut this hoped-for curative encounter with the mirror by never really giving us any kind of successful reflection that produces anchored, autonomous selfhood. Instead, reflections produce dissociational visions of interconnection and fractured temporalities. In other words, Diop's texts want mirrors to work in both ways. The act of reading these texts is figured as a process of looking into a mirror but with the suggestion that this will lead not to greater clarity but to a kind of stumbling further into a darkness from which the reader may not emerge wholly themselves.

Drawing out both of these aspects of the mirrors helps us approach the entire project's maddeningly complex form. Both versions of the text abound in stories within stories, many of which are awfully similar to each other. One way to understand this is through the figure of the mirror. The story of Yaasin's two children who become monkeys is an eerie copy of another dreamlike tale in which two human-like monkeys terrorize an elderly man. An episode that focuses on a dictator named Daour Diagne has its dream-world counterpart in the figure of the autocrat Dibi-Dibi. Even the two main narrators of the text—Ngiraan and the madman Aali Këbóoy—double each other in a similar fashion. The multiple and mutually encasing narratives that populate Ngiraan's notebooks are *reflections* of each other, but in an ontology of reflection in which the relation between reflections is one of reenactment and refashioning, not equivalence or original/copy.

Reflection also helps us conceptualize the curious relationship that exists between the Wolof and French versions of the text. The two versions resemble each other in their overall structure but are clearly not identical— they begin differently, introduce motifs and refrains in different orders, and at times have rather different content and stylistic approaches. As Diop himself describes, the process of creating the French version was not about imitating or recreating what could be said in Wolof. Diop has called the French version a "translation which is not a translation."[55] The Wolof and French versions duplicate each other, but much in the same manner that mirrors work in these texts themselves—the relationship between them becomes a process of substitution, distortion, and eventual emancipation of the supposedly derivative copy that in turn reinvents the original. We can then read the two versions as reflections of each other, but in the special sense of reflection that they themselves put into play. Such a perspective would not privilege the Wolof version as the original. Instead of thinking of *Doomi Golo* and *Les Petits* as distinct texts, we can see them as two facets of a larger work whose composition and life appear to be ongoing.

The theory of nonreflective semblance that Diop's texts develop can also help us rethink how we compare vernacular literary movements across time and space. We have a tendency to think of vernacular movements as always being derivative of some past model. For Casanova, all modern vernacularizations seem to be reflections of Herder (or her understanding of Herder).[56] Wherever the language question appears, it always seems to be a copy of this original model. This is in keeping with Casanova's attention to the broad patterns of world literary space. In a later essay responding to her critics, Casanova clarified this focus on large-scale patterns by expanding on the analogy that opens *The World Republic of Letters*—the Persian rug at the center of Henry James's short story "The Figure in the Carpet." When viewed from the correct position, this textile offers its viewer a "superb intricacy . . . the one right combination."[57] For Casanova, world literary space works like James's carpet: "Each figure can be grasped only in terms of the position it occupies within the whole, and its interconnections with all the others."[58] This way of imagining literature as a textile is quite helpful, because it allows me to clarify how my own approach differs. Rather than trying to view the intricate tapestry from a great distance and from the exact right angle, I am arguing for unwinding the textile itself. Throughout this book, I have endeavored to show how the strands of a literary world come to be woven together as they are and to attend to the ways in which a seemingly tightly bound whole can be opened to new configurations in which negative spaces and the texture of frayed edges constellate a pattern as significant as the overall design.

What if the relationship between vernacular literary movements were closer to the kind of "reflection" that exists both within and between *Doomi Golo* and *Les Petits*? What if it were a kind of "translation which is not a translation" rather than a relationship of filiation or reproduction of the same? In other words, vernacular literary movements resemble each other because they reflect *each other*, with reflection here being understood through the prism of a nonreflective semblance. The kinship that many scholars observe in vernacular literary movements is clearly not illusory. The language question does reveal a kinship between literary traditions but not one that can be understood through the logic of original and copy and its linear temporality. Such kinship is not about resemblance since, as Walter Benjamin puts it, "resemblance does not necessarily appear where there is kinship."[59] Instead the bond between vernacular movements exists by virtue of their shared exposure of the contingency and historicity of any shared sense of literature. This kind of kinship is not derivation or filiation so much as copies emancipating themselves from the original and transforming both themselves and the original such that we can no longer assign one primacy over the other. Each instance of the language question restages the process of making a literary tradition, a process that extends existing literary norms and creates opportunities for their radical undoing. To put that another way, the model that everyone is copying is not in fact Herder, it is the Herder that Yeats reinvents, the Marx of *The German Ideology* that Ngũgĩ wa Thiong'o reworks. The "model" is nothing but a reflection that has emancipated itself from the original. The language question is fundamentally about absconding with and remaking the existing models for fashioning a literary tradition, not merely repeating them. But in the untimely temporality of such reflection, Herder would be as much a translation of Diop as the other way around. To put that in *Doomi Golo*'s terms, the language question means bringing your own ancestors into the world.

If we think of the relationship between vernacular literature movements in this way, it becomes easier to understand why we often detect an untimeliness around the language question. A vernacular literature movement seems to involve a kind of time-space compression or dislocation. One treats precedents of successful vernacularization that occurred centuries ago or continents away as if they were one's contemporaries; one calls out to audiences that may be decades or even centuries in the future as if they were just there, beyond that door. Both of these impulses have often been bound up with nationalism. But in this chapter, I have argued that this is not their essential nature. The politics of language defamiliarizes our sense of a shared literary present by suggesting that literature as it currently exists is not given but made, and as such, it always contains the possibility of being remade differently.

The untimeliness of the language question has both persisted and evolved in Senegal since 1980, past structural adjustment and beyond the decline of state-centered cultural nationalism. In the *Doomi Golo* project, we can start to see the outlines of new trajectories for many of the tendencies I have traced. Diop's texts are an experiment in what vernacular writing can be or do with the nature of address, audience, and textuality. This does not make them a telos for the language question so much as a restaging that calls back to and intermingles with earlier iterations. As a work of vernacular literature, the project seems to be both a radical departure from the past and in strong continuity with what has come before. As we saw in the figure of the mirror, Diop seems to want to continue the effort to make vernacular writing a committed project of disalienation. But in holding up a mirror to his readers, Diop's writings offer not self-recognition, nor uncomplicated cultural rootedness, nor even a return to a more perfect fusion of language and community that would have supposedly existed in the past. Instead, they make the very act of reading into a difficult, disjunctive act of losing yourself and your place in time.

DOOMI GOLO 4: AFTERLIVES

In 2016, an English translation of Diop's novel appeared. This seemed to mark a signal moment for Wolof literature on the world stage—at long last, that most coveted mode of consecration: the translation of a work into Global English. Entitled *Doomi Golo: The Hidden Notebooks*, the book's back cover and promotional materials proclaimed it to be "the first novel to be translated from Wolof to English."[60] The situation was a bit more complicated. Despite the bold announcement, this was not a translation of a Wolof text at all. It was rather a translation done from Diop's French version, *Les Petits de la guenon*.[61] The simplest explanation for the oddly misleading marketing of this text is that we generally do not view the practice of translating from a translation to be legitimate. But given the complexity of the relationship between the two versions—with Diop himself calling the French a "translation which is not a translation"—an English translation of *Les Petits* would seem to be a defensible, even exciting endeavor. What might it tell us about the terms in which African-language literatures can appear as world literature that "the first novel to be translated from Wolof to English" is in fact no such thing?

One of the English translators, Vera Wülfing-Leckie, makes no effort to hide the true source of the translation in an introduction to the new version (despite the considerable dissonance this produces with the loud proclamation on the book's back cover). Wülfing-Leckie acknowledges that she and her cotranslator, El Hadji Moustapha Diop, worked from *Les Petits*. Although she describes the French version as "a liberal adaptation" of *Doomi Golo*, Wülfing-Leckie seems in general to be intent on minimizing any differences between the two novels, presumably to legitimize the choice of the French version. And yet despite the translation having been done from *Les Petits*, the major focus of the introduction is the Wolof text. A great deal is made of the fact that this text was originally written in Wolof, a pedigree that is presented as grounding the novel's status as a work of authentic, rooted, anticolonial resistance. Somewhat perversely, this leads to dismissals of the French version that the translators actually worked from. For example, Wülfing-Leckie suggests that the French title Diop chose, *Les petits de la guenon*, is somehow compromised. By contrast, the title of their new English version—*Doomi Golo: The Hidden Notebooks*—is said to restore "the foreignizing Wolof element" of the original title and resist "the hegemonic, exclusionary 'linguistic imperialism' of the past."[62] Perhaps. But might we not also say that this new title erases its own conditions of possibility? Is it not a bit curious, to say the least, that the English title begins with those two untranslated Wolof words, when it is not a translation of *Doomi Golo* but rather of *Les Petits*?

In the effort to market this book as a novel originally written in an African language, the new translation actively obscures the entanglement of languages that actually made it possible. What gets elided is the importance of translation to the *Doomi Golo* project. Instead of a view of Diop's work that recognizes the interplay between the two versions, what we get is a vision of a singular, authentic African-language text that has been passed along to us, its English readers. Although the translator's introduction is slightly more ingenuous than the back cover, both minimize the trajectory that actually made this English-language version possible. The phrase used to market the book—"the first novel to be translated from Wolof to English"—thus remains a curiously unfulfilled promise as well as an unintentionally clear articulation of the terms through which Diop's work had to pass to emerge in English. Only by minimizing the dense tangle of translation from which this project emerged does the text have a chance at becoming world literature.

But the English translation is not the only new version of the *Doomi Golo* project to appear in the last few years. In the fall of 2014, another *Doomi Golo* made its way into the world. This was an audio version of the Wolof text, read by Diop himself, that was broadcast weekly in and around Dakar. The Senegalese filmmaker and director of E-Book Afrika, Joseph Gaï Ramaka, indicated that the purpose of the serialization was to "reach a public that had not necessarily been to school."[63] Given the density and opacity of Diop's work, the choice of this text as material for radio might initially appear surprising; how would a work that is demanding enough in print fare in a serialized format, with listeners tuning in and out?

The broadcasts captured a different stage of the *Doomi Golo* project and its ongoing experiment with exploring the nature of its public.[64] First, the weekly episodes were a mix of discussion and performance. The portion of each episode devoted to the audiobook itself was often truncated. An announcer would sometimes pause the recording of the book to have a debate with a variety of guests, give context for a particular passage, or even take a minute to read out the station's phone number and take a call from a listener. Some of the callers were excited about the project, while others were simply confused. As the broadcasts continued, all these interruptions became part of the performance.[65]

The remaking of *Doomi Golo* as a series of radio broadcasts seemed to have two principle effects: first, it made the novel porous to other voices, and second, it attempted to give the work a destiny beyond that of a silent, private reader. These are both strategies and desires we find in the original text. The broadcasts continued the larger project of *Doomi Golo* by experimenting with new models for vernacular literature; rather than envisioning the work of a vernacular writer as one of collecting and preserving folk traditions, the radio broadcasts took the printed text and gave it the same treatment that other stories and traditions receive within the text itself. *Doomi Golo* as radio became a conversation with an uncertain audience, prone to unexplained opacity, susceptible to digression and interruption, and apt to never quite reach its end. The new format thus conserved much of what *Doomi Golo* already did as a text but only by translating these same features into a new medium.

The decision to make a literary text into a series of radio broadcasts at all is a reminder of the precarious place of literature and book culture in contemporary Senegal. But it is also a sign of the diversity and creativity of responses to this situation. Putting the *Doomi Golo* project on the radio has the potential to reach a broader audience, to short-circuit the frustrating absence of the reading public by doing away with literacy as a criterion of participation in the work. But this is only a possibility, and it only opens up because the work risks itself. On the radio, the "novel" must share space with everything else on the airwaves, contend with different uptakes and forms of attention, and try to fashion a public for itself amid a din of other voices.

This change of medium transforms *Doomi Golo*, but the metamorphosis it undergoes is also a continuation of a central project of the text itself: making the work of fiction into a struggle for the creation of an audience. The passage of Diop's text onto the airwaves recalls the figure of Khadidja, driven mad by a missing echo and seething with both rage and love as she tries to conjure her listener with just the sound of her own voice. But the serialization of *Doomi Golo* extends the performative dimension of Khadidja's storytelling with an important difference: an audience for *Doomi Golo* will not be the creation of a lone storyteller. No reader can be summoned from silence by the power of narrative alone. This is the strategy that drives Khadidja mad. Diop has said that a text always precedes its public. In the case of his *Doomi Golo* project, this precedence takes the form of an ongoing attempt to invent an audience and to make this invention part of the work of fiction—without the sense that such a public could be conjured into being by a commanding and heroic storyteller. Rather, the work itself becomes a space in which author and public must move toward each other in the darkness, without being assured that they will meet. The position of the listener in this structure is thus no more certain than that of the storyteller.

Which afterlife are we to privilege, the translation into Global English or the radio broadcasts in Dakar? And which is legible to us as the beginning of the text's entry into world literature? The temptation would be to align the broadcasts with the local and the translation with the global. But such a schema is too simple. In fact, both new versions converge in the way that they reconfigure the project for new spaces of circulation, altering the character of the work itself in the process. The radio version stretches the text to accommodate the give-and-take of a broadcast format, which recalls the call-and-response format of oral storytelling. The English version acclimates itself to a new readership that appears to demand a certain narrative about the project's origins as the price of entry. Both of these new versions capture the *Doomi Golo* project mutating as it searches for an audience. In this respect, both respond to and refract the poesis of audience at the core of Diop's work.

In this chapter, I have read Diop's *Doomi Golo* as an attempt to reconfigure rather than overcome the separation between the work of vernacular fiction and its uncertain public. Across the project's many facets and versions, these attempts coalesce around a tendency to invite a reader (or even a listener) into a strange and sometimes disorienting experience of mutual invention, in which it is difficult to discern what is reflection or echo. Only then can the very nature of the distance that divides the storyteller and the public be brought into the work of poetics itself.

Out of Time: Decolonization and the Future of World Literature

Il n'est au pouvoir de personne de faire que ce qui s'est
passé ne se soit pas passé.

(No one has the power to make it such that what has
happened will not have happened.)

—AIMÉ CÉSAIRE, *Une saison au Congo*

Ndox tuuru na, an bàq a des.

(Rain has fallen, all that remains is to clean up the puddle.)

—AIMÉ CÉSAIRE, *Nawetu Deret*, Wolof trans. Boubacar Boris Diop

In this book, I have explored the dense knot of the language issue in Senegal, tracing its many threads and following their changing configurations. I have argued that the politics of language unwinds the literary present; by exposing the contingency of literature, the language question both extends the reach of global literary patterns and imagines how they might be rewoven otherwise. By reframing the language question as a struggle over literature's past, its present, and its future, this book also gestures toward a more capacious understanding of translation, which I recast to include reconfigurations of literary institutions, practices, and dispositions. This more expansive perspective on translation in turn has helped me outline the contours of a different approach to literary comparison that focuses on the variability of literature across time and space.

Across these readings in the politics of language, I have studied the variations among many different literary conventions, from textuality and authorship to orthography and reading. In this epilogue, I turn to a more evanescent variable. My focus will be on the shifting nature of the separation between a text's address and its audience. By address, I mean the quality of a text that seems to be speaking to someone; by audience, I mean the recipient of this address.[1] I have explored versions of this relationship throughout the book, from the call-and-response structure that changes in David Boilat's text collections to the figure of the future reader in colonial-era newspapers to the question of the audience in works by Mariama Bâ and Boubacar Boris Diop. In this conclusion, I tie together many of these main threads with a reading of the two texts that make up my epigraph above—Aimé Césaire's 1966 play *Une saison au Congo* (*A Season in the Congo*) and its recent Wolof translation by Boubacar Boris Diop. By comparing how a separation between audience and address that exists in the play changes across the work's different versions and circumstances, I end this book with an illustration of what a different comparative method might look like. This will in turn allow me to conclude with a reflection on Erich Auerbach's question: What is the future of world literature?

The separation between a text's address and its audience can vary in quite dramatic ways. Under certain circumstances, such a rift is barely apparent at all; while on other occasions, the division can seem like a chasm. But my point here is that such variability is not just quantitative, it is qualitative. The separation between a text and its audience can be configured as space, time, or a combination of both. When it is configured spatially, the separation becomes a kind of distance between the writer and his or her publics. When it is configured temporally, it emerges as a delay between a text's appearance and its reception.

The study of world literature has tended to privilege the first dimension of this separation—its spatiality. We have tended to think about literary cultures on a global scale in spatial terms, which is in part what allows us to conceive of world literature as a world-system through which texts, forms, and literary capital circulate. Over the course of this book, I have argued for a different understanding of world literature that approaches it temporally as well. This has been founded on my reading of the politics of language as a disruption of a literary present. For the language question, the separation between address and public tends to assume a temporal rather than spatial character; the separation is often configured as a sense of waiting for a public that is yet to come. The language question allows us to attend to the temporality of literature in its becoming—to study how literary pasts are produced and how future audiences are assembled.

Spatial configurations of the separation between address and audience seem to prevail wherever the institutionality of literature can be taken for granted. When writers address audiences they presume are already familiar with the institutions, practices, and sensibilities that subtend literary modernity, the division between address and audience tends to be minimal and thought of in terms of distance. Similarly, when we as scholars assume that texts from far-flung points are all already equivalently literary and need only to find literary audiences elsewhere in translation, then we tend to view the movement of texts and forms in terms of distance.

But when the literary cannot or will not be taken for granted, then the separation between address and audience often assumes a more temporal character. When writers must project a literary public that they sense is not yet there, the division of texts and audience appears as a postponement. Similarly, when we as scholars do not assume that every literary work exists for an audience in a commensurably literary way, then we begin to see the separation between address and audience in temporal terms as well. We see that literariness itself exists in time, that it must be made and remade in and by literary institutions and practices.

What might it look like to take the separation between a literary address and its public as a site of comparison itself? To do so, we have to conceive of this separation as more than the lack of an immediate or unmediated relationship to an audience. Although the wait for a future audience can be experienced as a deficiency, the division between address and audience is also where the world of the text and the world around the text are woven into each other. When writers or critics can assume that literary readers are already there, then the process of a text finding its audience tends to be configured in terms of a journey across a distance. But where there is a sense that a literary audience for a text is not given in advance or not there yet, then this same dynamic becomes a matter of a text not only waiting for its readers but also of trying to project its public. A spatial configuration tends to locate the separation between address and audience *outside* the text in the world itself, while a temporal configuration tends to draw the missing audience *inside* the text and transform the text itself into a site from which to project or assemble that future audience. In both cases, the separation between address and audience exists both inside and outside the text, of course, since this negative space/time is the very boundary of the work itself. To give substance to this approach, I will give a brief reading of a remarkable sequence of transformations in the separation between a work and its audience.

In 2016, Boubacar Boris Diop published *Nawetu Deret* (*Rainy Season of Blood*), a Wolof translation of one of the great literary works about decolonization, Aimé Césaire's play *Une saison au Congo* (*A Season in the Congo*). *A Season* is part of a trilogy of plays Césaire wrote in the 1960s and early 1970s on the subject of colonization and the struggle for freedom. The other two plays in this sequence—*La Tragédie du roi Christophe* (*The Tragedy of King*

Christophe) and *Une Tempête* (*A Tempest*)—took as their focus historical events or classic literary plots (the Haitian revolution and Shakespeare's *The Tempest*, respectively). *A Season*'s subject matter was a rather more contemporary event that was almost ripped from the headlines when Césaire began work on the play. *A Season* stages the rise and fall of the Congolese independence leader Patrice Lumumba—from his brief, tumultuous tenure as prime minister in 1960 to his imprisonment and assassination by rebel forces with the complicity of Belgium and the United States in 1961.[2] The play depicts Lumumba's tragic fate as intertwined with that of the Congo, which passes, in the course of the play's three acts, from colonial rule to independence and then into a civil war, a coup, and finally a dictatorship. In interviews, Diop insists that one reason he wanted to translate *A Season* was that the play is not only relevant to our present moment, it is actually contemporary of this moment (*actuel*).[3] This is a striking claim to make about a play that was both produced and set in the early 1960s. To understand Diop's assertion, we have to reconstruct the relationship between the play's audience, Césaire's composition process, and the history of decolonization.

A Season was first published in 1966, just three years after Lumumba's murder. It was first staged the following year in Brussels to some controversy.[4] But Césaire would continue to revise the play for a further seven years even as it continued to be performed. Until 1973, the script of *A Season* appears to have been in a state of open composition. The revisions Césaire made in the late 1960s and early 1970s were quite significant. They included new scenes, revisions to existing scenes, and even a new ending. The changes were made both in response to performances of the play and to the unfolding of decolonization in the Congo and elsewhere. Césaire continued to alter his play as new information about Lumumba's death came to light and as other African countries faced military coups that seemed to echo events depicted in the play.[5] For a nearly a decade, *A Season* reflected on the era of decolonization as this moment of radical possibility passed into history.

Even in its earliest incarnations, Césaire's play was concerned with the relationship between time and decolonization. Lumumba is forever running out of time in *A Season*. He and his ministers are constantly worrying that decolonization is not moving fast enough or that it is moving too fast. Lumumba also seems to be in a perpetual mismatch with events that unfold around him, always arriving at the decisive moment too late. This is captured memorably by President Kala, Lumumba's erstwhile ally, who betrays him. After Kala has removed Lumumba as prime minister, he gives Lumumba a piece of advice: "No one has the power to make it such that what has happened will not have happened." (Il n'est au pouvoir de personne de faire que ce qui s'est passé ne se soit pas passé.) Lumumba responds defiantly: "I hate time!"[6] This exchange remained in the text throughout the revision process, and yet the many changes Césaire would later introduce seem designed to work against the limits of Kala's thought. Instead of accepting that the era of possibility that Lumumba represented to many had simply become history, Césaire's revisions worked to produce an ongoing reflection on decolonization's relationship to time.

Césaire's revisions explore the turning points of the Lumumba narrative—moments where the story might have gone otherwise. Over the course of Césaire's revisions, such turning points start to become more and more about the separation between Lumumba and an audience. In the final version of *A Season*, the play bookends its vision of decolonization with two moments: one in which a radically new temporality opens up and another in which it starts to close. The two turning points are, not accidentally, two speeches—one successful and the other thwarted. The first is Lumumba's speech to an ecstatic audience on Congolese independence day. This first scene is based on historical events; Lumumba did make a passionate speech, out of turn and against protocol, in 1960. In the play, Lumumba proclaims independence as a step forward into a "new time" (*temps neuf*) and speaks in a declamatory mode that is reminiscent of the language of Césaire's visionary poem *Cahier d'un retour au pays natal*. Lumumba is greeted with joy by the people and consternation by the bankers and counterrevolutionaries who are already beginning to plot his downfall.[7]

Lumumba's jubilant speech stands in stark contrast with a later scene in which he tries but fails to address the nation on the radio after he is arrested during a coup. This scene of unsuccessful address is one of Césaire's many later additions. In the earliest versions of the play, there was no such attempt to make a radio address; Lumumba was simply arrested. Césaire added the scene partly in response to new information coming to light, but far from giving a more accurate picture of Lumumba's arrest, the revision he added is actually counterfactual. Lumumba really did address the nation on the radio several times after his initial detention, although he was also later prevented from doing so.[8] Césaire's revision alters historical events, and in so doing, he asks the play's audience to examine its own relationship to history.

A Season assumes an audience for whom decolonization has already become history. This is the source of the play's extraordinary prescience. Even in the early 1960s, Césaire seems to have had the sense that what was

at stake in Lumumba's tragedy was the becoming-history of decolonization, the closing of a certain moment of radical possibility. Césaire's play
assumes that its audience will take for granted that that era lies in the past.
But the revisions he made in the 1960s and 1970s largely challenge this
presumed sense of temporal detachment from the events depicted onstage.
Through the counterfactual scene of Lumumba's failed address, Césaire's
play suggests that all Lumumba would have to have done to change the
course of history was to speak on the radio and be heard. By this point,
the play as a whole has already made this case: Lumumba declares that
his only weapon is his speech and reassures his worried wife that if he is
arrested, all he will have to do is speak to the people to be understood.[9]
Césaire's revision invites the audience to believe it actually could have
been enough *if only* Lumumba had addressed the people.

Césaire's revision asks an audience to imagine how decolonization might
have gone differently—and how it still might. The revised text produces
this effect through a kind of substitution between two different separa-
tions of address and audience. In the scene of Lumumba's failed radio
speech, the audience *of* the play is made to stand in for the public that Lumumba cannot reach *within* the play. Although Lumumba fails to be heard
within the play's diegesis, this very failure stages his address reaching a
very different public—the audience of the play itself—in a displaced manner. This substitution forces a realignment in the audience's own sense of
temporal detachment from the events depicted in the play. The revision
frustrates the assumption that decolonization has become what Reinhart
Koselleck called a "future past," a superseded future. The revision asks the
audience to imagine itself as the public that Lumumba could have had—as
the public that could have changed everything. Through this disjunctive
temporality, the play attempts to rescue decolonization from being a superseded past and transform it into a future that has yet to unfold. *A Season* therefore makes a counterclaim against our sense of temporal separation
from the era of decolonization. It does this by trying to absorb into itself
the separation that always exists between a work and its audience. By absorbing this untimely division, the play asks its audience to recalibrate its
own separation from the moment of decolonization the play depicts. The
"new time" that Lumumba proclaims in the play continues to exist in a
new form, as the time that separates the work from its audience. In this
substitution, Césaire's revisions suggest that decolonization is a future that
is yet to be invented. This is one source of the untimeliness that makes *A
Season* paradoxically "of this moment," as Diop puts it.

Diop's *Nawetu Deret* is a Wolof translation of the final version of *Une saison* and includes all Césaire's changes. The Wolof translation responds to Césaire's refusal to let decolonization become history. But Diop's translation does this not by following the script word-for-word but by participating in Césaire's reworking of temporality and address. We can see this most clearly in the way Diop handles Lumumba's death scene. As he dies, Lumumba confronts his murderer, Msiri. Even with Msiri's knife at his throat, Lumumba makes a defiant speech: "We are two forces! The two forces! You are the invention of the past, and I am an inventor of the future!" (Nous sommes deux forces! Les deux forces! Tu es l'invention du passé, et je suis un inventeur du futur!)[10] These lines appeared in the first text of the play and remained unchanged across Césaire's many revisions. They allow the audience a last glimpse of Lumumba as a tragic hero. But there is something disingenuous about this final speech. Lumumba's final speech seems to sift historical actors into two neat temporal categories: either one is on the right or the wrong side of history, a mere passive invention of the past or an active inventor of the future. But Césaire's later revisions often pulled in a more ambiguous direction, suggesting that the challenge of decolonization was knowing whether the future one is trying to create has broken sufficiently with the past.

Diop's translation pulls away from the schematism of past/future that Lumumba's final speech introduces and offers a version of this same thought in a more multilayered temporality:

> Weddiwuma ne ponkal nga, Misiri. Wànte su ma la xoolee xottu nit kese laay gis. Ba nga faatoo du tey! Man nag, daanaka juddoguma sax. Démb ak Ëllëg mënuñoo bokk àtte.[11]

> I do not deny that you are a force, Misiri. But if I look at you deeply, I see only a human. That which you are killing is not today! As for me, it is as if I had not yet even been born. Yesterday and tomorrow cannot share in justice.

In Diop's translation, today, yesterday, and tomorrow are all superimposed. Although Lumumba's death is also the death of a certain vision of decolonization in the play, the Wolof version tells us that it is "as if" (*daanaka*) Lumumba has not yet even been born. The Wolof version seems less sure that it can sustain a stark difference between someone either being a creation of the past or a creator of the future. In Diop's translation, the struggle between past and future is allegorized as the inability of Yesterday (*Démb*) and Tomorrow (*Ëllëg*) to share an *àtte*. An *àtte* can mean a judgment, a law, a decree, or even justice itself. (The constitution of Senegal, for example, is translated into Wolof as the *ndeyu àtte*, [mother of judgment or law]). In a more literal sense, an *àtte* is also a separation. It refers to the way one might resolve a conflict between two individuals who are fighting by dragging them apart. We could then also translate *àtte* as "critique"—if we recall that the original sense of "critique" also included judging, deciding, separating, and distinguishing. In Diop's translation, these two senses of *àtte* threaten to pull Lumumba's speech apart. On the one hand, Lumumba suggests that yesterday and tomorrow will never share in the same judgment, that no earthly justice will ever extend between them. But he also seems to suggest that yesterday and tomorrow cannot be made to separate, that they are like two warring parties that we cannot pull apart.

Diop's translation undoes the neat parallelism and opposition between "invention of the past/inventor of the future." It traces instead an entangled vision in which neither the past nor the future is the mere creation of the other. Although Diop's translation is a departure from Césaire's text, it also seems to harmonize in a profound way with the spirit of the many revisions Césaire made to the play, which seem to work against our sense that we can separate ourselves from the moment of decolonization.

When we read *A Season in the Congo* and *Nawetu Deret* through the separation of address and audience, the play appears to us as a moving thing. It is a work that has changed in response to the closing of decolonization as a "new time," and yet it also continues to intervene in our sense of remove from that temporality. The reworkings of key scenes that we find in Diop's translation are not outside interventions onto a preexisting text; they are rather part of a series of shifts in the temporality of the work that also includes Césaire's revisions. For a comparative perspective that traces changes in the nature of the separation between address and audience, Diop's translation and Césaire's revisions are part of the same continuum. When we work in this way, we are not looking for or at a boundaried text that reflects its context. Instead, we see how the world of the text and the world around the text are constantly being woven into and out of each other. In this work of winding and unwinding, the text and its world continue to make claims on us and our relationship to time. Césaire's play and Diop's translation explore what it means for a text to be of a given moment but also how a text might refuse the contours of a given present. They do this by exploring the temporal nature of a separation between audience and address, which they develop into a way of reactivating the "new time" of decolonization.

Decolonization and the language question are of roughly the same historical vintage, and they face similar challenges in making a case for their continued actuality. Césaire wrote *A Season in the Congo* for an audience for whom decolonization would already be fading into history. Much of Diop's recent work has struggled against a related sense that the language issue and vernacular writing also belong to a past that has been superseded. *Nawetu Deret* was published by Céytu Editions, a new publishing venture founded by Diop and his fellow writer Felwine Sarr in 2016. The aim of the Céytu project seems to be to translate world literature into Wolof.[12] Its other two initial offerings are *Baay Sama, Doomu Afrig*, a translation of the French Nobel laureate J. M. G. Le Clézio's *L'Africain*, and a new edition of *Bataaxal bu gudde nii*, Maam Yunus Dieng and Arame Fal's Wolof version of Mariama Bâ's *So Long a Letter*.[13] Diop has promoted Céytu in a series of interviews and essays, in which he mixes the different registers of vernacular literary activism that I have traced throughout this book. He frames the Céytu project both as a continuation of a long tradition of literary activism and as an attempt to take part in universal literary culture.

What is the future of world literature? Is it a future of increasing standardization, the use of just a few literary languages, and the rise of a global literary monoculture? Drawing on the temporality of decolonization in Césaire's play, Diop asks us to imagine the future of world literature otherwise. He traces the outlines of a vernacular world literature in which the standardization dynamics that Auerbach warned of are present but not preordained, and the making and unmaking of the literary remains open as a temporal separation between text and public. Césaire's refusal to accept the passing of decolonization into history finds its echo in the challenge the language question continues to pose to world literature. In its persistence past the era of cultural nationalism, the language question and the writers who respond to it ask us to imagine that the moment for reinventing the literary has not passed us by, that other futures besides the standardization of literary cultures and languages remain possible. This is the language question's untimely intervention: to invite the temporality of decolonization into the unfolding of world literature.

ACKNOWLEDGMENTS

This book took shape over a decade of research and writing. The debts of gratitude that I have incurred over this time—in both life and work—are impossible to capture and would surely fill another volume by themselves. What follows is not a complete accounting, but a way of gesturing toward the gratitude I feel for the generosity of so many people who helped make this book possible.

I was fortunate to have the early mentorship of Natalie Melas and Naoki Sakai. Their encouragement of my interests in comparison and translation were foundational for the work I do today. *The Tongue-Tied Imagination* began to take shape in the graduate program in Comparative Literature at the University of California, Berkeley. I am grateful to my teachers there who shaped the early stages of this project with their discerning comments and generous mentoring—especially to Karl Britto, Judith Butler, Samba Diop, Susan Maslan, and Gautam Premnath. Karl's insightful and meticulous feedback left a deep impression on this book. Michael Lucey's Mellon seminar sparked new directions in my work, and I have continued to benefit from our conversations. At Berkeley and in Senegal, I had the incredible privilege of learning the Wolof language and studying its literature from a number of gifted teachers, including Sana Camara, Birane Gassama, Lamane Mbaye, and Oumoul Sow. Of all these teachers, I owe the most to Paap Alsaan Sow. I am so grateful to Paap for our thought-provoking conversations over the years and for his corrections to many of the translations included here. All mistakes are mine alone.

A variety of friends and colleagues read or listened to portions of this book in various stages: Michael Allan, Jennifer Bajorek, Juan Caballero, Nijah Cunningham, Vincent Debaene, Jeremy Dell, Jonathan Cole, Katrina Dodson, Sam England, Rosalind Fredericks, Andrea Gadberry, Isabel Hofmeyr, Javier Jiménez, Stephanie Newell, Fallou Ngom, Derek Peterson, Caitlin Scholl, David Simon, Maya Smith, Richard Terdiman, Tristram Wolff, Duncan Yoon, Livi Yoshioka, and Sarah Zimmerman. Among these interlocutors, I owe a special thank-you to the participants in the 2013 Wolof Literature Working Group—Ivy Mills, Cullen Goldblatt, Jonathon Repinecz, and Fatoumata Seck—and to the University of California Research Institute and the Mellon Foundation for supporting the project. Chapter 7 would not have been possible without you.

I'm grateful for the friendships that sustained me in Senegal, with Sophie Coly, Habib Bâ, Alioune Bâ, Ousmane Fall, and Nicki List. I still miss Abdou Mbodj's humor. Above all, I am thankful for the support and long-term hospitality of the *waa kër* Bâ—Fatoumata Beye especially—who have provided a home away from home for many years. I would also like to thank the writers and publishers in Dakar who generously agreed to speak with me—Arame Fal, Maam Yunus Dieng, Cheikh Aliou Ndao, and Seydou Nourou Ndiaye.

While writing this book, I spent more time than I care to remember in dusty collections of various kinds. I am grateful to Laurent Bismuth at the Archives françaises du film for helping me locate the French version of *Mandabi* and to the staff at the Institut fondamental d'Afrique Noire (especially Elhadji Birame Diouf) for their support and patience during my time working on the Cahiers Ponty. I am also grateful to James Currey and Mary Jay for pointing me to the Noma Award archive and to Alessandro Meregaglia for his assistance with it.

At UC Davis, I am thankful for colleagues like Jeff Fort, David Gundry, Claire Goldstein, Noah Guynn, Sven-Erik Rose, Eric Russell, Juliana Schiesari, Julia Simon, Chunjie Zhang, Carrie Seal, Corrie Decker, Rachel Jean-Baptiste, and John Marx, who read portions or helped with aspects of the project. I also wish to thank the participants in the faculty research seminar at the Davis Humanities Institute, who provided much-needed feedback in the later stages of writing.

Research for *The Tongue-Tied Imagination* was supported by a number of institutions. Rocca fellowships from the Center for African Studies at UC Berkeley supported time in Senegal in the early stages. A Robert L. Platzman Fellowship at the Regenstein Library at the University of Chicago allowed me to work in the International Association for Cultural Freedom collection. A Hellman Family Fellowship was invaluable in freeing me up for the final push of research and writing. The publication of this book was also made possible by two generous awards—the Helen Tartar First Book Subvention Award from the American Comparative Literature Association and a Publication Assistance grant from UC Davis. Earlier versions of portions of Chapters 2 and 6 appeared in *Research in African Literatures* and *PMLA*, respectively. I'm enormously grateful to Thomas Lay for his enthusiasm and dedication to this book and to the staff at Fordham University Press for their careful work on the manuscript.

My parents, Isabel Downs and Bob Warner, have served as lifelong models of curiosity and commitment. I owe them my love of language and my inclination to study a question from multiple angles—as well the conviction that a life of intellectual work must also leave room for laughter. The creativity of my siblings Andy and Olivia are sources of constant inspiration. Andrew and Kathy have been great and constant friends. Jeanne's generosity with her time allowed me to finish this book. Of all the people who have contributed in ways large and small, I owe the most to Lauren, who has been there from the very beginning. Her love, encouragement, and support have meant everything. I see her remarkable curiosity about the world in Sophie, who interrupted me in the final stages of writing this book to show me that she had just written her very own first letter.

INTRODUCTION: UNWINDING THE LANGUAGE QUESTION

1. Congress for Cultural Freedom, *The Writers Speak [Unedited]*, Box 442, Folder 1, "Report on Dakar and Freetown Conferences 1963," International Association for Cultural Freedom Records, JRL, 67. Unless otherwise noted, all translations are my own.

2. On India, see Rashmi Sadana, *English Heart, Hindi Heartland: The Political Life of Literature in India* (Berkeley: University of California Press, 2012), pp. 107–8; and Debjani Ganguly, "The Language Question in India," in *The Cambridge History of Postcolonial Literature*, ed. Ato Quayson (Cambridge: Cambridge University Press, 2012), pp. 649–80. On Ngũgĩ's intervention in Kenya, see Simon Gikandi, *Ngugi wa Thiong'o* (Cambridge: Cambridge University Press, 2000), pp. 247–85; on Lusophone Africa, see Russell G. Hamilton, *Literatura Africana, Literatura Necessária*, vol. 1, edições 70, 1984, pp. 1–29; on créolité and the francophone Caribbean, see Jean Bernabé, Patrick Chamoiseau, and Raphaël Confiant, *Éloge de la créolité* (Paris: Gallimard, 1989). On the Maghreb, see Réda Bensmaïa, *Experimental Nations: Or, the Invention of the Maghreb* (Princeton, N.J.: Princeton University Press, 2009), pp. 11–26; and Anne Donadey, "The Multilingual Strategies of Postcolonial Literature: Assia Djebar's Algerian Palimpsest," *World Literature Today*, vol. 74, no. 1, 2000, pp. 27–36. On South Africa, see Bhekizizwe Peterson, "The Language Question in Africa," in *The Cambridge History of Postcolonial Literature*, ed. Ato Quayson (Cambridge: Cambridge University Press, 2012), pp. 689–91.

3. Congress for Cultural Freedom, *Mbari Writers' Conference in Uganda*, Mbari Writers Conference, Kampala, 1961, Container 1.3, Transcription Centre Archive, HRC, p. 3. In this introduction, I refer to "What is African literature?" as Okigbo's question for clarity's sake, but the attribution is murky. This was less "his" question than the initial item on the agenda for the first session. In other places in the unpublished report on Makerere, Gabriel Okara is described as presiding over this session.

4. Obiajunwa Wali, "The Dead End of African Literature?," *Transition*, no. 10, Sept. 1963, p. 13.

5. See especially Chinua Achebe, "English and the African Writer," *Transition*, no. 18, 1965, pp. 27–30; and Ngũgĩ wa Thiong'o, *Decolonising the Mind: The Politics of Language in African Literature* (Nairobi: East African Publishers), 1994. For a collection of the initial replies to Wali, see Barry Reckord et al., "Polemics: The Dead End of African Literature," *Transition*, no. 75/76, 1997, pp. 335–41. For excellent surveys of the language question in African literatures, see B. Peterson, "The Language Question in Africa," 681–702; Abiola Irele, "African Literature and the Language Question," in *The African Experience in Literature and Ideology* (Bloomington: Indiana University Press, 1990), pp. 43–65; and Moradewun Adejunmobi, "Routes: Language and the Identity of African Literature," *The Journal of Modern African Studies*, vol. 37, no. 4, Dec. 1999, pp. 581–96, as well as the 1992 special issue of *Research in African Literatures*.

6. Helon Habila, "Tradition and the African Writer," Caine Prize, http://caineprize.com/blog/2015/12/1/tradition-and-the-african-writer-by -2014-judge-helon-habila.

7. Of his use of a modified French, Patrice Nganang says, "I do not describe the language I use. I simply use it." Peter Wuteh Vakunta, "The Ramifications of Linguistic Innovation in African Literature: An Interview with Patrice Nganang," *Journal of the African Literature Association* vol. 3, no. 2, 1 Jan. 2009, pp. 206–12. Of her writing in English, Chimamanda Ngozi Adichie notes, "I have taken ownership of English." Ada Uzoamaka Azodo, "Creative Writing and Literary Activism: Interview with Chimam- anda Ngozi Adichie," *Journal of the African Literature Association*, vol. 2, no. 1, Winter-Spring 2008, pp. 146–151. Maryse Condé famously declared that she wrote in "my language, the language of Maryse Condé." Marie Poinsot and Nicolas Treiber, "Entretien avec Maryse Condé," *Hommes et migrations. Revue française de référence sur les dynamiques migratoires*, no. 1301, Jan. 2013, pp. 182–88.

8. Chinua Achebe, *Morning Yet on Creation Day: Essays* (Garden City, N.Y.: Anchor Press, 1975), pp. xi–xii.

9. This scripted quality allows J. M. Coetzee to transform the "what is African literature" debate into a literary trope in his novel *Elizabeth Costello: Eight Lessons* (New York: Random House, 2004).

10. For an important recent exception—which unfortunately appeared too far into the production phase of this book for me to discuss it here—see Mukoma Wa Ngugi, *The Rise of the African Novel: Politics of Language, Identity, and Ownership* (Ann Arbor: University of Michigan Press, 2018).

11. In the preface to the language section of the revised *Post-Colonial Studies Reader*, Ashcroft, Griffiths, and Tiffin identify rejection and subver- sion as the two strategies of response to the domination of a former imperial

language. The first option they associate with Ngũgĩ's break with English, which they read as an attempt to restore an ethnic or national identity embedded in an essentialized vision of the precolonial past. The second strategy, which they seem to prefer, centers around an appropriation of the colonizing language. Bill Ashcroft, Gareth Griffiths, and Helen Tiffin, eds., *The Post-Colonial Studies Reader*, 2nd ed. (London: Routledge, 2006), pp. 261–62.

12. Harry Garuba, "The Critical Reception of the African Novel," in *The Cambridge Companion to the African Novel*, ed. F. Abiola Irele (Cambridge: Cambridge University Press, 2009), p. 253.

13. For an exception to the sense of critical fatigue surrounding the language issue, see Gikandi's insightful recent work. Simon Gikandi, "Provincializing English," Editor's Column, *PMLA*, vol. 129, no. 1, 2014, pp. 7–17.

14. Pascale Casanova. *La République mondiale des Lettres* (Paris: Points, 2008), pp. 122–25.

15. John F. Povey, "How Do You Make a Course in African Literature?" *Transition*, no. 18, 1965, p. 39.

16. Frantz Fanon, *Œuvres* (Paris: La Découverte, 2011), p. 88.

17. The critical literature on translation is vast. My approach here emerges from the confluence of several different scholarly traditions. Throughout the book, I propose a dialogue between work on translation that will be more familiar to literary scholars and research from other disciplines—notably anthropology, linguistic anthropology, and actor-network theory. For a helpful and concise overview of the contributions of these latter fields to the study of translation, see Susan Gal, "Politics of Translation," *Annual Review of Anthropology* 44, 2015, pp. 225–40.

18. Congress, *Mbari Writers' Conference*, HRC; Congress, "Report on Dakar," JRL.

19. Both Makerere and Dakar were convened by the Congress for Cultural Freedom (CCF), an American foundation that was also a front for the soft power projects of the US Central Intelligence Agency. During the Cold War, the CCF promoted literary institutions and projects across the globe. The Dakar and Makerere conferences (as well as a third conference in Freetown) were part of these initiatives. The CIA backing was not widely known at the time, although some writers had their suspicions. For studies of the CCF, see Peter Coleman, *The Liberal Conspiracy* (New York: Free Press, 1989); and Frances Stonor Saunders, *The Cultural Cold War: The CIA and the World of Arts and Letters* (New York: New Press, 2013). On the CCF's work in anglophone Africa and its connections to modernism, see Peter Kalliney, "Modernism, African Literature, and the Cold War," *Modern*

Language Quarterly 76, no. 3, 1 Sept. 2015, pp. 333–68. For a discussion of the role of the CCF in African literary relations across French and English, see Ruth Bush, *Publishing Africa in French: Literary Institutions and Decolonization 1945–1967* (Oxford: Oxford University Press, 2016), pp. 187–188.

20. There are many earlier examples of the language issue being raised. To cite only the francophone ones, we can point to the Senegalese poet David Diop's 1956 essay in *Présence Africaine* or the Malagasy poet Jacques Rabemananjara's speech at the First Congress of Black Writers, also in 1956. Dakar and Makerere seem to be where the question developed into a polemic in the context of literary institutionalization. David Diop, "Contribution au débat sur la poésie nationale," *Présence Africaine*, no. 6, 1956, pp. 113–15; Jacques Rabemananjara, "L'Europe et Nous," *Présence Africaine*, no. 8/10, 1956, pp. 20–28.

21. Joseph Slaughter makes a complementary argument in a recent article in which he suggests that "for African literature to make its way in the world" it had to "become literature by comparison." Joseph R. Slaughter, "Locations of Comparison," *Cambridge Journal of Postcolonial Literary Inquiry* 5, no. 2, Apr. 2018, p. 218. Patrice Nganang also offers an insightful reading of Okigbo's "What is African literature?" question by insisting on the noun *literature* rather than the adjective *African*. Nganang's approach differs from mine in that it quickly dispenses with the category of literature for a fascinating inquiry into the history of alphabetic writing. Patrice Nganang, "In Praise of the Alphabet," in *Rethinking African Cultural Production* (Bloomington: Indiana University Press, 2015), p. 80.

22. This is partly the sense of Simon Gikandi's often-misunderstood claim that Chinua Achebe "invented" African literature in the 1960s. Gikandi never argued that there were no other writers or texts of value before Achebe came along, but rather that Achebe was a central (for Gikandi, *the* central) figure in establishing "the terms by which African literature was produced, circulated, and interpreted." Simon Gikandi, "Chinua Achebe and the Invention of Modern African Literature," in *Things Fall Apart* (Oxford: Heinemann, 1996), p. 5. We can debate, as Ruth Bush does, whether the impact of Achebe was quite the same on the francophone side, but Gikandi's location of the beginnings of the field in the early 1960s seems correct. Bush, *Publishing Africa in French*, 196–202.

23. Bloke Modisane referred to East African literature at Makerere as an "embryonic body." At these gatherings, conversations that would change the course of literary history were just beginning—Ngũgĩ famously handed the manuscript of *Weep Not, Child* to Achebe at Makerere, an exchange that eventually led to Achebe becoming the editorial advisor for Heinemann's landmark African Writers Series. James Currey, *Africa Writes Back: The*

African Writers Series and the Launch of African Literature (Athens: Ohio University Press, 2008), p. 3. The inchoate and even improvised aspect of these conversations about "African literature" was polarizing. Nkosi described Makerere as an "improbable circus," while Sembène complained of the heavy focus on academic papers. Both conferences featured personal attacks, most famously Soyinka's satire of a "negritude" poem, but also camaraderie. Nkosi refers to Makerere as an "unlikely collection of open shirts, sandals, goatees, sunglasses . . . gathered in the dining hall, learning to sing in Zulu, crowded into a local nightclub." Bloke Modisane, *Critic's Time: The East African Short Story*, Mbari Writers Conference, Kampala, 1961, MAK/III(3), Container 1.3, Transcription Centre Archive, HRC, p. 2.; Lewis Nkosi, *Press Report*, Mbari Writers Conference, Kampala, 1961; MAK V (1), Container 1.3, Transcription Centre Archive, HRC, pp. 1, 3; Congress, *The Writers Speak [Unedited]*, JRL, p. 64.

24. Ezekiel Mphahlele, *Press Report*, Mbari Writers Conference, Kampala, 1961, Container 1.3, Transcription Centre Archive, HRC, p. 2. The format was called "Critic's Time" in Makerere.

25. Congress, *The Writers Speak [Unedited]*, JRL, p.128.

26. Congress for Cultural Freedom. *Conference for African Writers of English Expression*, Mbari Writers Conference, Kampala, 1961, TC/127, Container 1.3, Transcription Centre Archive, HRC, p. 2.

27. On Makerere, see Segun Olusola, *Reports from Conference Study Groups: Drama*, Mbari Writers Conference, Kampala, 1961, MAK/IV (1), Container 1.3, Transcription Centre Archive, HRC; John Pepper Clark, *Reports from Conference Study Groups: Poetry*, Mbari Writers Conference, Kampala, 1961, MAK/lV (2), Container 1.3, Transcription Centre Archive, HRC; Ulli Beier, *Contemporary African Poetry in English*, Mbari Writers Conference, Kampala, 1961, MAK/ll (4), Container 1.3, Transcription Centre Archive, HRC; Donatus Nwoga, *Critic's Time for The Short Story*, Mbari Writers Conference, Kampala, 1961, MAK/III, Container 1.3, Transcription Centre Archive, HRC; Ezekiel Mphahlele, *Critic's Time for the Novel*, Mbari Writers Conference, Kampala, 1961, Container 1.3, Transcription Centre Archive, HRC; and Mphahlele, *Press Report*. On Dakar, see Congress for Cultural Freedom, *Report on Dakar and Freetown Conferences 1963*, Box 442, Folder 1, International Association for Cultural Freedom Records, JRL; and Congress for Cultural Freedom, *The Writers Speak [Edited]*, Box 440, Folder 8, "Transcripts in French, 1953," International Association for Cultural Freedom Records, JRL. Also see the papers by Roger Mercier, Thomas Melone, and Louis Thomas in Congress for Cultural Freedom, *Actes du Colloque sur la littérature africaine d'expression française, Dakar, 26–29 mars 1963* (Dakar: Faculté des Lettres, 1965).

28. See the reports from the individual sessions on the novel, drama, and poetry by Mphahlele, Olusola, and Clark in *Mbari Writers Conference in Uganda*, HRC. Although Makerere is remembered as a conference of "African Writers of English Expression," the program and agenda both describe it as a gathering of "English-Speaking African Writers." In the press report that Mphahlele prepared later, the description shifts to "African Writers of English Expression." At least in the initial framing, the focus appears to have been on the writers' common *understanding* of English, rather than the language they wrote in.

29. It has gone largely unremarked that Wali's essay also attacks the institutionalization he correctly detected occurring at Makerere—he opens by declaring that African literature "as now defined and understood" at the Makerere conference will lead nowhere and later refers to literature "as now understood and practiced" after Makerere. Wali, "The Dead End of African Literature?," 13. My intent is not to endorse Wali's position but rather to point out that even his contribution to the debate, which is so closely associated with the nativist position, was also clearly a response to the insitutionalizing project of the conference.

30. Ngũgĩ, *Decolonising*, 4–6.

31. Gerald Moore, ed., *African Literature and the Universities* (Ibadan: Published for the Congress for Cultural Freedom by Ibadan University Press, 1965), p. 56. These edits were likely made in response to space restrictions rather than any intent on Moore's part to change the nature of the discussions. See Marion Bieber, *Letter to P. Edwards*, 24 Jan. 1964, Box 441, Folder 4, International Association for Cultural Freedom Records, JRL.

32. Compare Moore, *African Literature*, 56, with Congress, *The Writers Speak [Unedited]*, JRL, 64–71.

33. Compare the table of contents of Congress, *Actes du Colloque*, 275, with the full schedule of the conference, reproduced in Congress, *Actes du Colloque*, 9.

34. Jacques Golliet, *Letter to Françoise Robinet*, 16 May 1963, and undated letter, Box 440, Folder 6, International Association for Cultural Freedom Records, JRL.

35. Johann Wolfgang von Goethe, *Conversations of Goethe with Johann Peter Eckermann*, ed. J. K. Moorhead., trans. John Oxenford (London: Everyman's Library, 1930), p. 132.

36. See David Damrosch, *What Is World Literature?* (Princeton, N.J.: Princeton University Press, 2003); Franco Moretti, "Conjectures on World Literature," in *Distant Reading* (London: Verso, 2013), pp. 43–62; and Casanova, *La République mondiale des Lettres*.

37. Since these three interventions first appeared, there has been a second wave of work on world literature and comparison. Scholars such as Emily Apter, Alexander Beecroft, Pheng Cheah, and Aamir Mufti have all interrogated the possibilities and limitations of world literature as a framework. See Emily Apter, *Against World Literature: On the Politics of Untranslatability* (London: Verso, 2013); Alexander Beecroft, *An Ecology of World Literature: From Antiquity to the Present Day* (London: Verso Books, 2015); Pheng Cheah, *What Is a World? On Postcolonial Literature as World Literature* (Durham, N.C.: Duke University Press, 2016); Aamir R Mufti, *Forget English! Orientalisms and World Literatures* (Cambridge, Mass.: Harvard University Press, 2016); and Joseph R. Slaughter, "World Literature as Property," *Alif: Journal of Comparative Poetics*, no. 34, 2014, pp. 39–73. *The Tongue-Tied Imagination* joins this second generation of scholarship. The questions I ask about world literature have also been shaped in particular by two recent works. In *All the Difference in the World: Postcoloniality and the Ends of Comparison* (Stanford, Calif: Stanford University Press, 2007), Natalie Melas reflects on the challenge postcoloniality poses to the practice of comparison. Melas focuses on incommensurability (moments when there is a ground of comparison but not equivalence). My project draws on her understanding of incommensurability, but to explore the language question, I also look to sites of commensurability (where literary traditions, institutions, and practices come to be standardized and produced as comparable). Michael Allan's *In the Shadow of World Literature: Sites of Reading in Colonial Egypt* (Princeton, N.J.: Princeton University Press, 2016) asks us to think of world literature not as a neutral meeting ground of national traditions but as a disciplinary framework that exerts a particular normative force linked to a semiotic ideology of secular reading. Allan's approach is to trace the emergence of a literary world in Egypt as it joins the world of world literature. Although I follow a similar trajectory here, by working through a history of the language question rather than of secular reading, my focus expands to include other literary institutions and practices, such as authorship and textuality.

38. Damrosch, *What Is World Literature*, 14.

39. Erich Auerbach, "The Philology of World Literature," in *Time, History, and Literature: Selected Essays of Erich Auerbach*, ed. James I. Porter, trans. Jane O. Newman (Princeton, N.J.: Princeton University Press, 2016), p. 253.

40. For this reason, Auerbach has become a pivotal interlocutor in many "second wave" studies of world literature. See Allan, *In the Shadow*, 138–40; Apter, *Against World Literature*, 193–210; Cheah, *What Is a World*, 24–27; and Mufti, *Forget English*, 203–42.

41. Marx and Engels's formulation also shared this sense of levelling. See Aijaz Ahmad, "The Communist Manifesto and 'World Literature.'" *Social Scientist*, vol. 28, no. 7/8, 2000, pp. 3–30.

42. Auerbach, "The Philology of World Literature," 254.

43. Auerbach, 261–64.

44. Pathé Diagne, *Teerebtanu ladab ci wàlàf: anthologie wolof de littérature* (Dakar: Université de Dakar, Institut fondamental d'Afrique noire, Séminaire sur l'adaptation des langues africaines, 1971) pp. 35–7. The *Teerebtanu* includes *xasida*—a Wolof term (derived from the Arabic *qaṣida*) for poetry/songs that express Islamic themes. The anthologized works by Musaa Ka, Ahmadu Bamba, and others are examples of living performance genres that continue to be widely read, recited, recorded, and collectively chanted. See Fallou Ngom, *Muslims Beyond the Arab World: The Odyssey of Ajami and the Muridiyya* (Oxford: Oxford University Press, 2016), pp. 29–32. Diagne also includes modern poems by his contemporaries Cheikh Aliou Ndao and Cheikh Anta Diop.

45. Even the word Diagne chooses to express "literature" in Wolof is a conceptual translation. He uses *ladab*, a loanword from the Arabic *adab*. But other writers and literacy activists have used *mbind* (writing, creation), *woy* (song, poetry), or other terms.

46. Benedict Anderson, *Imagined Communities: Reflections on the Origin and Spread of Nationalism* (London: Verso, 2006) pp. 67–82.

47. Casanova, *La République mondiale des Lettres*, 127–87.

48. See, among many others, Moradewun Adejunmobi, *Vernacular Palaver: Imaginations of the Local and Non-Native Languages in West Africa* (Clevedon, UK: Multilingual Matters, 2004); Adélékè Adéèkó, *Proverbs, Textuality, and Nativism in African Literature* (Gainesville: University Press of Florida, 1998); and Karin Barber, *The Anthropology of Texts, Persons, and Publics: Oral and Written Culture in Africa and Beyond* (Cambridge: Cambridge University Press, 2007).

49. For notable exceptions, see Lisa McNee, *Selfish Gifts* (Albany, N.Y.: SUNY Press, 2000); and Papa Samba Diop, *Archéologie du roman sénégalais* (Paris: L'Harmattan, 2010) and *Glossaire du roman sénégalais* (Paris: L'Harmattan, 2010).

50. For a critique of the first aspect, see Adejunmobi, "Routes."

51. The conflict with French is not the earliest language question relative to Wolof. Besides the Latin-based script that is used by the self-identified literary writers that I study in this book, Wolof is also written using Arabic characters in a much older script known as Wolofal. The Wolofal religious poets of the late nineteenth and early twentieth centuries were in a similar position with regard to Arabic as later Wolof writers would be with regard to

French. They had to make the case that Wolof could be a language of religious devotion, over and against the assumption that Arabic was the only possible pious language. The poet Musaa Ka is famously said to have declared: "Bépp làkk rafet na buy yee ci nit xel ma / Di tudd ci jaam ngor la." (Every language is beautiful if it enlarges the intellectual horizon of the human / And returns to the slave the taste of freedom.) Although I do not focus on it here, the Wolof-Arabic tension could be considered an earlier vernacularization: the struggle was over the proper language of religious life rather than of literary expression. On Ka's poetry, see Diâo Faye, "L'Œuvre poétique wolofal de Moussa Ka ou l'épopée de Cheikh Ahmadou Bamba," Thèse de doctorat de troisième cycle (Université Cheikh Anta Diop, 1999); and Sana Kamara, *Sëriñ Muusaa Ka: melokaani roytéef* (Dakar: Éditions Papyrus Afrique, 2008). For a comprehensive study of Wolofal, see F. Ngom, *Muslims Beyond the Arab World*.

52. Throughout this book I will refer to Wolof sometimes as a "vernacular" and sometimes as an "African language." There are no value-neutral terms for discussing languages, but these choices invite clarification. When I use "vernacular," I am implicitly writing in a comparative mode in order to point out how the case of Wolof illustrates something about the language question more generally. The term *vernacular* came into English to describe the structurally inferior position of many European languages with regard to Latin, a state of affairs that began to unravel in the sixteenth century. Today, "vernacular" is used to refer to a linguistic ecology in which the language(s) of everyday life differ from those used in certain specialized and privileged milieu. When my frame of discussion is limited to Senegal, I often refer to Wolof as an "African language." This choice is also worth nuancing, since Senegal does not officially recognize languages as being "African" or otherwise. The preferred terminology, which I also invoke, is "national languages" (*langues nationales*).

53. See, for example, Ndao's comments as reported in Samory, "Le Wolof n'est pas une langue ethnique," 29 Dec. 2010, Xalima.com, http:// xalimasn.com/cafe-litteraire-du-festival-mondial-des-arts-negres-le-wolof -n%e2%80%99est-pas-une-langue-ethnique/.

54. Fiona McLaughlin, "Haalpulaar Identity as a Response to Wolo-fization," *African Languages and Cultures*, vol. 8, no. 2, 1995, pp. 153–68.

55. Ibrahima Diallo, *The Politics of National Languages in Postcolonial Senegal* (Amherst, N.Y.: Cambria Press, 2010), p.19.

56. McLaughlin, "Haalpulaar Identity"; Donal B. Cruise O'Brien, "The Shadow-Politics of Wolofisation," in *Symbolic Confrontations: Muslims Imagining the State in Africa* (New York: Palgrave Macmillan, 2003), pp. 120–40.

1. THE FETISH OF TEXTUALITY: DAVID BOILAT'S NOTEBOOKS
AND THE MAKING OF A LITERARY PAST

1. David Boilat, *Notes du Fouta Toro*, 1843, Société de Géographie Ms 8 48–49, Département des Cartes et Plans (Richelieu), BNF.

2. *Signares* were an important and relatively economically powerful class of mixed-race women in Saint-Louis and Gorée. As in many French colonies before the twentieth century, there were a variety of racial categorizations and privileges at work in Saint-Louis in Boilat's lifetime. For a history of the métis communities of Saint-Louis and Gorée, see Hilary Jones, *The Métis of Senegal: Urban Life and Politics in French West Africa* (Bloomington: Indiana University Press, 2013).

3. Yvon Bouquillon and Robert Cornevin, *David Boilat, 1814–1901: le précurseur.* (Dakar: Les Nouvelles éditions africaines du Sénégal, 1981).

4. The Wolof term *woy* (song, poetry) is internally diverse, covering a wide variety of distinct performance genres. These include songs of satire and praise, songs that accompany certain events or activities, and songs performed only by certain social groups. For an introduction to Wolof song and performance, see Momar Cisse, *Parole chantée et communication sociale chez les Wolof du Sénégal* (Paris: L'Harmattan, 2010).

5. David Boilat, *Esquisses sénégalaises: physionomie du pays, peuplades, commerce, religions, passé et avenir, récits et légendes* (Paris: Karthala, 2000), pp. 247–50.

6. *Marabout* is a polyvalent term in Senegal and much of West Africa. It can refer to an Islamic teacher, a Sufi religious leader, or an occult practitioner.

7. Until recently, Boilat's notebooks remained unknown to scholars and historians of Senegal. I found them again in the course of my research for this book and have since shared them with other scholars and writers. I am grateful to those who generously took the time to discuss Boilat's archive with me—Arame Fal, Souleymane Gaye, Fallou Ngom, and Boubacar Boris Diop. The French Bibliothèque Nationale (which took possession of the Society's archives) has since digitized the notebooks, which will hopefully make them more widely available.

8. Boilat, *Esquisses Sénégalaises*; David Boilat, *Grammaire de la langue Woloffe* (Paris: Imprimerie Impériale, 1858).

9. Boilat, *Grammaire*, vi; Boilat, *Esquisses Sénégalaises*, xvi.

10. Valentin-Yves Mudimbe, *The Idea of Africa* (Bloomington: Indiana University Press, 1994), p. xii.

11. Mudimbe, *Idea of Africa*, xii.

12. There is enormous variation among intellectual engagements with the colonial library, ranging from repetition and reflection to contestation

and critique. See Gaurav Desai, *Subject to Colonialism: African Self-Fashioning and the Colonial Library* (Durham, N.C.: Duke University Press, 2001).

13. At the beginning of his notebooks, Boilat includes portraits of two *marabouts* whom he says helped gather his texts. Boilat's research drew on kinship and friendship ties as well as his ecclesiastical authority. Some of his collection practices appear coercive: he indicates that he confiscated at least one of the *gris gris* from a *signare*. Boilat, *Notes Du Fouta Toro*, BNF.

14. For more on the textuality of *gris gris* (known as *téere* in Wolof) and other practices of protection and divination, see (Alfâ) Ibrahima Sow, *Divination marabout destin: aux sources de l'imaginaire* (Dakar: IFAN Cheikh Anta Diop, 2009); Allen F. Roberts and Mary Nooter Roberts, *A Saint in the City: Sufi Arts of Urban Senegal* (Los Angeles: UCLA Fowler Museum of Cultural History, 2003), published in conjunction with an exhibition of the same title, presented at the Fowler Museum at UCLA, February 27–July 27, 2003; Constant Hamès, *Coran et talismans: textes et pratiques magiques en milieu musulman* (Paris: Karthala, 2007).

15. La Société de géographie, *Instructions générales aux voyageurs* (Paris: Ch. Delagrave, 1875), p. 260.

16. Judith Irvine, "Genres of Conquest: From Literature to Science in Colonial African Linguistics," in *Verbal Art Across Cultures: The Aesthetics and Proto-Aesthetics of Communication*, ed. Hubert Knoblauch and Helga Kotthoff (Tübingen: Gunter Narr Verlag, 2001), p. 65.

17. Irvine, 65.

18. La Société de géographie, *Instructions générales*.

19. Boilat, *Grammaire*, 407.

20. Boilat, *Esquisses Sénégalaises*, illustrations.

21. The ceddo were originally a category of royal slaves who served as warriors to the crown in the pre-colonial Wolof kingdoms. For more on the etymology of the term and its stakes, see Chapter 4.

22. Boilat, *Esquisses Sénégalaises*, xv.

23. On the concept of the fetish and its origins on the frontiers of colonial contact in West Africa, see William Pietz, "The Problem of the Fetish, I," *RES: Anthropology and Aesthetics*, no. 9, Spring 1985, pp. 5–17. On accusations of fetishism as a way of distinguishing between subjects and objects, see Webb Keane, *Christian Moderns: Freedom and Fetish in the Mission Encounter* (Berkeley: University of California Press, 2007), p. 77.

24. Ann Laura Stoler, "Colonial Archives and the Arts of Governance." *Archival Science*, vol. 2, no. 1–2, 2002, p. 87.

25. On translation as controlled equivocation—"the mode of communication . . . between different perspectival positions"—see Eduardo Viveiros de Castro, "Perspectival Anthropology and the Method of Controlled

Equivocation," *Tipití: Journal of the Society for the Anthropology of Lowland South America*, vol. 2, no. 1, 2004. On radical translation—a "struggle . . . to characterize the social nature of the interaction"—see Elizabeth Povinelli, "Radical Worlds: The Anthropology of Incommensurability and Inconceivability," *Annual Review of Anthropology*, 2001, pp. 319–34. For translation and actor-network-theory, see Michel Callon, "Éléments pour une sociologie de la traduction: la domestication des coquilles saint-jacques et des marins-pêcheurs dans la baie de Saint-Brieuc," *L'Année Sociologique*, vol. 36, 1986, pp. 169–208. As Callon puts it, to translate is to "express in one's own language what others say and want, why they act in the way they do and how they associate with each other: it is to establish oneself as a spokesperson" (204). On "transduction" as conversion across semiotic frameworks, see Michael Silverstein, "Translation, Transduction, Transformation: Skating 'Glossando' on Thin Semiotic Ice," in *Translating Cultures: Perspectives on Translation and Anthropology*, ed. Paula G. Rubel and Abraham Rosman (Oxford: Berg, 2003), 75–105.

26. Jacques Louis Hymans, *Léopold Sédar Senghor: An Intellectual Biography* (Edinburgh: University Press, 1971), p. 248.

27. Léopold Sédar Senghor, "Afrique Noire," in *Les plus beaux écrits de l'Union Française et du Maghreb* (Paris: Éditions du Vieux Colombier, 1947), pp. 163–262.

28. Senghor, 214.

29. See Ursula Baumgardt, Françoise Ugochukwu, and Jean Derive, *Approches littéraires de l'oralité africaine* (Paris: Karthala Editions, 2005), p. 102; and Lilyan Kesteloot and Chérif Mbodj, *Contes et Mythes Wolof* (Dakar: Nouvelles Éditions Africaines du Sénégal, 1983).

30. Senghor, "Afrique Noire," 232; Boilat, *Grammaire*, 423.

31. Senghor, 232.

32. Senghor, 214.

33. Boilat's description of Wolof as his "maternal tongue" hints at how deeply gendered and at times conflicted his thinking on language was. He likely owed to his own mother both his fluency in Wolof and the kinship networks on which his research depended, but he gave virtually no indication of this in his writings. He also gave public lectures in which he called on mothers in Saint-Louis to stop speaking Wolof to their children, even as he was gathering the collections to produce a grammar of the language. Boilat, *Esquisses Sénégalaises*, 11–18.

34. Bernard Mouralis, "Les esquisses sénégalaises de l'abbé Boilat, ou le nationalisme sans la négritude," *Cahiers d'études Africaines*, vol. 35, no. 140, 1995, pp. 832–34.

35. Boilat insists that his work has neither "science nor elegance" while clearly aspiring to both these qualities. Boilat, *Esquisses Sénégalaises*, xiv. In

this sense, he was more of a precursor to the para-literary writers studied in Chapter 2 than to any self-consciously literary tradition.

36. David Murphy, "Birth of a Nation? The Origins of Senegalese Literature in French," *Research in African Literatures*, vol. 39, no. 1, 2008, p. 49.

37. I adapt "entextualization"—a "process of rendering a given instance of discourse as text, detachable from its local context"—from Michael Silverstein and Greg Urban, eds. *Natural Histories of Discourse* (Chicago: University of Chicago Press, 1996), p. 21. As Karin Barber points out, though, entextualization takes many forms. Script-based or text-focused recontextualizations are just one way that we make discourse object-like. Barber, *The Anthropology of Texts, Persons, and Publics: Oral and Written Culture in Africa and Beyond* (Cambridge: Cambridge University Press, 2007), pp. 1–31. While acknowledging the internal diversity of entextualization, my own use here is strategically more limited to focus our attention on the particular practice we see in Boilat.

38. The term "literarization" was coined nearly simultaneously by Sheldon Pollock and Pascale Casanova. See Alexander Beecroft, *An Ecology of World Literature: From Antiquity to the Present Day* (London: Verso Books, 2015), pp. 12–13. Casanova uses *"littérarisation"* (somewhat confusingly rendered as *littérisation* in the English translation from Harvard University Press), while Pollock opts for "literarization." Although both mean "to describe the process of texts, practices, or languages becoming 'literary,'" Casanova and Pollock diverge markedly in their focus. For Casanova, *littérarisation* refers primarily to the "magic transmutation" by which a language or a text becomes literary through proper recognition in her world republic of letters. Casanova, *La République mondiale des Lettres* (Paris: Points, 2008), p. 190. Pollock defines *literarization* as the emergence of new literatures through "conformity with a literary paradigm"—a process he distinguishes from *literization* (the breakthrough to writing). Sheldon Pollock, *The Language of the Gods in the World of Men: Sanskrit, Culture, and Power in Premodern India* (Berkeley: University of California Press, 2006), pp. 4–5. As will become clear in this chapter, my sense of literarization is distinct from both of these accounts. For a related discussion of *littérarisation* in the translations of the Rosetta Stone and the Quran, see Michael Allan, *In the Shadow of World Literature: Sites of Reading in Colonial Egypt* (Princeton, N.J.: Princeton University Press, 2016), pp. 30–32.

39. Practices of gathering texts as specimens are traceable back to the Enlightenment, if not farther. See Richard Bauman and Charles L. Briggs, *Voices of Modernity: Language Ideologies and the Politics of Inequality* (Cambridge: Cambridge University Press, 2003). But such practices seem to

become intensive with regard to African lifeworlds in the late nineteenth and early twentieth centuries with the rise of the colonial library. See Judith Irvine, "Subjected Words: African Linguistics and the Colonial Encounter," *Language & Communication*, vol. 28, no. 4, 2008, pp. 323–43.

40. Casanova. *La République mondiale des Lettres*, 202. Pascale Casanova, *The World Republic of Letters*, trans. M. B. Debevoise (Cambridge, Mass.: Harvard University Press, 2007), 136.

41. Casanova. *La République mondiale des Lettres*, 190.

42. Casanova. *La République mondiale des Lettres*, 336–40.

43. Boilat, *Grammaire*, 391–93; Jacques-François Roger, *Fables sénégalaises* (Paris: Nepveu, 1828), p. 400.

2. PARA-LITERARY AUTHORSHIP: COLONIAL EDUCATION AND THE USES OF LITERATURE

1. See, for example, Patrick Corcoran, *The Cambridge Introduction to Francophone Literature* (Cambridge: Cambridge University Press, 2007); and Malcom Offord et al., eds., *Francophone Literatures: A Literary and Linguistic Companion* (London: Routledge, 2001).

2. Léopold Sédar Senghor, "Afrique Noire," in *Les plus beaux écrits de l'Union Française et du Maghreb* (Paris: Éditions du Vieux Colombier, 1947), pp. 233–34.

3. Senghor, "Afrique Noire," 233. On ethnology and the emergence of a colonial public space, see Vincent Debaene, "Les écrivains contre l'ethnologie? Ethnographie, ethnologie et littérature d'Afrique et des Antilles, 1921–1948," *Romanic Review*, vol. 104, no. 3–4, 2013, pp. 362–70.

4. Senghor, "Afrique Noire," 233.

5. See Lilyan Kesteloot, *Les écrivains noirs de langue française: naissance d'une littérature* (Brussels: Editions de l'Université de Bruxelles, 1983); and Corcoran, *Cambridge Introduction to Francophone Literature*. But other critics have argued for connecting these earlier works to later francophone literary production. See Lydie Moudileno, "The Francophone Novel in Sub-Saharan African," in *The Cambridge Companion to the African Novel*, ed. F. Abiola Irele (Cambridge: Cambridge University Press, 2009), pp. 125–8; and Christopher L. Miller, *Theories of Africans: Francophone Literature and Anthropology in Africa* (Chicago: University of Chicago Press, 1993).

6. Bouillagui Fadiga, "Une circoncision chez les markas du soudan," *Bulletin Du Comité d'Études Historiques et Scientifiques d'Afrique Occidentale Française*, vol. 18, no. 4, 1934, p. 565.

7. Senghor notes that the literature of school teachers is "more scientific in a way than literary" but that "philological and ethnographic research is at the origin of every *renaissance*." Senghor, "Afrique Noire," 233. As Debaene

points out, the implicit comparison here is to the emergence of European national traditions in the sixteenth through nineteenth centuries. Vincent Debaene, "Le point de vue de l'indigène ou comment on écrit l'histoire de la littérature," *Romanic Review*, vol. 100, no. 1–2, 2009, pp. 15–28.

8. I first used "para-literary" in 2016 to describe the curious entanglement and disavowal of literary technique that I saw in the Ponty notebooks. Tobias Warner, "Para-Literary Ethnography and Colonial Self-Writing: The Student Notebooks of the William Ponty School," *Research in African Literatures*, vol. 47, no. 1, 2016, pp. 1–20. Since then, Merve Emre has adopted a similar term in *Paraliterary: The Making of Bad Readers in Postwar America* (Chicago: University of Chicago Press, 2017). Focusing on the United States, Emre concentrates on readers rather than authors and uses "paraliterary" to describe practices that thrive outside the central institutions of the literary world. Our uses appear complementary, and I take the convergence to be an indication that our critical lexicon needed expansion.

9. See Warner, "Para-Literary Ethnography." This research was conducted in the Ponty archive at the Institut Fondamental d'Afrique Noire (IFAN) in Dakar. During my two periods of research at IFAN, the collection was in the process of being recatalogued. The citations here reflect the new catalogue system. Since Ponty students did not always specify the year in which they were writing, it is not always possible to identify exactly when certain notebooks were written. A guide to the Cahiers does exist, but it covers only the Senegalese section of the notebooks. See François Afanou and Raymond Togbé Pierre, *Catalogue des "Cahiers William Ponty": extrait Sénégal* (Dakar: Département de documentation de l'I.F.A.N., 1967).

10. Ann Laura Stoler, *Along the Archival Grain: Epistemic Anxieties and Colonial Common Sense* (Princeton, N.J.: Princeton University Press, 2008), p. 65.

11. Michel Foucault, "Qu'est-ce qu'un auteur?" *Bulletin de la Société Française de Philosophie*, vol. 63, no. 3, 1969, p. 73.

12. On these foundational points, see Edward Said, *Culture and Imperialism* (New York: Vintage, 1994); Gauri Viswanathan, *Masks of Conquest: Literary Study and British Rule in India* (New York: Columbia University Press, 1989); and Simon Gikandi, *Maps of Englishness: Writing Identity in the Culture of Colonialism* (New York: Columbia University Press, 1996).

13. Georges Hardy, *Une conquête morale* (Paris: A. Colin, 1917), p. 189.

14. Reprinted in André Davesne and Joseph Gouin, *Mamadou et Bineta sont devenus grands: livre de français à l'usage des cours moyens et supérieurs des écoles de l'Afrique noire* (Strasbourg, France: Istra, 1939), p. 21.

15. Reprinted in Davesne and Gouin, 4.

16. Abdoulaye Sadji, *Commentez cette parole de Montaigne: savoir par cœur n'est pas savoir,* Student Composition, Serie O 150 (31), ANS.

17. "Sçavoir par cœur n'est pas sçavoir; c'est tenir ce qu'on a donné en garde à sa mémoire. Ce qu'on sçait droittement, on en dispose, sans regarder au patron, sans tourner les yeux vers son livre." Michel de Montaigne, *Les Essais* (Paris: Gallimard, 2007), p. 157.

18. M. M. Bakhtin, *The Dialogic Imagination: Four Essays* (Austin: University of Texas Press, 1982), p. 341.

19. Amadou Booker Sadji, *Abdoulaye Sadji: Biographie, 1910–1961* (Paris: Présence Africaine, 1997), pp. 23–24.

20. Peggy Sabatier, "Educating a Colonial Elite: The William Ponty School and Its Graduates," PhD diss., University of Chicago, 1977, p. 14. First established in Saint-Louis, the campus moved to Gorée Island in 1913 and finally to Sébikotane near Rufisque in 1931. Boubacar Ly, *La formation au métier d'instituteur: Tome III - Les instituteurs au Sénégal de 1903 à 1945* (Paris: L'Harmattan, 2009), pp. 61–84. For a reading of contemporary projects to found a university on the Sébikotane site, see Ferdinand De Jong and Brian Quinn, "Ruines d'utopies: l'École William Ponty et l'Université du Futur africain," trans. Jean-Nicolas Bach, *Politique africaine,* no. 135, Dec. 2014, pp. 71–94.

21. Alice Conklin, *A Mission to Civilize* (Stanford, Calif: Stanford University Press), p. 85.

22. Sabatier, "Educating a Colonial Elite," 31. The exception was Lamine Guèye, who taught mathematics for a year at Ponty in 1920. Africans did hold the disciplinary post of *surveillant général / moniteur* beginning in the 1920s. Ly, *La formation au métier d'instituteur,* 36; Sabatier, 99–100.

23. Sabatier, 27; Jean-Hervé Jézéquel, "Grammaire de la distinction coloniale. L'organisation des cadres de l'enseignement en Afrique occidentale française (1903-fin des années 1930)," *Genèses,* no. 69, 2007, pp. 7–14.

24. In his memoir, the future Senegalese Prime Minister Mamadou Dia writes of his years as a student at Ponty as a defining period in in his life. Dia presents it as a time when he encountered the reality of colonial racism and began many of the friendships that would be pivotal in his career. Mamadou Dia, *Mémoires d'un militant du tiers-monde* (Paris: Publisud, 1985), pp. 20–27.

25. Albert Charton, "Les Etudes indigènes à l'Ecole Normale William Ponty," *Bulletin de l'Enseignement de l'Afrique Occidentale Française,* no 84, 1933, p.199.

26. Senghor, "Afrique Noire," 233.

27. Sabatier, "Educating a Colonial Elite," 28–29; Ly, *La formation au métier d'instituteur,* 104–8.

28. Sabatier, 10.

29. For a study of the interplay between ethnography and administration, see Gary Wilder, "Colonial Ethnology and Political Rationality in French West Africa," *History and Anthropology*, vol. 14, no. 3, 2003, pp. 228–40.

30. Gary Wilder, *The French Imperial Nation-State: Negritude and Colonial Humanism between the Two World Wars* (Chicago: University of Chicago Press, 2005), pp. 18, 49; James E. Genova, *Colonial Ambivalence, Cultural Authenticity, and the Limitations of Mimicry in French-Ruled West Africa, 1914–1956* (New York: Peter Lang, 2004), pp. 90–94.

31. Genova, Wilder, and Gamble have all studied various aspects of the long-running "crisis" of the colonial education system. See Genova, 111–22; Wilder, 119–29; and Harry Gamble, *Contesting French West Africa: Battles Over Schools and the Colonial Order, 1900–1950* (Lincoln: University of Nebraska Press, 2017). For an earlier era, see Conklin, *A Mission to Civilize*, 77–81; Kelly Duke Bryant, *Education as Politics: Colonial Schooling and Political Debate in Senegal, 1850s–1914* (Madison: University of Wisconsin Press), 2015; and Denise Bouche, "L'enseignement dans les territoires français de l'Afrique occidentale de 1817 à 1920: mission civilisatrice ou formation d'une élite," PhD diss., Université de Lille, 1975. For a helpful overview of the historiography on French colonial education, see Pascale Barthélémy, "L'enseignement dans l'Empire colonial français: une vieille histoire?," *Histoire de l'éducation*, no. 128, Oct. 2010, pp. 5–28.

32. Owen White, *Children of the French Empire: Miscegenation and Colonial Society in French West Africa 1895–1960* (Oxford: Oxford University Press, 1999), pp. 62–63.

33. Wilder, *French Imperial*, 120.

34. Harry Gamble, "Peasants of the Empire. Rural Schools and the Colonial Imaginary in 1930s French West Africa," *Cahiers d'Études Africaines*, no. 195, 2009, p. 776.

35. Wilder, *French Imperial*, 129.

36. Wilder, 129; Genova, *Colonial Ambivalence*, 111.

37. Albert Charton, "Rôle social de l'enseignement en Afrique Occidentale Française," *Outre-Mer* 6, no. 2, June 1934, pp. 194–95.

38. Quoted in Gamble, "Peasants of the Empire," 781.

39. Genova, *Colonial Ambivalence*, 121; Gamble, 781.

40. Wilder, *French Imperial*, 120.

41. Mamadou Diouf's study of the civility of the *originaires* is foundational here, albeit with a focus on the nineteenth century. Mamadou Diouf, "The French Colonial Policy of Assimilation and the Civility of the Originaires of the Four Communes (Senegal): A Nineteenth-Century Globalization Project," *Development and Change*, vol. 29, no. 4, 1998, pp. 671–96. For

the politics of citizenship after 1945, see Frederick Cooper, *Citizenship between Empire and Nation: Remaking France and French Africa, 1945–1960* (Princeton, N.J.: Princeton University Press, 2014); and Gary Wilder, *Freedom Time: Negritude, Decolonization, and the Future of the World* (Durham, N.C.: Duke University Press, 2015).

42. Wilder, *French Imperial*, 129; Genova, *Colonial Ambivalence*, 27–28.

43. Wilder, 124–39.

44. Genova, *Colonial Ambivalence*, 99. Edwards suggests that the wariness toward the *évolués* was also a reaction to the Pan-African Congress movement of the 1920s. Brent Hayes Edwards, *The Practice of Diaspora: Literature, Translation, and the Rise of Black Internationalism* (Cambridge, Mass.: Harvard University Press, 2003), 75.

45. Wilder, *French Imperial*, 131.

46. Wilder, 120–21.

47. Aristide Prat, "Concours et examens en 1921: commentaires," *Bulletin de l'Enseignement de l'Afrique Occidentale Française*, vol. 9, no. 47, Sept. 1921, pp. 67–71.

48. Ly, *La formation au métier d'instituteur*, 123.

49. Sabatier, "Educating a Colonial Elite," 128–29.

50. Charton, "Rôle social de l'enseignement," 201.

51. Sabatier, "Educating a Colonial Elite," 135.

52. Roger Dumargue, "L'enseignement du français à l'Ecole William Ponty (A.O.F.)," *Information d'outre-mer pour l'enseignement* 1, Jan.–Feb. 1939, pp. 27–28, quoted in Sabatier, "Educating a Colonial Elite," 144.

53. Ly, *La formation au métier d'instituteur*, 124–25.

54. See Stephen Bulman, "A School for Epic? The École William Ponty and the Evolution of the Sunjata Epic, 1913–1960," in *Epic Adventures: Heroic Narrative in the Oral Performance Traditions of Four Continents*, ed. Jan Jansen and Henk M. J. Maier (Münster: Lit Verlag, 2004), pp. 34–45; Joshua Cohen, "Stages in Transition: Les Ballets Africains and Independence, 1959 to 1960," *Journal of Black Studies*, vol. 43, no. 1, Jan. 2012, pp. 11–48; John Conteh-Morgan, *Theatre and Drama in Francophone Africa: A Critical Introduction* (Cambridge: Cambridge University Press, 1994); Robert Cornevin, *Le théâtre en Afrique noire et à Madagascar* (Paris: Le livre africain, 1970); F. J. Amon D'Aby, *La Côte d'Ivoire dans la cité africaine* (Paris: Larose, 1951); Bernard Mouralis, "William Ponty Drama," in *European-Language Writing in Sub-Saharan Africa*, ed. A. S. Gérard (Budapest: Akadémiai Kiadó, 1986), pp. 130–40; Wole Soyinka, "Theatre in African Traditional Cultures: Survival Patterns," in *Twentieth Century Performance Reader*, ed. Teresa Brayshaw and Noel Witt (London: Routledge, 1996), pp. 430–43; and Bakary Traoré, *Le théâtre négro-africain et ses fonctions sociales* (Paris: Présence Africaine, 1958).

55. Student-written plays were staged both at Ponty and in public performances attended by Dakarois society. Mouralis, 132. A troupe of students toured France, performing in Paris during the 1937 Colonial Exposition. Traoré, 49–51. In the late 1940s, *Présence Africaine* consecrated some of Ponty's output by reprinting a number of plays. Mouralis, 139–40. Ponty students drew on the research they conducted over the summer to produce both their plays and their notebooks, but the exact overlap between the two is unclear. This has led some scholars to speculate that the notebooks were merely an "important phase" of the theater. Mouralis, 134. Studies of Ponty as an institution suggest that the notebooks were a significant assignment in their own right, and not subordinated to the theater. Sabatier, "Educating a Colonial Elite," 137–42; Ly, *La formation au métier d'instituteur*, 123–24; 232–33.

56. There are a number of precedents for the assignment. The regional or ethnic monograph was a key genre for future colonial administrators studying at the Ecole Coloniale in the interwar years. Wilder, *French Imperial*, 70. Another model may be the regional monographs that student-teachers in France wrote in the late nineteenth century, when the social sciences were cultivated at the Ecoles Normales of the Third Republic. Anne-Marie Thiesse, *Ils apprenaient la France: l'exaltation des régions dans le discours patriotique* (Paris: Les Editions de la MSH, 1997), pp. 10–15. I am grateful to Vincent Debaene for suggesting this latter parallel. What distinguishes the notebooks from these analogues is that Ponty students had to simultaneously establish their own authority as ethnographic observers while supplying information as native informants.

57. Charton, "Les Etudes indigènes," 199.

58. Quoted in Afanou and Togbé Pierre, *Catalogue*, iii.

59. Charton, "Les Etudes indigènes," 199.

60. Charton, 199.

61. Sabatier, "Educating a Colonial Elite," 137. However, some students cite work by colonial anthropologists such as Maurice Delafosse. Samba Diack, *A Podor, vestiges de quelques événements historiques et leurs conséquences dans la vie actuelle*, Cahiers Ponty, n.d., XXVI-SE- 766, carton N°5, IFAN, p. 2; and Larba Ouattara, *L'Alimentation en pays Lobi*, Cahiers Ponty, 1945, I-CI-27, carton N°68, IFAN, p. 4.

62. Lokho Damey, *Mémoire de fin d'études: Le système d'éducation traditionnelle chez les Manons*, Cahiers Ponty, n.d., XV-G-551, carton N°14, IFAN, p. 21.

63. Céline Labrune-Badiane and Etienne Smith's survey of the writings of schoolteachers in French West Africa unfortunately appeared too late in the production stages of this book for me to engage with it in a systematic

way, but it looks to be an exciting contribution to the historiography of French West Africa. Céline Labrune-Badiane and Etienne Smith, *Les Hussards noirs de la colonie: Instituteurs africains et petites patries en AOF* (Paris: Karthala, 2018). Nevertheless, I will comment briefly here on two points they raise regarding my work, since they touch directly on the arguments of this chapter. Labrune-Badiane and Smith discuss an earlier and condensed version of my research on the Ponty notebooks—Warner, "Para-Literary Ethnography"—that focused primarily on the interaction between the *bildungsroman* and ethnography. First, they question the extent to which the Ponty archive as a whole is para-literary (288). They suggest that the traces of literary techniques that I highlighted are mainly limited to notebooks on education. They are quite right that hints of the *bildungsroman* are more abundant in compositions on education. But their objection does not hold if we think about the para-literary more expansively, as I do in this chapter. By "para-literary," I mean more than a text "looks like" a novel of formation or an autobiography. Some of the seemingly "sober and impersonal" notebooks they point to could thus be understood as para-literary in the fuller sense I detail here. Second, Labrune-Badiane and Smith suggest that I argue that ethnography was merely "a simple pretext" for exercises in self-writing at Ponty (289). Quite the opposite. It would flatten a constitutive tension of the Ponty archive to read the notebooks as literature or creative writing in any kind of transparent way. My point remains that our existing categories of thought—literature, history, ethnography—are simply not capacious enough to capture the epistemological friction at work in these compositions.

64. Ibrahima Sow, *Mémoire de fin d'études: Type d'éducation Foulah*, Cahiers Ponty, n.d. XV-G-553, carton N°14, IFAN, pp. 48–49.

65. Amadou Sakhir Cissé, *Education de l'enfant Gourou en Côte d'Ivoire*, Cahiers Ponty, n.d., XV-CI-536, carton N°14, IFAN, p. 245.

66. Joseph Batiéno, *Devoir de vacances: Education et instruction des enfants dans le milieu indigène*, Cahiers Ponty, n.d., XV-G-535, carton N°14, IFAN, pp. 27–29.

67. Students also draw on other narrative forms besides the realist novel. M'bengue Mbaye, for example, uses an epistolary structure to relate his experiences as a soldier in the Second World War. M'bengue Mbaye, *La Méditerranée vue par un noir*, Cahiers Ponty, n.d., XXV-SE-751, carton N°26, IFAN.

68. Jules (Kouaho) Ossoh'ou, *Devoir de vacances*, Cahiers Ponty, 1945, C15. XV CI 5, IFAN, p. 1.

69. Cheikhou Tidiane Dieng, *Le Génie des eaux*, Cahiers Ponty, n.d., XXIV-SE-713, carton N°36, IFAN, pp. 47–48.

70. For a discussion on the "Flaubertian omniscience" of ethnography, see James Clifford, "On Ethnographic Authority," *Representations*, no. 2, 1983, p. 50.

71. Michael Silverstein observes that asking subjects who attended colonial schools to write about ritual events they remember from childhood produces "a confrontation in the narrating present of a *recuperated consciousness* situated within earlier childhood events in relation to the *narrating consciousness* of the present." Michael Silverstein, "The Fieldwork Encounter and the Colonized Voice of Indigeneity," *Representations*, vol. 137, no. 1, 2017, p. 31.

72. Barbara Johnson, "Bringing Out D. A. Miller," *Narrative*, vol. 10, no. 1, 2002, p. 7.

73. Specifically, the theatre was described as a way of requiring students to search for "the French image that will render as closely as possible the Mandingue, Agnie or Nago image." Charles Béart, "Le théâtre indigène et la culture franco-africaine," *L'Education africaine*, Apr.–Jun. 1936, p. 12.

74. Kalifa Keïta, *Ce que racontent les griots*, Cahiers Ponty, n.d., XXVI-SO-772, carton N°74, IFAN.

75. Sabatier, "Educating a Colonial Elite," 145.

76. Diakité's notebook was written at the Ecole Normale Rurale Frédéric Assomption de Katibougou, but he uses the play in the same way that Ponty students would have been taught. Although the archive is known as the Cahiers Ponty, this type of assignment appears to have been in use at other schools.

77. Mamadi Diakité, *Devoir de vacances: L'Education du garçon et de la fille dans la famille indigène*, Cahiers Ponty, 1945, XV-G-543, carton N°14, IFAN, pp. 42–43; Molière translation by Richard Wilbur.

78. Diakité, 43.

79. Ponty never had female students in the colonial period, but its "sister school," the Ecole Normale de jeunes filles de Rufisque, opened in 1938. For an excellent overview of this institution, see Pascale Barthélémy, *Africaines et diplômées à l'époque coloniale* (Rennes, France: Presses Universitaires de Rennes, 2010). Rufisque had no equivalent to the notebook assignment, but Germaine le Goff, the school's headmistress, did have a habit of asking her most promising students to write her long letters over their summer vacations. For an analysis of these compositions, see Pascale Barthélémy, "Je suis une africaine . . . j'ai vingt ans," *Annales. Histoire, Sciences Sociales*, vol. 64, 2009, pp. 825–852. Barthélémy suggests that Rufisque students wrote such letters not only to their headmistress but also to each other. We can perhaps detect an echo of this practice in one of the earliest francophone African novels written by a woman—Mariama Bâ's *Une si longue lettre*,

studied in Chapter 6—which is constructed as a long letter or diary written by one Rufisque graduate to another.

80. As this example suggests, these assignments were also attempts to produce a comparative discourse on gender across "African societies" among the all-male student body. This is particularly true of the notebooks on marriage, which offer occasions for the young men to reflect on their own masculinity and describe the "kind of woman" they would like to marry.

81. Ambivalence toward literature has long been a defining feature of the French anthropological tradition. See Vincent Debaene, *Far Afield: French Anthropology between Science and Literature* (Chicago: University of Chicago Press, 2014), pp. 1–22. But this tension operates slightly differently in the notebooks: literary traces at the level of style and form give substance to the notebooks as works of "personal experience," while the structural restrictions ensure that each one still has "a certain documentary value."

82. Edouard Aquereburu, *Le Noir évolué*, Cahiers Ponty, 1941, XVIII-D-602, carton N°5, IFAN, p. 10.

83. Serigne Fall Seck begins his notebook with an appeal to his "lecteurs et correcteurs" (readers and graders). Serigne Fall Seck, *Formation morale de l'enfant*, Cahiers Ponty, 1949, XV-SE-584, carton N°3, IFAN, p. 1.

84. Larba Ouattara planned to write on the topic of indigenous pharmacopeia until his uncle refused to tell him any secrets. Ouattara, *L'Alimentation en pays Lobi*, p. 2.

85. In his notebook on "Ce que racontent les griots," Kalifa Keïta describes how difficult it was to gather knowledge on his topic. He writes that he had to learn to listen in on "historical conversations" without asking questions or even appearing interested, because whenever "an auxiliary of the whites" asks "old people and griots" for information about the historical past, they reply, "I don't know!" Keïta, *Ce que racontent les griots*, p. 6.

86. Amadou Babaheine Ibn Alfa Diallo, for instance, complains of the difficulties he encountered in doing a "demographic study." Asking families how many children they had generated fears of increased taxes and conscription—but also ran up against the widespread prohibition on counting living children. Amadou Babaheine Ibn Alfa Diallo, *L'enfant dans le milieu familial*, Cahiers Ponty, 1949, XV-G-544, carton N°14, IFAN, p. 5.

87. Amadou Arona Sy, *Monographie du village de Poukhan*, Cahiers Ponty, 1941, XII-SE-488, carton N°16, IFAN, p. 1.

88. Baffa Gaye, *Le Noir évolué*, Cahiers Ponty, 1941, XVIII-SE-606, carton N°31, IFAN, p. 1.

89. Yapi Kouassi, *Les animaux de la brousse autour de Zékrézessou*, Cahiers Ponty, 1938, XIII-CI-504, carton N°59, IFAN, p. 1.

90. Lompolo Koné, *Devoir de fin d'année: L'Ancien tirailleur revenu au village*, Cahiers Ponty, n.d., XVIII-CI-600, carton N°12, IFAN, p. 1.

91. Ly, *La formation au métier d'instituteur*, 111.

92. Quoted in Ly, 111–12.

93. From the schedule reproduced in Barthélémy, *Africaines et diplômées*, 294, the study of French took up the greater part of the day. In the institution's early years, students mainly encountered excerpts—apparently taken from Philippon's *Les Lectures littéraires de l'école*—with occasional readings of longer works such as *Le bourgeois gentilhomme* and *Emile*. Ly, 374. More sustained engagements with literary texts were introduced by the 1920s, but it was not until well after World War II that studies on the level of a *lycée* were formalized. The curricula reproduced by Ly indicate that the readings were a mix of French classics (Zola, Daudet, Colette, Balzac) and so-called colonial literature written by French authors (André Demaison, Jérôme Tharaud, and Pierre Loti seem to have been popular). Early francophone African novels were never taught, although students were well aware of their existence and cultivated their own private reading habits outside the classroom. Sabatier, "Educating a Colonial Elite," 81, 145; Ly 111–114. In their interviews with Ly, former students recall reading widely and actively searching for books not contained in Ponty's library—notably for Maran's *Batouala* (403–4).

94. Ibrahima Ben Mady Cissé, *Mémoire de fin d'études normales: Système d'éducation traditionnelle d'une société*, Cahiers Ponty, 1949, XV-SE-562, carton N°30. IFAN, p. 2.

95. Ibrahima Cissé, 4–5.

96. Mahélor Diouf N'Dofène, *Système d'éducation traditionnellle d'une société: Sine Saloum*, Cahiers Ponty, n.d., XV-SE-570, carton N°30, IFAN, p. 25.

97. Habibou Bâ, *Mémoire de fin d'études normales: Le Systéme d'éducation traditionnelle au Fouta Djallon*, Cahiers Ponty, n.d., XV-G-540, carton N°14, IFAN, p. 25.

98. Jacques-Marie Ndiaye, *Le peuple sérère*, Cahiers Ponty, 1940, XI-SE-421, carton N°34, IFAN, p. 1.

99. Ndiaye does not entirely reject a racialized frame so much as dispute its exactitude. After quarreling with the prompt in his preface, Ndiaye goes on to write a fairly conventional study of a Sérère community in the notebook itself. In his case at least, the dissent appears to have been fleeting.

100. Wilder, *French Imperial*, 116.

101. Gregory Mann, *Native Sons: West African Veterans and France in the Twentieth Century* (Durham, N.C.: Duke University Press, 2006), p. 9.

102. See, for example, the exam questions from 1930, many of which asked students to recall experiences from their native village. Prat,

"Concours et examens," pp. 69–70. In 1921 and 1925, students were asked questions such as "Describe the kind of home your parents live in. What feelings does it inspire in you?" and "It is Sunday in the village. What does one do, see, and hear?" Anon, "Compositions françaises," *Bulletin de l'Enseignement de l'Afrique Occidentale Française*, vol. 13, no. 60, Jan.–June, 1925, pp. 100–4; and Anon, "Concours et examens en 1930." *Bulletin de l'Enseignement de l'Afrique Occidentale Française*, no. 72, June 1930, pp. 69–70.

103. Among many possible examples, see Robin, "Le développement de l'esprit d'observation chez l'enfant," *Education Africaine*, no. 104, 1940, pp. 59–60; and R. Guiffray, "Extraits de la conférence pédagogique de Bamako," *Education Africaine*, no. 15, 1952, pp. 61–63.

104. See, respectively, the issues from Jan.–Mar. 1935, Jan.–Mar. 1934, Apr.–June 1930, Apr.–June 1932, Apr.–Sept. 1935, July–Dec. 1933, and July–Dec. 1929.

105. Albert Charton, "La Vie et hygiène intellectuelles," *Bulletin de l'Enseignement de l'Afrique Occidentale Française*, vol. 19, no. 72, Mar. 1930, pp. 10–14.

106. See the recurring sections Etudes du milieu and Variétés et folklore in *L'Education Africaine* no. 14, 1952, through no. 25, 1954.

107. Déborah Lifchitz, "Projet d'une enquête sur la littérature orale en Afrique Noire," *Outre-Mer*, vol. 9, no. 2, Sept. 1937.

108. Antoine [pseud.], "L'Histoire de l'AOF," *Le Cœur de Dahomey*, Aug. 1935, pp. 1–2.

109. For an analysis of these patronage relationships, see Vincent Debaene, "Entre informateur et auteur. Discours ethnographique indigène et littérature en AOF," in *Ethnologues en situation coloniale*, ed. Daniel Fabre et al. (Paris: CNRS Editions, 2016).

110. Wilder, *French Imperial*, 129–34.

111. Jules Carde, *Demande d'accession à la qualité de citoyen français de M. Dim Delobson*, 13 Dec. 1929, Fonds Ministériels, Affpol148, ANOM.

112. Ousmane Socé, "Un témoignage: l'évolution culturelle de l'AOF," *Dakar-Jeunes*, 29 Jan. 1942.

113. On the debate in *Dakar-Jeunes*, see Harry Gamble, "The National Revolution in French West Africa: *Dakar-Jeunes* and the Shaping of African Opinion," *International Journal of Francophone Studies*, vol. 10, no. 1–2, Mar. 2007, pp. 85–103.

114. Anon, "Le Courrier de Nos Amis." *Dakar-Jeunes*, 23 July 1942, p. 4, and 17 Sept. 1942, p. 4.

115. Hamidou Dia, "Littérature et préjugés," *Dakar-Jeunes*, 14 May 1942, p. 3.

116. Charles Béart, "A propos d'une littérature indigène d'expression française," *Dakar-Jeunes*, 18 June 1942, p. 4.

117. Béart, 4.

118. Léopold Sédar Senghor, "Nuit de Sine" and "Chant d'ombre," in *Œuvre Poétique* (Paris: Points, 2006), pp. 16, 44.

119. Birago Diop, "Les Mamelles," in *Anthologie de la nouvelle poésie nègre et malgache de langue française*, ed. Léopold Sédar Senghor, 5th ed. (Paris: Presses Universitaires de France, 2002), p. 137.

120. Paul Hazoumé, "Tata Ajachè Soupo Ma Ha Awouinyan," *Reconnaissance Africaine*, no. 1, Aug. 1925; Hazoumé, "Journal de Voyage de Cotonou à Dassa-Zoumé," *Reconnaissance Africaine*, no. 13, Mar. 1926.

121. Paul Hazoumé, *Doguicimi* (Washington D.C.: Three Continents Press, 1990).

122. Dorothy S. Blair, *African Literature in French: A History of Creative Writing in French from West and Equatorial Africa* (Cambridge: Cambridge University Press, 1976), p. 75; Eleni Coundouriotis, *Claiming History: Colonialism, Ethnography, and the Novel* (New York: Columbia University Press, 1999), p. 110.

123. Georges Hardy, "Préface," in *Doguicimi* (Paris: Larose, 1938). Much of the praise that greeted *Doguicimi* upon its publication systematically recast Hazoumé's achievement as ethnography, rather than history—because to a European audience Africa did not have a history. Coundouriotis, *Claiming History*, 9, 11.

124. Paul Hazoumé, "Causerie aux instituteurs sur des recherches ethnographiques et historiques," 9 Jan. 1942, Series O 334 (31), ANS.

125. Hazoumé, 2.

126. Abdoulaye Sadji, "Ce que dit la musique africaine," *L'Education Africaine*, no. 94, Apr. 1936, pp. 119–72; Abdoulaye Sadji, "Ce que disent les vielles mélopées sénégalaises," *Paris-Dakar*, May 1938, p. 3.

127. Abdoulaye Sadji, "Ce que dit la musique africaine," 148–49.

128. Abdoulaye. Sadji, "Ce que disent les vielles mélopées sénégalaises," 3. French translation is by Sadji; English translation is my own.

129. Cooper, *Citizenship between Empire and Nation*, 6; Wilder, *French Imperial*, 148.

130. For a complementary and insightful reading of Sadji's commentaries, see Hans-Jürgen Lüsebrink, *La Conquête de l'espace public colonial: prises de parole et formes de participation d'écrivains et d'intellectuels africains dans la presse à l'époque coloniale (1900–1960)* (Frankfurt: IKO-Verlag für Internationale Kommunikation, 2003), pp. 128–37.

131. Bernard Dadié, *Composition Française*. Series O, Archives de l'Ecole Normale William Ponty, ANS.

132. Berndard Dadié, *Légendes et poèmes, Afrique debout! Légendes Afric-aines. Climbié. La Ronde des jours* (Paris: Seghers, 1966), p. 221; Bernard Dadié, *Climbié*, trans. Karen Chapman (London: Heinemann, 1971), p. 149.

133. Mildred P. Mortimer, *Journeys through the French African Novel* (Portsmouth, N.H.: Heinemann, 1990), p. 45.

134. Camara Laye, *L'Enfant noir* (Paris: Pocket, 2007), pp. 73–74.

135. Laye, 80.

136. Beti dismissed *L'Enfant noir* as an "idyllic universe" filled with "initiations, circumcisions, excisions, superstitions" that seemed to him borrowed from a colonial school reader. Mongo Beti, *Le Rebelle: Tome 1* (Paris: Editions Gallimard, 2007), p. 28.

137. Adèle King, *Rereading Camara Laye* (Lincoln: University of Nebraska Press, 2003).

138. Abiola Irele, "In Search of Camara Laye," *Research in African Litera-tures*, vol. 37, no. 1, 2006, pp. 110–27.

139. Kesteloot is far from the only scholar to trace the origins of franco-phone African literature this way. For overviews that begin with *Légitime défense, L'Etudiant noir,* and negritude, see also Corcoran, *Cambridge Introduc-tion to Francophone Literature,* 76; and Offord et al., *Francophone Literatures,* 78. See Coundouriotis, *Claiming History,* 12, for a discussion on how the judg-ment of "insufficient" literariness affected the later reputation of Hazoumé.

140. Kesteloot, *Les écrivains noirs,* 11, quoted in Christopher L. Miller, *Nationalists and Nomads: Essays on Francophone African Literature and Culture* (Chicago: University of Chicago Press, 1999), p 11.

141. C. L. Miller, 12. On the interface between literary and ethnographic writing in the colonial period, see Lüsebrink, *La Conquête de l'espace public colonial;* János Riesz, *De la littérature coloniale à la littérature africaine: pré-textes, contextes, intertextes* (Paris: Karthala, 2007); and Kusum Aggarwal, *Amadou Hampâté Bâ et l'africanisme: de la recherche anthropologique à l'exercice de la fonction autoriale* (Paris: L'Harmattan, 1999).

142. C. L. Miller, 12.

143. Franco Moretti, "Conjectures on World Literature," in *Distant Reading* (London: Verso, 2013), pp. 50, 57.

144. Moretti, 56. For a critical reading of Moretti's observations about the exceptional status of African literature, see Joseph R. Slaughter, "Locations of Comparison," *Cambridge Journal of Postcolonial Literary Inquiry* 5, no. 2, Apr. 2018, p. 218.

145. David Diop, "Contribution au débat sur la poésie nationale," *Présence Africaine,* no. 6, 1956, p. 116.

146. Léopold Sédar Senghor, *Liberté, Tome 1. Négritude et Humanisme* (Paris: Seuil, 1964), p. 241.

3. TOWARD THE FUTURE READER: PRINT NETWORKS
AND THE QUESTION OF THE AUDIENCE

1. Hans-Jürgen Lüsebrink estimates that 95 percent of the literary production of Africans working in French between 1913 and 1960 appeared in periodicals rather than as books. If we were to include para-literary writings, the figure would likely be even higher. Hans-Jürgen Lüsebrink, *La Conquête de l'espace public colonial: prises de parole et formes de participation d'écrivains et d'intellectuels africains dans la presse à l'époque coloniale (1900–1960)* (Frankfurt: IKO-Verlag für Internationale Kommunikation, 2003), p. 13.

2. I adopt and extend Michael Warner's understanding of a public as a "self-organized relationship among strangers . . . a social space that is constituted by the reflexive circulation of discourse itself." Michael Warner, *Publics and Counterpublics* (New York: Zone Books, 2002), pp. 67, 90. Understood in this way, all publics are virtual and all public speech is necessarily reflexive. But not all modes of address are equally aware of the reflexive nature of their relationship to their audiences, and fewer still insist on it.

3. Bruce Hall and Charles Stewart, "The Historic 'Core Curriculum' and the Book Market in Islamic West Africa." *The Trans-Saharan Book Trade* (Leiden, Netherlands: Brill, 2010), pp. 109–74; Henri Sene, *Le livre et l'écrit de langue arabe dans la société sénégalaise, des origines au début du XXe siècle*, Thèse de doctorat de troisième cycle, Université de Dakar, 1982.

4. Ghislaine Lydon, "A Thirst for Knowledge: Arabic Literacy, Writing Paper and Saharan Bibliophiles in the Southwestern Sahara," in *The Trans-Saharan Book Trade: Manuscript Culture, Arabic Literacy, and Intellectual History in Muslim Africa* (Leiden, Netherlands: Brill, 2010), pp. 35–72.

5. Roger Pasquier, "Les débuts de la presse au sénégal," *Cahiers d'études Africaines*, 1962, pp. 477–490.

6. Derek R. Peterson, Emma Hunter, and Stephanie Newell, "Print Culture in Colonial Africa," in *African Print Cultures: Newspapers and Their Publics in the Twentieth Century* (Ann Arbor: University of Michigan Press, 2016), pp. 1–45.

7. Benedict Anderson, *Imagined Communities: Reflections on the Origin and Spread of Nationalism* (London: Verso, 2006), pp. 24–36.

8. See Frederick Cooper, *Citizenship between Empire and Nation: Remaking France and French Africa, 1945–1960* (Princeton, N.J.: Princeton University Press, 2014); and Gary Wilder, *Freedom Time: Negritude, Decolonization, and the Future of the World* (Durham, N.C.: Duke University Press, 2015).

9. Karin Barber, *The Anthropology of Texts, Persons, and Publics: Oral and Written Culture in Africa and Beyond* (Cambridge: Cambridge University Press, 2007), p. 152.

10. My understanding of network draws on Caroline Levine, *Forms: Whole, Rhythm, Hierarchy, Network* (Princeton, N.J.: Princeton University Press, 2015), pp. 112–31.

11. French West Africa was not a "literary field" in Bourdieu's sense. Instead of relative autonomy, we find entanglement. There was no group of writers who were remotely autonomous from the market or the state, and even the revered journal and publishing house *Présence Africaine* sought subventions from the colonial administration. Governor of Upper Volta to Governor General of AOF, 14 October, 1949, 14MIOM/3097, 21 G 173, ANOM. Nor was there a public sphere in a Habermasian sense either. As we saw in Chapter 2, the modes of written public discourse available in French diverged from the ideal Habermas outlines in nearly every way. Instead of universal access, autonomy, equal footing, and a common discourse, we find limited access, surveillance, coercion of various kinds, and participation limited to a small number of elites. This being said, the frameworks of the literary field and the public sphere have been productively modified by scholars studying African literature in French in the late colonial era. Both Ruth Bush and Claire Ducournau offer invigorating and necessary reappraisals of the emergence of African literature in French by adjusting Bourdieu's approach. Ruth Bush, *Publishing Africa in French: Literary Institutions and Decolonization 1945–1967* (Oxford: Oxford University Press, 2016); Claire Ducournau, *La Fabrique des classiques africains: Ecrivains d'Afrique subsaharienne francophone* (Paris: CNRS, 2017). The concept of the public sphere has also been usefully adapted by Gary Wilder, who convincingly shows that some of the metropolitan papers and journals run by colonized intellectuals tended to act as if they were already members of a universal forum of equals to which they could in reality only claim a provisional form of belonging. Gary Wilder, *The French Imperial Nation-State: Negritude and Colonial Humanism between the Two World Wars* (Chicago: University of Chicago Press, 2005). My use of the network in this chapter is not intended to foreclose on other approaches but rather to illuminate a different set of dynamics and concerns.

12. Trish Loughran, *The Republic in Print: Print Culture in the Age of U.S. Nation Building, 1770–1870* (New York: Columbia University Press, 2009), p. 115.

13. Jules Carde, *Circulaire sur le décret du 27 mars 1928 sur le régime de la presse*, 14MIOM 3034, 21 G 44 1, ANOM.

14. On the internationalist dimension of these periodicals, see Brent Hayes Edwards, *The Practice of Diaspora: Literature, Translation, and the Rise of Black Internationalism* (Cambridge, Mass.: Harvard University Press, 2003).

15. These are collected in SLOTFOM, 2MIA/241, ANOM.

16. Anon, "Au secours de votre journal!" *Le Cri des nègres,* July–Aug. 1933, p. 2.

17. Anon, "Chaque travailleur nègre a un devoir à accomplir envers son journal," *Le Cri des nègres,* June 1934, p. 1.

18. Anon, "Le cri des nègres justifie son titre de journal des travailleurs nègres," *Le Cri des nègres,* July 1934, p. 1.

19. See the reports collected in 14MIOM/3034, 21 G 44 1, ANOM.

20. This should not be confused with a value judgment on my part. Part of the usefulness of the figure of the network is that it lets us describe different qualities of address without having to argue that they ought to have been otherwise.

21. On *La Dépêche Africaine* and *La Revue du Monde noir,* see Edwards, *Practice of Diaspora.*

22. See Gregory Mann, "What Was the Indigénat? The 'Empire of Law' in French West Africa," *The Journal of African History,* vol. 50, no. 3, 2009, pp. 331–53.

23. See the article under the pseudonym "Fiat Justitia" (let there be justice), "Les Délits de la presse et les coutumes," *L'Etoile du Dahomey,* 1933.

24. Patrick Manning, *Slavery, Colonialism and Economic Growth in Dahomey, 1640–1960* (Cambridge: Cambridge University Press, 2004), pp. 271–72.

25. Henri Dubois, "Affaire *Voix du Dahomey,* rapport du directeur adjoint de police sur les menées anti-françaises au Dahomey et au Togo," 14MIOM/3103 FM, 21 G 140, ANOM. While the police intended to press charges relating to these documents, only a copy of a 1932 budget proved to be actionable. Instead, the *Voix* staff were prosecuted for other violations of the 1928 press law. Manning, *Slavery, Colonialism and Economic Growth,* 273.

26. Anon, *Reports on the* Voix Du Dahomey *Affair, 1934–6,* 14MIOM/3103 FM, 21 G 140, ANOM.

27. Cooper, *Citizenship between Empire and Nation,* 165–214.

28. Governor General of AOF to Minister of Overseas France, 13 Sept. 1950, 14MIOM/3097, 21 G 173, ANOM.

29. Anon, "Renseignements du service de la sûreté du soudan," 6 Oct. 1950, 14MIOM/3097, 21 G 173, ANOM.

30. Anon, Bobards, *L'Essor,* 17 June 1952, 29 Aug. 1952, and 10 June 1952.

31. Bobards,14 Nov. 1952.

32. Bobards, 16 Apr. 1952 and 30 Apr. 1943.

33. Bobards, 18 Nov. 1952.

34. On pseudonyms in anglophone West Africa in the colonial period, see Stephanie Newell, *The Power to Name: A History of Anonymity in Colonial West Africa* (Athens: Ohio University Press, 2013).

35. The series often uses passive voice to avoid direct accusations that could be construed as libel. Speaking of a bribe that was supposed have been paid to an official, one of the Bobards says, "It has been talked about now for more than a month." Anon, Bobards, 16 Oct. 1951.

36. Bobards, 12 Sept. 1952.

37. Ecole normale supérieure de Bamako, *Bamako* (Pessac, France: Presses Universitaires de Bordeaux, 1993), p. 21.

38. Lüsebrink, *La Conquête de l'espace public colonial*, 11–30.

39. In addition to Ousmane Socé, other literary writers published in installments: Abdoulaye Sadji, Félix Couchouro, Massyla Diop (elder brother of Birago), and Fodéba Keïta, to name just a few. Even writers who did not work directly in serials often published their first texts in periodicals, from Mariama Bâ and Ousmane Sembène to the para-literary writers Dim Delobson and Fily Dabo Sissako. Christopher L. Miller, *Nationalists and Nomads: Essays on Francophone African Literature and Culture* (Chicago: University of Chicago Press, 1999), p. 20; Lüsebrink, 11–20.

40. Ousmane Socé, *Karim: roman sénégalais* (Paris: Nouvelles éditions latines, 1966); Ousmane Socé, "Karim: roman sénégalais," *Paris-Dakar* Jan.–July 1935.

41. See C. L. Miller, *Nationalists and Nomads*, 55–89.

42. Socé, *Karim: roman sénégalais*, 100; Socé, "Karim: roman sénégalais," *Paris-Dakar*, 11 June 1935, 5.

43. Socé, *Karim: roman sénégalais*, 103; Socé, "Karim: roman sénégalais," *Paris-Dakar*, 18 June 1935, 5.

44. Socé, *Karim: roman sénégalais*, 103; Socé, "Karim: roman sénégalais," *Paris-Dakar*, 18 June 1935, 5.

45. Socé explains the proverb to his readers in a footnote, but with a definition that is arguably incomplete. He says the proverb means "do what everyone else does" and yet it clearly also includes the thought "as someone in a new place or situation." Socé, *Karim: Roman Sénégalais*, 103.

46. Socé, *Karim: Roman Sénégalais*, 17.

47. Socé, "Karim: roman sénégalais," *Paris-Dakar*, 22 Jan. 1935, 5.

48. "Ah! C'est toi Ousmane Socé: tu as écrit dernièrement qu'il faut que nous devenions tous des toubabs?" Socé, "Karim 1942," *Dakar-Jeunes*, 7 May 1942.

49. Socé, "Karim 1942."

50. Socé, "Karim 1942."

51. On printed works that dramatize the limits of their own circulation, see Michael Warner, *Publics and Counterpublics*, 109; Isabel Hofmeyr, *The Portable Bunyan: A Transnational History of "The Pilgrim's Progress"* (Princeton, N.J.: Princeton University Press, 2003), p. 25.

52. Léopold Sédar Senghor, "Appel aux lecteurs," *Condition Humaine*, 5 Oct. 1948, pp. 1–2; Jean-Paul Sartre, "Orphée noir," *Condition Humaine*, 5 Oct. 1948; Jean-Paul Sartre, "Orphée noir, suite," *Condition Humaine*, 14 Nov. 1948, pp. 2–3; Jean-Paul Sartre, "Orphée noir, suite et fin," *Condition Humaine*, 30 Nov. 1948, pp. 2–3.

53. Sartre, "Orphée noir, suite"; Sartre, "Orphée noir, suite et fin."

54. Abiola Irele, "The Negritude Debate," in *European Language Writing in Sub-Saharan Africa*, ed. Albert S. Gerard (Budapest: Akadémiai Kiadó, 1986).

55. Sartre, "Orphée noir, suite."

56. Lamine Diakhate, "Chronique littéraire," *Condition Humaine*, 12 Jan. 1955, p. 4.

57. Ousmane Socé, "Ce Que Pensent Nos . . . Futurs Lecteurs . . ." *Bingo*, Feb. 1953.

58. See Jaji on *Bingo* and "sheen reading." Tsitsi Ella Jaji, "Bingo: Francophone African Women and the Rise of the Glossy Magazine," in *Popular Culture in Africa: The Episteme of the Everyday*, ed. Stephanie Newell and Onookome Okome (New York: Routledge, 2013), pp. 111–30.

59. Anon, "Nos Lecteurs et Nous," *Bingo* N°31.

60. Anon, "Nos Lecteurs et Nous."

61. Anon, "Nos Lecteurs et Nous."

62. On the political imaginary of *Bingo*'s photography, see Jennifer Bajorek, "'Ca Bouscoulait!': Democratization and Photography in Senegal," in *Photography in Africa: Ethnographic Perspectives*, ed. Richard Vokes (Woodbridge, Suffolk: James Currey, 2012), pp. 140–66.

63. See, for example, Ruth Bush on the pioneering women's magazine *Amina*. Ruth Bush, "'Mesdames, Il Faut Lire!' Material Contexts and Representational Strategies in Early Francophone African Women's Magazines," *Francosphères*, vol. 5, no. 2, 2016, pp. 213–36.

64. Congress for Cultural Freedom, *Report on Dakar and Freetown Conferences 1963*, Box 442, Folder 1, International Association for Cultural Freedom Records, JRL.

65. Boroom Yoon, "Ubbi," *Kaddu*, no. 2, Jan. 1972, pp. 1–2.

4. SENGHOR'S GRAMMATOLOGY: THE POLITICAL IMAGINARIES
OF WRITING AFRICAN LANGUAGES

1. The Senegalese constitution was amended again in 2001 to include within the national language designation any regional language that was "codified." There are currently eighteen that fit this description. Ibrahima Diallo, *The Politics of National Languages in Postcolonial Senegal* (Amherst, N.Y.: Cambria Press, 2010), p. 62.

2. On patronage under Senghor, see Elizabeth Harney, *In Senghor's Shadow: Art, Politics, and the Avant-Garde in Senegal, 1960–1995* (Durham, N.C.: Duke University Press, 2004).

3. Jacques Derrida, *De la grammatologie* (Paris: Minuit, 1967).

4. Derrida, 156.

5. Karin Barber, *The Anthropology of Texts, Persons, and Publics: Oral and Written Culture in Africa and Beyond* (Cambridge: Cambridge University Press, 2007), pp. 75–102. Barber's work is part of a rich conversation on literacy and writing in African studies. See also Neil Ten Kortenaar, *Postcolonial Literature and the Impact of Literacy: Reading and Writing in African and Caribbean Fiction* (Cambridge: Cambridge University Press, 2011); Isabel Hofmeyr, *The Portable Bunyan: A Transnational History of "The Pilgrim's Progress"* (Princeton, N.J.: Princeton University Press, 2003); Stephanie Newell, *Literary Culture in Colonial Ghana* (Bloomington: Indiana University Press, 2002); Derek R. Peterson, *Creative Writing: Translation, Bookkeeping, and the Work of Imagination in Colonial Kenya* (London: Heinemann, 2004); and Sean Hawkins, *Writing and Colonialism in Northern Ghana* (Toronto: University of Toronto Press, 2002).

6. Fallou Ngom, *Muslims Beyond the Arab World: The Odyssey of Ajami and the Muridiyya* (Oxford: Oxford University Press, 2016), pp. 1–41.

7. See Ngom, 4–5.

8. The Wolofal tradition does not figure heavily in the debates about orthography of the 1970s. Although Wolofal writers had been making decisions on phonetics and word separation for a very long time, the postcolonial argument over spelling tended to proceed as if it were the year zero in such matters.

9. Susan Gal and Judith Irvine, "The Boundaries of Languages and Disciplines: How Ideologies Construct Difference," *Social Research*, vol. 62, no. 4, 1995, p. 414.

10. Roger Pasquier, "Les débuts de la presse au sénégal," *Cahiers d'études Africaines*, 1962, pp. 477–490.

11. See Boisson, "Détermination des noms des indigènes," 16 Mar. 1942, and Delmond, "Etat civil indigène," 29 July 1942, 14MIOM/3211, 23G 6, ANOM. Another impetus for colonial attempts to develop a better writing system for African languages was a rise in cases of "patronym theft"—in which a young métis would begin using the last name of a colonial administrator whom he claimed as his biological father. See reports and correspondence in Anon, "Orthographie des noms propres indigènes," 14MIOM/3211, 23G 6, ANOM.

12. Anon, *Reports on Patronym Theft*, 14MIOM/3211, 23G 6, ANOM. Some African names were also modified to make them easier to spell. The

novelist Abdoulaye Sadji apparently added an "i" to his Sérère surname to help his Ponty teachers pronounce it. Amadou Booker Sadji, *Abdoulaye Sadji: Biographie, 1910–1961* (Paris: Présence Africaine, 1997), pp. 14–15.

13. Léopold Sédar Senghor and Mohamed Aziza, *La poésie de l'action: conversations avec Mohamed Aziza* (Paris: Stock, 1980), p. 48.

14. Senghor and Aziza, 55–58.

15. Senghor and Aziza, 60.

16. Cheikh M'Backé Diop, *Cheikh Anta Diop: l'homme et l'oeuvre* (Paris: Présence Africaine, 2003).

17. Diop was eventually accorded only an honorable mention for his defense. Senghor never let him forget this. Even years later, Senghor apparently used this slight to prevent Diop from teaching at the University of Dakar, a deep irony considering the same institution is today named after him.

18. Gary Wilder, *Freedom Time: Negritude, Decolonization, and the Future of the World* (Durham, N.C.: Duke University Press, 2015), pp. 49–73; Cheikh Anta Diop, *Nations nègres et culture: De l'antiquité nègre égyptienne aux problèmes culturels de l'Afrique Noire d'aujourd'hui*, 4th ed. (Paris: Présence Africaine, 2000), pp. 13–24.

19. See Donna V. Jones, *The Racial Discourses of Life Philosophy: Négritude, Vitalism, and Modernity* (New York: Columbia University Press, 2010); Souleymane Bachir Diagne, *African Art as Philosophy: Senghor, Bergson and the Idea of Negritude*, trans. Jeffers Chike (London: Seagull Books, 2011); and Wilder, *Freedom Time*.

20. See Frantz Fanon, *Œuvres* (Paris: La Découverte, 2011), p. 79; and Aimé Césaire, *Discours sur le colonialisme* (Paris: Présence Africaine, 1955), p. 21. Diop was also a delegate at the Second Congress of Black Writers and Artists in 1959, where he helped draft a resolution for a pan-African linguistic policy. Anon, "Résolution de Linguistique," *Présence Africaine*, no. 24/25, 1959, pp. 397–98.

21. Mamadou Diouf and Mohamed Mbodj, "The Shadow of Cheikh Anta Diop," in *The Surreptitious Speech. Présence Africaine and the Politics of Otherness 1947-1987*, ed. V. Y. Mudimbe (Chicago: University of Chicago Press. 1992), pp. 118–135.

22. Léopold Sédar Senghor, *Liberté, Tome 1. Négritude et Humanisme* (Paris: Seuil, 1964).

23. Senghor, 165.

24. S. B. Diagne, *African Art as Philosophy*, 93.

25. Senghor, *Liberté, Tome 1*, 168.

26. Senghor notes how "supple" and "rich" African languages are and that some of them are written, but he adds that he prefers "popular

literature," which awaits "only linguists" to codify it in order for it to become the "well" from which future generations will develop a new literature using "new instruments" imported from France. Senghor, *Liberté, Tome 1*, 68.

27. "La vielle Afrique se meurt. Les coutumes et les langues se transforment avec une incroyable rapidité. Oui, il n'est que temps de photographier son visage actuel, visage où ses traits éternels sont encore si accusés. Demain, il sera trop tard." Senghor, 66.

28. Senghor, 331.

29. For a helpful survey of linguistic naturalisms, see Lia Formigari and Gabriel Poole, *A History of Language Philosophies* (Amsterdam: John Benjamins Publishing, 2004).

30. C. A. Diop, *Nations nègres et culture*, 405–13.

31. While Diop intended for his work to be repeated with other African languages, this existed in tension with his wish for linguistic unity in a future federal African state. For Diop, not all African languages could enjoy the same status in his hypothetical polity, and this led him to some moments of remarkable linguistic chauvinism. For example, he writes admiringly of the "suffocation" of Breton and Basque in France in the nineteenth century and observes that languages with both "internal possibilities" and "literatures" are more worthy than certain "dialects." Cheikh Anta Diop, *Alerte sous les tropiques: articles 1946–1960* (Paris: Présence Africaine, 1990), p. 119.

32. C. A. Diop, *Nations nègres et culture*, 413–37.

33. C. A. Diop, *Alerte sous les tropiques*, 36.

34. Senghor, "L'esthétique négro-africaine," 208–9. Senghor makes it clear that his vision of a Negro-African aesthetic—in which all artistic forms present stylistic affinities—derived from his linguistic research on languages. Although he went on to demonstrate the idea through the study of sculpture, painting, music, and dance, it is the linguistic proofs that initially secure the claim.

35. Senghor, *Liberté, Tome 1*, 210–13.

36. The way Senghor scales up linguistic differences into corresponding patterns of cultural and civilizational difference is an example of what Susan Gal and Judith Irvine call "fractal recursivity." This is a language ideology in which "an opposition, salient at some level of relationship" is projected "onto some other level." Judith T. Irvine and Susan Gal, "Language Ideology and Linguistic Differentiation," in Paul Kroskrity, ed. *Regimes of Language: Ideologies, Polities, and Identities* (Santa Fe, N.Mex.: School for Advanced Research Press, 2000), p. 38.

37. Senghor, *Liberté, Tome 1*, 165.

38. C. A. Diop, *Nations nègres et culture*, 246.

39. In his address to the Second Congress of Black Writers and Artists, Senghor defended his much-criticized statement that *l'émotion est nègre comme la raison est héllène* through a reading of the rhythm of a greeting exchange (called *nuyu*, in Wolof) that he found to be untranslatable. Senghor, *Liberté, Tome 1*, 260–62. On translation and the *nuyu*, see Chapter 5.

40. Gary Wilder, *The French Imperial Nation-State: Negritude and Colonial Humanism between the Two World Wars* (Chicago: University of Chicago Press, 2005), pp. 335–38.

41. Senghor, *Liberté, Tome 1*, 19.

42. Senghor, 19. Senghor would later revisit two of these claims when this speech was reprinted in his collected writings in 1963. First, Senghor indicated that he had rethought his argument that there could be no civilization worthy of the name without a written literature; second, he indicated that he had reconsidered his position that "native" languages would be mainly used to write poetry, theater, and tales in the future. Senghor gave no indication as to *how* his positions might have evolved, just that in 1963 he found them too reductive or simplistic (*trop sommaire*). Remarkably, these are the only two revisions signaled in this way in the entire first volume of Senghor's collected essays. The footnotes Senghor adds are a temporal marker—decolonization has transformed the terrain in which languages and literatures are being debated. When he originally gave this speech in 1937, it was a call to reform colonial educational policy. But by 1963, he was the president of a newly sovereign nation just emerging from its first constitutional crisis, and he had to defend his policies from critics.

43. Senghor, *Liberté, Tome 1*, 20.

44. C. A. Diop, *Alerte sous les Tropiques*, 34.

45. C. A. Diop, 34.

46. C. A. Diop, 33.

47. C. A. Diop, 35.

48. C. A. Diop, *Nations nègres et culture*, 533.

49. C. A. Diop, 413.

50. Léopold Sédar Senghor, "Lettre au premier ministre relative à la revue mensuelle Kaddu, à propos des langues nationales, 19 mai 1972," in *Education et Culture*, ed. A. Raphaël Ndiaye and Doudou Joseph Ndiaye (Paris: Presence Africaine, 2014), p. 60.

51. Senghor, 60.

52. Léopold Sédar Senghor, "Exposé des motifs," *Transcription des langues nationales* (Dakar: CLAD, 1972), pp. 7–9.

53. Cheikh Aliou Ndao, Interview by Tobias Warner, 28 July 2008, Dakar, Senegal. Despite his focus on modernizing Wolof, Diop never gave his reader an explicit guide in *Nations* to the transcription scheme he was

using. *Ijjib* set out to fix this by creating the institutional and pedagogical tools that Diop had skipped right past.

54. Association des étudiants sénégalais en France, *Ijjib Volof* (Grenoble: Imprimerie des Deux-Ponts, 1959). Unlike some earlier script standardization projects, *Ijjib* alluded to the fact that the use of Latin characters came after a longer history of writing in Arabic script. The group framed its choice of the Latin alphabet as a "souci de commodité."

55. Association des étudiants, *Ijjib Volof*, "Avant-propos."

56. The full title is "Loi N° 77–55 du 10 Avril 1977 relative à l'application de la reglementation en matière de transcription des langues." Quoted in Pathé Diagne, "Défense et illustration des langues sénégalaises," *Andë Soppi*, Feb. 1978.

57. I. Diallo, *Politics of National Languages*, 61.

58. For initial coverage of the censorship, see B. Biram Gassama, "'Ceddo' Baillonné!" *Andë Soppi*, June 1977.

59. Ousmane Sembène, "Sembène s'exprime," *Andë Soppi*, Nov. 1977.

60. Abd'el Kader Fall, "A chacun son métier," *Le Soleil*, 19 Dec. 1977.

61. P. Diagne, "Défense." Many of these commentaries are included in a special section of *Andë Soppi* in May 1978, entitled "Débat sur les langues." See also Pathé Diagne, "Siggi nag faf!" *Siggi*, Feb. 1977, pp. 17–21.

62. Arame Fal, "A propos des consonnes géminées du wolof: opinion d'un linguiste," *Taxaw*, no. 11, 1978, p. 3.

63. Ibrahima Gaye, "Un contre-décret du peuple," *Taxaw*, no. 12, 1978, p. 3.

64. Léopold Sédar Senghor, "Une lettre de M. Léopold Sedar Senghor," *Le Monde*, 14 Aug. 1979.

65. See Boubacar Barry, *La Sénégambie du XVe au XIXe siècle: traite négrière, Islam et conquête coloniale* (Paris: L'Harmattan, 1988); James F. Searing, *West African Slavery and Atlantic Commerce* (Cambridge: Cambridge University Press, 2003); and Mamadou Diouf, *Le Kajoor Au XIXe Siècle* (Paris: Karthala, 1990).

66. See Searing, 206.

67. Jean-Leopold Diouf's Wolof dictionary defines *ceddo* simply as "animist," while Sana Camara's defines it as "pagan." Jean Léopold Diouf, *Dictionnaire wolof-français et français-wolof* (Paris: Karthala, 2003); Sana Camara, *Wolof Lexicon and Grammar* (Bloomington, Ind.: NALRC Press, 2006).

68. Deleuze seems to make this assumption in his reading of *Ceddo*. Gilles Deleuze, *Cinema 2: The Time Image* (London: Continuum International Publishing Group, 2005), p. 244.

69. Mamadou Diouf, "History and Actuality in Ousmane Sembene's *Ceddo* and Djibril Diop Mambety's *Hyenas*," in *African Experiences of Cinema*,

ed. Imrah Bakari and Mbye Cham (London: British Film Institute, 1996), p. 244.

70. Gregor Ulrich, "Interview with Ousmane Sembène," *Framework*, no. 7/8, 1978, quoted in *Ousmane Sembène: Interviews*, ed. Annett Busch and Max Annas (Jackson: University Press of Mississippi, 2008), p. 107.

71. David Murphy, *Sembène: Imagining Alternatives in Film and Fiction* (Oxford: James Currey Publishers, 2000), p. 178.

72. Ousmane Sembène, *Ceddo*, Filmi Doomireew, 1976.

73. Focusing on Bengali, Partha Chatterjee suggests that when a vernacular language has been set up during a period of colonization to be an inner domain of cultural identity for a bilingual elite, then a postcolonial state will then turn toward the vernacular as "a zone over which the nation first ha[s] to declare its sovereignty . . . to transform in order to make it adequate for the modern world." Partha Chatterjee, *The Nation and Its Fragments: Colonial and Postcolonial Histories* (Princeton, N.J.: Princeton University Press, 1993), p. 7. The Senegalese case is somewhat different. While there is no question that the Senghorian state wished to declare sovereignty over the nation's linguistic infrastructure, the project seems to have emanated less from a desire to master collective inner identity than as an effort to establish dominion over the capacity to produce history, both in a backward- and a forward-looking sense.

5. COUNTERPOETICS: TRANSLATION AS AESTHETIC CONSTRAINT IN SEMBÈNE'S *MANDABI* AND NDAO'S *BUUR TILLEEN*

1. Bill Ashcroft, Gareth Griffiths, and Helen Tiffin, eds., *The Post-Colonial Studies Reader*, 2nd ed. (London: Routledge, 2006), pp. 261–22.

2. Chantal Zabus, *The African Palimpsest: Indigenization of Language in the West African Europhone Novel* (Amsterdam: Rodopi, 1991), pp. 210–11.

3. Cheikh Aliou Ndao, "Ousmane Sembène, véritable griot d'hommes" and "Langues et littérature," in *Les étudiants africains et La littérature négro-africaine d'expression française*, ed. Amady Aly Dieng (Cameroon: Langaa RPCIG, 2009), pp. 126–30.

4. I am grateful to Laurent Bismuth of the AFF for helping me locate a copy.

5. Édouard Glissant, *Le discours antillais* (Paris: Gallimard, 1997), pp. 401–10. On Glissant and counterpoetics, see Celia Britton, *Edouard Glissant and Postcolonial Theory: Strategies of Language and Resistance* (Charlottesville: University of Virginia Press, 1999), pp. 30–34; and Simon Gikandi, *Slavery and the Culture of Taste* (Princeton, N.J.: Princeton University Press, 2011), p. 235.

6. Glissant, 414.

7. David Murphy, *Sembène: Imagining Alternatives in Film and Fiction* (Oxford: James Currey Publishers, 2000), p. 65.

8. Tobias Warner, "Enacting Postcolonial Translation: Voice, Color and Free Indirect Discourse in the Restored Version of Sembène's *La Noire de . . .* ," in *Translating the Postcolonial in Multilingual Contexts*, ed. Judith Misrahi-Barak and Srilata Ravi (Montpellier: Presses Universitaires de la Méditerranée, 2017).

9. Paulin Vieyra ended up making *L'Afrique sur Seine* (1955) because he was denied permission to film in Africa. The decree was also invoked to ban *Les statues meurent aussi* (1955), the collaboration between Chris Marker, Alain Resnais, and the publishing house Présence Africaine. Manthia Diawara, *African Cinema: Politics and Culture* (Bloomington: Indiana University Press, 1992), pp. 22–23.

10. Diawara, 21–35.

11. See "Un entretien avec T. M'Bissine Diop" in the DVD extras on the Médiathèque des Trois Mondes edition of *La Noire de . . . .* Ousmane Sembène, *La Noire de . . .* (Paris: Médiathèque des Trois Mondes, [1966] 2008).

12. T. Warner, "Enacting Postcolonial Translation."

13. See Diawara, *African Cinema*, 32; S. Diallo, "Jeune Afrique fait parler Sembène Ousmane," *Jeune Afrique*, no. 629, 1973, pp. 48–49. It was partly Sembène's negative experience shooting *Mandabi* that led him to vow never again to accept funding from France. This put him in the position of seeking funding from the Senegalese state, which would result in the *Ceddo* affair.

14. Ousmane Sembène, *Le Mandat précédé de Véhi-Ciosane* (Paris: Présence Africaine, 1966).

15. See production credits in Ousmane Sembène, *Mandabi*, Wolof version, Filmi Domireew/Comptoir Français du Film, 1968.

16. Paulin Soumanou Vieyra, *Ousmane Sembène, cinéaste: première période, 1962–1971* (Paris: Présence Africaine, 1972), p. 96.

17. Vieyra, 97–98.

18. Judith Irvine defines a language ideology as "a cultural system of ideas about social and linguistic relationships, together with their loading of moral and political interests." Judith Irvine, "When Talk Isn't Cheap: Language and Political Economy," *American Ethnologist*, vol. 16, no. 2, May 1, 1989, p. 255, quoted in Webb Keane, *Christian Moderns: Freedom and Fetish in the Mission Encounter* (Berkeley: University of California Press, 2007), p. 16.

19. Ousmane Sembène, *Le Mandat*, French version, Filmi Domireew/ Comptoir Français du Film, 1968, AFF. Because Sembène's production

company had accepted CNC funding, it was required by French law to deposit a copy of the final film with the CNC. It is for this reason that a copy of the French print is still held by the AFF. My thanks again to Laurent Bismuth for sharing a copy of the *Mandabi* contract.

20. The relationship between Dieng and his cousin, for example, is entirely different. The Wolof version makes the cousin's habit of speaking French into an indication of his social class, but in the French version this difference between the characters' speech is erased.

21. Ato Quayson, *Oxford Street, Accra: City Life and the Itineraries of Transnationalism* (Durham, N.C.: Duke University Press, 2014), p. 130.

22. Sembène, *Le Mandat*, French version.

23. Kwate Nee Owoo, "The Language of Real Life," in *Framework*, vol. 36, 1989, and *Framework*, vol. 49, no. 1, Fall 2007, quoted in Annett Busch and Max Annas, *Ousmane Sembène: Interviews* (Jackson: University Press of Mississippi, 2008), p. 129.

24. Judith Irvine, "Strategies of Status Manipulation in the Wolof Greeting," in *Explorations in the Ethnography of Speaking*, ed. Richard Bauman and Joel Sherzer (Cambridge: Cambridge University Press, 1974), pp. 167–91. *Nuyu* also involve more than the manipulation of status. They may serve to index kinship relations, express friendship, and or just convey the joy of meeting someone again. Increasingly, a lengthy greeting might also imply a shared rural background, as the longer versions are less common in cities.

25. Compare the same scene in the French version of the film and in the French script. Sembène, *Le Mandat*, French version; and Ousmane Sembène, *Le Mandat (Scénario)*, La Bibliothèque du film, 1968, CF.

26. Michael Dembrow and Klaus Troller, "Interview with Ousmane Sembène," quoted in Busch and Annas, *Ousmane Sembène: Interviews*, 69–70.

27. For further indications that Sembène's self-reflexivity is anything but accidental, see *Xala* (1975). In that film, a minor character walks the streets of Dakar trying to sell copies of *Kaddu*, the Wolof-language magazine that Sembène was editing at the time with Pathé Diagne. Given the difficulties *Kaddu* faced, it is not surprising that the character selling the journal in the film is arrested for presumed vagrancy.

28. Samba Gadjigo, "Interview with Ousmane Sembène," *Rabat*, 11 Apr. 2004, quoted in Busch and Annas, *Ousmane Sembène: Interviews*, 194.

29. According to Ndao, the project of writing in national languages progressed as it did in this period partly because of the difficulty of directly confronting the Senghor regime. Ndao's involvement with linguistic research developed out of an interest in finding a way to write creatively in Wolof. Ndao was raised in a Mouride milieu and aware of the existence of the Wolofal alphabet and the poetic and scholarly traditions that exist in it.

He opted for a romanized system to "reach a larger public." Cheikh Aliou Ndao, Interview by Tobias Warner, 28 July 2008, Dakar, Senegal.

30. Ndao, Interview.

31. Cheikh Aliou Ndao, *Buur Tilleen* (Dakar: IFAN Cheikh Anta Diop, 1993), p. 7.

32. "Waaye céy léegi! Soo toppandooqul say moroom ñu teg la nitu àll, naan danga dellu gannaaw. Ndeysaan!" Ndao, 9.

33. This mode of narration is used for Maram's reminiscences as well, in the very early sections of the novel, with similar framing clauses: "démb ak tey day jaxasoo ci xelam, léttante ni fàlley." Ndao, 9. I am focusing on Gorgui's reverie here since it is the space of free indirect discourse in which the cop directly intervenes. After the policeman arrests Gorgui, the narrator's voice is distinguished more easily from both main characters.

34. Ndao, 16.

35. Ndao, 24.

36. D. A. Miller, *Jane Austen, or the Secret of Style* (Princeton, N.J.: Princeton University Press, 2005), p. 60.

37. Lauren Berlant, *Cruel Optimism* (Durham, N.C.: Duke University Press, 2011), pp. 26–27.

38. Ndao, *Buur Tilleen*, 26.

39. On free indirect style and legal interpolation, consider the prosecution's case in Flaubert's trial for obscenity, which insisted on "the dangers of a realism that abandoned the controlling observations of the author." Roy Pascal, *The Dual Voice: Free Indirect Speech and Its Functioning in the Nineteenth-Century European Novel* (Manchester: Manchester University Press, 1977), p. 99.

40. Cheikh Aliou Ndao, *Buur Tilleen: Roi de La Médina* (Paris: Présence Africaine, 1988), p. 9.

41. See, for example, Ndao, *Buur Tilleen: Roi de la Médina*, 76: "Bougouma et Raki mesurent leur isolement. . . . Leur horizon est obstrué, l'infortune les emprisonne comme dans un filet; ils butent contre l'incompréhension, la méchanceté."

42. For an exception to this dynamic, see the very end of the French novel as the narrative responds to the tragedy of Raki's death.

43. Ndao, *Buur Tilleen: Roi de la Médina*, 24–25.

44. Ndao, 43.

45. Ndao, *Buur Tilleen*, 24; Ndao, *Buur Tilleen: Roi de la Médina*, 43.

46. Barbara Johnson, "Bringing Out D. A. Miller," *Narrative*, vol. 10, no. 1, 2002, pp. 7–8.

47. V. N. Volosinov, *Marxism and the Philosophy of Language* (Cambridge, Mass.: Harvard University Press, 1986), pp. 146, 151.

48. Volosinov discusses a variety of direct and indirect modes. The closest of these to what we normally refer to as free indirect style is what he calls quasi-direct discourse.

49. Volosinov's approach resonates with Eve Sedgwick, who in *Touching Feeling* developed a complementary understanding of what she called "texxture" and texture. Drawing on an essay by Renu Bora, Sedgwick divides her understanding of texture into two categories. "Texxture" with two *x*'s is described as being "dense with offered information about how, substantively, historically, materially, it came into being." "Texture" with one *x*, by contrast, "blocks or refuses such information"—it "signifies the willed erasure of its history." Whereas texture is "usually glossy if not positively tacky," the example Sedgwick gives of "texxture" is of "a brick or a metal-work pot that still bears the scars and uneven sheen of its making." Sedgwick's attention to the "ineffaceable historicity" of "texxture" helps capture what is at stake in counterpoetics: the circumstances of the making of an artwork remain legible in the work as a certain roughness or density, qualities that can in turn be a spur toward further reflection on how such a consistency came to be. Eve Kosofsky Sedgwick, *Touching Feeling: Affect, Pedagogy, Performativity* (Durham, N.C.: Duke University Press, 2003), pp. 14–15.

50. For proposals on the intersection of literary studies and linguistic anthropology, see Michael Lucey, Tom McEnaney, and Tristram Wolff, eds., "Language-in-Use and the Literary Artifact," special issue, *Representations*, no. 137, Winter 2017.

51. See Irvine, "Strategies of Status Manipulation."

52. Pragmatics is the study of how meaning emerges from a given utterance's context of use, especially the ways in which that relevant context is itself subject to renegotiation. Pragmatic meaning is typically distinguished from semantic or referential meaning. On metapragmatics and metapragmatic awareness, see Michael Silverstein and Greg Urban, eds., *Natural Histories of Discourse* (Chicago: University of Chicago Press, 1996), pp. 1–17; Michael Silverstein, "Metapragmatic Discourse and Metapragmatic Function," in *Reflexive Language: Reported Speech and Metapragmatics*, ed. John A. Lucy (Cambridge: Cambridge University Press, 1993), p. 33–58; and Michael Silverstein, "The Limits of Awareness," *Linguistic Anthropology: A Reader* (Malden, Mass.: Blackwell, 2001), pp. 382–401.

6. HOW MARIAMA BÂ BECAME WORLD LITERATURE: TRANSLATION AND THE LEGIBILITY OF FEMINIST CRITIQUE

1. A 2012 edition estimates that Bâ's work now appears in sixteen languages. Mariama Bâ, *So Long a Letter*, trans. Modupé Bodé-Thomas (Long Grove, Ill.: Waveland Press, 2012).

2. A 1980 review in *World Literature Today* is emblematic of the first trend: Bâ's "principal subject matter [is] the problem of polygamy." Emeka Abanime, "Review: Une Si Longue Lettre," *World Literature Today*, vol. 54, no. 2, Spring 1980, p. 327. Examples of studies that take the novel to be about polygamy include Miriam Murtuza, "The Marriage and Divorce of Polygamy and Nation: Interplay of Gender, Religion, and Class in Sembene Ousmane and Manama Ba," in Azodo, *Emerging Perspectives on Mariama Bâ*, p. 176; Keith Louis Walker, *Countermodernism and Francophone Literary Culture: The Game of Slipknot* (Durham, N.C.: Duke University Press, 1999), p. 136; Kathryn R. Fleming, "Exorcising Institutionalized Ghosts and Redefining Female Identity in Mariama Bâ's *So Long a Letter* and Toni Morrison's *Beloved*," in Azodo, *Emerging Perspectives on Mariama Bâ*, p. 206; Cyril Mokwenye, "La Polygamie et la révolte de la femme africaine moderne: Une Lecture d'Une Si Longue Lettre de Mariama Bâ," *Peuples Noirs Peuples Africains, Paris*, vol. 31, 1983, p. 88; Eva Rueschmann, "Female Self-Definition and the African Community in Mariama Bâ's Epistolary Novel *So Long a Letter*," in *International Women's Writing: New Landscapes of Identity*, ed. Anne E. Brown and Marjanne E. Goozé (Westport, Conn.: Greenwood Press, 1995), p. 5; Helen Chukwuma, "Feminism and Change in Mariama Bâ's So Long A Letter," in *Accents in the African Novel* (Enugu, Nigeria: New Generation Books, 1991), p. 35; and Glenn W. Fetzer, "Women's Search for Voice and the Problem of Knowing in the Novels of Mariama Ba," *CLA Journal*, vol. 35, no. 1, 1991, p. 39. All of these critics offer different readings, and polygamy is not always their primary focus, which makes it all the more intriguing that the framing occurs across incommensurable approaches. Even Ojo-Ade's antifeminist reading takes the novel to be an attack on polygamy. Femi Ojo-Ade, "Still a Victim? Mariama Bâ's *Une Si Longue Lettre*," *African Literature Today*, no. 12, 1982, p. 79.

Salvific interpretations of writing and print culture are a less pronounced but still common trend in Bâ criticism. For example, Opara writes of "the clogs of repressive tradition" that are "decidedly surmounted by the weight of the dynamic woman's mighty pen." Chioma Opara, "The Emergence of the Female Self: The Liberating Pen in Mariama Bâ's *Une Si Longue Lettre* and Sembene Ousmane's 'Lettres de France,'" in *Feminism and Black Women's Creative Writing: Theory, Practice, and Criticism* (Ibadan: AMO, 1996), p. 165. Some further examples include Ada Uzoamaka Azodo, "Lettre Senegalaise de Ramatoulaye: Writing as Action in Mariama Bâ's 'Une Si Longue Lettre,'" in Azodo, *Emerging Perspectives on Mariama Bâ*, p. 3; Rebecca Wilcox, "Women and Power in Mariama Bâ's Novels," in Azodo, *Emerging Perspectives on Mariama Bâ*, p. 124; Rueschmann, "Female Self-

Definition," 7; and Fetzer, "Women's Search for Voice," 39. For more ambivalent appraisals, see Christopher L. Miller, *Theories of Africans: Francophone
Literature and Anthropology in Africa* (Chicago: University of Chicago Press,
1993); Shaun Irlam, "Mariama Bâ's *Une Si Longue Lettre*": The Vocation of
Memory and the Space of Writing," *Research in African Literatures*, vol. 29,
no. 2, 1998, pp. 76–93.

    3. The critical conversation on Bâ ranges far beyond the two trends
singled out here. As Andrade points out, there have been at least 150 articles,
chapters, and monographs on Bâ since *Letter* was first published. Susan Z.
Andrade, "The Loved and the Left: Sembène, Bâ, Sow Fall," in *The Nation
Writ Small: African Fictions and Feminisms, 1958–1988* (Durham, N.C.: Duke
University Press, 2011). For example, topics such as choice and personal
happiness have been examined by critics including Irène Assiba d'Almeida,
"The Concept of Choice in Mariama Ba's Fiction," in *Ngambika: Studies of
Women in African Literature*, ed. Carol Boyce Davies and Anne Adams
Graves (Trenton, N.J.: Africa World Press, 1986), pp. 161–71; and Edris
Makward, "Marriage, Tradition and Woman's Pursuit of Happiness in the
Novels of Mariama Bâ," also in *Ngambika*, pp. 271–82. For topics such as
space, see Mildred P. Mortimer, "The Nurturing Hearth: Mariama Bâ," in
*Writing from the Hearth: Public, Domestic, and Imaginative Space in Franco-
phone Women's Fiction of Africa and the Caribbean* (Lanham, Md.: Lexington
Books, 2007), pp. 71–116; and Obioma Nnaemeka, "Urban Spaces, Women's
Places: Polygamy as Sign in Mariama Bâ's Novels," in *The Politics of (M)
Othering: Womanhood, Identity, and Resistance in African Literature* (London:
Routledge, 1997), pp. 162–191. For feminism, friendship, and solidarity, see
Nicki Hitchcott, "'Confidently Feminine'? Sexual Role-Play in the Novels of
Mariama Bâ," in *African Francophone Writing: A Critical Introduction*, ed.
Nicki Hitchcott and Laïla Ibnlfassi (Oxford: Berg, 1996), pp. 139–41; and for
gender and national identity, see Eileen Julien, "When a Man Loves a
Woman: Gender and National Identity in Wole Soyinkas's *Death and the
King's Horseman* and Mariama Bâ's *Scarlet Song*," in *Africa after Gender?*, ed.
Catherine M. Cole et al. (Bloomington: Indiana University Press, 2007),
pp. 205–22. For micropolitics and public critique, see Andrade, "The Loved
and the Left"; and for marginality and canonicity, see C. L. Miller, *Theories of
Africans*. Bâ's posthumously published second novel, *Un chant écarlate (Scarlet
Song)*, has received far less attention (and fewer translations), although it does
"silk-screen" many aspects of *Letter* (Julien, 216). Since the present chapter
aims to trace how Bâ became world literature, my own exclusive focus on
Letter is a response to the outsize role that first text played. For excellent
studies of both novels, see Hitchcott, "'Confidently Feminine'?"; Julien,

"When a Man Loves a Woman"; and Juliana Makuchi Nfah-Abbenyi, "Women Redefining Difference: Mariama Bâ, Miriam Tlali, and Bessie Head," in *Gender in African Women's Writing: Identity, Sexuality, and Difference* (Bloomington: Indiana University Press, 1997), pp. 108–47.

4. See C. L. Miller, *Theories of Africans*, on this aspect of Bâ's poetics.

5. On literary worldedness, see Eric Hayot, *On Literary Worlds* (New York: Oxford University Press, 2012).

6. "Matchet's Diary." *West Africa*, Oct. 1980. Noma Award Mss, LL.

7. Ada Uzoamaka Azodo, ed. *Emerging Perspectives on Mariama Bâ: Postcolonialism, Feminism, and Postmodernism* (Trenton, N.J.: Africa World Press, 2003), pp. 403, 407.

8. The Heinemann edition is enmeshed with Bâ's status as world literature. It has achieved a life of its own, remaining a fixture on syllabi when the original briefly went out of print in the 1990s. Hitchcott, "'Confidently Feminine'?," 71. A 1994 translation into Swahili was even made directly from the English. African Books Collective, "*Barua Ndefu Kama Hii*," 29 June 2015, www.africanbookscollective.com/books/barua-ndefu-kama-hii.

9. Mariama Bâ, *So Long a Letter*, trans. Modupé Bodé-Thomas (Oxford: Heinemann, 1989).

10. As Joseph Slaughter observes, "italics, glosses, and glossaries are formal marks of the passage of minority ethnic, regional, and national literatures into World Literature." Joseph R. Slaughter, "World Literature as Property," *Alif: Journal of Comparative Poetics*, no. 34, 2014, 21.

11. Hans Zell, "Senegalese Woman Writer Wins First Noma Award," The Noma Award for Publishing in Africa, Press release, 7 Oct. 1980, Noma Award Mss, LL.

12. Based on a comparison of Zell, "Senegalese Woman Writer," and "Readers' Assessments" for the 1980 Noma Award, both in Noma Award Mss, LL.

13. On Ramatoulaye's subversion of her widow's seclusion, or *mirasse*, see Mbye B. Cham, "Contemporary Society and the Female Imagination: A Study of the Novels of Mariama Bâ," *African Literature Today*, no. 15, 1987, pp. 89–101.

14. Mariama Bâ, *Une si longue lettre* (Dakar: Les Nouvelles éditions africaines du Sénégal, 1980), p. 28; Bâ, *So Long a Letter*, 16. Unless otherwise noted, English quotations from *So Long a Letter* are from the 1989 Heinemann edition of Modupé Bodé-Thomas's translation.

15. See Mame Coumba Ndiaye, *Mariama Bâ, ou les allées d'un destin: essai* (Dakar: Les nouvelles éditions africaines du Sénégal, 2007). For a study of Bâ's generation at Rufisque, see Pascale Barthélémy, *Africaines et diplômées à l'époque coloniale* (Rennes, France: Presses Universitaires de Rennes, 2010).

16. On "the emancipatory potential of the French school system," see János Riesz, "Mariama Bâ's 'Une Si Longue Lettre': An Erziehungsroman," trans. Richard Bjornson, *Research in African Literatures* 22, no. 1, Spring 1991, p. 29.

17. Wilcox, "Women and Power in Mariama Bâ's Novels," 134.

18. Fleming, "Exorcising Institutionalized Ghosts," 207–12.

19. Nnaemeka continues, "Even on the two occasions that Ramatoulaye makes references to the institution, *la polygamie* is not used; she chooses instead to speak about the modalities of its operation." Nnaemeka, "Urban Spaces, Women's Places," 167.

20. Jeff Fort, David Gundry, Sven-Erik Rose, Eric Russell, and Juliana Schiesari helped me compare the first wave of Bâ translations. The Dutch translation diverges slightly from this pattern, rendering *le problème polygamique* as "de problemen van het polygame huwelijk" (the problems of polygamous marriage). Mariama Bâ, *Een lange Brief: Roman*, trans. Sonja Pos (Maasbree, Netherlands: Corrie Zelen, 1981), p. 90. Yet while the adjective *polygamique* remains an adjective, *problème*, as in the other translations, becomes the problem(s) of an institution. My thanks to Eric Russell for help with the Dutch.

21. Walker, *Countermodernism and Francophone Literary Culture*, 136.

22. For an analysis of these "instincts," see Hitchcott, "'Confidently Feminine'?"

23. Bâ, *Une si longue lettre*, 50–51; Bâ, *So Long a Letter*, 32.

24. "Books have a salvific power . . . the book-object is an instrument of liberty for the Senegalese woman." Chantal Zabus, "La langue avant la lettre: 'Une si longue lettre' de Mariama Bâ," *Notre librairie*, vol. 119, 1994, p. 97.

25. For Coulis, Ramatoulaye "is willing to accept . . . polygyny." For Wilcox, "Ramatoulaye never really accepts polygyny." Shari Coulis, "The Impossibility of Choice: Gender and Genre in Mariama Bâ's So Long a Letter," in Azodo, *Emerging Perspectives on Mariama Bâ*, p. 41; Wilcox, "Women and Power in Mariama Bâ's Novels," 134.

26. Fleming suggests Ramatoulaye acts in accordance with "traditional Islamic precepts." Fleming, "Exorcising Institutionalized Ghosts," 215. Ajayi-Soyinka notes that it "is hard to imagine that her subjection to polygyny is not a factor." O. Ajayi-Soyinka, "Negritude, Feminism, and the Quest for Identity: Re-Reading Mariama Bâ's *So Long a Letter*," in Azodo, *Emerging Perspectives on Mariama Bâ*, p. 197.

27. Bâ, *Une si longue lettre*, 61.

28. Igolima T. D. Amachree, "Mariama Bâ and the Marginal Person: A New Examination and Social Interpretation of Her Novels," in Azodo, *Emerging Perspectives on Mariama Bâ*, p. 81.

29. By "world literary public," I mean the public that is constituted in the global and uneven circulation of texts and practices of reading that we collectively call world literature.

30. But see Hitchcott, who reads friendship as a model of female solidarity that transcends the modernity/tradition binary. Hitchcott, "'Confidently Feminine'?," 89.

31. D'Almeida, "Concept of Choice," 165.

32. For an exception, see Edson, who notes the relevance of the Family Code but not its entanglement with the plot. Laurie Edson, "Mariama Bâ and the Politics of the Family," *Studies in 20th & 21st Century Literature*, vol. 17, no. 1, 1993, p. 3.

33. On Senegalese engagements with the colonial legal system, see Mamadou Diouf, "The French Colonial Policy of Assimilation and the Civility of the Originaires of the Four Communes (Senegal): A Nineteenth-Century Globalization Project," *Development and Change*, vol. 29, no. 4, 1998, pp. 671–96. Also see Mamdani's foundational analysis of multi-tiered colonial legal regimes across Africa. Mahmood Mamdani, *Citizen and Subject* (Princeton, N.J.: Princeton University Press, 1996).

34. On the colonial construction of customary law and its focus on family form, see Gary Wilder, *The French Imperial Nation-State: Negritude and Colonial Humanism between the Two World Wars* (Chicago: University of Chicago Press, 2005); David Robinson, "Ethnography and Customary Law in Senegal," *Cahiers d'Études Africaines*, vol. 32, no. 126, 1992, pp. 221–37; Emily S. Burrill, *States of Marriage: Gender, Justice, and Rights in Colonial Mali* (Athens: Ohio University Press, 2015); S. R. Wooten, "Colonial Administration and the Ethnography of the Family in the French Soudan," *Cahiers d'Études Africaines*, vol. 33, no. 131, 1993, pp. 419–46; and F. G. Snyder, "Colonialism and Legal Form: The Creation of Customary Law in Senegal," *Journal of Legal Pluralism*, vol. 19, 1981, pp. 49–90.

35. On these controversies, see Roman Loimeier, "The Secular State and Islam in Senegal," in *Questioning the Secular State: The Worldwide Resurgence of Religion and Politics*, ed. David Westerlund (London: Hurst, 1996), pp. 183–197.

36. In her debate with Daouda, Ramatoulaye declares, "Et voilà que l'on a promulgé le Code de la famille, qui restitue, à la plus humble des femmes, sa dignité combien de fois bafouée." M. Bâ, *Une si longue lettre*, 89. The tone appears celebratory, but Ramatoulaye's larger point in this scene concerns the limits of legal reform as a feminist strategy. As Gayatri Spivak puts it, "It is good to change laws, but social change cannot be achieved merely by changing the laws. Changing the laws is not the same as teaching the general public to will the law, to want the law." Gayatri Chakravorty Spivak,

"Can There Be a Feminist World?" *Public Books*, 15 May 2015, http://www .publicbooks.org/can-there-be-a-feminist-world/.

37. Bâ was clearly aware of the Family Code and, in addition to introducing the structural homologies between the novel and the law, she invokes it frequently in interviews following the publication of *Letter*. See Alioune Toure Dia, "Succès littéraire de Mariama Ba pour son livre *Une si longue lettre*," *Amina*, no. 86, 1979, p. 14; Djib Diédhiou, "Echo des voix féminines de détresse," *Le soleil*, 13 June 1980, p. 2; Laye Bamba Diallo and E. B. Sow, "Mariama Ba: Sous chaque homme qui pointe, il y a l'action d'une femme méritante," *Zone 2*, no. 26, July 1979, p. 13; Barbara Harrell-Bond, "Mariama Bâ: Winner of the First Noma Award for Publishing in Africa for Her Novel *Une si longue lettre*," *African Book Publishing Record*, vol. 6, nos. 3–4, 1980, p. 210. All clippings collected in Noma Award Mss, LL.

38. Fatou Sow makes this point, in slightly different terms. Fatou Sow, "Family and Law in Senegal: Continuity and Change," in *Shifting Boundaries in Marriage and Divorce in Muslim Communities* (Grabels, France: Women Living Under Muslim Laws, 1996), pp. 142–157. For a critique of the Family Code, see Fatou K. Camara, "Women and the Law: A Critique of Senegalese Family Law," *Social Identities*, vol. 13, no. 6, 2007, pp. 787–800. For an ethnography of Muslim families in contemporary Senegal, see Beth A. Buggenhagen, *Muslim Families in Global Senegal: Money Takes Care of Shame* (Bloomington: Indiana University Press, 2012).

39. Bâ, *Une si longue lettre*, 90.

40. On the use of apostrophe to address Aïssatou *and* Modou, see Andrade, "The Loved and the Left."

41. My use of "critique" here is informed by Judith Butler's reading of Foucault's "What Is Critique?" Butler describes critique as "that perspective on established and ordering ways of knowing which is not immediately assimilated into that ordering function." Judith Butler, "What Is Critique? An Essay on Foucault's Virtue," in *The Political*, ed. David Ingram (Oxford: Blackwell, 2001), p. 5.

42. Bâ, *Une si longue lettre*, 85.

43. Bâ, 48, 52.

44. For instance, Ramatoulaye declines Daouda's offer of marriage through a letter that is hand delivered by a *géwél* (a griot, in Wolof). Since *géwél* are a casted group, this gesture reinforces Ramatoulaye's status as a *géer* (a non-casted person). A *géwél* would traditionally mediate between a *géer* subject and public space. Thus, even the novel's iconic gesture of refusal is overlaid with a patron-client relationship based on caste status. On the caste system, see Abdoulaye Bara Diop, *La sociéte wolof: tradition et changement* (Paris: Karthala, 1981).

45. For a reading of *Letter* as a response to the political malaise of post-independence Senegal, see Andrade, "The Loved and the Left."

46. Bâ, *Une si longue lettre*, 14, 82, 63, 78, 76.

47. Talal Asad makes a related point about the limits of free speech as a liberal virtue: "The enjoyment of free speech presupposes not merely the physical ability to speak but *to be heard*, a condition without which speaking to some effect is not possible." Talal Asad, *Formations of the Secular: Christianity, Islam, Modernity* (Stanford, Calif: Stanford University Press, 2003), p. 184.

48. Bâ, *Une si longue lettre*, 50–51; Bâ, *So Long a Letter*, 32; Mariama Bâ, *Bataaxal bu gudde nii*, trans. Maam Yunus Dieng and Arame Fal (Dakar: Les Nouvelles éditions africaines du Sénégal, 2007), p. 62.

49. On these figures, see C. L. Miller, *Theories of Africans*, 275.

50. The first wave of translations all follow the original closely here. The drift in Dieng and Fal's version appears to be an outlier.

51. On these difficulties, see Arame Fal, "OSAD's Experience in the Publishing of Books in National Languages," in *Literacy and Linguistic Diversity in a Global Perspective: An Intercultural Exchange with African Countries*, ed. Neville Alexander and Brigitta Busch (Strasbourg: Council of Europe, 2007), p. 31.

52. On addressivity—"the quality of turning to someone"—see M. M. Bakhtin, *Speech Genres and Other Late Essays* (Austin: University of Texas Press, 2010), p. 99. Following Bakhtin, by "address" here, I mean the way in which a text presumes to speak to a particular audience. On address and world literature, see also Michael Allan, "Reading with One Eye, Speaking with One Tongue: On the Problem of Address in World Literature," *Comparative Literature Studies*, vol. 44, no. 1, 2007, pp. 1–19.

53. Walter Benjamin, *Selected Writings, Volume 1: 1913–1926* (Cambridge, Mass.: Belknap Press of Harvard University Press, 2004), p. 75.

54. As in earlier chapters, my use of "public" here takes its cue from Michael Warner, *Publics and Counterpublics* (New York: Zone Books, 2002), pp. 65–124.

55. On Bâ's "projective" relationship to her audience and the "virtuality" of her letter, see C. L. Miller, *Theories of Africans*, 291; and Irlam, "Mariama Bâ's *Une Si Longue Lettre*," 78.

56. Dieng's novel appeared in the 1990s alongside several other Wolof prose manuscripts that used the Latin-character script standardized by Arame Fal.

57. When I asked Dieng about *Letter*, she positioned Bâ as an elder sister—*sama mag la*—before clarifying that she did not share Bâ's views on family form and that her own novel was partly intended to counter *Letter*'s

rather narrow account. Maam Yunus Dieng, Interview by Tobias Warner, 26 Oct. 2010, Dakar, Senegal.

58. *Géwél* is the Wolof name for the endogamous social group of performers and musicians who are traditionally the custodians of what is today defined as oral tradition. A *géwél* might also be called *griot*, a term of French origin. *Griot* is used to describe the traditional oral performers who are found across a range of Sahelian societies.

59. For example, "Man dey xaar naa la ba tàyyi, xàddi woon naa sax; ragal naa ni sunu létt yii du yegg tey; foo jogéeti bay jooy?" (I'm exhausted waiting for you, I had actually given up; I was afraid our hairbraiding session would not happen today; but where are you coming from like this, in tears?) Maam Yunus Dieng, *Aawo Bi* (Dakar: IFAN Cheikh Anta Diop, 1992), p. 5. As Guedj Fall points out, the conversation that forms the narrative is doubled by the hairbraiding. Guedj Fall, "Aawo Bi de Mame Younousse Dieng, un récit fondateur en langue wolof," *Ethiopiques*, no. 76, 2006, http://ethiopiques.refer.sn/spip.php?page=imprimer-article&id _article=1496. At the end of the text, Fama makes the analogy explicit: "Man bu saa létt yi baaxut tey it, neex na ndax waxtaan wi." (For me, even if my braids are terrible today, it was all worth it because of this conversation.) M. Y. Dieng, *Aawo bi*, 70.

60. M. Y. Dieng, 5.

61. Jean Léopold Diouf, *Dictionnaire wolof-français et français-wolof* (Paris: Karthala, 2003), p. 170.

62. M. Y. Dieng, *Aawo bi*, 5.

63. For instance: "Ku roy ci Ndéela doo juum. Ab aawo noonu lay mel." (Whoever models herself on Ndeela would not do so in error. A first wife should be like her.) M. Y. Dieng, 70.

64. Mariama Bâ, *Bataaxal bu gudde nii*, trans. Maam Yunus Dieng and Arame Fal (Dakar: Les Nouvelles éditions africaines du Sénégal, 2007), pp. 3–4.

7. AESTHETICS AFTER AUSTERITY: BOUBACAR BORIS DIOP AND THE WORK OF LITERATURE IN NEOLIBERAL SENEGAL

1. "L'histoire de toutes les littératures humaines montre que ce sont toujours les textes qui précédent le public—parfois avec plusieurs siècles d'avance—et non l'inverse." Boubacar Boris Diop, "Langues Africaines et Création Littéraire," Unpublished manuscript, n.d.

2. See Nicolas Van De Walle, *African Economies and the Politics of Permanent Crisis, 1979–1999* (Cambridge: Cambridge University Press, 2001); and Momar Coumba Diop and Mamadou Diouf, *Le Sénégal sous Abdou Diouf: Etat et société* (Paris: Karthala, 1990).

3. The work on neoliberalism focused on the North Atlantic is enormously generative but not necessarily a reliable guide to developments in West Africa. See Wendy Brown, *Undoing the Demos* (Durham, N.C.: Duke University Press, 2015); and David Harvey, *A Brief History of Neoliberalism* (Oxford: Oxford University Press, 2005). Throughout this chapter, I draw more on research on neoliberalism in African contexts, which has tended to foreground the *temporal* dislocations and transformations that occurred in the wake of structural adjustment. Jean Comaroff and John L. Comaroff, *Theory from the South: Or, How Euro-America Is Evolving Toward Africa* (Boulder, Colo.: Paradigm Publishers, 2011); Mamadou Diouf, "Les jeunes dakarois, la scène urbaine et le temps du monde a la fin du XXe siècle," in *Les arts de la citoyenneté au Sénégal: espaces contestés et civilités urbaine*, ed. Mamadou Diouf and Rosalind Fredericks (Paris: Karthala, 2013), pp. 49–92; James Ferguson, *Global Shadows: Africa in the Neoliberal World Order* (Durham, N.C.: Duke University Press, 2006); Jane I. Guyer, "Prophecy and the Near Future: Thoughts on Macroeconomic, Evangelical, and Punctuated Time," *American Ethnologist*, vol. 34, no. 3, 2007, pp. 409–21.

4. See Comaroff and Comaroff, *Theory from the South*, 1–19.

5. Pascale Casanova, *La République mondiale des Lettres* (Paris: Points, 2008), pp. 120–125.

6. Casanova, 123; Pascale Casanova, *The World Republic of Letters*, trans. M. B. Debevoise (Cambridge, Mass.: Harvard University Press, 2007), p. 79.

7. Casanova, *La République mondiale des Lettres*, 123, 384. Casanova, *The World Republic of Letters*, 274.

8. Guyer, "Prophecy and the Near Future," 409–11.

9. Mamadou Diouf and Rosalind Fredericks, eds., *The Arts of Citizenship in African Cities: Infrastructures and Spaces of Belonging* (Basingstoke: Palgrave Macmillan, 2014), p. 5.

10. Diop and Diouf, *Le Sénégal sous Abdou Diouf*, 9, 178.

11. On these shifts, see Diop and Diouf, *Le Sénégal sous Abdou Diouf*.

12. Makhtar Diouf, "La Crise de l'ajustement," *Politique Africaine*, no. 45, 2002, pp. 78–81.

13. On the World Bank's Women's Literacy Project, see Bjorn Harald Nordtveit, "Producing Literacy and Civil Society: The Case of Senegal," *Comparative Education Review*, vol. 52, no. 2, May 2008, pp. 175–98.

14. Arame Fal, "OSAD's Experience in the Publishing of Books in National Languages," in *Literacy and Linguistic Diversity in a Global Perspective: An Intercultural Exchange with African Countries*, ed. Neville Alexander and Brigitta Busch (Strasbourg: Council of Europe, 2007, p. 31.

15. Other major publishers of Wolof texts include larger, international NGOs such as Enda, which mainly publishes collections of fables for

children, and TOSTAN, which uses vernacular language content as part of a broader program that aims to empower women to understand themselves as rights-bearing subjects. The orientation of national language publishing toward basic literacy is not universally shared. Editions Papyrus Afrique, which published *Doomi Golo* and other vernacular texts in Wolof and Pulaar, distances itself from the NGO book market by not including a phonetic syllabary with its works.

16. Mamadou Diouf, "Les jeunes dakarois," 88.

17. Etienne Smith, "La nationalisation par le bas: un nationalisme banal?," *Raisons Politiques*, vol. 37, no. 1, 2010, p. 65.

18. Pathé Diagne, *Teerebtanu ladab ci wàlàf: anthologie wolof de littérature* (Dakar: Université de Dakar, Institut fondamental d'Afrique noire, Séminaire sur l'adaptation des langues africaines, 1971), pp. I–XI.

19. P. Diagne, 106.

20. P. Diagne, 106.

21. Diagne presents his text as an example to be followed for other "africophone" literatures rather than a demonstration of any special excellence on the part of Wolof. P. Diagne, 1.

22. Although the anthology as a whole is entirely in Wolof, except for a short bilingual preface, the section on Wolof literature is in fact quite small. P. Diagne, 1, 54–63.

23. Cheikh Aliou Ndao, *Taaral ak ladab ci làmmiñu wolof: esthétique et littérature de langue wolof* (Dakar: OSAD, 2002), pp. 9–12.

24. Ndao, 47–48.

25. Ferguson, *Global Shadows*, 20.

26. David Scott, *Omens of Adversity: Tragedy, Time, Memory, Justice* (Durham, N.C.: Duke University Press, 2013), pp. 1–29.

27. Jennifer Wenzel, *Bulletproof: Afterlives of Anticolonial Prophecy in South Africa and Beyond* (Chicago: University of Chicago Press, 2010), pp. 1–9.

28. Boubacar Boris Diop, *Le Cavalier et son ombre* (Abidjan: Nouvelles Editions Ivoiriennes, 2000), p. 61.

29. See Eileen Julien, "The Extroverted African Novel," in *The Novel, Volume 1: History, Geography, and Culture*, ed. Franco Moretti (Princeton, N.J.: Princeton University Press, 2007), pp. 692–93. As Nasrin Qader lucidly observes, Khadidja's dilemma also recalls Franz Kafka's parables and paradoxes, in which messages, desires, and bodies never quite seem to reach their hoped-for destinations. In Diop's novel, it is as if Kafka's petitioner waiting before the law had been transformed into a storyteller. See Boubacar Boris Diop, *The Knight and His Shadow*, trans. Alan Furness (East Lansing: Michigan State University Press, 2015), p. xii; and Nasrin Qader, *Narratives*

of Catastrophe: Boris Diop, Ben Jelloun, Khatibi (New York: Fordham University Press, 2009), pp. 100–1.

30. Boubacar Boris Diop and Charles J. Sugnet, "Dances with Wolofs: A Conversation with Boubacar Boris Diop," *Transition*, 87, vol. 10, no. 3, 2001, pp. 147, 158.

31. Boubacar Boris Diop, "Écrire entre deux langues. De Doomi Golo aux Petits de la guenon," *Rèperes-Dorifs*, http://www.dorif.it/ezine/ezine _articles.php?art_id=40.

32. On some of these differences and similarities, see Cullen Goldblatt, "Lëndëmtu: réflexions sur *Doomi Golo* et *Les Petits de la guenon*," in *Des Mondes et des langues: l'écriture de Boubacar Boris Diop* (Paris: Présence Africaine, 2014), pp. 61–83; and Jonathon Repinecz, "'The Tales of Tomorrow': Towards a Futurist Vision of Wolof Tradition," *Journal of African Cultural Studies*, vol. 27, no. 1, 2015, pp. 56–70.

33. "Man bokkuma ci bindkat yi ñuy soow. Doore ca Musaa Ka ba agsi ei Séex Aliyu Ndaw, jaar ci ñoomin Sëriñ Mbay Jaxate ak Maabo Gise, ñu ma gën a aay fuuf ñoo saxal seeni kàddu yu rafet ci biir xolu askan wi, jëmbët leen ci xeli doomi Aadama yi." Boubacar Boris Diop, *Doomi Golo* (Dakar: Editions Papyrus, 2003), p. 19. "N'étant pas un de ces poètes fameux dont notre peuple est si fier, qu'ils se nomment Serigne Moussa Kâ, Mabo Guissé ou Cheik Aliou Ndao, je me suis senti désemparé quand, au fil des semaines, d'autres événements ont en quelque sorte exigé d'être racontés, eux aussi." Boubacar Boris Diop, *Les petits de la guenon* (Paris: P. Rey, 2009), pp. 18–19.

34. Goldblatt, "Lëndëmtu," 67–69.

35. "Je pourrais dire, pour utiliser un langage imagé, qu'ils frappaient à la porte comme des sourds et essayaient de sauter par-dessus les bords de mes Carnets pour y resquiller une place et que ça faisait tout de même un drôle de vacarme. De guerre lasse et sans doute encore une fois par inexpérience, je les ai laissés avoir le dernier mot." B. B. Diop, *Les Petits*, 19.

36. B. B. Diop, *Doomi Golo*, 37.

37. B. B. Diop, 32, 286.

38. See B. B. Diop, *Doomi Golo*, 29–33, 27–28, 270, 191; and B. B. Diop, *Les Petits*, 30–37, 325, 213.

39. Nathalie Carré, "Between Mother Tongue and 'Ceremonial Tongue': Boubacar Boris Diop and the Self-Translation of Doomi Golo," *International Journal of Francophone Studies*, vol. 18, no. 1, 2015, pp. 101–114; Ousmane Ngom, "Militantisme Linguistique et Initiation Littéraire Dans Doomi Golo—Roman Wolof de Bubakar Bóris Jóob," *Repères-Dorif*, 2012, http:// www.dorif.it/ezine/ezine_articles.php?art_id=34.

40. Repinecz, "'The Tales of Tomorrow,'" 5–10.

41. Badu does "appear" briefly late in the novel, but this is one of many of scenes narrated by the madman Aali that has a highly uncertain relationship to reality. B. B. Diop, *Les Petits*, 398–99.

42. Narratives that feature migrant narrators and diasporic address have become increasingly common in Senegalese literature, from Ken Bugul to Fatou Diome. See Mahriana Rofheart, *Shifting Perceptions of Migration in Senegalese Literature, Film, and Social Media* (Lanham, Md.: Lexington Books, 2013).

43. B. B. Diop, *Doomi Golo*, 346; B. B. Diop, *Les Petits*, 438.

44. B. B. Diop, *Doomi Golo*, 232; B. B. Diop, *Les Petits*, 273.

45. B. B. Diop, *Doomi Golo*, 24; B. B. Diop, *Les Petits*, 27.

46. B. B. Diop, *Doomi Golo*, 315–23; B. B. Diop, *Les Petits*, 380–97.

47. B. B. Diop, *Les Petits*, 27.

48. B. B. Diop, *Doomi Golo*, 107; B. B. Diop, *Les Petits*, 108.

49. B. B. Diop, *Doomi Golo*, 107; B. B. Diop, *Les Petits*, 108. The idea is expressed in nearly the same way in both versions, but the Wolof version is just a bit more disorienting. Cast in the "A" conjugation, which emphasizes the subject of a phrase, "Yaay man. Maay yow" could be literally translated as "it is you who is me, it is me who is you."

50. B. B. Diop, *Les Petits*, 70.

51. Both *foofe* and *ailleurs* are spatial deictics: parts of speech that indicate the positioning of a designated object with regard to the speaker, hearer, or referent. Different languages accomplish deixis in different ways, with varying combinations of semantic language, referential language, and indices. The Wolof version puts an additional level of disorientation into play by taking advantage of the nuances of deictic space the language affords. It is obligatory in Wolof to refer to where an object is in space relative to the speaker, which is accomplished through a system of affixes that indicate the proximity of a referent relative to both the speaker and the addressee. To put that more concisely, *foofe* means something like "over there" for *both* the listener and the speaker, but with an added nuance that one could translate as "far from both of us, but closer to you than to me." Stéphane Robert, "Deictic Space in Wolof: Discourse, Syntax and the Importance of Absence," *Typological Studies in Language*, vol. 66, 2006, p. 155. The French version signals its inability to capture the same precision by noting that Yaasin's transformation must be called *ailleurs*, "for lack of a better word" (faute de mieux). B. B. Diop, *Doomi Golo*, 319; B. B. Diop, *Les Petits*, 390.

52. B. B. Diop, *Doomi Golo*, 317; B. B. Diop, *Les Petits*, 387.

53. Diop and Sugnet, "Dances with Wolofs," 146.

54. B. B. Diop, *Doomi Golo*, 120; B. B. Diop, *Les Petits*, 126.

55. "Ce processus de traduction où je me découvrais à chaque seconde en train de traduire sans traduire tout en traduisant." B. B. Diop, "Écrire entre deux langues."

56. For a revisionist account of Herder's thinking on language and collective will, see Tristram Wolff, "Arbitrary, Natural, Other: J. G. Herder and Ideologies of Linguistic Will," *European Romantic Review*, vol. 27, no. 2, 2016, pp. 259–80.

57. Casanova, *La République mondiale des Lettres*, 17–20; Henry James, *The Figure in the Carpet* (London: Martin Secker, 1916), p. 44.

58. Pascale Casanova, "Literature as a World," *New Left Review*, vol. 31, 2005, p. 72.

59. Walter Benjamin, *Selected Writings, Volume 1: 1913–1926* (Cambridge, Mass.: Belknap Press of Harvard University Press, 2004), p. 256.

60. Boubacar Boris Diop, *Doomi Golo—The Hidden Notebooks*, trans. Vera Wülfing-Leckie and El Hadji Moustapha Diop (East Lansing: Michigan State University Press, 2016); and Michigan State University Press, email message "Doomi Golo—The Hidden Notebooks Offered by Michigan State University Press," 12 Oct. 2016.

61. This English version has been followed by a Spanish translation, also done from *Les Petits*. Boubacar Boris Diop, *El Libro De Los Secretos*, trans. Wenceslao Carlos Lozano González (Córdoba, Spain: Almuzara, 2015).

62. B. B. Diop, *Doomi Golo—The Hidden Notebooks*, xxvii.

63. "Montrer aux créateurs qu'il existe cette possibilité de diffuser leurs livres, en s'appuyant sur les technologies de l'information et de la communication, pour atteindre un public qui n'a pas forcément été à l'école." Agence de Presse Sénégalaise, "La version audio du roman 'Doomi Golo' diffusée à partir de lundi sur des radios dakaroises," Seneweb.com, http://www .seneweb.com/news/culture/la-version-audio-du-roman-quot-doomi-golo -quot-diffusee-a-partir-de-lundi-sur-des-radios-dakaroises_n_131806.html.

64. Ramaka proposed the project to Diop at a symposium at Indiana University in 2007. The two collaborated on it later that year at Indiana, and Ramaka would go on to orchestrate the diffusion of the recording in Senegal in 2014. Many thanks to Eileen Julien for this information.

65. My analysis here examines the November broadcasts on AFIA FM. I am very grateful to Jeremy Dell for his help recording them. Boubacar Boris Diop, *Doomi Golo*, Radio broadcasts, AFIA FM, Dakar, Senegal, Nov. 2014.

EPILOGUE. OUT OF TIME: DECOLONIZATION AND THE FUTURE OF WORLD LITERATURE

1. On addressivity, see M. M. Bakhtin, *Speech Genres and Other Late Essays* (Austin: University of Texas Press, 2010), p. 99; and Michael Allan,

"Reading with One Eye, Speaking with One Tongue: On the Problem of Address in World Literature," *Comparative Literature Studies*, vol. 44, no. 1, 2007, pp. 1–19.

2. Suzanne Brichaux-Houyoux, *Quand Césaire écrit, Lumumba parle: édition commentée de Une saison au Congo* (Paris: L'Harmattan, 1993).

3. "Il n'existe pas de texte plus *actuel* qu'*Une saison au Congo* de Césaire." Katia Touré, "Céytu: là où le wolof tutoie les grandes œuvres francophones," *Le Point Afrique*, http://afrique.lepoint.fr/culture/litterature-ceytu-quand-le -wolof-tutoie-les-grandes-oeuvres-francophones-19-02-2016-2019620_2256 .php; "La pièce de Césaire sur l'assassinat de Lumumba a beau dater des années 70, elle reste *actuelle*." Anne Bocandé, "L'écrivain sénégalais Boubacar Boris Diop lance une collection en langue wolof," *Altermondes*, 9 Mar. 2016, http://www.altermondes.org/lecrivain-senegalais-boubacar-boris -diop-lance-une-collection-en-langue-wolof/.

4. A. Tshitungu Kongolo, "Présentation," in *Poésie, théâtre, essais et discours*, ed. Albert-James Arnold (Paris : CNRS, 2014), p. 1105.

5. Césaire added a new ending after Lumumba was rehabilitated as a national icon by the dictator Mobutu Sese Seko; he also added a confrontation between Lumumba and a Ghanaian soldier after Kwame Nkrumah, the first president of Ghana, was toppled in an officers' coup. For an overview of evolution of the play, see Kongolo, "Présentation," 1107–11, in the CNRS edition of Césaire's collected works. As should become clear, I do not endorse this edition's preference for the 1966 version of the play as the "original." If Césaire's revisions "obscured the initial message," as Kongolo puts it in an otherwise very helpful entry, then perhaps this was their point. See also Christopher L. Miller, "Editing and Editorializing: The New Genetic Cahier of Aimé Césaire," *South Atlantic Quarterly*, vol. 115, no. 3, 2016, pp. 441–55, in which Miller faults the CNRS edition's preference for the earliest versions of Césaire's *Cahier*.

6. Aimé Césaire, *Une saison au Congo* (Paris: Editions du Seuil, 2001), pp. 111–12.

7. Césaire, 32–33.

8. Brichaux-Houyoux, *Quand Césaire écrit, Lumumba parle*, 174.

9. Césaire, *Une saison au Congo*, 106, 80.

10. Césaire, 123.

11. Aimé Césaire, *Nawetu deret*, trans. Boubacar Boris Diop (Paris: Céytu, 2016), p. 154.

12. The Céytu venture has affinities with a variety of contemporary projects that promote creative writing, publishing, and translating in and from African languages. See, for example, *Jalada*'s issue on translation, which features a story by Ngũgĩ wa Thiong'o translated into thirty-three

different languages. "Jalada Translation Issue 01: Ngũgĩ wa Thiong'o," *Jalada*, March 22, 2016, https://jaladaafrica.org/2016/03/22/jalada-translation -issue-01-ngugi-wa-thiongo/.

13. Touré, "Céytu"; Bocandé, "L'écrivain sénégalais Boubacar Boris Diop."

ARCHIVAL SOURCES
France
Archives Françaises du Film, Centre National du Cinéma, Bois-d'Arcy (AFF)
Archives Nationales d'Outre-Mer, Aix-en-Provence (ANOM)
Bibliothèque du Film, Cinémathèque Française, Paris (CF)
Bibliothèque Nationale de France, Paris (BNF)

Senegal
Archives Nationales du Sénégal, Dakar (ANS)
Cahiers Ponty Collection, Institut Fondamental d'Afrique Noire, Université Cheikh Anta Diop, Dakar (IFAN)
Centre de Linguistique Appliquée de Dakar, Université Cheikh Anta Diop, Dakar (CLAD)

United States
International Association for Cultural Freedom Records, Joseph Regenstein Library, University of Chicago Library (JRL)
Noma Award Manuscripts, The Lilly Library, Indiana University, Bloomington (LL)
Transcription Centre Archive, Harry Ransom Center, University of Texas at Austin (HRC)

BIBLIOGRAPHY OF PRIMARY AND SECONDARY SOURCES
Abanime, Emeka. "Review: Une Si Longue Lettre." *World Literature Today*, vol. 54, no. 2, Spring 1980, p. 327.
Achebe, Chinua. "English and the African Writer." *Transition*, no. 18, 1965, pp. 27–30.
———. *Morning Yet on Creation Day: Essays*. Garden City, N.Y.: Anchor Press, 1975.
Adéèkọ́, Adélékè. *Proverbs, Textuality, and Nativism in African Literature*. Gainesville: University Press of Florida, 1998.

Adejunmobi, Moradewun. "Routes: Language and the Identity of African Literature." *The Journal of Modern African Studies*, vol. 37, no. 4, Dec. 1999, pp. 581–96.

———. *Vernacular Palaver: Imaginations of the Local and Non-Native Languages in West Africa*. Clevedon, UK: Multilingual Matters, 2004.

Afanou, François, and Raymond Togbé Pierre. *Catalogue des "Cahiers William Ponty": extrait Sénégal*. Dakar: Département de documentation de l'I.F.A.N., 1967.

African Books Collective. "*Barua Ndefu Kama Hii.*" 29 June 2015. www .africanbookscollective.com/books/barua-ndefu-kama-hii.

Agence de Presse Sénégalaise. "La version audio du roman 'Doomi Golo' diffusée à partir de lundi sur des radios dakaroises." Seneweb.com. http://www.seneweb.com/news/culture/la-version-audio-du-roman-quot -doomi-golo-quot-diffusee-a-partir-de-lundi-sur-des-radios-dakaroises _n_131806.html.

Aggarwal, Kusum. *Amadou Hampâté Bâ et l'africanisme: de la recherche anthropologique à l'exercice de la fonction autoriale*. Paris: L'Harmattan, 1999.

Ahmad, Aijaz. "The Communist Manifesto and 'World Literature.'" *Social Scientist*, vol. 28, no. 7/8, 2000, pp. 3–30.

Ajayi-Soyinka, O. "Negritude, Feminism, and the Quest for Identity: Re-Reading Mariama Bâ's *So Long a Letter*." In Azodo, *Emerging Perspectives on Mariama Bâ*, pp. 153–74.

Allan, Michael. *In the Shadow of World Literature: Sites of Reading in Colonial Egypt*. Princeton, N.J.: Princeton University Press, 2016.

———. "Reading with One Eye, Speaking with One Tongue: On the Problem of Address in World Literature." *Comparative Literature Studies*, vol. 44, no. 1, 2007, pp. 1–19.

Amachree, Igolima T. D. "Mariama Bâ and the Marginal Person: A New Examination and Social Interpretation of Her Novels." In Azodo, *Emerging Perspectives on Mariama Bâ*, pp. 73–88.

Anderson, Benedict. *Imagined Communities: Reflections on the Origin and Spread of Nationalism*. London: Verso, 2006.

Andrade, Susan Z. "The Loved and the Left: Sembène, Bâ, Sow Fall." In *The Nation Writ Small: African Fictions and Feminisms, 1958–1988*. Durham, N.C.: Duke University Press, 2011.

Anon. "Au secours de votre journal!" *Le cri des nègres*, Aug. 1933, p. 2.

———. "Bobards." *L'Essor*, 16 Oct. 1951, 16 April 1952, 10 June 1952, 17 June 1952, 29 Aug. 1952, 12 Sept. 1952, 14 Nov. 1952, 18 Nov. 1952, 30 April 1943.

———. "Chaque travailleur nègre a un devoir à accomplir envers son journal." *Le cri des nègres*, June 1934, p. 1.

———. "Compositions françaises." *Bulletin de l'Enseignement de l'Afrique Occidentale Française*, vol. 13, no. 60, Jan.–June, 1925, pp. 100–4.

———. "Concours et examens en 1930." *Bulletin de l'Enseignement de l'Afrique Occidentale Française*, no. 72, June 1930, pp. 69–70.

———. "Concours et examens: session du 13 juin 1921." *Bulletin de l'Enseignement de l'Afrique Occidentale Française*, vol. 9, no. 47, Apr.–Sept. 1921, p. 60.

———. "Le Courrier de Nos Amis." *Dakar-Jeunes*, 23 July 1942, p. 4, and 17 Sept. 1942, p. 4.

———. "Le cri des nègres justifie son titre de journal des travailleurs nègres." *Le cri des nègres*, July 1934, p. 1.

———. "Nos Lecteurs et Nous." *Bingo* N°31.

———. "Orthographie des noms propres indigènes." 14MIOM/3211, 23G 6, ANOM.

———. *Readers' Assessments of Mariama Bâ: Une si longue lettre*. Noma Award Mss, LL.

———. *Renseignements du service de la sûreté du soudan*. 9 Sept. and 6 Oct. 1950. 14MIOM/3097, 21 G 173, ANOM.

———. *Reports on the* Voix du Dahomey *Affair, 1934–6*, 14MIOM/3068, 3069, 21 G 140, ANOM.

———. *Reports on Patronym Theft*. 14MIOM/3211, 23G 6, ANOM.

———. *Reports on Publications in Circulation*. 14MIOM/3111, 21G 204, ANOM.

———. "Résolution de Linguistique." *Présence Africaine*, no. 24/25, 1959, pp. 397–98.

Antoine [pseud.]. "L'Histoire de l'AOF." *Le Cœur de Dahomey*, Aug. 1935, pp. 1–2.

Apter, Emily. *Against World Literature: On the Politics of Untranslatability*. London: Verso, 2013.

Aquereburu, Edouard. *Le Noir évolué*. Cahiers Ponty, 1941, XVIII-D-602, carton N°5, IFAN.

Asad, Talal. *Formations of the Secular: Christianity, Islam, Modernity*. Stanford, Calif: Stanford University Press, 2003.

Ashcroft, Bill, Gareth Griffiths, and Helen Tiffin, eds. *The Post-Colonial Studies Reader*. 2nd ed. London: Routledge, 2006.

Association des étudiants sénégalais en France. *Ijjib Volof*. Grenoble: Imprimerie des Deux-Ponts, 1959.

Auerbach, Erich. "The Philology of World Literature." In *Time, History, and Literature: Selected Essays of Erich Auerbach*, edited by James I. Porter, translated by Jane O. Newman. Princeton, N.J.: Princeton University Press, 2016.

Azodo, Ada Uzoamaka. "Creative Writing and Literary Activism: Interview with Chimamanda Ngozi Adichie." *Journal of the African Literature Association*, vol. 2, no. 1, Winter-Spring 2008, pp. 146–51.

Azodo, Ada Uzoamaka, ed. *Emerging Perspectives on Mariama Bâ: Postcolonialism, Feminism, and Postmodernism*. Trenton, N.J.: Africa World Press, 2003.

Azodo, Ada Uzoamaka. "Lettre Senegalaise de Ramatoulaye: Writing as Action in Mariama Bâ's 'Une Si Longue Lettre.'" In Azodo, *Emerging Perspectives on Mariama Bâ*, pp. 3–18.

Bâ, Habibou. *Mémoire de fin d'études normales: Le Systéme d'éducation traditionnelle au Fouta Djallon*. Cahiers Ponty, n.d., XV-G-540, carton N°14, IFAN.

Bâ, Mariama. *Bataaxal bu gudde nii*. Translated by Maam Yunus Dieng and Arame Fal. Dakar: Les Nouvelles éditions africaines du Sénégal, 2007.

———. *So Long a Letter*. Translated by Modupé Bodé-Thomas. Oxford: Heinemann, 1989.

———. *So Long a Letter*. Translated by Modupé Bodé-Thomas. Long Grove, Ill.: Waveland Press, 2012.

———. *Een lange Brief: Roman*. Translated by Sonja Pos. Maasbree, Netherlands: Corrie Zelen. 1981.

———. *Un chant écarlate*. Dakar: Les Nouvelles éditions africaines du Sénégal, 1981.

———. *Une si longue lettre*. Dakar: Les Nouvelles éditions africaines du Sénégal, 1980.

Bajorek, Jennifer. "'Ca Bouscoulait!': Democratization and Photography in Senegal." In *Photography in Africa: Ethnographic Perspectives*, edited by Richard Vokes. Woodbridge, Suffolk: James Currey, 2012, pp. 140–66.

Bakhtin, M. M. *The Dialogic Imagination: Four Essays*. Austin: University of Texas Press, 1982.

———. *Speech Genres and Other Late Essays*. Austin: University of Texas Press, 1986.

Barber, Karin. *The Anthropology of Texts, Persons, and Publics: Oral and Written Culture in Africa and Beyond*. Cambridge: Cambridge University Press, 2007.

Barry, Boubacar. *La Sénégambie du XVe au XIXe siècle: traite négrière, Islam et conquête coloniale*. Paris: L'Harmattan, 1988.

Barthélémy, Pascale. *Africaines et diplômées à l'époque coloniale*. Rennes, France: Presses Universitaires de Rennes, 2010.

———. "Je suis une africaine . . . j'ai vingt ans." *Annales. Histoire, Sciences Sociales*, vol. 64, 2009, pp. 825–52.

———. "L'enseignement dans l'Empire colonial français: une vieille histoire?" *Histoire de l'éducation*, no. 128, Oct. 2010, pp. 5–28.

Batiéno, Joseph. *Devoir de vacances: éducation et instruction des enfants dans le milieu indigène*. Cahiers Ponty, n.d., XV-G-535, carton N°14, IFAN.

Bauman, Richard, and Charles L. Briggs. *Voices of Modernity: Language Ideologies and the Politics of Inequality*. Cambridge: Cambridge University Press, 2003.

Baumgardt, Ursula, Françoise Ugochukwu, and Jean Derive. *Approches littéraires de l'oralité africaine*. Paris: Karthala Editions, 2005.

Béart, Charles. "A Propos d'une littérature indigène d'expression française." *Dakar-Jeunes*, 18 June 1942.

———. "Le théâtre indigène en A.O.F. Les problèmes de l'éducation aux colonies." *L'Information d'Outre-Mer*, no. 2, Apr. 1939, pp. 128–39.

———. "Le théâtre indigène et la culture franco-africaine." *L'Education africaine*, Apr.–June 1936, p. 12.

Beecroft, Alexander. *An Ecology of World Literature: From Antiquity to the Present Day*. London: Verso Books, 2015.

Beier, Ulli. *Contemporary African Poetry in English*. Mbari Writers Conference, Kampala, 1961, MAK/ll (4), Container 1.3, Transcription Centre Archive, HRC.

Benjamin, Walter. *Selected Writings, Volume 1: 1913–1926*. Cambridge, Mass.: Belknap Press of Harvard University Press, 2004.

Bensmaïa, Réda. *Experimental Nations: Or, the Invention of the Maghreb*. Princeton, N.J.: Princeton University Press, 2009.

Berlant, Lauren. *Cruel Optimism*. Durham, N.C.: Duke University Press, 2011.

Bernabé, Jean, Patrick Chamoiseau, and Raphaël Confiant. *Éloge de la créolité*. Paris: Gallimard, 1989.

Beti, Mongo. *Le Rebelle: Tome 1*. Paris: Gallimard, 2007.

Bieber, Marion. *Letter to P. Edwards*. 24 Jan. 1964. Box 441, Folder 4, International Association for Cultural Freedom Records, JRL.

Blair, Dorothy S. *African Literature in French: A History of Creative Writing in French from West and Equatorial Africa*. Cambridge: Cambridge University Press, 1976.

Bocandé, Anne. "L'écrivain sénégalais Boubacar Boris Diop lance une collection en langue wolof." *Altermondes*. 9 Mar. 2016. http://www.altermondes.org/lecrivain-senegalais-boubacar-boris-diop-lance-une-collection-en-langue-wolof/.

Boilat, David. *Esquisses sénégalaises: physionomie du pays, peuplades, commerce, religions, passé et avenir, récits et légendes*. Paris: Karthala, 2000.

———. *Grammaire de la langue Woloffe*. Paris: Imprimerie Impériale, 1858.

———. *Notes du Fouta Toro*. 1843. Société de Géographie Ms 8 48–49, Département des Cartes et Plans (Richelieu), BNF.

Boisson. "Détermination des noms des indigènes," 16 Mar. 1942, 14MIOM/3211, 23G 6, ANOM.

Bouche, Denise. "L'enseignement dans les territoires français de l'Afrique occidentale de 1817 à 1920: mission civilisatrice ou formation d'une élite." PhD diss., Université de Lille, 1975.

Bouquillon, Yvon, and Robert Cornevin. *David Boilat, 1814–1901: le précurseur.* Dakar: Les Nouvelles éditions africaines du Sénégal, 1981.

Brichaux-Houyoux, Suzanne. *Quand Césaire écrit, Lumumba parle: édition commentée de Une saison au Congo.* Paris: L'Harmattan, 1993.

Britton. Celia. *Edouard Glissant and Postcolonial Theory: Strategies of Language and Resistance.* Charlottesville: University of Virginia Press, 1999.

Brown, Wendy. *Undoing the Demos.* Durham, N.C.: Duke University Press, 2015.

Bryant, Kelly Duke. *Education as Politics: Colonial Schooling and Political Debate in Senegal, 1850s–1914.* Madison: University of Wisconsin Press, 2015.

Buggenhagen, Beth A. *Muslim Families in Global Senegal: Money Takes Care of Shame.* Bloomington: Indiana University Press, 2012.

Bulman, Stephen. "A School for Epic? The École William Ponty and the Evolution of the Sunjata Epic, 1913–1960." In *Epic Adventures: Heroic Narrative in the Oral Performance Traditions of Four Continents,* edited by Jan Jansen and Henk M. J. Maier. Münster: Lit Verlag, 2004, pp. 34–45.

Burrill, Emily S. *States of Marriage: Gender, Justice, and Rights in Colonial Mali.* Athens: Ohio University Press, 2015.

Busch, Annett, and Max Annas, eds. *Ousmane Sembène: Interviews.* Jackson: University Press of Mississippi, 2008.

Bush, Ruth. "'Mesdames, Il Faut Lire!' Material Contexts and Representational Strategies in Early Francophone African Women's Magazines." *Francosphères,* vol. 5, no. 2, 2016, pp. 213–36.

———. *Publishing Africa in French: Literary Institutions and Decolonization 1945–1967.* Oxford: Oxford University Press, 2016.

Butler, Judith. "What Is Critique? An Essay on Foucault's Virtue." In *The Political,* edited by David Ingram. Oxford: Blackwell, 2001, pp. 212–26.

Callon, Michel. "Éléments pour une sociologie de la traduction: la domestication des coquilles saint-jacques et des marins-pêcheurs dans la baie de Saint-Brieuc." *L'Année Sociologique,* vol. 36, 1986, pp. 169–208.

Camara, Fatou K. "Women and the Law: A Critique of Senegalese Family Law." *Social Identities,* vol. 13, no. 6, 2007, pp. 787–800.

Camara, Sana. *Wolof Lexicon and Grammar.* Bloomington, Ind: NALRC Press, 2006.

———. *See also* Kamara, Sana.

Carde, Jules. *Circulaire sur le décret du 27 mars 1928 sur le régime de la presse.* 14MIOM/3034, 21 G 44 1, ANOM.

———. *Demande d'accession à la qualité de citoyen français de M. Dim Delobson.* 13 Dec. 1929, Fonds Ministériels, Affpol148, ANOM.

Carré, Nathalie. "Between Mother Tongue and 'Ceremonial Tongue': Boubacar Boris Diop and the Self-Translation of Doomi Golo." *International Journal of Francophone Studies,* vol. 18, no. 1, 2015, pp. 101–14.

Casanova, Pascale. *La République mondiale des Lettres.* Paris: Points, 2008.

———. "Literature as a World." *New Left Review,* vol. 31, 2005, pp. 71–90.

———. *The World Republic of Letters.* Translated by M. B. Debevoise. Cambridge, Mass.: Harvard University Press, 2007.

Césaire, Aimé. *Discours sur le colonialisme.* Paris: Présence Africaine, 1955.

———. *Nawetu deret.* Translated by Boubacar Boris Diop. Paris: Céytu, 2016.

———. *Une saison au Congo.* Paris: Editions du Seuil, 2001.

Cham, Mbye B. "Contemporary Society and the Female Imagination: A Study of the Novels of Mariama Bâ." *African Literature Today,* no. 15, 1987, pp. 89–101.

Charton, Albert. "La vie et hygiène intellectuelles." *Bulletin de l'Enseignement de l'Afrique Occidentale Française,* vol. 19, no. 72, Mar. 1930, pp. 10–14.

———. "Les études indigènes à l'Ecole Normale William Ponty." *Bulletin de l'Enseignement de l'Afrique Occidentale Française,* no. 84, 1933, p. 199.

———. "Rôle social de l'enseignement en Afrique Occidentale Française." *Outre-Mer,* no. 2, June 1934, pp. 188–202.

Chatterjee, Partha. *The Nation and Its Fragments: Colonial and Postcolonial Histories.* Princeton, N.J.: Princeton University Press, 1993.

Cheah, Pheng. *What Is a World? On Postcolonial Literature as World Literature.* Durham, N.C.: Duke University Press, 2016.

Chukwuma, Helen. "Feminism and Change in Mariama Bâ's So Long A Letter." In *Accents in the African Novel.* Enugu, Nigeria: New Generation Books, 1991, pp. 31–38.

Cissé, Amadou Sakhir. *Education de l'enfant Gourou en Côte d'Ivoire.* Cahiers Ponty, n.d., XV-CI-536, carton N°14, IFAN.

Cissé, Ibrahima Ben Mady. *Mémoire de fin d'études normales: Système d'éducation traditionnelle d'une société.* Cahiers Ponty, 1949, XV-SE-562, carton N°30. IFAN.

Cisse, Momar. *Parole chantée et communication sociale chez les Wolof du Sénégal.* Paris: L'Harmattan, 2010.

Clark, John Pepper. *Reports from Conference Study Groups: Poetry.* Mbari Writers Conference, Kampala, 1961, MAK/IV (2), Container 1.3, Transcription Centre Archive, HRC.

Clifford, James. "On Ethnographic Authority." *Representations*, no. 2, 1983, pp. 118–46.

Coetzee, John Maxwell. *Elizabeth Costello: Eight Lessons.* New York: Random House, 2004.

Cohen, Joshua. "Stages in Transition: Les Ballets Africains and Independence, 1959 to 1960." *Journal of Black Studies*, vol. 43, no. 1, Jan. 2012, pp. 11–48.

Coleman, Peter. *The Liberal Conspiracy.* New York: Free Press, 1989.

Comaroff, Jean, and John L. Comaroff. *Theory from the South: Or, How Euro-America Is Evolving Toward Africa.* Boulder, Colo.: Paradigm Publishers, 2012.

Congress for Cultural Freedom. *Actes du Colloque sur la littérature africaine d'expression française, Dakar, 26–29 mars 1963*, Dakar: Faculté des Lettres, 1965.

———. *Conference for African Writers of English Expression.* Mbari Writers Conference, Kampala, 1961, TC/127, Container 1.3, Transcription Centre Archive, HRC.

———. *Mbari Writers' Conference in Uganda.* Mbari Writers Conference, Kampala, 1961, Container 1.3, Transcription Centre Archive, HRC.

———. *Report on Dakar and Freetown Conferences 1963.* Box 442, Folder 1, International Association for Cultural Freedom Records, JRL.

———. *The Writers Speak [Edited].* Box 440, Folder 8, "Transcripts in French, 1953." International Association for Cultural Freedom Records, JRL.

———. *The Writers Speak [Unedited].* Box 442, Folder 1, "Report on Dakar and Freetown Conferences 1963." International Association for Cultural Freedom Records, JRL.

Conklin, Alice L. *A Mission to Civilize.* Stanford, Calif: Stanford University Press, 1997.

Conteh-Morgan, John. *Theatre and Drama in Francophone Africa: A Critical Introduction.* Cambridge: Cambridge University Press, 1994.

Cooper, Frederick. *Citizenship between Empire and Nation: Remaking France and French Africa, 1945–1960.* Princeton, N.J.: Princeton University Press, 2014.

Corcoran, Patrick. *The Cambridge Introduction to Francophone Literature.* Cambridge: Cambridge University Press, 2007.

Cornevin, Robert. *Le théâtre en Afrique noire et à Madagascar.* Paris: Le livre africain, 1970.

Coulis, Shari. "The Impossibility of Choice: Gender and Genre in Mariama Bâ's So Long a Letter." In Azodo, *Emerging Perspectives on Mariama Bâ*, p. 19.

Coundouriotis, Eleni. *Claiming History: Colonialism, Ethnography, and the Novel*. New York: Columbia University Press, 1999.

Currey, James. *Africa Writes Back: The African Writers Series and the Launch of African Literature*. Athens: Ohio University Press, 2008.

D'Aby, F. J. Amon. *La Côte d'Ivoire dans la cité africaine*. Paris: Larose, 1951.

Dadié, Bernard. *Climbié*. Translated by Karen Chapman. London: Heinemann, 1971.

———. *Composition Française*. Series O, Archives de l'Ecole Normale William Ponty, ANS.

———. *Légendes et poèmes, Afrique debout! Légendes Africaines. Climbié. La Ronde des jours*. Paris: Seghers, 1966.

D'Almeida, Irène Assiba. "The Concept of Choice in Mariama Ba's Fiction." In *Ngambika: Studies of Women in African Literature*, edited by Carole Boyce Davies and Anne Adams Graves. Trenton, N.J.: Africa World Press, 1986, pp. 161–71.

Damey, Lokho. *Mémoire de fin d'études: Le système d'éducation traditionnelle chez les Manons*. Cahiers Ponty, n.d., XV-G-551, carton N°14, IFAN.

Damrosch, David. *What Is World Literature?* Princeton, N.J.: Princeton University Press, 2003.

Davesne, André. "L'enseignement du français." *Bulletin de l'Enseignement de l'Afrique Occidentale Française*, Dec. 1930, pp. 20–26.

Davesne, André, and Joseph Gouin. *Mamadou et Bineta sont devenus grands: livre de français à l'usage des cours moyens et supérieurs des écoles de l'Afrique noire*. Strasbourg, France: Istra, 1939.

Debaene, Vincent. "Entre informateur et auteur. Discours ethnographique indigène et littérature en AOF." In *Ethnologues en situation coloniale*, edited by Daniel Fabre, et al. Paris: CNRS Editions, 2016.

———. *Far Afield: French Anthropology between Science and Literature*. Chicago: University of Chicago Press, 2014.

———. "Le point de vue de l'indigène ou comment on écrit l'histoire de la littérature." *Romanic Review*, vol. 100, no. 1–2, 2009, pp. 15–28.

———. "Les écrivains contre l'ethnologie? Ethnographie, ethnologie et littérature d'Afrique et des Antilles, 1921–1948." *Romanic Review*, vol. 104, no. 3–4, 2013, pp. 353–74.

De Jong, Ferdinand, and Brian Quinn. "Ruines d'utopies: l'École William Ponty et l'Université du Futur africain." Translated by Jean-Nicolas Bach. *Politique africaine*, no. 135, Dec. 2014, pp. 71–94.

Delmond. "Etat civil indigène," 29 July 1942, 14MIOM/3211, 23G 6, ANOM.

Deleuze, Gilles. *Cinema 2: The Time Image*. London: Continuum International Publishing Group, 2005.

Dembrow, Michael, and Klaus Troller. "Interview with Ousmane Sembène." In Busch and Annas, *Ousmane Sembène*, pp. 63–71.

Derrida, Jacques. *De la grammatologie*. Paris: Minuit, 1967.

———. *Of Grammatology*. Translated by Gayatri Chakravorty Spivak. Baltimore: Johns Hopkins University Press, 1998.

Desai, Gaurav. *Subject to Colonialism: African Self-Fashioning and the Colonial Library*. Durham, N.C.: Duke University Press, 2001.

Dia, Alioune Toure. "Succès littéraire de Mariama Ba pour son livre *Une si longue lettre*." *Amina*, no. 86, 1979, pp. 12–14.

Dia, Hamidou. "Littérature et préjugés." *Dakar-Jeunes*, 14 May 1942, p. 3.

Dia, Mamadou. *Mémoires d'un militant du tiers-monde*. Paris: Publisud, 1985.

Diack, Samba. *A Podor, vestiges de quelques événements historiques et leurs conséquences dans la vie actuelle*. Cahiers Ponty, n.d., XXVI-SE- 766, carton N°5, IFAN.

Diagne, Pathé. "Défense et illustration des langues sénégalaises." *Andë Soppi*, Feb. 1978.

———. "Siggi nag faf!" *Siggi*, Feb. 1977, pp. 17–21.

———. *Teerebtanu ladab ci wàlàf: anthologie wolof de littérature*. Dakar: Université de Dakar, Institut fondamental d'Afrique noire, Séminaire sur l'adaptation des langues africaines, 1971.

Diagne, Souleymane Bachir. *African Art as Philosophy: Senghor, Bergson and the Idea of Negritude*. Translated by Jeffers Chike. London: Seagull Books, 2011.

Diakhate, Lamine. "Chronique littéraire." *Condition Humaine*, 12 Jan. 1955, p. 4.

Diakité, Mamadi. *Devoir de vacances: L'Education du garçon et de la fille dans la famille indigène*. Cahiers Ponty, 1945, XV-G-543, carton N°14, IFAN.

Diallo, Amadou Babaheine Ibn Alfa. *L'enfant dans le milieu familial*. Cahiers Ponty, 1949, XV-G-544, carton N°14, IFAN.

Diallo, Ibrahima. *The Politics of National Languages in Postcolonial Senegal*. Amherst, N.Y.: Cambria Press, 2010.

Diallo, Laye Bamba, and E. B. Sow. "Mariama Ba: Sous chaque homme qui pointe, il y a l'action d'une femme méritante." *Zone 2*, no. 26, July 1979, p. 13.

Diallo, S. "Jeune Afrique fait parler Sembène Ousmane." *Jeune Afrique*, no. 629, 1973, pp. 44–49.

Diawara, Manthia. *African Cinema: Politics and Culture*. Bloomington: Indiana University Press, 1992.

Diédhiou, Djib. "Echo des voix féminines de détresse." *Le soleil*, 13 June 1980, p. 2.

Dieng, Cheikhou Tidiane. *Le Génie des eaux*. Cahiers Ponty, n.d., XXIV-SE-713, carton N°36, IFAN.

Dieng, Maam Yunus. *Aawo Bi*. Dakar: IFAN Cheikh Anta Diop, 1992.

———. Interview by Tobias Warner. 26 Oct. 2010. Dakar, Senegal.

Diop, Abdoulaye Bara. *La sociéte wolof: tradition et changement*. Paris: Karthala, 1981.

Diop, Birago. "Les Mamelles." In *Anthologie de la nouvelle poésie nègre et malgache de langue française*, edited by Léopold Sédar Senghor, 5th ed. Paris: Presses Universitaires de France, 2002, pp. 135–42.

Diop, Boubacar Boris. *Doomi Golo*. Dakar: Editions Papyrus, 2003.

———. *Doomi Golo*. Radio Broadcasts, AFIA FM, Dakar, Senegal. Nov. 2014.

———. *Doomi Golo—The Hidden Notebooks*. Translated by Vera Wülfing-Leckie and El Hadji Moustapha Diop. East Lansing: Michigan State University Press, 2016.

———. "Écrire entre deux langues. De Doomi Golo aux Petits de la guenon." *Rèperes-Dorifs*. http://www.dorif.it/ezine/ezine_articles.php?art_id=40.

———. *El Libro De Los Secretos*. Translated by Wenceslao Carlos Lozano González. Córdoba, Spain: Almuzara, 2015.

———. *The Knight and His Shadow*. Translated by Alan Furness. East Lansing: Michigan State University Press, 2015.

———. "Langues africaines et création littéraire." unpublished manuscript, n.d.

———. *Le Cavalier et son ombre*. Abidjan: Nouvelles Editions Ivoiriennes, 2000.

———. *Les petits de la guenon*. Paris: P. Rey, 2009.

Diop, Boubacar Boris, and Charles J. Sugnet. "Dances with Wolofs: A Conversation with Boubacar Boris Diop." *Transition*, 87, vol. 10, no. 3, 2001, pp. 138–59.

Diop, Cheikh Anta. *Alerte sous les tropiques: articles 1946–1960*. Paris: Présence Africaine, 1990.

———. *Nations nègres et culture: De l'antiquité nègre égyptienne aux problèmes culturels de l'Afrique Noire d'aujourd'hui*. 4th ed. Paris: Présence Africaine, 2000.

Diop, Cheikh M'Backé. *Cheikh Anta Diop: l'homme et l'oeuvre*. Paris: Présence Africaine, 2003.

Diop, David. "Contribution au débat sur la poésie nationale." *Présence Africaine*, no. 6, 1956, pp. 113–15.

Diop, Momar Coumba, and Mamadou Diouf. *Le Sénégal sous Abdou Diouf: Etat et société*. Paris: Karthala, 1990.

Diop, Papa Samba. *Archéologie du roman sénégalais*. Paris: L'Harmattan, 2010.

———. *Glossaire du roman sénégalais*. Paris: L'Harmattan, 2010.

Diouf, Jean Léopold. *Dictionnaire wolof-français et français-wolof.* Paris: Karthala, 2003.

Diouf, Makhtar. "La Crise de l'ajustement." *Politique Africaine,* no. 45, 2002, pp. 62–85.

Diouf, Mamadou. "The French Colonial Policy of Assimilation and the Civility of the Originaires of the Four Communes (Senegal): A Nineteenth-Century Globalization Project." *Development and Change,* vol. 29, no. 4, 1998, pp. 671–96.

———. "History and Actuality in Ousmane Sembene's *Ceddo* and Djibril Diop Mambety's *Hyenas.*" In *African Experiences of Cinema,* edited by Imrah Bakari and Mbye Cham. London: British Film Institute, 1996, pp. 239–51.

———. *Le Kajoor Au XIXe Siècle.* Paris: Karthala, 1990.

———. "Les jeunes dakarois, la scène urbaine et le temps du monde à la fin du XXe siècle." In *Les arts de la citoyenneté au Sénégal: espaces contestés et civilités urbaine,* edited by Mamadou Diouf and Rosalind Fredericks. Paris: Karthala, 2013, pp. 49–92.

Diouf, Mamadou, and Rosalind Fredericks, eds. *The Arts of Citizenship in African Cities: Infrastructures and Spaces of Belonging.* Basingstoke: Palgrave Macmillan, 2014.

Diouf, Mamadou, and Mohamed Mbodj. "The Shadow of Cheikh Anta Diop." In *The Surreptitious Speech. Présence Africaine and the Politics of Otherness 1947–1987,* edited by V. Y. Mudimbe. Chicago: University of Chicago Press, 1992, pp. 118–35.

Diouf N'Dofène, Mahélor. *Système d'éducation traditionnellle d'une société: Sine Saloum.* Cahiers Ponty, n.d., XV-SE-570, carton N°30, IFAN.

Donadey, Anne. "The Multilingual Strategies of Postcolonial Literature: Assia Djebar's Algerian Palimpsest." *World Literature Today,* vol. 74, no. 1, 2000, pp. 27–36.

Dubois, Henri. "Affaire *Voix du Dahomey,* rapport du directeur adjoint de police sur les menées anti-françaises au Dahomey et au Togo," 14MIOM/3103 FM, 21 G 140, ANOM.

Ducournau, Claire. *La Fabrique des classiques africains: Ecrivains d'Afrique subsaharienne francophone.* Paris: CNRS, 2017.

Ecole normale supérieure de Bamako. *Bamako.* Pessac, France: Presses Universitaires de Bordeaux, 1993.

Edson, Laurie. "Mariama Bâ and the Politics of the Family." *Studies in 20th & 21st Century Literature,* vol. 17, no. 1, 1993, p. 3.

Edwards, Brent Hayes. *The Practice of Diaspora: Literature, Translation, and the Rise of Black Internationalism.* Cambridge, Mass.: Harvard University Press, 2003.

Emre, Merve. *Paraliterary: The Making of Bad Readers in Postwar America.* Chicago: University of Chicago Press, 2017.

Fadiga, Bouillagui. "Une circoncision chez les markas du soudan." *Bulletin Du Comité d'Études Historiques et Scientifiques d'Afrique Occidentale Française*, vol. 18, no. 4, 1934, pp. 565–77.

Fal, Arame. *Alphabétisation en wolof: guide orthographique.* Dakar: OSAD, 1991.

———. "A propos des consonnes géminées du wolof: opinion d'un linguiste." *Taxaw*, no. 11, 1978, p. 3.

———. "OSAD's Experience in the Publishing of Books in National Languages." In *Literacy and Linguistic Diversity in a Global Perspective: An Intercultural Exchange with African Countries*, edited by Neville Alexander and Brigitta Busch. Strasbourg: Council of Europe, 2007, p. 31.

———. "Phonetic Correspondences Between Wolof and English." In *Nawetu deret*. Translated by Boubacar Boris Diop. Paris: Céytu, 2016, pp. 172–74.

Fall, Abd'el Kader. "A chacun son métier." *Le Soleil*, 19 Dec. 1977.

Fall, Guedj. "Aawo Bi de Mame Younousse Dieng, un récit fondateur en langue wolof." *Ethiopiques*, no. 76, 2006. http://ethiopiques.refer.sn/spip .php?page=imprimer-article&id_article=1496.

Fanon, Frantz. *Œuvres.* Paris: La Découverte, 2011.

Faye, Diâo. "L'euvre poétique wolofal de Moussa Ka ou l'épopée de Cheikh Ahmadou Bamba." Thèse de doctorat de troisième cycle, Université Cheikh Anta Diop, 1999.

Ferguson, James. *Global Shadows: Africa in the Neoliberal World Order.* Durham, N.C.: Duke University Press, 2006.

Fetzer, Glenn W. "Women's Search for Voice and the Problem of Knowing in the Novels of Mariama Ba." *CLA Journal*, vol. 35, no. 1, 1991, pp. 31–41.

Fiat Justitia [pseud.]. "Les Délits de la presse et les coutumes." *L'Etoile du Dahomey*, 1933.

Fleming, Kathryn R. "Exorcising Institutionalized Ghosts and Redefining Female Identity in Mariama Bâ's *So Long a Letter* and Toni Morrison's *Beloved*." In Azodo, *Emerging Perspectives on Mariama Bâ*, p. 205.

Formigari, Lia, and Gabriel Poole. *A History of Language Philosophies.* Amsterdam: John Benjamins Publishing, 2004.

Foucault, Michel. "Qu'est-ce qu'un auteur?" *Bulletin de la Société Française de Philosophie*, vol. 63, no. 3, 1969, p. 73.

Gadjigo, Samba. "Interview with Ousmane Sembène," *Rabat*, 11 Apr. 2004. Quoted in Busch and Annas, pp. 190–96.

Gal, Susan. "Politics of Translation." *Annual Review of Anthropology*, vol. 44, 2015, pp. 225–40.

Gal, Susan, and Judith Irvine. "The Boundaries of Languages and Disciplines: How Ideologies Construct Difference." *Social Research*, vol. 62, no. 4, 1995, pp. 967–1,001.

Gamble, Harry. *Contesting French West Africa: Battles Over Schools and the Colonial Order, 1900–1950.* Lincoln: University of Nebraska Press, 2017.

———. "The National Revolution in French West Africa: *Dakar-Jeunes* and the Shaping of African Opinion." *International Journal of Francophone Studies*, vol. 10, no. 1–2, Mar. 2007, pp. 85–103.

———. "Peasants of the Empire. Rural Schools and the Colonial Imaginary in 1930s French West Africa." *Cahiers d'Études Africaines*, no. 195, 2009, pp. 775–804.

Ganguly, Debjani. "The Language Question in India." In *The Cambridge History of Postcolonial Literature*, edited by Ato Quayson. Cambridge: Cambridge University Press, 2012, pp. 649–80.

Garuba, Harry. "The Critical Reception of the African Novel." In *The Cambridge Companion to the African Novel*, edited by F. Abiola Irele. Cambridge: Cambridge University Press, 2009, pp. 243–62.

Gassama, B. Biram. "'Ceddo' Baillonné!" *Andë Soppi*, June 1977.

Gaye, Baffa. *Le Noir évolué.* Cahiers Ponty, 1941, XVIII-SE-606, carton N°31, IFAN.

Gaye, Ibrahima. "Un contre-décret du peuple." *Taxaw*, no. 12, 1978, p. 3.

Genova, James E. *Colonial Ambivalence, Cultural Authenticity, and the Limitations of Mimicry in French-Ruled West Africa, 1914–1956.* New York: Peter Lang, 2004.

Gikandi, Simon. "Chinua Achebe and the Invention of Modern African Literature." In *Things Fall Apart.* Oxford: Heinemann, 1996.

———. *Maps of Englishness: Writing Identity in the Culture of Colonialism.* New York: Columbia University Press, 1996.

———. *Ngugi wa Thiong'o.* Cambridge: Cambridge University Press, 2000.

———. "Provincializing English." Editor's Column. *PMLA*, vol. 129, no. 1, 2014, pp. 7–17.

———. *Slavery and the Culture of Taste.* Princeton, N.J.: Princeton University Press, 2011.

Glissant, Édouard. *Le discours antillais.* Paris: Gallimard, 1997.

Goethe, Johann Wolfgang von. *Conversations of Goethe with Johann Peter Eckermann.* Edited by J. K. Moorhead. Translated by John Oxenford. London: Everyman's Library, 1930.

Goldblatt, Cullen. "Lëndëmtu: réflexions sur *Doomi Golo* et *Les Petits de la guenon.*" In *Des Mondes et des langues: l'écriture de Boubacar Boris Diop.* Paris: Présence Africaine, 2014, pp. 61–83.

Golliet, Jacques. *Letter to Françoise Robinet.* 16 May 1963. Box 440, Folder 6, International Association for Cultural Freedom Records, JRL.

Governor General of AOF to Minister of Overseas France, 13 Sept. 1950, 14MIOM/3097, 21 G 173, ANOM.

Governor of Upper Volta to Governor General of AOF, 14 Oct. 1949, 14MIOM/3097, 21 G 173, ANOM.

Guiffray, R. "Extraits de la conférence pédagogique de Bamako." *Education Africaine,* no. 15, 1952, pp. 61–72.

Guyer, Jane I. "Prophecy and the Near Future: Thoughts on Macroeconomic, Evangelical, and Punctuated Time." *American Ethnologist,* vol. 34, no. 3, 2007, pp. 409–21.

Habila, Helon. "Tradition and the African Writer." Caine Prize. 11 June 2014. http://caineprize.com/blog/2015/12/1/tradition-and-the -african-writer-by-2014-judge-helon-habila.

Hall, Bruce S., and Charles C. Stewart. "The Historic 'Core Curriculum' and the Book Market in Islamic West Africa." In *The Trans-Saharan Book Trade: Manuscript Culture, Arabic Literacy, and Intellectual History in Muslim Africa,* edited by Graziano Krätli and Ghislaine Lydon. Leiden, Netherlands: Brill, 2010, pp. 109–74.

Hamès, Constant. *Coran et talismans: textes et pratiques magiques en milieu musulman.* Paris: Karthala, 2007.

Hamilton, Russell G. *Literatura Africana, Literatura Necessária,* vol. 1, edições 70, 1984.

Hardy, Georges. "Préface." In *Doguicimi.* Paris: Larose, 1938.

———. *Une conquête morale.* Paris: A. Colin, 1917.

Harney, Elizabeth. *In Senghor's Shadow: Art, Politics, and the Avant-Garde in Senegal, 1960–1995.* Durham, N.C.: Duke University Press, 2004.

Harrell-Bond, Barbara. "Mariama Bâ: Winner of the First Noma Award for Publishing in Africa for Her Novel *Une si longue lettre.*" *African Book Publishing Record,* vol. 6, nos. 3–4, 1980, pp. 209–14.

Harvey, David. *A Brief History of Neoliberalism.* Oxford: Oxford University Press, 2005.

Hawkins, Sean. *Writing and Colonialism in Northern Ghana.* Toronto: University of Toronto Press, 2002.

Hayot, Eric. *On Literary Worlds.* New York: Oxford University Press, 2012.

Hazoumé, Paul. "Causerie aux instituteurs sur des recherches ethnographiques et historiques." 9 Jan. 1942. Series O 334 (31), ANS.

———. *Doguicimi.* Washington, D.C.: Three Continents Press, 1990.

———. "Journal de Voyage de Cotonou à Dassa-Zoumé." *Reconnaissance Africaine,* no. 13, Mar. 1926.

———. "Tata Ajachè Soupo Ma Ha Awouinyan." *Reconnaissance Africaine*, no. 1, Aug. 1925.

Hitchcott, Nicki. "'Confidently Feminine'? Sexual Role-Play in the Novels of Mariama Bâ." In *African Francophone Writing: A Critical Introduction*, edited by Nicki Hitchcott and Laïla Ibnlfassi. Oxford: Berg, 1996, pp. 139–41.

Hofmeyr, Isabel. *The Portable Bunyan: A Transnational History of "The Pilgrim's Progress."* Princeton, N.J.: Princeton University Press, 2003.

Hymans, Jacques Louis. *Léopold Sédar Senghor: An Intellectual Biography.* Edinburgh: University Press, 1971.

Irele, Abiola. "African Literature and the Language Question." In *The African Experience in Literature and Ideology*. Bloomington: Indiana University Press, 1990, pp. 43–65.

———. "In Search of Camara Laye." *Research in African Literatures*, vol. 37, no. 1, 2006, pp. 110–27.

———. "The Negritude Debate." In *European Language Writing in Sub-Saharan Africa*, edited by Albert S. Gerard. Budapest: Akadémiai Kiadó, 1986, pp. 379–94.

Irlam, Shaun. "Mariama Bâ's *Une Si Longue Lettre*": The Vocation of Memory and the Space of Writing." *Research in African Literatures*, vol. 29, no. 2, 1998, pp. 76–93.

Irvine, Judith. "Genres of Conquest: From Literature to Science in Colonial African Linguistics." In *Verbal Art across Cultures: The Aesthetics and Proto-Aesthetics of Communication*, edited by Hubert Knoblauch and Helga Kotthoff. Tübingen, Germany: Gunter Narr Verlag, 2001, pp. 63–90.

———. "Strategies of Status Manipulation in the Wolof Greeting." In *Explorations in the Ethnography of Speaking*, edited by Richard Bauman and Joel Sherzer. Cambridge: Cambridge University Press, 1974, pp. 167–91.

———. "Subjected Words: African Linguistics and the Colonial Encounter." *Language & Communication*, vol. 28, no. 4, 2008, pp. 323–43.

———. "When Talk Isn't Cheap: Language and Political Economy." *American Ethnologist* 16, no. 2, May 1, 1989, p. 255.

Irvine, Judith T., and Susan Gal. "Language Ideology and Linguistic Differentiation." In *Regimes of Language: Ideologies, Polities, and Identities*, edited by Paul Kroskrity. Santa Fe, N.Mex.: School for Advanced Research Press, 2000, pp. 35–83.

Jaji, Tsitsi Ella. "*Bingo*: Francophone African Women and the Rise of the Glossy Magazine." In *Popular Culture in Africa: The Episteme of the Everyday*, edited by Stephanie Newell and Onookome Okome. New York: Routledge, 2013, pp. 111–30.

"Jalada Translation Issue 01: Ngũgĩ Wa Thiong'o." *Jalada*, March 22, 2016. https://jaladaafrica.org/2016/03/22/jalada-translation-issue-01-ngugi-wa -thiongo/.

James, Henry. *The Figure in the Carpet*. London: Martin Secker, 1916.

Jézéquel, Jean-Hervé. "Grammaire de la distinction coloniale. L'organisation des cadres de l'enseignement en Afrique occidentale française (1903-fin des années 1930)." *Genèses*, no. 69, 2007.

Johnson, Barbara. "Bringing Out D. A. Miller." *Narrative*, vol. 10, no. 1, 2002, pp. 3–8.

Jones, Donna V. *The Racial Discourses of Life Philosophy: Négritude, Vitalism, and Modernity*. New York: Columbia University Press, 2010.

Jones, Hilary. *The Métis of Senegal: Urban Life and Politics in French West Africa*. Bloomington: Indiana University Press, 2013.

Julien, Eileen. "The Extroverted African Novel." In *The Novel, Volume 1: History, Geography, and Culture*, edited by Franco Moretti. Princeton, N.J.: Princeton University Press, 2007, pp. 667–700.

———. "When a Man Loves a Woman: Gender and National Identity in Wole Soyinkas's *Death and the King's Horseman* and Mariama Bâ's *Scarlet Song*." In *Africa after Gender?*, edited by Catherine M. Cole, Takyiwaa Manuh, and Stephan F. Miescher. Bloomington: Indiana University Press, 2007, pp. 205–22.

Kalliney, Peter. "Modernism, African Literature, and the Cold War." *Modern Language Quarterly*, vol. 76, no. 3, 1 Sept. 2015, pp. 333–68.

Kamara, Sana. *Sëriñ Muusaa Ka: melokaani roytéef*. Dakar: Éditions Papyrus Afrique, 2008.

———. *See also* Camara, Sana.

Keane, Webb. *Christian Moderns: Freedom and Fetish in the Mission Encounter*. Berkeley: University of California Press, 2007.

Keïta, Kalifa. *Ce que racontent les griots*. Cahiers Ponty, n.d., XXVI-SO-772, carton N°74, IFAN.

Kesteloot, Lilyan. *Les écrivains noirs de langue française: naissance d'une littérature*. Brussels: Editions de l'Université de Bruxelles, 1983.

Kesteloot, Lilyan and Chérif Mbodj. *Contes et Mythes Wolof*. Dakar: Nou-velles Éditions Africaines du Sénégal, 1983.

King, Adèle. *Rereading Camara Laye*. Lincoln: University of Nebraska Press, 2003.

Koné, Lompolo. *Devoir de fin d'année: L'Ancien tirailleur revenu au village*. Cahiers Ponty, n.d., XVIII-CI-600, carton N°12, IFAN.

Kongolo, A. Tshitungu. "Présentation." In *Poésie, théâtre, essais et discours*, edited by Albert-James Arnold. Paris: CNRS, 2014.

Kouassi, Yapi. *Les animaux de la brousse autour de Zékrézessou.* Cahiers Ponty, 1938, XIII-CI-504, carton N°59, IFAN.

La Société de géographie. *Instructions générales aux voyageurs.* Paris: Ch. Delagrave, 1875.

Labrune-Badiane, Céline, and Etienne Smith. *Les Hussards noirs de la colonie: Instituteurs africains et petites patries en AOF.* Paris: Karthala, 2018.

Laye, Camara. *L'Enfant noir.* Paris: Pocket, 2007.

Levine, Caroline. *Forms: Whole, Rhythm, Hierarchy, Network.* Princeton, N.J.: Princeton University Press, 2015.

Lifchitz, Déborah. "Projet d'une enquête sur la littérature orale en Afrique Noire." *Outre-Mer,* vol. 9, no. 2, Sept. 1937.

Loimeier, Roman. "The Secular State and Islam in Senegal." In *Questioning the Secular State: The Worldwide Resurgence of Religion and Politics,* edited by David Westerlund. London: Hurst, 1996, pp. 183–97.

Loughran, Trish. *The Republic in Print: Print Culture in the Age of U.S. Nation Building, 1770–1870.* New York: Columbia University Press, 2009.

Lucey, Michael, Tom McEnaney, and Tristram Wolff, eds. "Language-in-Use and the Literary Artifact." Special issue, *Representations,* no. 137, Winter 2017.

Lüsebrink, Hans-Jürgen. *La Conquête de l'espace public colonial: prises de parole et formes de participation d'écrivains et d'intellectuels africains dans la presse à l'époque coloniale (1900–1960).* Frankfurt: IKO-Verlag für Internationale Kommunikation, 2003.

Ly, Boubacar. *La formation au métier d'instituteur: Tome III - Les instituteurs au Sénégal de 1903 à 1945.* Paris: L'Harmattan, 2009.

Lydon, Ghislaine. "A Thirst for Knowledge: Arabic Literacy, Writing Paper and Saharan Bibliophiles in the Southwestern Sahara." In *The Trans-Saharan Book Trade: Manuscript Culture, Arabic Literacy, and Intellectual History in Muslim Africa,* edited by Graziano Krätli and Ghislaine Lydon. Leiden, Netherlands: Brill, 2010, pp. 35–72.

Makward, Edris. "Marriage, Tradition and Woman's Pursuit of Happiness in the Novels of Mariama Bâ." In *Ngambika: Studies of Women in African Literature,* edited by Carol Boyce Davies and Anne Adams Graves. Trenton, N.J.: Africa World Press, 1986, pp. 271–82.

Mamdani, Mahmood. *Citizen and Subject.* Princeton, N.J.: Princeton University Press, 1996.

Mann, Gregory. *Native Sons: West African Veterans and France in the Twentieth Century.* Durham, N.C.: Duke University Press, 2006.

———. "What Was the Indigénat? The 'Empire of Law' in French West Africa." *The Journal of African History,* vol. 50, no. 3, 2009, pp. 331–53.

Manning, Patrick. *Slavery, Colonialism and Economic Growth in Dahomey, 1640–1960*. Cambridge: Cambridge University Press, 2004.

"Matchet's Diary." *West Africa*, Oct. 1980. Noma Award Mss, LL.

Mbaye, M'bengue. *La Méditerranée vue par un noir*. Cahiers Ponty, n.d., XXV-SE-751, carton N°26, IFAN.

McLaughlin, Fiona. "Haalpulaar Identity as a Response to Wolofization." *African Languages and Cultures*, vol. 8, no. 2, 1995, pp. 153–68.

McNee, Lisa. *Selfish Gifts*. Albany, N.Y.: SUNY Press, 2000.

Melas, Natalie. *All the Difference in the World: Postcoloniality and the Ends of Comparison*. Stanford, Calif.: Stanford University Press, 2007.

Miller, Christopher L. "Editing and Editorializing: The New Genetic Cahier of Aimé Césaire." *South Atlantic Quarterly*, vol. 115, no. 3, 2016, pp. 441–55.

———. *Nationalists and Nomads: Essays on Francophone African Literature and Culture*. Chicago: University of Chicago Press, 1999.

———. *Theories of Africans: Francophone Literature and Anthropology in Africa*. Chicago: University of Chicago Press, 1993.

Miller, D. A. *Jane Austen, or the Secret of Style*. Princeton, N.J.: Princeton University Press, 2005.

Modisane, Bloke. *Critic's Time: The East African Short Story*, Mbari Writers Conference, Kampala, 1961, MAK/III(3), Container 1.3, Transcription Centre Archive, HRC.

Mokwenye, Cyril. "La Polygamie et la révolte de la femme africaine moderne: Une Lecture d'Une Si Longue Lettre de Mariama Bâ." *Peuples Noirs Peuples Africains, Paris*, vol. 31, 1983.

Montaigne, Michel de. *Les Essais*. Paris: Gallimard, 2007.

Moore, Gerald, ed. *African Literature and the Universities*. Ibadan: Published for the Congress for Cultural Freedom by Ibadan University Press, 1965.

Moretti, Franco. "Conjectures on World Literature." In *Distant Reading*. London: Verso, 2013, pp. 43–62.

Mortimer, Mildred P. *Journeys through the French African Novel*. Portsmouth, N.H.: Heinemann, 1990.

———. "The Nurturing Hearth: Mariama Bâ." In *Writing from the Hearth: Public, Domestic, and Imaginative Space in Francophone Women's Fiction of Africa and the Caribbean*. Lanham, Md.: Lexington Books, 2007, pp. 71–116.

Moudileno, Lydie. "The Francophone Novel in Sub-Saharan African." In *The Cambridge Companion to the African Novel*, edited by F. Abiola Irele. Cambridge: Cambridge University Press, 2009, pp. 125–40.

Mouralis, Bernard. "Les esquisses sénégalaises de l'abbé Boilat, ou le nationalisme sans la négritude." *Cahiers d'études Africaines*, vol. 35, no. 140, 1995, pp. 819–37.

——. "William Ponty Drama." In *European-Language Writing in Sub-Saharan Africa*, edited by A. S. Gérard. Budapest: Akadémiai Kiadó, 1986, pp. 130–40.

Mphahlele, Ezekiel. *Critic's Time for the Novel*. Mbari Writers Conference, Kampala, 1961, Container 1.3, Transcription Centre Archive, HRC.

——. *Press Report*. Mbari Writers Conference, Kampala, 1961, Container 1.3, Transcription Centre Archive, HRC.

Mudimbe, Valentin-Yves. *The Idea of Africa*. Bloomington: Indiana University Press, 1994.

Mufti, Aamir R. *Forget English! Orientalisms and World Literatures*. Cambridge, Mass.: Harvard University Press, 2016.

Murphy, David. "Birth of a Nation? The Origins of Senegalese Literature in French." *Research in African Literatures*, vol. 39, no. 1, 2008, pp. 48–69.

——. *Sembène: Imagining Alternatives in Film and Fiction*. Oxford: James Currey Publishers, 2000.

Murtuza, Miriam. "The Marriage and Divorce of Polygamy and Nation: Interplay of Gender, Religion, and Class in Sembene Ousmane and Manama Ba." In Azodo, *Emerging Perspectives on Mariama Bâ*, p. 175.

Ndao, Cheikh Aliou. *Buur Tilleen*. Dakar: IFAN Cheikh Anta Diop, 1993.

——. *Buur Tilleen: Roi de La Médina*. Paris: Présence Africaine, 1988.

——. Interview by Tobias Warner. 28 July 2008. Dakar, Senegal.

——. "Langues et littérature." In *Les étudiants africains et La littérature négro-africaine d'expression française*, edited by Amady Aly Dieng. Cameroon: Langaa RPCIG, 2009, pp. 128–30.

——. "Ousmane Sembène, véritable griot d'hommes." In *Les étudiants africains et La littérature négro-africaine d'expression française*, edited by Amady Aly Dieng, Cameroon: Langaa RPCIG, 2009, pp. 126–27.

——. *Taaral ak ladab ci làmmiñu wolof: esthétique et littérature de langue wolof*. Dakar: OSAD, 2002.

Ndiaye, Jacques-Marie. *Le peuple sérère*. Cahiers Ponty, 1940, XI-SE-421, carton N°34, IFAN.

Ndiaye, Mame Coumba. *Mariama Bâ, ou les allées d'un destin: essai*. Dakar: Les nouvelles éditions africaines du Sénégal, 2007.

Newell, Stephanie. *Literary Culture in Colonial Ghana*. Bloomington: Indiana University Press, 2002.

——. *The Power to Name: A History of Anonymity in Colonial West Africa*. Athens: Ohio University Press, 2013.

Nfah-Abbenyi, Juliana Makuchi. "Women Redefining Difference: Mariama Bâ, Miriam Tlali, and Bessie Head." In *Gender in African Women's Writing: Identity, Sexuality, and Difference*. Bloomington: Indiana University Press, 1997, pp. 108–47.

Nganang, Patrice. "In Praise of the Alphabet." In *Rethinking African Cultural Production*. Bloomington: Indiana University Press, 2015, pp. 78–94.

Ngom, Fallou. *Muslims Beyond the Arab World: The Odyssey of Ajami and the Muridiyya*. Oxford: Oxford University Press, 2016.

Ngom, Ousmane. "Militantisme Linguistique et Initiation Littéraire Dans Doomi Golo—Roman Wolof de Bubakar Bóris Jóob." *Repères-Dorif*, 2012, http://www.dorif.it/ezine/ezine_articles.php?art_id=34.

Ngugi, Mukoma Wa. *The Rise of the African Novel: Politics of Language, Identity, and Ownership*. Ann Arbor: University of Michigan Press, 2018.

Ngũgĩ wa Thiong'o. *Decolonising the Mind: The Politics of Language in African Literature*. Nairobi: East African Publishers, 1994.

Nkosi, Lewis. *Press Report*. Mbari Writers Conference, Kampala, 1961; MAK V (1); Container 1.3, Transcription Centre Archive, HRC.

Nnaemeka, Obioma. "Urban Spaces, Women's Places: Polygamy as Sign in Mariama Bâ's Novels." In *The Politics of (M)Othering: Womanhood, Identity, and Resistance in African Literature*. London: Routledge, 1997, pp. 162–191.

Nordtveit, Bjorn Harald. "Producing Literacy and Civil Society: The Case of Senegal." *Comparative Education Review*, vol. 52, no. 2, May 2008, pp. 175–98.

Nwoga, Donatus. *Critic's Time for The Short Story*. Mbari Writers Conference, Kampala, 1961, MAK/III, Container 1.3, Transcription Centre Archive, HRC.

O'Brien, Donal B. Cruise. "The Shadow-Politics of Wolofisation." In *Symbolic Confrontations: Muslims Imagining the State in Africa*. New York: Palgrave Macmillan, 2003, pp. 120–140.

Offord, Malcom, Rosemary Chapman, Laïla Ibnlfassi, and Nicki Hitchcott, eds. *Francophone Literatures: A Literary and Linguistic Companion*. London: Routledge, 2001.

Ojo-Ade, Femi. "Still a Victim? Mariama Bâ's *Une Si Longue Lettre*." *African Literature Today*, no. 12, 1982, pp. 71–87.

Olusola, Segun. *Reports from Conference Study Groups: Drama*. Mbari Writers Conference, Kampala, 1961, MAK/IV (1), Container 1.3, Transcription Centre Archive, HRC.

Opara, Chioma. "The Emergence of the Female Self: The Liberating Pen in Mariama Bâ's *Une Si Longue Lettre* and Sembene Ousmane's 'Lettres de

France.'" In *Feminism and Black Women's Creative Writing: Theory, Practice, and Criticism*. Ibadan: AMD, 1996, pp. 153–67.

Ossoh'ou, Jules (Kouaho). *Devoir de vacances*. Cahiers Ponty, 1945, C15. XV CI 5, IFAN.

Ouattara, Larba. *L'Alimentation en pays Lobi*. Cahiers Ponty, 1945, I-CI-27, carton N°68, IFAN.

Owoo, Kwate Nee. "The Language of Real Life" in *Framework*, vol. 36, 1989, and *Framework*, vol. 49, no. 1, Fall 2007. Quoted in Busch and Annas, pp. 131–33.

Pascal, Roy. *The Dual Voice: Free Indirect Speech and Its Functioning in the Nineteenth-Century European Novel*. Manchester: Manchester University Press, 1977.

Pasquier, Roger. "Les débuts de la presse au sénégal." *Cahiers d'études Africaines*, 1962, pp. 477–490.

Peterson, Bhekizizwe. "The Language Question in Africa." In *The Cambridge History of Postcolonial Literature*, edited by Ato Quayson. Cambridge: Cambridge University Press, 2012, pp. 681–702.

Peterson, Derek R. *Creative Writing: Translation, Bookkeeping, and the Work of Imagination in Colonial Kenya*. London: Heinemann, 2004.

Peterson, Derek R., Emma Hunter, and Stephanie Newell. "Print Culture in Colonial Africa." In *African Print Cultures: Newspapers and Their Publics in the Twentieth Century*. Ann Arbor: University of Michigan Press, 2016.

Pietz, William. "The Problem of the Fetish, I." *RES: Anthropology and Aesthetics*, no. 9, Spring 1985, pp. 5–17.

Poinsot, Marie, and Nicolas Treiber. "Entretien avec Maryse Condé." *Hommes et migrations. Revue française de référence sur les dynamiques migratoires*, no. 1301, Jan. 2013, pp. 182–88.

Pollock, Sheldon. *The Language of the Gods in the World of Men: Sanskrit, Culture, and Power in Premodern India*. Berkeley: University of California Press, 2006.

Povey, John F. "How Do You Make a Course in African Literature?" *Transition*, no. 18, 1965, pp. 39–42.

Povinelli, Elizabeth A. "Radical Worlds: The Anthropology of Incommensurability and Inconceivability." *Annual Review of Anthropology*, vol. 30, 2001, pp. 319–34.

Prat, Aristide. "Concours et examens en 1921: commentaires." *Bulletin de l'Enseignement de l'Afrique Occidentale Française*, vol. 9, no. 47, Sept. 1921, pp. 67–71.

Qader, Nasrin. *Narratives of Catastrophe: Boris Diop, Ben Jelloun, Khatibi*. New York: Fordham University Press, 2009.

Quayson, Ato. *Oxford Street, Accra: City Life and the Itineraries of Transnationalism*. Durham, N.C.: Duke University Press, 2014.

Rabemananjara, Jacques. "L'Europe et nous." *Presence Africaine*, no. 8/10, 1956, pp. 20–28.

Reckord, Barry, Ezekiel Mphahlele, Gerald Moore, Wole Soyinka, Denis Williams, and Jan Knappert. "Polemics: The Dead End of African Literature." *Transition*, no. 75/76, 1997, pp. 335–41.

Repinecz, Jonathon. "'The Tales of Tomorrow': Towards a Futurist Vision of Wolof Tradition." *Journal of African Cultural Studies*, vol. 27, no. 1, 2015, pp. 56–70.

Riesz, János. *De la littérature coloniale à la littérature africaine: prétextes, contextes, intertextes*. Paris: Karthala, 2007.

———. "Mariama Bâ's 'Une Si Longue Lettre': An Erziehungsroman." Translated by Richard Bjornson. *Research in African Literatures*, vol. 22, no. 1, Spring 1991, pp. 27–42.

Robert, Stéphane. "Deictic Space in Wolof: Discourse, Syntax and the Importance of Absence." *Typological Studies in Language*, vol. 66, 2006, p. 155.

Roberts, Allen F., and Mary Nooter Roberts. *A Saint in the City: Sufi Arts of Urban Senegal*. Los Angeles: UCLA Fowler Museum of Cultural History, 2003. Published in conjunction with an exhibition of the same title, presented at the Fowler Museum at UCLA, February 27–July 27, 2003.

Robin. "Le développement de l'esprit d'observation chez l'enfant." *Education Africaine*, no. 104, 1940, pp. 59–64.

Robinson, David. "Ethnography and Customary Law in Senegal." *Cahiers d'Études Africaines*, vol. 32, no. 126, 1992, pp. 221–37.

Rofheart, Mahriana. *Shifting Perceptions of Migration in Senegalese Literature, Film, and Social Media*. Lanham, Md.: Lexington Books, 2013.

Roger, Jacques-François. *Fables sénégalaises*. Paris: Nepveu, 1828.

Rueschmann, Eva. "Female Self-Definition and the African Community in Mariama Bâ's Epistolary Novel *So Long a Letter*." In *International Women's Writing: New Landscapes of Identity*, edited by Anne E. Brown and Marjanne E. Goozé. Westport, Conn.: Greenwood Press, 1995.

Sabatier, Peggy. "Educating a Colonial Elite: The William Ponty School and Its Graduates." PhD diss., University of Chicago, 1977.

Sadana, Rashmi. *English Heart, Hindi Heartland: The Political Life of Literature in India*. Berkeley: University of California Press, 2012.

Sadji, Abdoulaye. "Ce que disent les vielles mélopées sénégalaises." *Paris-Dakar*, May 1938, p. 3.

———. "Ce que dit la musique africaine." *L'Education Africaine*, no. 94, Apr. 1936, pp. 119–72.

————. *Commentez cette parole de Montaigne: savoir par coeur n'est pas savoir.*
    Student Composition, Serie O 150 (31), ANS.
Sadji, Amadou Booker. *Abdoulaye Sadji: Biographie, 1910–1961.* Paris:
    Présence Africaine, 1997.
Said, Edward W. *Culture and Imperialism.* New York: Vintage, 1994.
Sall, Adjaratou Oumar. "Multilinguism, Linguistic Policy, and Endangered
    Languages in Senegal." *Journal of Multicultural Discourses,* vol. 4, no. 3, 1
    Nov. 2009, pp. 313–30.
Samory. "Le Wolof n'est pas une langue ethnique." 29 Dec. 2010. Xalima
    .com. http://xalimasn.com/cafe-litteraire-du-festival-mondial-des-arts
    -negres-le-wolof-n%e2%80%99est-pas-une-langue-ethnique/.
Sartre, Jean-Paul. "Orphée noir." *Condition Humaine,* 5 Oct. 1948, pp. 2–3.
————. "Orphée noir, suite." *Condition Humaine,* 14 Nov. 1948, pp. 2–3.
————. "Orphée noir, suite et fin." *Condition Humaine,* 30 Nov. 1948, pp. 2–3.
Saunders, Frances Stonor. *The Cultural Cold War: The CIA and the World of
    Arts and Letters.* New York: New Press, 2013.
Scott, David. *Omens of Adversity: Tragedy, Time, Memory, Justice.* Durham,
    N.C.: Duke University Press, 2013.
Searing, James F. *West African Slavery and Atlantic Commerce.* Cambridge:
    Cambridge University Press, 2003.
Seck, Serigne Fall. *Formation morale de l'enfant.* Cahiers Ponty, 1949,
    XV-SE-584, carton N°3, IFAN.
Sedgwick, Eve Kosofsky. *Touching Feeling: Affect, Pedagogy, Performativity.*
    Durham, N.C.: Duke University Press, 2003.
Sembène, Ousmane. *Ceddo.* Filmi Doomireew, 1976.
————. *La Noire de . . .* Les Films Domirev/Les Actualités françaises, 1966.
————. *La Noire de . . .* Paris: Médiathèque des Trois Mondes, [1966] 2008.
    DVD.
————. *Le Mandat.* French version. Filmi Domireew/Comptoir Français du
    Film, 1968, AFF.
————. *Le Mandat précédé de Véhi-Ciosane.* Paris: Présence Africaine, 1966.
————. *Le Mandat (Scénario).* La Bibliothèque du film, 1968, CF.
————. *Mandabi.* Wolof version. Filmi Domireew/Comptoir Français du
    Film, 1968.
————. "Sembène s'exprime." *Andë Soppi,* Nov. 1977.
————. *Xala.* La Médiathèque des Trois Mondes, 1975.
Sene, Henri. "Le livre et l'écrit de langue arabe dans la société sénégalaise,
    des origines au début du XXe siècle." Thèse de doctorat de troisième
    cycle, Université de Dakar, 1982.
Senghor, Léopold Sédar. "Afrique Noire." In *Les plus beaux écrits de l'Union
    Française et du Maghreb.* Paris: Éditions du Vieux Colombier, 1947.

———. "Appel aux lecteurs." *Condition Humaine*, 5 Oct. 1948, pp. 1–2.

———. "Chant d'ombre." In *Œuvre Poétique*. Paris: Points, 2006, pp. 42–44.

———. "Exposé des motifs." *Transcription des langues nationales*. Dakar: CLAD, 1972.

———. "Lettre au premier ministre relative à la revue mensuelle Kaddu, à propos des langues nationales, 19 mai 1972." In *Education et Culture*, edited by A. Raphaël Ndiaye and Doudou Joseph Ndiaye. Paris: Presence Africaine, 2014, pp. 60–77.

———. *Liberté, Tome 1. Négritude et Humanisme*. Paris: Seuil, 1964.

———. "Nuit de Sine." In *Œuvre Poétique*. Paris: Points, 2006, pp. 16–17.

———. "Une lettre de M. Léopold Sedar Senghor." *Le Monde*, 14 Aug. 1979.

Senghor, Léopold Sédar, and Mohamed Aziza. *La poésie de l'action: conversations avec Mohamed Aziza*. Paris: Stock, 1980.

Silverstein, Michael. "The Fieldwork Encounter and the Colonized Voice of Indigeneity." *Representations*, vol. 137, no. 1, 2017, pp. 23–43.

———. "The Limits of Awareness." *Linguistic Anthropology: A Reader*. Malden, Mass.: Blackwell, 2001, pp. 382–401.

———. "Metapragmatic Discourse and Metapragmatic Function." In *Reflexive Language: Reported Speech and Metapragmatics*, edited by John A. Lucy. Cambridge: Cambridge University Press, 1993, pp. 33–58.

———. "Translation, Transduction, Transformation: Skating 'Glossando' on Thin Semiotic Ice." In *Translating Cultures: Perspectives on Translation and Anthropology*, edited by Paula G. Rubel and Abraham Rosman. Oxford: Berg, 2003, pp. 75–105.

Silverstein, Michael, and Greg Urban, eds. *Natural Histories of Discourse*. Chicago: University of Chicago Press, 1996.

Slaughter, Joseph R. "Locations of Comparison." *Cambridge Journal of Postcolonial Literary Inquiry*, vol. 5, no. 2, April 2018, pp. 209–26.

———. "World Literature as Property." *Alif: Journal of Comparative Poetics*, no. 34, 2014, pp. 39–73.

Smith, Etienne. "La nationalisation par le bas: un nationalisme banal?" *Raisons Politiques*, vol. 37, no. 1, 2010, p. 65.

Snyder, F. G. "Colonialism and Legal Form: The Creation of Customary Law in Senegal." *Journal of Legal Pluralism*, vol. 19, 1981, pp. 49–90.

Socé, Ousmane. "Ce Que Pensent Nos . . . Futurs Lecteurs . . ." *Bingo*, Feb. 1953.

———. "Karim 1942." *Dakar-Jeunes*, 7 May 1942.

———. *Karim: roman sénégalais*. Paris: Nouvelles éditions latines, 1966.

———. "Karim: roman sénégalais." *Paris-Dakar*, 11 June 1935, p. 5.

———. "Karim: roman sénégalais." *Paris-Dakar*, 18 June 1935, p. 5.

———. "Un témoignage: l'évolution culturelle de l'AOF." *Dakar-Jeunes*, 29 Jan. 1942.

Sow, Fatou. "Family and Law in Senegal: Continuity and Change." In *Shifting Boundaries in Marriage and Divorce in Muslim Communities.* Grabels, France: Women Living Under Muslim Laws 1996, pp. 142–157.

Sow, (Alfâ) Ibrahima. *Divination marabout destin: aux sources de l'imaginaire.* Dakar: IFAN Cheikh Anta Diop, 2009.

Sow, Ibrahima. *Mémoire de fin d'études: Type d'éducation Foulah.* Cahiers Ponty, n.d. XV-G-553, carton N°14, IFAN.

Soyinka, Wole. "Theatre in African Traditional Cultures: Survival Patterns." In *Twentieth Century Performance Reader,* edited by Teresa Brayshaw and Noel Witt. London: Routledge, 1996, pp. 430–43.

Spivak, Gayatri Chakravorty. "Can There Be a Feminist World?" *Public Books,* 15 May 2015. http://www.publicbooks.org/can-there-be-a-feminist -world/.

Stoler, Ann Laura. *Along the Archival Grain: Epistemic Anxieties and Colonial Common Sense.* Princeton, N.J.: Princeton University Press, 2008.

———. "Colonial Archives and the Arts of Governance." *Archival Science,* vol. 2, no. 1–2, 2002, pp. 87–109.

Sy, Amadou Arona. *Monographie du village de Poukhan.* Cahiers Ponty, 1941, XII-SE-488, carton N°16, IFAN.

Ten Kortenaar, Neil. *Postcolonial Literature and the Impact of Literacy: Reading and Writing in African and Caribbean Fiction.* Cambridge: Cambridge University Press, 2011.

Thiesse, Anne-Marie. *Ils apprenaient la France: l'exaltation des régions dans le discours patriotique.* Paris: Les Editions de la MSH, 1997.

Touré, Katia. "Céytu: là où le wolof tutoie les grandes œuvres francophones." *Le Point Afrique.* http://afrique.lepoint.fr/culture/litterature -ceytu-quand-le-wolof-tutoie-les-grandes-oeuvres-francophones-19-02 -2016-2019620_2256.php.

Traoré, Bakary. *Le théâtre négro-africain et ses fonctions sociales.* Paris: Présence Africaine, 1958.

Ulrich, Gregor. "Interview with Ousmane Sembène." *Framework,* no. 7/8, 1978.

Vakunta, Peter Wuteh. "The Ramifications of Linguistic Innovation in African Literature: An Interview with Patrice Nganang." *Journal of the African Literature Association,* vol. 3, no. 2, 1 Jan. 2009, pp. 206–12.

Vieyra, Paulin Soumanou. *Ousmane Sembène, cinéaste: première période, 1962–1971.* Paris: Présence Africaine, 1972.

Viswanathan, Gauri. *Masks of Conquest: Literary Study and British Rule in India.* New York: Columbia University Press, 1989.

Viveiros de Castro, Eduardo. "Perspectival Anthropology and the Method of Controlled Equivocation." *Tipití: Journal of the Society for the Anthropology of Lowland South America*, vol. 2, no. 1, 2004, pp. 3–21.

Volosinov, V. N. *Marxism and the Philosophy of Language*. Cambridge, Mass.: Harvard University Press, 1986.

Wali, Obiajunwa. "The Dead End of African Literature?" *Transition*, no. 10, Sept. 1963, pp. 13–16.

Walker, Keith Louis. *Countermodernism and Francophone Literary Culture: The Game of Slipknot*. Durham, N.C.: Duke University Press, 1999.

Walle, Nicolas Van De. *African Economies and the Politics of Permanent Crisis, 1979–1999*. Cambridge: Cambridge University Press, 2001.

Warner, Michael. *Publics and Counterpublics*. New York: Zone Books, 2002.

Warner, Tobias. "Enacting Postcolonial Translation: Voice, Color and Free Indirect Discourse in the Restored Version of Sembène's *La Noire de . . .*" In *Translating the Postcolonial in Multilingual Contexts*, edited by Judith Misrahi-Barak and Srilata Ravi. Montpellier: Presses Universitaires de la Méditerranée, 2017.

———. "Para-Literary Ethnography and Colonial Self-Writing: The Student Notebooks of the William Ponty School." *Research in African Literatures*, vol. 47, no. 1, 2016, pp. 1–20.

Wenzel, Jennifer. *Bulletproof: Afterlives of Anticolonial Prophecy in South Africa and Beyond*. Chicago: University of Chicago Press, 2010.

White, Owen. *Children of the French Empire: Miscegenation and Colonial Society in French West Africa 1895–1960*. Oxford: Oxford University Press, 1999.

Wilcox, Rebecca. "Women and Power in Mariama Bâ's Novels." In Azodo, *Emerging Perspectives on Mariama Bâ*, pp. 121–42.

Wilder, Gary. "Colonial Ethnology and Political Rationality in French West Africa." *History and Anthropology*, vol. 14, no. 3, 2003, pp. 219–52.

———. *Freedom Time: Negritude, Decolonization, and the Future of the World*. Durham, N.C.: Duke University Press, 2015.

———. *The French Imperial Nation-State: Negritude and Colonial Humanism between the Two World Wars*. Chicago: University of Chicago Press, 2005.

Wolff, Tristram. "Arbitrary, Natural, Other: J. G. Herder and Ideologies of Linguistic Will." *European Romantic Review*, vol. 27, no. 2, 2016, pp. 259–80.

Wooten, S. R. "Colonial Administration and the Ethnography of the Family in the French Soudan," *Cahiers d'Études Africaines*, vol. 33, no. 131, 1993, pp. 419–46.

Yoon, Boroom [pseud.]. "Ubbi." *Kaddu*, no. 2, Jan. 1972, pp. 1–2.

Zabus, Chantal. *The African Palimpsest: Indigenization of Language in the West African Europhone Novel*. Amsterdam: Rodopi, 1991.

———. "La langue avant la lettre: 'Une si longue lettre' de Mariama Bâ."
    Notre librairie, vol. 119, 1994, pp. 95–97.
Zell, Hans. "Senegalese Woman Writer Wins First Noma Award." The
    Noma Award for Publishing in Africa. Press Release. 7 Oct. 1980. Noma
    Award Mss, LL.

CPSIA information can be obtained
at www.ICGtesting.com
Printed in the USA
BVHW071930240119
538631BV00001B/6/P

9 780823 284290